COMPANY ACCOUNTING & FINANCIAL STATEMENTS

COMPANY ACCOUNTING & FINANCIAL STATEMENTS

PAUL DE LANGE | **ROBERT RODGERS** | **EDWARD A. CLARKE**

FOURTH EDITION

THOMSON

Australia · Canada · Mexico · Singapore · Spain · United Kingdom · United States

Level 7, 80 Dorcas St
South Melbourne, Victoria, 3205

Email: highereducation@thomsonlearning.com.au
Website: www.thomsonlearning.com.au

First published in 2005
10 9 8 7 6 5 4 3 2 1
09 08 07 06 05

Copyright © 2005 Nelson Australia Pty Limited.

COPYRIGHT

Reproduction and Communication for educational purposes
The Australian *Copyright Act 1968* (the Act) allows a maximum of one chapter or 10% of the pages of this work, whichever is the greater, to be reproduced and/or communicated by any educational institution for its educational purposes provided that the educational institution (or the body that administers it) has given a remuneration notice to Copyright Agency Limited (CAL) under the Act.

For details of the CAL licence for educational institutions contact:

Copyright Agency Limited
Level 19, 157 Liverpool Street
Sydney NSW 2000
Telephone: (02) 9394 7600
Facsimile: (02) 9394 7601
E-mail: info@copyright.com.au

Reproduction and Communication for other purposes
Except as permitted under the Act (for example a fair dealing for the purposes of study, research, criticism or review) no part of this book may be reproduced, stored in a retrieval system, communicated or transmitted in any form or by any means without prior written permission. All enquiries should be made to the publisher at the address above.

Copyright owners may take legal action against a person who infringes on their copyright through unauthorised copying. Enquiries should be directed to the publisher.

National Library of Australia
Cataloguing-in-Publication data

De Lange, Paul
Company accounting and financial statements

4th ed.
Includes index
ISBN 0 17 012375 8.

1. Corporations – Accounting. 2. Corporations – Accounting – Problems, exercises, etc. 3. Financial statements.
4. Financial statements – Problems, exercises, etc. I. Rodgers, Robert. II. Clarke, Ted, 1945 – . III. Title.

657.95

Editor: Juliet West
Project editor: Tony Davidson
Publishing editor: Anthony Hey
Publishing manager: Michael Tully
Indexer: John E Simkin
Text designer: Linda Hamley
Cover designer: Sonia Juraja
Revised cover art: Olga Lavecchia
Typeset in Birka 10/12pt by Linda Hamley
Production controller: Jodie Tamblyn
Printed in China by China Translation & Printing Services Ltd
This title is published under the imprint of Thomson.
Nelson Australia Pty Limited ACN 058 280 149 (incorporated in Victoria) trading as Thomson Learning Australia.

The URLs contained in this publication were checked for currency during the production process.
Note, however, that the publisher cannot vouch for the ongoing currency of URLs.

Contents

Preface		ix
Chapter 1	**Introduction to companies**	**1**
	Objectives	1
	Introduction	2
	Non-incorporated forms of business ownership	2
	Nature of an incorporated company	3
	Types of companies	3
	Proprietary and public companies limited by shares	4
	Other forms of public companies	5
	Conversion of a proprietary company to a public company	5
	Procedures for the incorporation of a company	8
	Costs associated with establishing a company	10
	Authorities governing companies	11
	Company statutory records and registers	13
Chapter 2	**Accounting for share and debenture issues**	**16**
	Objectives	16
	Introduction	17
	Share capital	17
	Classes of shares	18
	Issuing shares	19
	Costs associated with a share issue	55
	Issuing debentures	60
	Types of debt	61
	Contrast of funds from equity and debt	62
	Accounting entries for the issuing and redemption of debentures	64
Chapter 3	**Accounting for the conversion of a business to a company**	**79**
	Objectives	79
	Introduction	80
	Converting a business into a company	80
	Approved accounting standards	80
	Purchase consideration in excess of fair values	81
	Purchase consideration below fair values	89

Chapter 4	Finalisation of a company's profit and loss account	93
	Objectives	93
	Introduction	94
	Finalisation of the profit and loss account	94
	Adjustments to income tax	100
Chapter 5	Accounting for company income tax	112
	Objectives	112
	Introduction	113
	Permanent differences	113
	Temporary differences	117
	Deductible temporary differences and deferred tax assets	119
	Assessable temporary differences and deferred tax liabilities	123
	Reversal of temporary differences	140
	Combined deferrals of tax assets and tax liabilities	149
	Accounting for taxation on losses	154
	Summary of taxation outcomes	156
Chapter 6	Appropriation of company profits and changing shareholders' wealth	158
	Objectives	158
	Introduction	159
	Transfer of profit (loss) after income tax	159
	Appropriation of profits	160
	Revaluation of property, plant and equipment	166
	Bonus share dividends	168
	The balance sheet and shareholders' equity	169
Chapter 7	Corporate reporting	173
	Objectives	173
	Introduction	174
	Corporate reporting requirements	174
	The accounting standards	174
	The income statement	175
	The statement of changes in equity	187
	The balance sheet	194

Chapter 8	The cash flow statement	213
	Objectives	213
	Introduction	214
	The cash flow statement	214
	Cash defined	215
	Cash flow activities	215
	Cash flow statement format	216
	Completing a cash flow statement	217
Chapter 9	Consolidated accounts	250
	Objectives	250
	Introduction	251
	Obligation to present group accounts	251
	Consolidated accounts	251
	Capacity to control	252
	Elimination adjustments	253
	Summary of elimination entries on consolidation	298
Chapter 10	Consolidation with minority interests	306
	Objectives	306
	Introduction	307
	Minority interest	307
	Consolidation with minority interest	308
	Indirect minority interests	337
	Accounting for indirect minority interests on consolidation	338
	Consolidation with direct and indirect minority interests	343
Chapter 11	Share capital alterations	352
	Objectives	352
	Introduction	353
	Alteration to share capital	353
	Reduction of share capital	353
	Cancellation of lost share capital	355
	Redemption of shares	357
	Issuing bonus shares	365

Chapter 12	**Receivership and liquidation**	**373**
	Objectives	373
	Introduction	374
	Receivership	374
	Liquidation	374
	Treatment of assets on liquidation	374
	Treatment of liabilities on liquidation	379
	Treatment of shareholders on liquidation	386
Chapter 13	**Amalgamations and takeovers**	**394**
	Objectives	394
	Introduction	395
	The difference between an amalgamation and a takeover	395
	Purchase consideration	395
	Accounting for amalgamations	396
	Accounting for takeovers	409
Chapter 14	**Accounting for foreign currency translations**	**411**
	Objectives	411
	Introduction	412
	Translating foreign currency transactions	412
	Translation to Australian currency	412
	Translation to foreign currency	413
	Accounting for foreign currency transactions	414
	Capitalisation of exchange rate variations	420
	Accounting for foreign investments	424
	Disclosure of foreign exchange rate variations	432
Index		433

Preface

Company Accounting and Financial Statements is designed to meet the accounting and financial requirements of companies.

The chapters are written to conform with the main components of the regulatory frameworks affecting companies which are reporting entities. These main components are:

- the Corporations Law;
- the accounting standards; and
- the Australian Stock Exchange Listing Rules.

The Corporations Law

The Corporations Law governs all companies that are incorporated in Australia. This text examines the relevant sections of the Law as they relate to the formation of a company, the importance of specific company documentation, and the responsibilities of company directors in relation to accounting and reporting.

The accounting standards

Companies under the Corporations Law are required to abide by the accounting standards. The accounting standards contain detailed guidance on accounting matters.

The accounting standards which affect companies have legal status in that they are presented before federal parliament and become law.

The practical aspects of accounting standards which have a significant impact on the presentation of company financial statements are addressed in this book.

The Australian Stock Exchange Listing Rules

Companies listed with the Australian Stock Exchange are required to submit regular financial statements to the Exchange which comply with the requirements of the Corporations Law and the Australian Accounting Standards Board standards. This book deals with the presentation requirements of company financial statements that are suitable for submission to the Australian Stock Exchange.

CHAPTER 1
INTRODUCTION TO COMPANIES

Objectives

Upon satisfactory completion of this chapter you should be able to:

- define a company;
- compare the limited liability of a company with the liability of a sole trader or partnership;
- differentiate between the main types of companies under the Corporations Law;
- distinguish between small and large proprietary companies;
- explain the advantages of the company forms of business ownership;
- discuss the need for and content of a company constitution;
- describe the procedures required to register a company;
- identify and record costs of establishing a company;
- discuss the roles of the Australian Securities and Investments Commission (ASIC), the Australian Stock Exchange (ASX) and the Australian Accounting Standards Board (AASB); and
- describe and explain the records and registers required by the Corporations Law.

Introduction

When a business is commenced the business owner(s) must give careful consideration to a range of issues, including the name of the business, registration of the business name, rules and regulations relating to the operations of the business, and taxation issues, including the Goods and Services Tax (GST) and income tax.

The decisions of the owner(s) in relation to these issues will vary depending on the form of business ownership adopted by the owner(s).

There are two main categories of business ownership that the owner(s) may consider. These are non-incorporated, which include a sole trader or partnership form of business ownership, and incorporated, which relates to company forms of business ownership.

This chapter examines the differences between the two main categories of business ownership and provides a detailed examination of issues involved in establishing and operating a company form of business ownership.

Non-incorporated forms of business ownership

When a business is incorporated it is formed in accordance with the statutory requirements of the Corporations Law, which is applicable only to company forms of business ownership.

Non-incorporated forms of business ownership include a sole trader and a partnership. Unlike company forms of business ownership, sole trader and partnership businesses do not have to comply with the Corporations Law.

Sole trader

A sole trader form of business ownership is owned by one person. The distinctive characteristics associated with this form of business ownership include:

- the name of the business does not have to be registered if the business carries the name of the owner;
- the costs associated with the establishment are minimal;
- the owner normally operates and manages the business and takes all profits. If the business makes a loss the owner suffers the loss;
- if the business is unable to meet the debts of the business the owner is held personally liable for the unpaid business debts. This is referred to as unlimited liability;
- the business must register for GST if its annual sales turnover exceeds $50 000;
- the business does not pay income tax. The owner must prepare a personal individual tax return each year.

Partnership

A partnership form of business ownership is owned by between two and 20 people (although some special partnerships do exceed this maximum). The distinctive characteristics associated with this form of business ownership are the same as those for a sole trader with the following differences:

- The partnership is governed by the partnership agreement made between the partners. If no agreement exists, the *Partnership Act* applies.
- Profits and losses derived by the business are shared among the owners in accordance with the partnership agreement, or the *Partnership Act* if an agreement does not exist.
- All partners must abide by the actions and decisions of each partner made in relation to activities of the business. From a legal perspective, this is referred to as mutual agency.
- The partnership will cease to exist upon the retirement or death of one of the partners.

Nature of an incorporated company

An individual or group of individuals may choose to organise themselves for business purposes as a registered company in accordance with the Corporations Law. When a business is registered under the Corporations Law it becomes an incorporated company and the owner(s) are called shareholder(s).

Subject to limitations placed upon it by the Corporations Law, a company may exercise much the same powers as an individual person at law. The Corporations Law states that a company has the power to:

- a issue and cancel shares in the company
- b issue debentures
- c grant options over unissued shares in the company
- d distribute any of the property of the company among the members, in kind or otherwise
- e give security by charging uncalled capital
- f grant a floating charge over the company's property *[group of assets for security]*
- g arrange for the company to be registered or recognised as a body corporate in any place outside this jurisdiction
- h do any other act that it is authorised to do by any other law (including a law of a foreign country).

A company may enter into agreements with its owners (shareholders), hold property and incur debts in its own name, borrow and give security, and sue and be sued. Moreover, it is unaffected by the death or bankruptcy of a shareholder and does not cease to exist when there is a change in ownership. Although a company does enjoy perpetual succession, it is still possible for a company to be liquidated and wound up.

Because a company is an artificial legal person, having no mind of its own, the power that it possesses must be exercised through agents. The chief agents of the company (called directors) are elected by the shareholders to operate and manage the company on their behalf.

In relation to taxation issues a company must register for GST if its sales exceed $50 000 per annum. However, unlike sole trader or partnership forms of business ownership which do not pay income tax, a company must pay income tax on the profits earned by the business. Conversely, if the business suffers a loss the company can apply the loss against future years' profits to reduce income tax.

Types of companies

The Corporations Law lists two types of companies that can be registered under the Law. These are:
- proprietary companies; and
- public companies.

To be registered as a company the business must have a minimum of one member. Proprietary companies are restricted to a maximum of 50 (non-employee) shareholders, while there is no restriction on the maximum number of shareholders that a public company can have.

Proprietary companies must also be classified as either 'small' or 'large'. The classification as to the size of the proprietary company is important, as small proprietary companies will generally have reduced financial reporting requirements compared to large proprietary companies.

The distinction between large and small proprietary companies is based on the following three factors:
1. whether the company has a gross operating revenue exceeding $10 million;
2. whether the assets controlled by the company exceed $5 million; and
3. whether the company has 50 or more employees at the end of the financial year.

[passes 2 out of 3 tests.]

To be classified as a large proprietary company, the company must satisfy at least two of the above requirements. If the company cannot satisfy at least two of the requirements it is considered to be a small proprietary company.

The following table summarises the distinction between small and large proprietary companies.

Requirement	Small	Large
Value of gross operating revenue	Less than $10m	Greater than $10m
Value of gross assets	Less than $5m	Greater than $5m
Number of employees	Less than 50	Greater than 50

Proprietary and public companies limited by shares

Most companies registered in Australia are companies limited by shares, where the liability of each shareholder is limited to the maximum value of the shares acquired by the shareholder at the time of allotment and shareholders are not required to contribute to the funds of the company in excess of this amount.

In the event of a company liquidation, shareholders are only liable to contribute any unpaid amounts owing on their shares; their personal assets are thereby protected – that is, the shareholders have limited liability.

The advantages and disadvantages of forming, or converting an existing sole trader or partnership form of business ownership to, a proprietary or public company limited by shares are as follows.

Advantages of formation or conversion

Limited liability of shareholders

In a company limited by shares (both proprietary and public) the liability of shareholders for debts of the company is limited to any unpaid amounts owing on the shares. The shareholders (owners) are therefore protected against possible financial ruin if the company is unable to pay its debts.

Perpetual succession or continuity of existence

A company does not dissolve on the death or retirement of an owner, or on the transfer of ownership, because the company is a separate legal entity with an independent existence from that of its owners.

Although a company does enjoy a perpetual existence, it is still possible for a company to be liquidated and wound up voluntarily or by the creditors as stipulated by the Corporations Law.

Increased capital

A company offers the possibility of a greater number of owners of the business and therefore greater access to capital. It should be noted, however, that a proprietary company is prohibited from inviting the public to subscribe for shares or debentures in the company. A proprietary company is also prohibited from having more than 50 non-employee members.

Income tax

The income tax rate applied to companies may be lower than the personal income tax rates which are applied to the incomes of sole traders or partners. Companies currently incur an income tax rate of 30%, while individuals can pay up to 48.5%.

Transferability of shares

A proprietary company must restrict the right of its members to transfer shares to the public. This restriction usually means that shareholders can only transfer their shares to a person approved by the directors.

Disadvantages of formation or conversion

Cost of formation
Before a company can be registered, an application must be lodged with the Australian Securities and Investments Commission (ASIC) and the relevant lodgement fees must be paid. In addition to these fees, the legal costs of employing a solicitor or accountant to oversee the formation of the company may also be considerable.

Difficulty of formation
In some cases the formation may be quite involved and require the expertise of members of the legal and accounting professions. This may be particularly relevant where the shareholders require the drawing up of a specific and detailed company constitution.

Subject to regulations of the Corporations Law
A company incorporated under the Corporations Law must comply with the rules and regulations of the Law. These can be complex, and penalties may be imposed for contravention of sections of the Law.

Other forms of public companies

Three other forms of public company are the no liability, guarantee and unlimited liability company. Their characteristics are noted as follows.

No liability company.
No liability companies are restricted to the mining area. The company name of a no liability company must include the words 'No Liability' or the abbreviation 'NL'. The amount owing to the company by a shareholder is no greater than the amount already paid for the shares. If a shareholder decides not to pay a call, then they forfeit the shares which are then sold at public auction. There is also no liability if the company is liquidated.

Guarantee company.
Public companies limited by guarantee are formed mainly for charitable purposes, community service and by professional associations who have not-for-profit objectives. Members of such companies are not shareholders and do not share in any surplus of the guarantee company. If the company is liquidated and unable to pay all its debts, then each member pays up to an agreed sum to meet the shortfall on liquidation. The company limited by guarantee is rare.

Unlimited liability company.
Unlimited liability shareholders have the requirement to pay calls on shares, the same as shareholders in a limited liability company. However, as the name implies, shareholders have unlimited liability if the company is liquidated and cannot pay its debts. This is similar to that liability endured by sole traders and partners in a partnership. The unlimited company is very rare due to the risks involved.

Conversion of a proprietary company to a public company

The advantages and disadvantages of converting an existing proprietary company to a public company are as follows.

Advantages of conversion

Increased capital
A public company may issue prospectuses inviting the public to subscribe for shares, debentures or unsecured notes. A proprietary company cannot make invitations to the public.

Stock exchange listing
Only a public company can have its shares listed on the Australian Stock Exchange (ASX), which is the marketplace where shares and securities are bought and sold. A proprietary company must restrict the right of shareholders to transfer shares to the public. The mere act of incorporation does not, however, entitle a public company to be listed. The ASX has its own listing requirements, which some companies may not meet.

A public company listed on the ASX would generally have greater financial standing in the community than a company not listed. This listing is important if the company wishes to raise additional capital.

Transferability of shares
Shares held in a public company are freely transferable. That is, there are no restrictions placed on the transfer of shares as in a proprietary company.

No compulsion to pay dividends on ordinary shares
In accordance with the *Income Tax Assessment Act*, a public company is not compelled to distribute any part of its income or profits in the form of dividends to shareholders. A company's own constitution may, however, compel it to pay dividends on preference shares.

Disadvantages of conversion

Loss of control by shareholders
A proprietary company is generally subject to close control by its shareholders because its membership is limited to 50 shareholders. Many proprietary companies have, in fact, only one or two shareholders, with these same shareholders being directors in the company.

Because of the large number of shareholders in a public company, responsibility for the management of the company is left to a board of directors who are elected by the shareholders.

Question 1.1

From the following clues relating to the topic matters covered above, complete the crossword that follows.

Across
1. When a business is registered under the Corporations Law it becomes an … company.
4. The Corporations Law deals with this type of business entity.
8. A partnership is usually limited to between two and … people.
10. Shareholders in both proprietary and public companies have this (2 words).
12. A requirement for a large proprietary company is that the number of … is greater than 50.
14. A large proprietary company must satisfy two of three requirements regarding value and number. One of them is … … (2 words).
16. This business is owned by one person who is legally required to bear and to satisfy all losses; there is unlimited liability (2 words).
17. Most companies registered in Australia are limited by …
20. The owners of a company are its …
21. Details including capital contributions and the profit-sharing proportions should be included in the partnership …, otherwise the *Partnership Act* will apply.
22. The Corporations Law restricts the number of owners in this company.

Down

2. A company is registered because of it and it must comply with it. … … (2 words)
3. If not included in the partnership agreement, then the *Partnership* … applies.
5. There is no restriction on the maximum number of shareholders in this company.
6. Under the Corporations Law, before a company can commence it must be …
7. Both sole traders and partnerships have this in common. … … (2 words)
9. The maximum number of non-employee shareholders is … for a proprietary company.
11. A requirement for a large proprietary company is that the value of gross … is greater than $5 million.
13. Between two and 20 people can own this type of business and they all share in the losses and can each be held personally liable for the business debts; liability is unlimited.
15. This type of company must have not-for-profit objectives.
18. A proprietary company is classified as … or large.
19. A company is an artificial … person.

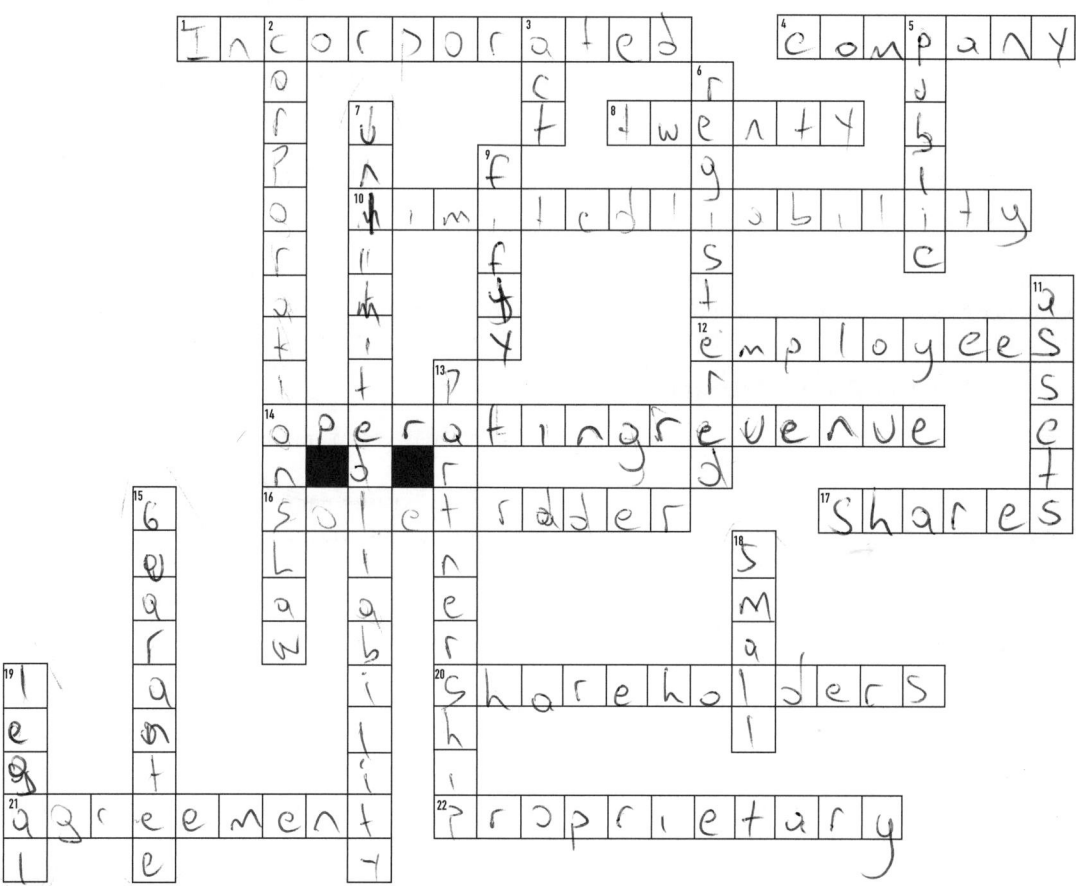

Question 1.2

Trigger and Sharon are contemplating converting their partnership business into a proprietary company limited by shares. List and explain two advantages that the company form of business organisation would have to offer them.

limited liability

Income Tax

Question 1.3

Ian and Paul have been trading in partnership and they are now contemplating converting their business to a proprietary company limited by shares. List and explain two disadvantages that the partners should consider before converting their business into such a company.

[handwritten: Corporations Law & Cost]

Question 1.4

Bill, Graham and George have been operating in partnership for three years. They are unhappy with the partnership form of business ownership and have decided to convert their existing business to a proprietary company limited by shares.
a   List and briefly explain two possible reasons for their decision. *[handwritten: Corporations Law & limited liabilities]*
b   State the minimum and maximum number of shareholders that a proprietary company may have. *[handwritten: 1-50]*
c   Explain how the partners will be able to ensure that they can maintain personal ownership and control of their business. *[handwritten: 1=50 33⅓ Share]*

Procedures for the incorporation of a company

The procedure for the incorporation of a company limited by shares under the Corporations Law involves the following steps:

1 Register the business.
2 Adopt the Replaceable Rules or prepare a constitution.
3 Allot shares to founding members.
4 Appoint director(s) and company secretary.
5 Complete and lodge the application form.
6 Commence business on the granting of the certificate of registration.

Step 1 Register the business

The registration of a company involves registering the business name and obtaining an Australian Business Number.

In order not to choose a name that is identical or similar to an existing name, it is advisable to consult the alphabetical listing of companies and business names available at ASIC Business Centres. ASIC will reject a name that is identical to another body corporate or business name.

It is important to note that ASIC is responsible for the reservation and recognition of corporate names and *not* business names. (This is a state responsibility.) With regard to the names of particular classes of companies, the Corporations Law provides that a company may use as its name one that is available. In addition:

- a limited company shall have the word 'Limited' or the abbreviation 'Ltd' as part of and at the end of its name; and
- a proprietary company shall have the word 'Proprietary' or the abbreviation 'Pty' as part of its name, inserted immediately before the word 'Limited' or before the abbreviation 'Ltd' or, in the case of an unlimited company, at the end of its name.

Step 2 Adopt the Replaceable Rules or prepare a constitution

When establishing a company the shareholders will need to establish the rules and procedures that it will put in place to govern its internal management, such as appointing, remunerating and removing directors, calling and conducting meetings of directors and meetings of members (shareholders), issuing shares and paying dividends.

The Corporations Law allows a new company to be governed by the Replaceable Rules contained within the Law, by a constitution, or by a combination of the Replaceable Rules and a constitution. Replaceable Rules apply to all companies with the exception of single shareholder/single director companies.

As the specially drafted constitution is now optional, shareholders of companies other than single shareholder/single director companies can either:

- adopt the Replaceable Rules as they appear in the Corporations Law without making any amendments; or
- amend any provisions of the Replaceable Rules as they see fit by preparing a constitution that varies the Replaceable Rules; or
- prepare a constitution that replaces the Replaceable Rules entirely. However, certain Replaceable Rules are mandatory for public companies.

Note that companies registered prior to 1998 were required to lodge a Memorandum of Association and Articles of Association when seeking incorporation. These companies are permitted under the current law to continue with these as their constitutional documents, or they may convert from using their Memorandum of Association and Articles of Association to adopting the Replaceable Rules as their constitution.

Step 3 Allot shares to founding members

The founding members of the newly formed company, known as subscriber shareholders, will need to determine the number of shares and the value of each share that they each will take in the newly formed company. In the past, these people were sometimes referred to as promoters.

Step 4 Appoint director(s) and company secretary

In accordance with the Law, a proprietary company will need to appoint a director who will be responsible for the day-to-day operations of the company. A public company must have at least three directors. In addition, the company directors will need to appoint a company secretary.

Step 5 Complete and lodge the application form

The registration of a company with ASIC must be made by a person, with the application including the following contents:

- the type of company to be registered;
- the proposed company name;
- the name and address of each person who consents to be a member;
- the name and address of each person who consents to be a director or company secretary;
- the address of the proposed registered office and principal place of business; and
- for a company limited by shares, the number of shares that each member agrees to take and the amount that each member agrees to pay (or owe) on each share.

Step 6 Commence business on the granting of the certificate of registration

If ASIC is satisfied with the application for registration of the company, it will register the company and issue the company with a Certificate of Registration.

The shares that are to be taken by the members named on the application form are deemed to be issued to the members on the date of registration of the company.

Question 1.5

Wendy and Bill operate a partnership and have decided to convert to a company limited by shares.

As their accountant, you are required to prepare a brief report that explains their options and the procedures that they will need to follow in order to obtain registration under the Corporations Law.

Costs associated with establishing a company

The formation of a company may involve costs associated with obtaining financial advice on establishing the business, legal advice in relation to company registration and adoption of a suitable constitution, and the actual costs of registration.

The initial payment of these establishment costs will give rise to an account specifically named to describe the costs associated with the formation of the company. These costs can be called formation costs, preliminary costs, establishment costs or set-up costs.

The accounting treatment for these costs has not yet been adequately determined in the accounting standards, which has resulted in alternative treatments of these costs. The alternative treatments include:

- capitalisation of the costs as an asset which is subsequently written off against profits over an extended period of time; and
- treating the costs as an expense in the period in which they were incurred.

The journal entry to record the payment of formation costs is:

General journal		
Cost of establishment	Dr	
Bank account		Cr

ILLUSTRATION

Albert Park Ltd was registered as a public company on 1 July 2003. In the weeks leading up to the registration and during the registration period the business incurred the following GST-inclusive establishment costs:

Accounting advice	$2 750 (includes $250 GST)
Legal costs	$4 250 (includes $386 GST)
Registration and other costs	$520 (includes $48 GST)
Total establishment costs	**$7 520 (includes $684 GST)**

These costs would be recorded in the journal and general ledger as follows:

General journal of Albert Park Ltd

Date	Particulars	Debit	Credit
2007		$	$
1 July	Costs of establishment	6 836	
	Input tax credit	684	
	Bank		7 520
	To record cost of establishing the company		

General ledger of Albert Park Ltd

Date	Particulars	Debit	Credit	Balance
Costs of establishment				
1 July 2007	Bank	6 836		6 836 Dr

Input tax credit				
1 July 2007	Bank	684		684 Dr
Bank				
1 July 2007	Costs of formation		7 520	7 520 Cr

Question 1.6

Harris Pty Ltd was incorporated on 18 May 2003. The business incurred $1 980 (inclusive of GST) in various costs during the establishment and registration of the company. You are required to:
a record the establishment costs in the general journal; and
b post the journal to the general ledger.

Authorities governing companies

The main authorities governing companies are:
- the Corporations Law, together with other related legislation, which contains most of the requirements relating to the formation, operation, record-keeping and reporting, grievance procedures and winding-up of private sector companies. Supervision of the *Corporations Act 2001* and the Law is the responsibility of ASIC;
- the Australian Stock Exchange, whose requirements are additional to those of ASIC and the Australian Accounting Standards Board (AASB) and apply to companies when their securities are traded on the stock exchange; and
- accounting standards made by the AASB, which are the main basis of accounting rules used in the recording of data and the production of company reports.

Australian Securities and Investments Commission

The federal government appoints between three and eight people as members of ASIC whose functions include:
- overall administration of matters relating to companies; these include registration formalities and the issue of certificates of registration, registration of business names, receipt and monitoring of companies' annual returns, and dealing with enquiries from the public about companies;
- investigation of companies suspected of non-compliance with the Corporations Law or accounting standards;
- formulation and issue of certain corporate reporting and compliance requirements in their ASIC releases; and
- the referral of matters to other statutory bodies, which include the Companies and Securities Advisory Panel and the Companies Auditors and Liquidators Disciplinary Board, and the provision of resources to these bodies.

Australian Stock Exchange

The Australian Stock Exchange provides a market for the sale and purchase of securities, including company shares. The ASX, through its listing and trading rules, has implemented its responsibility under the Corporations Law for the appropriateness of stock market activities.

Part of this responsibility entails the monitoring of companies and the transmission of information about them to existing and potential shareholders. The ASX maintains listing rules that govern certain aspects of share trading, company administration and compulsory reporting. The listing rules do not conflict with the Corporations Law or the accounting standards, but are complementary or additional to those authorities.

Financial Reporting Council

The federal government has established an agency called the Financial Reporting Council (FRC), which is responsible for advising the government on the process of setting and developing accounting standards. Council members are appointed by the federal government and consist of representatives from the accounting professions and from the private and public sectors. The FRC assists the AASB by approving its strategic directions, priorities, budget and staffing arrangements. Members of the AASB are appointed by the FRC.

Australian Accounting Standards Board

The AASB is responsible for the setting of accounting standards in Australia. The accounting standards established by the AASB are issued by the AASB, rather than codified in legislation, as:

- the process provides a mechanism for accounting standards to be set by a group of individuals who are specialists in financial reporting and provides these specialists with professional support;
- accounting standards need to be updated and corrected from time to time and this would generally be more difficult to do if they were embodied in legislation; and
- the AASB is able to act as a forum for canvassing diverse community views on the accounting standards.

The AASB must ensure that the standards it issues do not conflict with any of the requirements in the Corporations Law. The AASB standards apply by force of law to all entities regulated by the Law, including public companies and large proprietary companies formed under the Law, as well as managed investment schemes such as unit trusts.

Under the Corporations Law, AASB standards have the force of law, as:

- a company's directors must ensure that its financial statements comply with accounting standards;
- auditors of companies are required to state whether the accounts have been made out in accordance with accounting standards; and
- there are substantial penalties for company directors' non-compliance.

International Accounting Standards Board

Throughout the last century Australian companies and other reporting entities were obliged to comply with the Australian accounting standards developed by the AASB. In other countries companies adopted similar national measures. In the later part of the century pressure was mounting around the world for the harmonisation of accounting standards as the globalisation of capital markets increased.

An international accounting body was established called the International Accounting Standards Committee (IASC), taking its membership from a host of nations. The primary aim of the IASC was to develop a single set of International Accounting Standards (IAS) that would eventually replace the national standards used in different countries.

In 2000, the IASC was revamped and renamed the International Accounting Standards Board (IASB). This board is responsible for issuing international accounting standards called International Financial Reporting Standards (IFRS). In the coming years the IASB will be reviewing the former IAS and reissuing them as IFRS.

The Australian government, through the FRC and the AASB, has decreed that Australian domestic companies must, for the reporting year ending in 2005, report according to the standards laid down by the IASB.

Accordingly, the AASB is reissuing the Australian accounting standards so that they comply with the existing IFRS and IAS.

In 2005, six IFRS were issued which have been adopted by the AASB. These standards have single-digit references, such as AASB 1. There were also approximately 35 applicable IAS. These are identified with three-digit references such as AASB 101.

Where there are no IFRS or IAS to replace an existing accounting standard the AASB will remain in place. These standards have four-digit references such as AASB 1031.

Company statutory records and registers

Once a business becomes registered/incorporated it must continue to comply with the provisions of the law as detailed in the Corporations Law. Within the Law there are a range of records and registers that must be kept or maintained by a company. These are summarised as follows:

Register of members

The Corporations Law requires a company to set up and maintain a register of its members which contains:

- each member's name and address;
- the date of entry of the member to the register;
- the date of the allotment of shares to the member;
- the number of shares allotted to the member and the total number of shares held;
- the class of shares, share numbers or share certificate numbers held by each member; and
- the amount that remains unpaid on the shares.

Register of charges

Companies at times may raise finance, such as a mortgage, and secure the loan against the company's assets. This is referred to as a charge.

The Law requires a company to keep a register of charges on the property of the company, or upon the acquisition of property subject to a charge.

Register of debenture holders

A source of finance commonly used by larger companies is the issue of debentures. A debenture is essentially a document that is issued by a company that evidences or acknowledges the indebtedness of the company to the party that provided the finance. A debenture may be secured against the assets of the company or it may be unsecured.

The Corporations Law stipulates that a company that issues debentures must keep a register of holders of debentures by recording the name and address of the debenture holder and the amount of the debenture.

Register of option holders

Where a company grants options over unissued shares, a register of option holders and copies of options documents must be maintained. Because it is a register of the holders of options that are still exercisable, the register must be updated whenever options are exercised or expire.

Minutes of all proceedings of general meetings and meetings of directors

A company in accordance with the Law must keep minute books recording such things as proceedings and resolutions at meetings of members and directors, the details of which must be recorded within one month of the meeting.

Accounting records

The Corporations Law requires a company to keep written financial records that:

a   correctly record and explain its transactions and financial position and performance; and
b   would enable true and fair financial statements to be prepared and audited.

An overview of the obligations for financial reports and audit, described in the Law, includes:

1. the preparation of financial reports, including financial statements, disclosures and notes, and directors' declaration;
2. the preparation of the directors' report;
3. the auditing of the financial report and obtaining the auditor's report;
4. the forwarding of the financial reports and auditor's report to members; and
5. the lodging of the financial report, directors' report and auditor's report with ASIC.

The Corporations Law requires that all disclosing entities, public companies and large proprietary companies prepare annual financial reports and directors' reports, and that these organisations have their accounts audited.

Small proprietary companies, on the other hand, do not have to prepare annual financial reports and directors' reports unless requested to do so by their shareholders or ASIC, and they are exempt from having their accounts audited.

The financial reports referred to in the Corporations Law are:

- financial statements for the year;
- notes to financial statements; and
- directors' declaration about the statements and notes.

As there needs to be compliance with the accounting standards and regulations, the profit and loss statement will be the statement of financial performance (AASB 1018), the balance sheet will be the statement of financial position (AASB 1040) and the statement of cash flows will remain as that (AASB 1026).

These financial statements and notes for a financial year must give a true and fair view of the financial performance and position of the company and consolidated financial statements where required. Small proprietary companies may be exempt from complying with the accounting standards under certain conditions.

Question 1.7

From the following clues relating to the topic matters covered above, complete the crossword that follows:

Across

1. A function of the AASB is to participate and contribute to a single set of accounting standards for … use.
4. A company's … must ensure that the company's financial statements comply with accounting standards.
6. If directors do not comply with accounting standards, then there are substantial …
10. Before a company can commence, ASIC needs to issue a certificate of …
11. The body that is directed by the FRC to develop Australian accounting standards is the …
12. A company that raises finance through a mortgage or secures a loan over its assets must keep details in a register of …
13. Supervision of the Corporations Law is their responsibility (abbreviation).
16. A company that issues debentures must maintain a register of … … (2 words).
18. Legislation that is relevant to companies is the … Law.
19. They state whether the accounts have been made out in accordance with accounting standards.
20. The 'S' in AASB stands for …

Down

2. The 'X' in ASX stands for …
3. The AASB provides the main basis of accounting rules for the production of company …
5. AASB standards apply to both public companies and large … companies.

7 The initials of the organisation responsible for the supervision of the Corporations Law.
8 The 'I' in ASIC stands for …
9 ASX provides a market for the sale and purchase of securities, including company …
14 The ASX … … (2 words) do not conflict with the Law or the accounting standards, but are complementary or additional to those authorities.
15 AASB has the power to make accounting standards that have the … … … (3 words).
17 A shareholder's name, address and shareholding details are shown in the register of …

Question 1.8

Name the records and registers that are required to be kept by a large proprietary company under the Corporations Law.

CHAPTER 2
ACCOUNTING FOR SHARE AND DEBENTURE ISSUES

Objectives

Upon satisfactory completion of this chapter you should be able to:

- define the issue price of shares;
- differentiate between preference shares, ordinary shares and deferred shares;
- account for the issue of shares on incorporation;
- distinguish between issued capital, uncalled capital, and share capital or paid-up capital;
- describe the concept of partly paid shares and calls on unpaid share capital;
- account for public company share issues;
- define the various costs associated with share issues and account for those costs;
- define in relation to recent public issues:
  - bookbuilding
  - stapled securities;
- define and differentiate between debentures, mortgage debentures and unsecured notes; and
- account for the issue and redemption of debentures.

Introduction

All companies are involved in the issuing of shares to the owners on incorporation. In addition, public companies requiring capital to finance the operations of the company may issue shares to the public. Alternatively, capital may be raised through the issue of debentures.

This chapter concentrates on the various options that a company has in issuing shares and debentures to the public and their associated accounting requirements.

Share capital

Owners of a company are referred to as shareholders. To become a shareholder of a company, a person or entity must obtain a share or shares issued by that company.

For a company to be registered under the Corporations Law it must provide the names of the people who have consented to be members of the company. The founding members, also known as subscribers, become the first shareholders of the company and must be recorded in the Register of Members.

Shares in a public company can also be purchased when the company issues a prospectus offering shares in the company to the general public. Where a prospectus is issued, people or entities must complete and lodge an application form which specifies the number and type of shares that are to be bought, and forward payment for the shares in anticipation of the application being accepted by the company that issued the prospectus.

The share capital of a company refers to the shares issued and paid for by either the subscribers or the applicants who were successful in obtaining shares on a prospectus. Share capital is also referred to as owners' equity or paid-up share capital or, more specifically, shareholders' equity.

Issue price of shares

When a company issues shares the directors are free to place any terms and conditions they consider appropriate to the share issue. This includes placing a value on the shares under offer. In setting the price of a share the directors would need to give consideration to a range of factors, including:

- the maximisation of shareholder wealth;
- the effect on the market price of existing shares;
- the requirement to sell a desired volume of shares;
- the expectation of future profits and dividends to service the new shares;
- whether ASX listing is proposed or already exists; and
- the use of an underwriter, as this affects the directors' risk in underwriting the issue.

Consequently, all shares issued by a company may not have the same issue price. For example, a company may have issued a prospectus offering shares to the public at $1 each in 2005. Another prospectus may be issued in the next year offering shares at $1.20 each or even $0.90 each.

Uncalled and paid-up share capital

When a company issues shares, the directors may place conditions on the issue in relation to the amount(s) that must be paid for the shares.

The shares could be issued on the condition that they are paid in full, or could be issued partly paid with the balance payable at a future date(s). Amounts to be paid at a future date are referred to as calls.

A company's share capital, also referred to as paid-up capital, is equal to the number of shares issued, multiplied by the amount that the directors required as payment for the shares. The amount not required for payment is referred to as the uncalled amount.

For example, the directors of GB Ltd issued 100 000 $2 shares payable $0.50 on application and the balance in the future. The respective amounts of share capital and uncalled capital would be calculated as follows:

	Share capital	Uncalled capital
No. of shares issued	100 000	100 000
Amount called/uncalled	$0.50	$1.50
Total	$50 000	$150 000

Uncalled capital will be converted to share capital when payment is required for the amount owing. When a shareholder fails to pay the uncalled amount by the date required, the amount owing is classified as calls in arrears. Shareholders may forfeit their shares if calls remain unpaid; however, the conditions for forfeiture would need to be documented in the company's constitution.

Classes of shares

Companies can issue a variety of different classes of shares each with particular characteristics, benefits and advantages. Three classes of shares are:
1. ordinary shares;
2. preference shares; and
3. deferred or founder shares.

Ordinary shares

The ordinary share is the basic type of share and the most common. When only one type of share is issued, then it is by definition the ordinary share. The company decides the rights, duties and other terms on which ordinary shares are issued. Typically, ordinary shares give full voting rights and the right to receive dividends. However, the rate of dividend depends on the profit performance of the company and the decisions of the directors in relation to the distribution of profits.

Preference shares

This is the second most common type of share and usually gives the preference shareholder preferential rights to a fixed rate of dividends before dividends of the ordinary shareholders are declared. The rights attaching to preference shares, which must be set out in the constitution or by special resolution, are as follows:
- **Repayment of capital:** Shareholders may be entitled to preferential rights in regard to return of capital when a company is wound up.
- **Participation in surplus assets and profits:** Shares may be either participating or non-participating. Participating preference shares entitle holders to participate with ordinary shareholders in dividends declared in excess of the fixed preferential dividend rate, sometimes to a specific limit only.
- **Cumulative and non-cumulative dividends:** Cumulative preference shares entitle holders who receive less than the fixed preferential dividend in any one year to receive the arrears of preferential dividend, plus the current year's preferential dividend in the following period, before the ordinary shareholders receive any dividend.
- **Voting rights.**
- **Priority of payment of capital and dividends** in relation to other shares or classes of preference shares.

Deferred or founder shares

With this type of share, usually issued to the initial subscribers, founders or promoters of the company, dividends are often paid after they have been paid to other classes of shareholders. The founders are the very first shareholders who start the company before any shares are issued to the public.

The founders provide the money to establish and register the company and issue the prospectus. If the founders accept that their shares are deferred shares, they are trying to make a statement that they believe in the future profitability of the company.

The initial subscribers, founders or promoters of the company are not required to accept deferred shares and quite often will be issued with ordinary shares.

When accounting for the issue of different classes of shares, it is important that each class of share is identified separately in the financial records of the company.

Issuing shares

Companies will issue shares when they are initially registered and when raising additional capital.

Shares issued on registration

Both private and public companies are required to provide the name(s) of people who have agreed to become members of the company when it is seeking registration. These people, referred to as subscribers, are recorded in the Register of Members as the first shareholders of the company.

As the subscribers have agreed to their names being included on the application form, and to the acceptance of shares when the company is registered, they have legal ownership of the shares and have an obligation to pay for those shares.

The procedures and accounting entries to account for the issue of subscriber shares are as follows:

1. Issue the shares to the subscribers on the date that the company was incorporated (or the date on which the directors issued the shares).

General journal		
Subscribers	Dr	
Share capital		Cr

2. Issue receipts to the subscribers upon payment for the shares.

General journal		
Bank	Dr	
Subscribers		Cr

ILLUSTRATION

Albert Park Ltd was registered as a public company limited by shares on 1 July 2007. The application for registration of the company named three people who had agreed to be members. Each member had agreed to take the following:
- 50 000 ordinary shares each at an issue price of $1 per share;
- 10 000 preference shares at an issue price of $2.50 each; and
- 10 000 deferred shares at an issue price of $5 each.

Payment for the shares was required by 14 July 2007.
The journal and general ledger entries recording these transactions would be as follows:

1 Issue of shares to subscribers

General journal of Albert Park Ltd

Date	Particulars	Debit	Credit
2007 1 July	Subscribers	$ 375 000	$
	Share capital – Ordinary shares		150 000
	Share capital – Preference shares		75 000
	Share capital – Deferred shares		150 000
	Issued shares to subscribers on registration		

General journal of Albert Park Ltd

Date	Particulars	Debit	Credit	Balance
Subscribers				
1 July 2007	Share capital	375 000		375 000 Dr
Share capital – Ordinary shares				
1 July 2007	Subscribers		150 000	150 000 Cr
Share capital – Preference shares				
1 July 2007	Subscribers		75 000	75 000 Cr
Share capital – Deferred shares				
1 July 2007	Subscribers		150 000	150 000 Cr

2 *Receipt of subscribers' payments*

General journal of Albert Park Ltd

Date	Particulars	Debit	Credit
2007 14 July	Bank	$ 375 000	$
	Subscribers		375 000
	Receipted money paid by subscribers		

General ledger of Albert Park Ltd

Date	Particulars	Debit	Credit	Balance
Subscribers				
1 July 2007	Share capital	375 000		375 000 Dr
14 July 2007	Bank		375 000	Nil
Bank				
14 July 2007	Subscribers		375 000	375 000 Dr

The balance sheet of the company prepared for reporting to management could be presented as follows:

Albert Park Ltd
Balance sheet as at 14 July 2007

Shareholders' equity	$
Share capital	150 000
Ordinary shares (150 000)	150 000
Preference shares (30 000)	75 000
Deferred shares (30 000)	150 000
Total shareholders' equity	375 000
Assets	
Bank	375 000
Total assets	375 000

Question 2.1

Castaway Ltd was incorporated on 1 July 2006. The application for registration of the company listed five members who had each agreed to take 1 000 ordinary shares at an issue price of $2 each. Subscribers were required to pay for the shares by 31 July 2006. You are required to:

a prepare journal entries to record the share transactions;
b post the journal entries to the general ledger; and
c prepare a balance sheet as at 31 July 2006.

Question 2.2

Weffacol Suppliers Ltd was registered as a public company on 31 January 2006. The four members whose names were listed on the registration papers had each agreed to take the following shares in the company, with payment to be made by 28 February 2006:

- Ordinary shares: 100 000 each at an issue price of $0.50 each.
- Preference shares: 20 000 each at an issue price of $5 each.

You are required to:
a prepare journal entries to record the share transactions;
b post the journal entries to the general ledger; and
c prepare a balance sheet as at 28 February 2006.

Raising share capital

When a company wishes to raise additional share capital it will need to issue more shares. Private companies are not permitted under the Corporations Law to issue shares to the public. Public companies, however, are permitted to issue shares to the public. When a public company issues shares to the public, it must issue a prospectus in accordance with the requirements of the Corporations Law.

The prospectus sets out information relevant to the potential investor's understanding of the prospects of the company. Generally, the prospectus is required to include all the information that investors and their professional advisers would reasonably require to make an informed assessment of the matter.

The Corporations Law requires disclosure of the rights and liabilities attaching to the shares and disclosure of information, including the terms of the offer. The terms and conditions of the invitation would include:

- the class of share being issued;
- the share price and the number of shares to be issued;
- the amount that must be paid for each share with the application (on allotment and in future calls, if any);
- the minimum subscription (if any), being the minimum amount that must be raised by the prospectus before shares can be allotted;

- the allotment process; and
- the treatment of oversubscriptions (being money paid by the applicant in excess of the number of shares allotted).

Disclosure would also need to be made of specific details, such as the interests of directors and other persons named in the prospectus.

In contract law, a prospectus is an 'invitation to treat' and not strictly an offer by the company. Prospective shareholders must complete and lodge with the company or its solicitor the application form together with the amount required to be paid. The application constitutes an offer by the applicant. If the company accepts the offer, the applicant will be issued with shares in the company and become a member (shareholder) of the company. The company may not accept the offer made by the applicant, in which case the offer is refused and the applicant's money is refunded.

Before a company can invite applications from the public to purchase shares, it must lodge the prospectus with ASIC for approval.

Procedure for issuing shares under a prospectus

The accounting entries associated with issuing shares under a prospectus are directly associated with the legal requirements associated with the issue of shares under a prospectus. These requirements are as follows:

1. The company makes the approved prospectus, together with an application form attached, available to the general public. The application form inviting the public to apply for shares is completed by the prospective shareholder and forwarded together with money (usually) to the company and received as application monies.
2. The application monies are 'held in trust' until after the shares are allotted, or allocated, as the money does not belong to the company until the shares are allotted. Following the passing of the *Corporate Law Economic Reform Program Act 2003* (CLERP), the cash received can now be held in trust by deposit with any financial institution, as opposed to a bank which was the requirement prior to the Act. The company would therefore need to arrange for a trust account to be established with a financial institution and would need to include such an account in its Chart of Accounts.
3. If the invitation to apply for shares is subject to minimum subscription conditions, then the minimum subscription must be received before the shares can be allotted. If the minimum subscription is not reached, then the application money is returned to the applicants from the trust account and the share issue ceases. If the minimum subscription is exceeded or there was no minimum, then the directors allot the shares to the applicants. If the invitation is oversubscribed, the directors will have to decide which of the applications will be successful and applicants may receive all, some or none of the shares that they applied for.
4. When allotment is made and the advice is communicated to the applicant, the shares are then considered formally issued. The company can then transfer the application money from the trust account to their bank account for general use.
5. On allotment the successful applicant may be required to pay a further amount of money calculated on the shares allotted. This is processed through the accounts as allotment. Allotment money does not have to be held in trust as the shares have been granted to the shareholder, and the shareholder has a legal obligation to make payment for the shares as per the terms of the prospectus.

Question 2.3

a Explain the difference between subscriber shareholders and shareholders who obtained shares via a prospectus.

b A company has issued 100 000 ordinary shares via a prospectus at an issue price of $2.50 payable $1 on application and the balance when required. Explain the following terms in relation to the prospectus:
  i issue price;
  ii share capital; and
  iii uncalled capital.

c Differentiate between the following types of shares in reference to dividend payments:

      i   ordinary shares;
     ii   preference shares; and
    iii   deferred shares.
- **d** Briefly describe the five steps involved in issuing shares via a prospectus.
- **e** Explain the importance of achieving the minimum subscription on a prospectus.
- **f** Explain the difference between the terms 'application' and 'allotment' in relation to a prospectus.
- **g** In reference to the principles of contract law, explain the relevance of the following:
  - **i** the issue of a prospectus;
  - **ii** application to a prospectus; and
  - **iii** issuing shares on allotment.

Share capital issued by prospectus

Public companies may raise funds by issuing a prospectus inviting the public to make offers for shares in the company. The terms of payment for the shares would be included in the prospectus and may include the following scenarios:

- payment in full on application;
- part payment on application, with the balance payable on allotment of the shares; and
- part payment on application and allotment, with the balance payable in calls.

A company may also find that the number of shares applied for by the applicants to the prospectus may exceed the number of shares on offer. This is referred to as an oversubscription and may require the company to make refunds to people who were not successful in obtaining shares when allotment occurred.

The illustrations that follow explore a number of scenarios that may confront a public company that has issued a prospectus.

Shares issued fully paid on application

An ideal, simple situation is where shares are issued:

- fully paid on application; and
- the number of shares issued by the directors agrees exactly with the number applied for; and
- all applications have been received with the full amount.

Three entries are required to account for the transactions associated with this prospectus. They are as follows:

1. Record the receipt of monies forwarded by the applicants who make offers to purchase shares. Applicants' deposits must be held in a trust account until allotment of the shares occurs.

General journal		
Trust account	Dr	
Application		Cr

2. Formally allot shares to the applicants (acceptance of applicants' offers).

General journal		
Application	Dr	
Share capital		Cr

3. After the allotment of shares, the money held in the trust account can be transferred to the company's normal bank account as the company, by issuing shares, has met its contractual obligations and can legally take possession of the money.

General journal		
Bank	Dr	
Trust account		Cr

ILLUSTRATION

On 31 July 2007 Hyde Ltd issued a prospectus inviting applications for 100 000 ordinary shares at $1 each payable in full on application, with 31 August 2007 being the closing date for applications. Applications and money were received for exactly 100 000 shares. The directors formally allotted the shares to these applications on 1 September 2007.

1 Receipt of application monies

General journal of Hyde Ltd

Date	Particulars	Debit	Credit
2007		$	$
31 Aug	Trust account – Share applications	100 000	
	Applications – Ordinary shares		100 000
	Receipted money paid by subscribers		

General ledger of Hyde Ltd

Date	Particulars	Debit	Credit	Balance
Trust account – Share applications				
31 Aug 2007	Applications	100 000		100 000 Dr
Applications – Ordinary shares				
31 Aug 2007	Trust account		100 000	100 000 Cr

2 Allotment of shares

General journal of Hyde Ltd

Date	Particulars	Debit	Credit
2007		$	$
1 Sept	Applications – Ordinary shares	100 000	
	Share capital – Ordinary shares		100 000
	Allotted shares to applicants		

General ledger of Hyde Ltd

Date	Particulars	Debit	Credit	Balance
Applications – Ordinary shares				
31 Aug 2007	Trust account		100 000	100 000 Cr
	Share capital	100 000		Nil

Share capital – Ordinary shares

1 Sept 2007	Applications		100 000	100 000 Cr

3 *Transfer of trust account balance*

General journal of Hyde Ltd

Date	Particulars	Debit	Credit
2007		$	$
1 Sept	Bank	100 000	
	Trust account – Share applications		100 000
	Transfer of money held in trust		

General ledger of Hyde Ltd

Date	Particulars	Debit	Credit	Balance

Applications – Ordinary shares

| 31 Aug 2007 | Applications | 100 000 | | 100 000 Dr |
| 1 Sept 2007 | Bank | | 100 000 | Nil |

Share capital – Ordinary shares

| 31 Aug 2007 | Trust account | | 100 000 | 100 000 Dr |

The balance sheet prepared for internal management purposes after these share issue transactions could be presented as follows:

Hyde Ltd
Balance sheet as at 14 July 2007

	$
Shareholders' equity	
Share capital	
Ordinary shares (100 000)	100 000
Total shareholders' equity	100 000
Assets	
Bank	100 000
Total assets	100 000

Question 2.4

On 1 September 2007 Huskisson Ltd was registered as a public company limited by shares. A prospectus was issued on 1 October 2007 inviting applications for 300 000 preference shares at a price of $2 each payable in full on application. The closing date for receipt of applications was 31 October, and by that date application and money was received for 300 000 shares.

On 1 November 2007 the directors formally allotted the shares to the applicants.

You are required to:
a   record all appropriate journal entries; and
b   post journals to the general ledger.

Question 2.5

Caesia Ltd was registered on 1 July 2006 with five members recorded on the application for registration. Each member had agreed to take 20 000 ordinary shares at an issue price of $0.50 each. The money owing by the subscribers was received on 8 July.

On 15 July 2006 the directors met and agreed to issue a prospectus inviting offers for 100 000 preference shares at an issue price of $4 each. Applicants to the prospectus were required to make payment in full on application by 31 August 2006.

When applications closed, applications had been received for 100 000 shares. The directors met on 6 September and allotted all shares.

You are required to:
a prepare journal entries for the respective share issues;
b post the journal entries to the general ledger; and
c prepare a balance sheet as at 6 September 2006.

Undersubscribed and oversubscribed share issues

When a company issues a prospectus inviting the public to apply for shares, it is more than likely that the number of shares applied for by prospective shareholders will not be equal to the number of shares listed as being made available in the prospectus.

A share issue is said to be undersubscribed if the minimum subscription stated in the prospectus has not been met. The minimum subscription is the minimum number of shares (decided by the directors) that must be applied for before the prospectus can proceed. If the minimum subscription is not met, the prospectus is cancelled and all applicants are refunded their application money.

Alternatively, a share issue may be oversubscribed. This will occur when the amount of money received on application for shares is greater than the maximum amount that should have been received. For example, if ABC Ltd issued a prospectus seeking applications for 100 000 ordinary shares issued at $2 each and applications were received for 120 000 shares, the share issue would be oversubscribed by $40 000 (20 000 shares at $2 each).

Where a share issue is oversubscribed, when allotting the shares the directors can use their discretion as to which applicants are to receive shares and in what quantities. Although the company's constitution (if there is one) and the conditions of issue on the prospectus may indicate various alternatives, the directors should allot the shares in an impartial manner.

Applicants to a prospectus who were unsuccessful in obtaining shares when they were allotted by the directors, or because the prospectus was cancelled, must be refunded their application money from the trust account.

The procedure and accounting entries to record the receipt of application money and the allotment of shares to successful applicants is the same as described in the previous illustration. Three entries are required to account for the transactions associated with this prospectus. They are as follows:

1 Record the receipt of application monies to the trust account.

General journal		
Trust account	Dr	
Application		Cr

2 Allot shares to successful applicants.

General journal		
Application	Dr	
Share capital		Cr

3 When applicants are to be refunded their application money, an additional entry is required. The entry to refund applicants' money is:

General journal		
Application	Dr	
Trust account		Cr

4 After the allotment of shares, and after refunds to unsuccessful applicants have been made, the money held in the trust account can be transferred to the company's normal bank account.

General journal		
Bank	Dr	
Trust account		Cr

ILLUSTRATION

On 1 September 2007 Buronga Ltd issued a prospectus inviting applications for 200 000 preference shares at $4 each payable in full on application ($800 000).

By the closing date of 30 September, fully paid applications had been received for 230 000 shares ($920 000).

On 1 October the directors:
- allotted 200 000 shares to successful applicants; and
- refunded unsuccessful applicants for the 30 000 shares at $4 each ($120 000).

The journal entries recording these transactions would be as follows:

1 Receipt of application monies

General journal of Buronga Ltd

Date	Particulars	Debit	Credit
2007		$	$
30 Sept	Trust account – Share applications	920 000	
	Applications – Preference shares		920 000
	Receipt of $4 per share for 230 000 shares		

2 Allotment of shares to successful applicants

General journal of Buronga Ltd

Date	Particulars	Debit	Credit
2007		$	$
1 Oct	Applications – Preference shares	800 000	
	Share capital – Preference shares		800 000
	Allotted 200 000 shares at $4 each to successful applicants		

3 *Refunds of application monies to unsuccessful applicants*

General journal of Buronga Ltd

Date	Particulars	Debit	Credit
2007		$	$
1 Oct	Applications – Preference shares	120 000	
	Trust account – Share applications		120 000
	Refunded unsuccessful applicants for 30 000 shares at $4 per share		

4 *Transfer of trust account balance*

General journal of Buronga Ltd

Date	Particulars	Debit	Credit
2007		$	$
1 Oct	Bank	800 000	
	Trust account – Share applications		800 000
	Transfer of money held in trust		

The general ledger arising from these entries would appear as follows:

General ledger of Buronga Ltd

Date	Particulars	Debit	Credit	Balance
Trust account – Share applications				
30 Sept 2007	Applications	920 000		920 000 Dr
1 Sept 2007	Applications		120 000	800 000 Dr
	Bank		800 000	Nil
Applications – Preference shares				
30 Sept 2007	Trust account		920 000	920 000 Cr
1 Sept 2007	Share capital	800 000		120 000 Cr
	Trust account	120 000		Nil
Share capital – Preference shares				
1 Sept 2007	Applications		800 000	800 000 Cr
Bank				
1 Sept 2007	Trust account	800 000		800 000 Dr

Question 2.6

On 1 April 2007 Carreara Ltd issued a prospectus inviting applications for 500 000 ordinary shares at a price of $1.50 each payable in full on application, with applications closing on 30 May.

When applications closed, applications for 650 000 shares had been received with the appropriate amount of application money.

On 4 June 2007 the directors met and formally allotted shares to successful applicants and made refunds to unsuccessful applicants.

You are required to:
a   prepare all necessary journal entries;
b   post journal entries to the general ledger; and
c   prepare a balance sheet as at 30 June 2007.

Question 2.7

Drummond Ltd was registered on 1 September 2006 with three members agreeing to take 50 000 ordinary shares each at an issue price of $1 each. The money owing by the subscribers was received on 30 September.

On 20 October the directors met and agreed to issue a prospectus inviting offers for 200 000 preference shares at an issue price of $3 each. Applicants to the prospectus were required to make payment in full on application by 28 November.

The applicants, the number of shares applied for and the amount paid on application were as follows:

Applicant	Shares applied for	Amount paid on application
F. Harris	50 000	$150 000
B. & D. Holt	30 000	$90 000
Wozza Ltd	80 000	$240 000
Peter Garbo	20 000	$60 000
DB Pty Ltd	60 000	$180 000
	240 000	**$720 000**

The directors met on 30 November and allotted each applicant shares as shown in the following table. Refunds for over-applications were also made on this date.

Applicant	Shares allotted
F. Harris	40 000
B. & D. Holt	25 000
Wozza Ltd	65 000
Peter Garbo	20 000
DB Pty Ltd	50 000
	200 000

You are required to:
a   prepare journal entries for the respective share issues;
b   post the journal entries to the general ledger; and
c   prepare a balance sheet as at 30 November.

Shares issued partly paid on application with the balance payable on allotment

A company may issue a prospectus which requires applicants to make two payments for shares, the first payment to be included with the application form and the second to be made when the shares are allotted to the shareholder.

The journal entries to record the share transactions under these terms of payment are the same as in the previous illustration; however, two additional entries are required upon the allotment of the shares. These entries are to record the amount owing by the shareholders when the shares are allotted, and to record the receipt of money by the shareholders when the final payment is made.

The entries to account for the application for shares, the allotment of shares and the transfer of trust money are as follows:

1. Record the receipt of application money.

General journal		
Trust account	Dr	
Application		Cr

2. Allot shares to applicants.

General journal		
Application	Dr	
Share capital		Cr

3. Transfer trust account money.

General journal		
Bank	Dr	
Trust account		Cr

In addition to these first three entries it is necessary to prepare journal entries to record the additional amount owing by the new shareholders on the allotment of shares. As the new shareholders have agreed to the terms of payment in the prospectus and have taken ownership of the shares, the company can record the amount that they owe in an account called 'Allotment' and record the amount as an increase in share capital.

The following entry records the amount owing by the shareholders and the additional share capital associated with the allotment.

General journal		
Allotment	Dr	
Share capital		Cr

A final entry is required when the amount owing by the shareholders on allotment is received. This amount is recorded directly to the company bank account and not the trust account, as the amount represents a debt owing by the shareholders (legal obligation), not an amount owing to applicants to a prospectus. The required entry would be:

General journal		
Bank	Dr	
Allotment		Cr

ILLUSTRATION

On 15 April 2007 Annandale Ltd was registered as a public company limited by shares. On 1 May 2007 a prospectus inviting applications was issued for 100 000 ordinary shares at $3 each payable $2 on application and $1 on allotment, with 31 May being the closing date for applications.

Applications and an amount of $240 000 for 120 000 shares were received by the due date. On 1 June the directors allotted the shares and made refunds for oversubscriptions.

Allotment money was payable by 20 June 2007 and $100 000 due was received in full.

The journal entries to record the amount received on application, the initial allotment of shares and the transfer of trust money would be as follows:

General journal of Annandale Ltd

Date	Particulars	Debit	Credit
2007		$	$
31 May	Trust account – Share applications	240 000	
	Applications – Ordinary shares		240 000
	Receipted money paid by applicants for 120 000 shares at $2 each		
1 June	Applications – Ordinary shares	40 000	
	Trust account – Share applications		40 000
	Refunds for 20 000 shares at $2 each		
	Applications – Ordinary shares	200 000	
	Share capital – Ordinary shares		200 000
	Allotted 100 000 shares to applicants		
	Bank	200 000	
	Trust account – Share applications		200 000
	Transfer of money held in trust		

The resulting general ledger would be:

General ledger of Annandale Ltd

Date	Particulars	Debit	Credit	Balance
Trust account – Share applications				
31 May 2007	Applications	240 000		240 000 Dr
1 June 2007	Applications		40 000	200 000 Dr
	Bank		200 000	Nil
Applications – Ordinary shares				
31 May 2007	Trust account		240 000	240 000 Cr
1 June 2007	Trust account	400 000		200 000 Cr
	Share capital	200 000		Nil
Share capital – Ordinary shares				
1 June 2007	Applications		200 000	200 000 Cr
Bank				
1 June 2007	Trust account	200 000		200 000 Dr

Upon the allotment of shares, the entry to record the amount owing by the shareholders associated with the additional amount of share capital issued would be:

General journal of Annandale Ltd

Date	Particulars	Debit	Credit
2007		$	$
1 June	Allotment – Ordinary shares	100 000	
	Share capital – Ordinary shares		100 000
	To record the amount owing by shareholders on the allotment of 100 000 shares at $1		

The entry recording the payment by the shareholders for the amount owing on allotment would be:

General journal of Annandale Ltd

Date	Particulars	Debit	Credit
2007		$	$
20 June	Bank	100 000	
	Allotment – Ordinary shares		100 000
	Receipt of money owing on allotment		

The updated general ledger recording these transactions would be as follows:

General ledger of Annandale Ltd

Date	Particulars	Debit	Credit	Balance
Allotment – Ordinary shares				
1 June 2007	Share capital	100 000		100 000 Dr
15 June 2007	Bank		100 000	Nil
Share capital – Ordinary shares				
1 June 2007	Applications		200 000	200 000 Cr
	Allotment		100 000	300 000 Cr
Bank				
1 June 2007	Trust account	200 000		200 000 Dr
15 June 2007	Allotment	100 000		300 000 Dr

The balance sheet after these transactions could be presented as follows:

Annandale Ltd
Balance sheet as at 15 June 2007

Shareholders' equity	$
Share capital	
Ordinary shares (300 000)	300 000
Total shareholders' equity	300 000
Assets	
Bank	300 000
Total assets	300 000

Question 2.8

Inverloch Ltd was registered on 1 February 2007. On 1 March a prospectus was issued inviting applicants for 300 000 ordinary shares with an issue price of $2.50. The shares were payable $1.20 on application and $1.30 on allotment.

By the end of March, the closing date for application, the company had received applications for 400 000 shares, together with the application money.

On 1 April the directors allotted shares and made refunds to unsuccessful applicants. Allotment monies were received by 30 April.

You are required to:
a   prepare the journal entries to record the above share transactions; and
b   post the journals to the general ledger.

Question 2.9

Jackaroo Ltd was registered as a public company on 15 January 2006 with 10 subscribers taking 500 ordinary shares each at an issue price of $1 each. The subscribers paid for their shares on 20 January.

A prospectus was issued on 18 February inviting the public to apply for 100 000 ordinary shares at an issue price of $1.20 each payable $0.80 on application and $0.40 on allotment.

When applications closed on 1 March, 160 000 shares had been applied for. The directors formally allotted the shares on 5 March and made refunds for over-applications to the prospectus.

Shareholders allotted shares on 5 March made payment on 30 March.

You are required to:
a   prepare all journal entries;
b   post the journals to the general ledger; and
c   prepare a balance sheet as at 30 March 2006.

Shares issued payable on application and allotment and subject to future calls

When a company is raising capital via a share issue it may plan to collect some of the money in the future. This is referred to as a call. The prospectus would indicate the amount that should be paid for on application to the prospectus, the amount payable on allotment (if any) and the amount(s) to be called in the future.

The journal entries required for a share issue involving a call are initially the same as described in previous illustrations. However, additional entries are required to make the call on the shares and to record the money received in respect of the call.

The entries required to record receipt of application monies, allot shares and transfer trust money are as follows:

1   Record the receipt of application money.

General journal		
Trust account	Dr	
Application		Cr

2   Allot shares to applicants.

General journal		
Application	Dr	
Share capital		Cr

3 Transfer trust account money.

General journal		
Bank	Dr	
Trust account		Cr

The entries to record the amount owing on the allotment of shares and the subsequent payment for the amount owing on allotment are as follows:

4 Record the amount owing on allotment.

General journal		
Allotment	Dr	
Share capital		Cr

5 Record the receipt of allotment money.

General journal		
Bank	Dr	
Allotment		Cr

The final steps in recording shares subject to a call are to record the amount owing by shareholders in respect of the call and to record the receipt of money on payment of the call. As shareholders have been previously allotted shares, they have a legal obligation to make payment for the amount owing and the company can record the receipt of cash directly to the bank account, as is the case with allotment.

6 Record the amount owing by shareholders for the call.

General journal		
Call	Dr	
Share capital		Cr

7 Record the amounts received in respect of the call.

General journal		
Bank	Dr	
Call		Cr

ILLUSTRATION

On 1 March 2007 Anglesea Ltd issued a prospectus inviting applications for 50 000 shares at $6 each payable:
- $3 on application payable by 31 March 2007;
- $2 on allotment of shares on 1 April payable by 30 April; and
- $1 call to be made on 1 November and payable by 30 November.

Applications for 50 000 shares were received by the due date with the application money.
The journal entries recording the share transactions up to the date of the call are as follows:

General journal of Anglesea Ltd

Date	Particulars	Debit	Credit
2007		$	$
31 March	Trust account – Share applications	150 000	
	Applications – Ordinary shares		150 000
	Receipted money paid by applicants		
1 April	Applications – Ordinary shares	150 000	
	Share capital – Ordinary shares		150 000
	Allotted shares to applicants		
	Bank	150 000	
	Trust account – Share applications		150 000
	Transfer of money held in trust		
	Allotment – Ordinary shares	100 000	
	Share capital – Ordinary shares		100 000
	To record the amount owing by shareholders on the allotment of shares		
30 April	Bank	100 000	
	Allotment – Ordinary shares		100 000
	Receipt of money owing on allotment		

The entries to record the call on the shares on 1 November, the date specified in the prospectus, and the receipt of call money on 30 November are as follows:

General journal of Anglesea Ltd

Date	Particulars	Debit	Credit
2007		$	$
1 Nov	Call	50 000	
	Share capital – Ordinary shares		50 000
	Call on 50 000 shares at $1		
30 Nov	Bank	50 000	
	Call		50 000
	Receipt of money owing on call		

The updated general ledger recording these transactions would be as follows:

General ledger of Anglesea Ltd

Date	Particulars	Debit	Credit	Balance
Trust account – Share applications				
31 Mar 2007	Applications	150 000		150 000 Dr
1 April 2007	Bank		150 000	Nil
Applications – Ordinary shares				
31 Mar 2007	Trust account		150 000	150 000 Cr
1 April 2007	Share capital	150 000		Nil

Allotment – Ordinary shares					
1 April 2007	Share capital	100 000		100 000 Dr
30 April 2007	Bank		100 000	Nil

Share capital – Ordinary shares					
1 April 2007	Applications		150 000	150 000 Cr
	Allotment		100 000	250 000 Cr
1 Nov 2007	Call		50 000	300 000 Cr

Bank					
1 April 2007	Trust account	150 000		150 000 Dr
30 April 2007	Allotment	100 000		250 000 Dr
30 Nov 2007	Call	50 000		300 000 Dr

Call					
1 Nov 2007	Share capital	50 000		50 000 Dr
30 Nov 2007	Bank		50 000	Nil

Question 2.10

In 2007 OPQ Ltd was registered as a public company and also issued shares to the public in the same year.

OPQ Ltd was registered on 1 March 2007 with five subscribers agreeing to take 1 000 ordinary shares each at an issue price of $1 each, payable by 10 March.

On 31 March a prospectus was issued inviting applications for 150 000 $1.20 ordinary shares. The terms of payment were:
- $0.50 on application payable by 14 May, with allotment occurring on 21 May;
- $0.50 on allotment payable by 31 May; and
- $0.20 in one call to take effect on 31 July and payable by 31 August.

The company received applications for 200 000 ordinary shares. All monies were received by the due dates, with refunds being made on the date of allotment.

From the information provided, you are required to:
a   prepare journal entries to record the share transactions;
b   post the journals to the general ledger; and
c   prepare the shareholders' equity section of the balance sheet as at 31 August.

Calls in arrears

When a call on shares is made, the company may not receive all call money owing by shareholders – that is, the call money is owing. Where the call account remains with a debit balance after the final date for payment of a call, the balance should be transferred to an account named 'Calls in arrears'.

The calls in arrears account should be classified as a shareholders' equity account and be disclosed as a reduction of share capital in the balance sheet.

A company's constitution may include clauses specifying that shareholders who have not paid for calls on shares may forfeit the shares and that the shares can be reissued.

ILLUSTRATION

On 1 February 2007 Yamba Ltd issued a prospectus inviting applications for 200 000 shares at $2 each payable:
- $1.50 on application payable by 31 March 2007 with allotment on 15 April;
- a first call of $0.30 to be made on 1 June and payable by 30 June; and
- a final call of $0.20 to be made on 1 November and payable by 30 November.
Applications for 200 000 shares were received by the due date with the application money.
The journal entries recording the applications and allotment of shares would be as follows:

General journal of Yamba Ltd

Date	Particulars	Debit	Credit
2007		$	$
31 March	Trust account – Share applications	300 000	
	Applications – Ordinary shares		300 000
	Receipted money paid by applicants for 200 000 shares at $1.50 each		
15 April	Applications – Ordinary shares	300 000	
	Share capital – Ordinary shares		300 000
	Allotted 200 000 shares to applicants paid to $1.50 each		
	Bank	300 000	
	Trust account – Share applications		300 000
	Transfer of money held in trust		

The entries to record the first call, assuming that all call money was received by the due date, would be as follows:

General journal of Yamba Ltd

Date	Particulars	Debit	Credit
2007		$	$
1 June	First call	60 000	
	Share capital – Ordinary shares		60 000
	Call on 200 000 shares at $0.30 each		
30 June	Bank	60 000	
	First call		60 000
	Receipt of money owing on call		

The entries to record the final call, assuming that call money was received for only 180 000 shares, would be as follows:

General journal of Yamba Ltd

Date	Particulars	Debit	Credit
2007		$	$
1 Nov	Final call	40 000	
	Share capital – Ordinary shares		40 000
	Call on 200 000 shares at $0.20 each		
30 Nov	Bank	36 000	
	Final call		36 000
	To record receipt of call money of $0.20 per share on 180 000 shares		

The general ledger of Yamba Ltd would include the following accounts in respect of ordinary shares and the two call accounts.

General ledger of Yamba Ltd

Date	Particulars	Debit	Credit	Balance
Share capital – Ordinary shares				
15 April 2007	Applications		300 000	300 000 Cr
1 June 2007	First call		60 000	360 000 Cr
1 Nov 2007	Final call		40 000	400 000 Cr
First call				
1 June 2007	Share capital	60 000		60 000 Dr
30 June 2007	Bank		60 000	Nil
Final call				
1 Nov 2007	Share capital	40 000		40 000 Dr
30 Nov 2007	Bank		36 000	4 000 Dr

The balance of the final call account should be transferred to a calls in arrears account as shown in the following journal entry.

General journal of Yamba Ltd

Date	Particulars	Debit	Credit
2007		$	$
30 Nov	Calls in arrears	4 000	
	Final call		4 000
	Transfer of balance of final call account		

The balance sheet would show the shares issued and the calls in arrears as follows:

	$
Yamba Ltd	
Balance sheet as at 30 November 2007	
Shareholders' equity	
Share capital	
Ordinary shares (300 000)	400 000
less Calls in arrears (20 000 shares)	4 000
Total shareholders' equity	396 000
Assets	
Bank	396 000
Total assets	396 000

Question 2.11

On 1 May 2007 Jindabyne Ltd was registered as a public company limited by shares.

On 7 May 2007 the directors issued a prospectus inviting applicants for 250 000 shares with an issue price of $3.50 per share payable as follows:
- $2 on application;
- $1 on allotment; and
- two calls of $0.25 each.

On 15 June 2007 applications received for 300 000 shares with application money.

On 25 June 2007 directors allot shares and make refunds.

On 31 July 2007 all allotment money is received.

On 28 November 2007 directors made the first call for $0.25 per share to be received by 20 December.

On 20 December 2007 all call money on the first call is received.

On 15 April 2008 directors made the final call for $0.25 per share to be received by 15 May.

On 15 May 2008 call money was received on 200 000 shares.

You are required to prepare:
a   journal entries to account for all share transactions;
b   the general ledger; and
c   the shareholders' equity section of the balance sheet as at 30 June 2008.

Question 2.12

On 1 June 2007 Korumburra Ltd was registered, with 10 members each agreeing to take 20 000 preference shares at an issue price of $10 each. Payment for these shares was made on 15 June.

On 25 July 2007 the directors issued a prospectus to the public inviting applications for 400 000 ordinary shares with an issue price of $5 payable as follows:
- $2 on application;
- $1.50 on allotment;
- $0.80 in first call; and
- $0.70 in a second and final call.

By the closing date for applications on 31 August 2007 the company had received 450 000 applications together with the application money as disclosed in the table following.

Applicant	Shares applied for	Amount paid on application
M & M Ltd	150 000	$300 000
Pilsons	50 000	$100 000
R. Evans	150 000	$300 000
I. Willis	90 000	$180 000
ADC Pty Ltd	10 000	$20 000
	450 000	**$900 000**

The directors met on 10 September and allotted each applicant shares as shown in the following table. Refunds for over-applications were also made on this date.

Applicant	Shares allotted
M & M Ltd	150 000
Pilsons	50 000
R. Evans	120 000
I. Willis	80 000
ADC Pty Ltd	Nil
	400 000

Allotment money was due by 1 October 2007. By 1 October 2007 all allotment money had been received.

The directors made the first call on 15 April 2008. By 25 May 2008 all call money had been received.

The directors made the final call on 29 January 2009, which was payable by 1 March 2009. By 1 March 2009, call money had been received for 380 000 shares.

You are required to prepare:
a   general journal entries to record all share issues;
b   the general ledger; and
c   the shareholders' equity section of the balance sheet as at 30 June 2009.

Retention of excess application money

When a prospectus is issued which requires applicants to pay for shares on application, allotment and in future calls, some applicants may take the opportunity to pay for the amount owing on allotment and the future call, as well as the amount owing on application, in the hope that they may be given preferential treatment when shares are allotted.

In previous illustrations where money received on application was in excess of the maximum amount required, application money was returned to applicants. An alternative to refunding excess application money is to retain the excess and allocate it against money owing on allotment and future calls.

Company directors can only make this decision if it is permitted by the company constitution and it is notified to applicants in the prospectus.

To assist in determining the apportionment of money received against application, allotment, call(s) and refunds, the following table may be helpful in determining the various amounts that will give rise to journal entries.

Worksheet for the allocation of application monies received

| Shares applied for | Paid to $ | Amount received $ | Shares allotted | Amounts received from applications allocated to | | | | Application refund $ |
| | | | | Application of $... | Allotment of $... | Calls in advance | | |
						Call 1 $...	Call 2 $...	

A prospectus may specify that excess application money can be applied against allotment and future calls directly and in full. Where the excess amount cannot be applied in full it will be refunded.

ILLUSTRATION

On 1 November, Clematis Ltd issued a prospectus inviting applications for 100 000 shares at a price of $5 each, payable:
- $2 on application;
- $1 on allotment;
- $1.20 on call 1 as and when required; and
- $0.80 on call 2 as and when required.

The prospectus gave the directors the power to apportion excess application money against allotment and calls in full.

By the closing date of 30 November 2007 applications for 129 000 shares were received, made up as:
- 20 000 shares applied for and paid to $5 (being for application, allotment and calls);
- 30 000 shares applied for and paid to $4.20 (being for application, allotment and call 1);
- 24 000 shares applied for and paid to $3 (being for application and allotment); and
- 55 000 shares applied for and paid to $2 (being for application).

On 1 December 2007, the directors allotted the shares. These amounts would be entered into the worksheet for the allocation of allotted application monies received as follows:

Applications received		
Shares applied for and paid to	Amount received	Shares allotted
20 000 shares applied for and paid to $5.00	$100 000	16 000
30 000 shares applied for and paid to $4.20	$126 000	26 000
24 000 shares applied for and paid to $3.00	$72 000	12 000
55 000 shares applied for and paid to $2.00	$110 000	46 000
	$396 000	100 000

These amounts would be entered into the worksheet for the allocation of allotted application monies received as follows:

1. For the 20 000 shares applied for and paid to $5 (being for application, allotment and calls)

Worksheet for the allocation of application monies received

| Shares applied for | Paid to $ | Amount received $ | Shares allotted | Amounts received from applications allocated to | | | | Application refund $ |
| | | | | Application of $2.00 | Allotment of $1.00 | Calls in advance | | |
						Call 1 $1.20	Call 2 $0.80	
20 000	5.00	100 000	16 000	32 000	16 000	19 200	12 800	20 000

As $100 000 was received on application and 16 000 shares have been allotted, the application money can be applied in full against allotment and the calls – that is, 16 000 shares × $5 per share = $80 000, leaving $20 000 to be refunded.

2 For the 30 000 shares applied for and paid to $4.20 (being for application, allotment and call 1)

Worksheet for the allocation of application monies received

| Shares applied for | Paid to $ | Amount received $ | Shares allotted | Amounts received from applications allocated to ||||| Application refund $ |
| | | | | Application of $2.00 | Allotment of $1.00 | Calls in advance |||
						Call 1 $1.20	Call 2 $0.80	
30 000	4.20	126 000	26 000	52 000	26 000	31 200	16 800	Nil

The $126 000 received on application can be applied in full as follows:

On application: 26 000 shares × $2.00 = $52 000
On allotment: 26 000 shares × $1.00 = $26 000
On call 1: 26 000 shares × $1.20 = $31 200

This totals $109 200, leaving $16 800 ($126 000 − $109 200) to be applied against call 2. When call 2 is made by the directors the shareholders would have to make payment for the balance owing on call 2 of $4 000 (26 000 shares × $0.80 = $20 800 less $16 800 paid on application).

3 For the 24 000 shares applied for and paid to $3 (being for application and allotment)

Worksheet for the allocation of application monies received

| Shares applied for | Paid to $ | Amount received $ | Shares allotted | Amounts received from applications allocated to ||||| Application refund $ |
| | | | | Application of $2.00 | Allotment of $1.00 | Calls in advance |||
						Call 1 $1.20	Call 2 $0.80	
24 000	3.00	72 000	12 000	24 000	12 000	14 400	9 600	12 000

As $72 000 has been received and only 12 000 shares allotted, the application money can be applied in full against application, allotment and the calls (12 000 × 5 = $60 000), leaving $12 000 to be refunded.

4 For the 55 000 shares applied for and paid to $2 (being for application)

Worksheet for the allocation of application monies received

| Shares applied for | Paid to $ | Amount received $ | Shares allotted | Amounts received from applications allocated to ||||| Application refund $ |
| | | | | Application of $2.00 | Allotment of $1.00 | Calls in advance |||
						Call 1 $1.20	Call 2 $0.80	
55 000	2.00	110 000	46 000	92 000	18 000			

With $110 000 being received on application and 46 000 shares being allotted in respect of this amount, the amount can be applied in full against application, leaving $18 000 as excess application money. This balance, rather than being refunded, can be applied against the balance owing on allotment.

These shareholders would therefore need to make payment for the amount owing on allotment and calls when required as follows:
- Amount owing on allotment: 46 000 shares × $1.00 = $46 000 less $18 000 = $28 000
- Amount owing for calls 1 and 2: 46 000 shares × ($1.20 + $0.80) = $92 000

The completed worksheet relating to the prospectus showing totals of amounts received and applied against applications, allotment, calls and refunds would appear as in the worksheet below. These totals would be used to prepare appropriate journal entries.

Worksheet for the allocation of application monies received

| Shares applied for | Paid to $ | Amount received $ | Shares allotted | Amounts received from applications allocated to | | | | Application refund $ |
| | | | | Application of $2.00 | Allotment of $1.00 | Calls in advance | | |
						Call 1 $1.20	Call 2 $0.80	
20 000	5.00	100 000	16 000	32 000	16 000	19 200	12 800	20 000
30 000	4.20	126 000	26 000	52 000	26 000	31 200	16 800	
24 000	3.00	72 000	12 000	24 000	12 000	14 400	9 600	12 000
55 000	2.00	110 000	46 000	92 000	18 000			
129 000		408 000	100 000	200 000	72 000	64 800	39 200	32 000

The totals of the worksheet should be checked to ensure that the amount received on application has been applied against application, allotment, calls and refunds. The totals of this worksheet proof as follows:

Amount received		$408 000
less Amounts applied		
On application	$200 000	
On allotment	$72 000	
On call 1	$64 800	
On call 2	$39 200	
As refunds	$32 000	$408 000
Balance remaining		Nil

Question 2.13

Using the figures provided in the worksheet that follows, you are required to complete all necessary columns and cross balance to the total of the amount received.

Worksheet for the allocation of application monies received

| Shares applied for | Paid to $ | Amount received $ | Shares allotted | Amounts received from applications allocated to | | | | Application refund $ |
| | | | | Application of $2.00 | Allotment of $1.00 | Calls in advance | | |
						Call 1 $1.20	Call 2 $0.80	
125 000		250 000	125 000					
110 000		110 000	90 000					
200 000		100 000	185 000					

Question 2.14

A public company limited by shares issued a prospectus inviting applications for 800 000 ordinary shares at a price of $3 each payable:
- $1.50 on application;
- $0.90 on allotment;
- $0.40 on call 1 as and when required; and
- $0.20 on call 2 as and when required.

The prospectus indicated that in the event of an oversubscription the directors could make a pro rata issue of shares and excess application money could be applied to allotment and calls.

By the closing date, applications for 900 000 shares had been received. The directors exercised their powers and allocated the shares pro rata:

Shares applied for	Paid to	Shares allotted
200 000	$2.40	160 000
700 000	$2.80	640 000

You are required to complete the worksheet for the allocation of allotted application monies received.

Question 2.15

A public company issued a prospectus inviting applications for 175 000 shares at a price of $3.50 each payable:
- $1.50 on application;
- $1 on allotment;
- $0.75 on call 1 as and when required; and
- $0.25 on call 2 as and when required.

As indicated in the prospectus, if there is an oversubscription the directors can make a pro rata issue of shares and excess application money can be applied to allotment and calls.

By the closing date, applications for 210 000 shares had been received made up as follows:
- 33 500 shares applied for and paid to $3.50;
- 50 000 shares applied for and paid to $3;
- 34 000 shares applied for and paid to $2; and
- 92 500 shares applied for and paid to $1.50.

The directors allotted the shares as follows:

Shares applied for	Shares allotted
33 500	18 000
50 000	45 000
34 000	24 000
92 500	88 000

You are required to complete the worksheet for the allocation of allotted application monies received.

Accounting for the retention of excess application money

The journal entries to account for the retention of excess application money are similar to those applied when application money is received, shares are allotted and refunds made. These entries are as follows:

1 Record the receipt of application money.

General journal		
Trust account	Dr	
Application		Cr

2 Allot shares to applicants.

General journal		
Application	Dr	
Share capital		Cr

3 Issue shares on allotment.

General journal		
Allotment	Dr	
Share capital		Cr

4 Refund application money.

General journal		
Application	Dr	
Trust account		Cr

5 Transfer trust account money.

General journal		
Bank	Dr	
Trust account		Cr

When application money has been retained against allotment the following entry is required:

General journal		
Application	Dr	
Allotment		Cr

In respect of excess application money applied to future calls, it is necessary to record the amount applied to future calls as calls in advance. The journal entry to record excess application money applied to future calls is as follows:

General journal		
Application	Dr	
Calls in advance		Cr

The calls in advance account represents shareholders' funds received in advance and must be included under shareholders' equity with share capital in the balance sheet until the call is made.

When the directors make the call, the calls in advance account can be applied against the respective call account. When the directors make a call the required journal entry is as follows:

General journal		
Call	Dr	
Share capital		Cr

The entry to apply the calls in advance against the call is as follows:

General journal		
Cash in advance	Dr	
Calls		Cr

When call money owing is received the required journal entry is:

General journal		
Bank	Dr	
Calls		Cr

ILLUSTRATION

In the previous illustration, Clematis Ltd issued a prospectus inviting applications for 100 000 shares at a price of $5 each, payable:
- $2 on application;
- $1 on allotment;
- $1.20 on call 1 as and when required; and
- $0.80 on call 2 as and when required.

The worksheet for the allocation of allotted application monies received in that illustration was as follows:

Worksheet for the allocation of application monies received

Shares applied for	Paid to $	Amount received $	Shares allotted	Amounts received from applications allocated to				Application refund $
				Application of $2.00	Allotment of $1.00	Calls in advance		
						Call 1 $1.20	Call 2 $0.80	
20 000	5.00	100 000	16 000	32 000	16 000	19 200	12 800	20 000
30 000	4.20	126 000	26 000	52 000	26 000	31 200	16 800	
24 000	3.00	72 000	12 000	24 000	12 000	14 400	9 600	12 000
55 000	2.00	110 000	46 000	92 000	18 000			
129 000		408 000	100 000	200 000	72 000	64 800	39 200	32 000

The critical dates for the respective share transactions were as follows:

Date	Event
2007	
30 November	Application money received
1 December	Shares allotted, excess application money applied and refunds made
21 December	Outstanding allotment money received
2008	
1 May	Call 1 was made with payment due on 31 May
31 May	Call money received. Calls remain owing on 5 500 shares

The journal entries recording the receipt of application money, the allotment of shares, the application of excess application money and refunds, and the resulting general ledger, are as follows:

General journal of Clematis Ltd

Date	Particulars	Debit	Credit
2007		$	$
30 Nov	Trust account – Share applications	408 000	
	Applications – Ordinary shares		408 000
	Receipted money paid by applicants for 129 000 shares		
1 Dec	Applications – Ordinary shares	200 000	
	Share capital – Ordinary shares		200 000
	Allotted 100 000 shares to applicants at $2 each		

General journal of Clematis Ltd

Date	Particulars	Debit	Credit
2007		$	$
1 Dec	Allotment – Ordinary shares	100 000	
	Share capital – Ordinary shares		100 000
	Allotted 100 000 shares at $1 each		
	Application – Ordinary shares	72 000	
	Allotment – Ordinary shares		72 000
	Transfer of excess application money applied to allotment		
	Application – Ordinary shares	104 000	
	Calls in advance		104 000
	Transfer of excess application money applied to calls 1 ($64 800) and 2 ($39 200)		
	Application – Ordinary shares	32 000	
	Trust account – Share applications		32 000
	Refund of excess application money not applied to allotment or calls		
	Bank	376 000	
	Trust account – Share applications		376 000
	Transfer of application money held in trust		

General ledger of Clematis Ltd

Date	Particulars	Debit	Credit	Balance
	Trust account – Share applications			
30 Nov 2007	Applications	408 000		408 000 Dr
1 Dec 2007	Applications		32 000	376 000 Dr
	Bank		376 000	Nil
	Applications – Ordinary shares			
30 Nov 2007	Trust account		408 000	408 000 Cr
1 Dec 2007	Share capital	200 000		208 000 Cr
	Allotment	72 000		136 000 Cr
	Calls in advance	104 000		32 000 Cr
	Trust account	32 000		Nil
	Allotment – Ordinary shares			
1 Dec 2007	Share capital	100 000		100 000 Dr
	Applications		72 000	28 000 Dr
	Share capital – Ordinary shares			
1 Dec 2007	Applications		200 000	200 000 Cr
	Allotment		100 000	300 000 Cr

Calls in advance

1 Dec 2007	Applications		104 000	104 000 Cr

Bank

1 Dec 2007	Trust account	376 000		376 000 Dr

The journal entry recording the payment of allotment money owing and the resulting general ledger would be as follows:

General journal of Clematis Ltd

Date	Particulars	Debit	Credit
2007		$	$
21 Dec	Bank	28 000	
	Allotment – Ordinary shares		28 000
	Receipt of allotment money owing		

General ledger of Clematis Ltd

Date	Particulars	Debit	Credit	Balance
\multicolumn{5}{c}{Trust account – Share applications}				
30 Nov 2007	Applications	408 000		408 000 Dr
1 Dec 2007	Applications		32 000	376 000 Dr
	Bank		376 000	Nil
\multicolumn{5}{c}{Applications – Ordinary shares}				
30 Nov 2007	Trust account		408 000	408 000 Cr
1 Dec 2007	Share capital	200 000		208 000 Cr
	Allotment	72 000		136 000 Cr
	Calls in advance	104 000		32 000 Cr
	Trust account	32 000		Nil
\multicolumn{5}{c}{Share capital – Ordinary shares}				
1 Dec 2007	Applications		200 000	200 000 Cr
	Allotment		100 000	300 000 Cr
\multicolumn{5}{c}{Calls in advance}				
1 Dec 2007	Applications		104 000	104 000 Cr
\multicolumn{5}{c}{Allotment – Ordinary shares}				
1 Dec 2007	Share capital	100 000		100 000 Dr
	Applications		72 000	28 000 Dr
21 Dec 2007	Bank		28 000	Nil
\multicolumn{5}{c}{Bank}				
1 Dec 2007	Trust account	376 000		376 000 Dr
21 Dec 2007	Allotment	28 000		404 000 Dr

Recording the call

The first call on 1 May will be $1.20 per share on 100 000 shares, requiring $120 000 in share capital to be paid. As $64 800 has already been retained from excess application money, this can be transferred on the date of the call, leaving $55 200 owing on the calls. By the closing date of 31 May, calls on 5 500 shares at $1.20 each, or $6 600, remain unpaid. Hence, calls of $48 600 will have been received in addition to the $64 800 retained on application.

The journal entries recording the first call on shares, the transfer from calls in advance, receipt of call money and recognition of calls in arrears would be as follows:

General journal of Clematis Ltd

Date	Particulars	Debit	Credit
2008		$	$
1 May	Call 1	120 000	
	Share capital – Ordinary shares		120 000
	To record the first call of $1.20 on 100 000 shares		
	Calls in advance	64 800	
	Call 1		64 800
	Transfer of calls in advance		
31 May	Bank	48 600	
	Call 1		48 600
	Receipt of call money		
	Calls in arrears	6 600	
	Call 1		6 600
	Money owing on 5 500 shares at $1.20 each		

The updated general ledger after these call entries would be as follows:

General ledger of Clematis Ltd

Date	Particulars	Debit	Credit	Balance
Share capital – Ordinary shares				
1 Dec 2007	Applications		200 000	200 000 Cr
	Allotment		100 000	300 000 Cr
1 May 2008	Call 1		120 000	420 000 Cr
Calls in advance				
1 Dec 2007	Applications		104 000	104 000 Cr
1 May 2008	Call 1	64 800		39 200 Cr
Bank				
1 Dec 2007	Trust account	376 000		376 000 Dr
21 Dec 2007	Allotment	28 000		404 000 Dr
31 May 2008	Call 1	48 600		452 600 Dr

		Call 1			
1 May 2008	Share capital	120 000		120 000 Dr	
	Calls in advance		64 800	55 200 Dr	
31 May 2008	Bank		48 600	6 600 Dr	
	Calls in arrears		6 600	Nil	

		Calls in arrears			
31 May 2008	Call 1	6 600		6 600 Dr	

The balance sheet after the call would show the following accounts and amounts for shareholders' equity.

Clematis Ltd
Balance sheet as at 31 May 2008 (Extract)

Shareholders' equity	$
Share capital	
Ordinary shares (100 000 shares with an issue price of $5.00 paid to $4.20)	420 000
less Calls in arrears (5 500 shares called to $1.20)	6 600
Total share capital	413 400
add Calls in advance	39 200
Total shareholders' equity	452 600

Question 2.16

Macguiness Ltd issued a prospectus inviting applications for 450 000 preference shares issued at $2 each payable as follows:
- On application: $0.50 closing on 20 January 2007.
- On allotment: $0.50 on 5 February 2007 payable on 25 February 2007.
- On call 1: $0.50 on 15 May 2007 payable by 30 May 2007.
- On call 2: $0.50 at the directors' discretion.

The prospectus gave the directors the powers to make a pro rata distribution of shares in the event of an oversubscribed application and to allocate excess application money against allotment and calls.

The following worksheet shows the details of applications, share allocations and apportionment of application money.

Worksheet for the allocation of application monies received

				Amounts received from applications allocated to				
						Calls in advance		
Shares applied for	Paid to $	Amount received $	Shares allotted	Application of $2.00	Allotment of $1.00	Call 1 $1.20	Call 2 $0.80	Application refund $
130 000	2.00	260 000	125 000	62 500	62 500	62 500	62 500	10 000
180 000	1.50	270 000	140 000	70 000	70 000	70 000	60 000	
200 000	0.50	100 000	185 000	92 500	7 500			
510 000		630 000	450 000	225 000	140 000	132 500	122 500	10 000

You are required to:
a prepare journal entries to record all share transactions;
b post the journals to the general ledger; and
c show the shareholders' equity section of the balance sheet as at 30 June 2007.

Question 2.17

From the following information relating to the prospectus issued by Hanniker Ltd you are required to:
a prepare journal entries to record all share transactions;
b post the journals to the general ledger; and
c show the shareholders' equity section of the balance sheet as at 30 June 2009.

Prospectus terms and conditions

- Share type – Ordinary shares.
- Excess application money to be apportioned against allotment and future calls.
- Applications closed: 14 July 2007
- Allotment, refunds and transfer: 30 July 2007
- Allotment due by: 31 August 2007
- Call 1:
  - Effective: 1 December 2008
  - Due by: 31 December 2008
  - Calls remain owing on 10 000 shares.
- Call 2 dates yet to be determined.

Worksheet for the allocation of application monies received

Shares applied for	Paid to $	Amount received $	Shares allotted	Amounts received from applications allocated to					Application refund $
				Application of $2.00	Allotment of $1.00	Calls in advance			
						Call 1 $1.20	Call 2 $0.80	
700 000	2.80	1 960 000	640 000	960 000	576 000	256 000	128 000	40 000
100 000	2.40		240 000	90 000	135 000	81 000	24 000	
800 000		2 200 000	730 000	1 095 000	657 000	280 000	128 000	40 000

Question 2.18

Leeton Ltd was registered on 1 June 2007 as a public company limited by shares, with five members taking and paying for 10 000 ordinary shares at $1.75 each.

On 15 June a prospectus was issued inviting applications for 100 000 ordinary shares at an issue price of $2 each payable:
- $0.75 on application;
- $0.50 on allotment;
- $0.45 on call 1 as and when required; and
- $0.30 on call 2 as and when required.

Under the prospectus, if there is an oversubscription, the directors can make a pro rata issue of shares and excess application money can be applied to allotment and calls.

By the closing date of 31 July 2007 applications for 215 000 shares were received together with the correct application money.

On 1 August 2007 the directors decided to reject and refund applications for 15 000 shares from applicants whose applications were received last and to allot the remaining applicants on a pro rata basis half the number of shares they actually applied for.

On 30 April 2008 call 1 was made. By 31 May 2008 all outstanding call money was received.

You are required to:
a   prepare a worksheet showing the allotment of applications received;
b   prepare journal entries for transactions relating to the prospectus;
c   post the journal entries to the general ledger;
d   prepare a trial balance as at 31 May 2008; and
e   prepare the shareholders' equity section of the balance sheet as at 31 May 2008.

Question 2.19

On 19 February 2007 Mildura Ltd was registered as a public company limited by shares, with members taking 50 000 preference shares at $8 each.

On 1 March 2007 a prospectus was issued inviting applications for 350 000 ordinary shares at a price of $4.50 each payable:
- $2 on application;
- $1.50 on allotment; and
- $1 on call as and when required.

Under the prospectus, if there is an oversubscription, the directors can make a pro rata issue of shares and excess application money can be applied to allotment and call.

By 15 April 2007, the closing date for applications, there were applications for 410 000 shares. Analysis of the applications showed that there were differing amounts of application money received compared with shares applied for as follows:
- 25 000 shares applied for and paid to $4;
- 50 000 shares applied for and paid to $3.50;
- 30 000 shares applied for and paid to $3;
- 300 000 shares applied for and paid to $2; and
- 5 000 shares applied for and paid to $1.

On 17 April 2007 the directors allotted the shares as follows:

Shares applied for	Paid to	Shares allotted
25 000	$4.00	5 000
50 000	$3.50	20 000
30 000	$3.00	25 000
300 000	$2.00	300 000
5 000	$1.00	Nil

Outstanding allotment money was received by 31 May 2007.

You are required to:
a   complete a worksheet showing the allotment of applications received;
b   prepare journal entries relating to the share transactions;
c   post the journal entries to the general ledger and prepare a trial balance; and
d   prepare a balance sheet as at 31 May 2007 showing shareholders' equity.

Question 2.20

Narooma Ltd was registered as a public company limited by shares on 30 April 2007, with subscribers taking 100 000 deferred shares at $5 each.

On 26 May 2007 a prospectus was issued inviting applications for 500 000 ordinary shares at a price of $2.50 each payable:
- $1.25 on application payable by 11 July 2007;
- $0.75 on allotment on 14 July 2007;
- $0.30 on call 1 as and when required; and
- $0.20 on call 2 as and when required.

Under the prospectus, if there is an oversubscription, the directors could make a pro rata issue of shares and excess application money can be applied to allotment and calls.

When applications closed, 600 000 shares had been applied for. On 14 July 2007 the directors allotted shares as follows:

Shares applied for	Amount received $	Shares allotted
170 000	340 000	140 000
100 000	250 000	80 000
260 000	325 000	220 000
70 000	175 000	60 000

On 31 August 2007 all remaining allotment money was received.
On 29 January 2008 call 1 was made by directors and was receivable by 28 February 2008.
On 28 February 2008 call 1 money was received except for that owing on 8 000 shares.
You are required to:
a complete a worksheet showing the allotment of applications received;
b prepare all journal entries;
c post the journal entries to the general ledger;
d extract a trial balance as at 28 February 2008; and
e prepare the balance sheet showing shareholders' equity as at 28 February 2008.

Question 2.21

Eden Ltd was registered as a public company limited by shares on 30 May 2006. The share capital on this date consisted of 10 000 $5 preference shares taken by subscribers.

On 26 June 2007 a prospectus was issued inviting applications for 750 000 ordinary shares at a price of $6 each payable:
- $2.50 on application;
- $1.75 on allotment;
- $0.95 on call 1 as and when required; and
- $0.80 on call 2 as and when required.

The closing date for applications was 21 August 2007.

Under the prospectus, if there is an oversubscription, the directors can make a pro rata issue of shares and excess application money can be applied to allotment and calls.

On 21 August 2007 applications closed and 935 000 shares were applied for and $3 477 250 was received. On 23 August 2007 the directors allotted the shares as follows:

Shares applied for	Amount received $	Shares allotted
81 000	486 000	75 000
157 000	785 000	125 000
265 000	1 126 250	200 000
432 000	1 080 000	350 000

On 30 September 2007 all remaining allotment money was received.
On 6 February 2008 call 1 was made by directors and was due by 2 April 2008.
On 2 April 2008 all necessary call 1 money was received except for that owing on 12 500 shares.
You are required to:
a   complete a worksheet showing the allotment of applications received;
b   record all transactions in the general journal;
c   post to the general ledger;
d   extract a trial balance as at 2 April 2008; and
e   prepare an extract of the balance sheet showing the shareholders' equity as at 2 April 2008.

Question 2.22

Albury Ltd was registered as a public company limited by shares on 19 July 2007 with subscribers accepting 100 000 ordinary shares at $2 each, which were paid for on 25 July.

On 1 August 2007 a prospectus was issued inviting applications for 500 000 ordinary shares at a price of $2.50 each payable:
- $1.10 on application;
- $0.80 on allotment; and
- $0.60 on call as and when required.

Under the prospectus, if there is an oversubscription, the directors can make a pro rata issue of shares and excess application money can be applied to allotment and call.

On 15 September 2007, the closing date for applications, there were applications for 585 000 shares. Analysis of the applications showed that there were differing amounts of application money received compared with shares applied for as follows:
- 410 000 shares applied for and paid to $1.10;
- 50 000 shares applied for and paid to $1.90;
- 84 000 shares applied for and paid to $2; and
- 41 000 shares applied for and paid to $2.20.

On 17 September 2007 the directors allotted the shares as follows:

Shares applied for	Shares allotted
410 000	375 000
50 000	37 000
84 000	58 000
41 000	30 000

By 31 October 2007 all outstanding allotment money had been received.
You are required to:
a   complete a worksheet showing the allotment of applications received;
b   record all transactions in the general journal;
c   post to the general ledger;
d   extract a trial balance as at 2 April 2008; and
e   prepare an extract of the balance sheet showing the shareholders' equity as at 31 October 2007.

Costs associated with a share issue

When a company prepares a prospectus and issues shares (equity instruments) it will incur unavoidable costs for every event associated with the prospectus, including the preparation of the prospectus, its lodgement with ASIC, its publication, the receipt of money and the issue of shares.

These costs, referred to as transaction costs, include:
- stamp duty and taxes;
- professional advisers' fees;
- underwriting costs, including commission; and
- brokerage fees.

Professional advisers' fees often arise when they are used as experts to give considered favourable opinions which are included with the prospectus to encourage prospective applicants to go ahead and invest in the company through the application for shares.

A public company making a new issue of shares will often enter into an underwriting agreement with a stockbroker or financial institution. Underwriters guarantee to purchase any shares that the company cannot sell to the public during the issue period and charge a commission or fee to minimise the company's risk of having a share issue that is undersubscribed. Selling those shares then becomes the underwriter's problem and not the company's.

A brokerage fee is paid for negotiating the sale or purchase of shares between a party that wants to sell and a party that wants to buy. Both the seller and the buyer pay the fee. The transaction may take place through a stockbroker and even over the Internet, especially if the company is registered on the ASX.

Other indirect costs associated with the issue of an equity instrument, such as overheads, research costs, assessing of financial options and negotiating sources of finance, are not included as transaction costs.

The accounting treatment is the same and they should all be processed as transaction costs whether the account names used are:
- share issue expense;
- underwriting commission expense;
- brokerage expense; or
- transaction costs.

AASB 132: Financial Instruments: Disclosure and Presentation, clause 39 states: Transaction costs of an equity transaction shall be accounted for as a deduction from equity. Hence, transaction costs must not be capitalised on the balance sheet or expensed on the income statement but included as a reduction to shareholders' equity.

Transaction costs are paid from the business bank account and can be recorded as follows:

General journal		
Transaction costs	Dr	
Bank		Cr

ILLUSTRATION

Clematis Ltd's costs associated with the share issue in the previous illustration totalled $55 000, inclusive of GST, including legal fees, all costs relating to the prospectus, together with underwriting commission costs. The amount was paid on 15 December 2007.

The journal entry to record this payment would be as follows:

General journal of Clematis Ltd

Date	Particulars	Debit	Credit
2007		$	$
15 Dec	Transaction costs	50 000	
	GST receivable	5 000	
	Bank		55 000
	To record costs associated with share issue		

General ledger of Clematis Ltd

Date	Particulars	Debit	Credit	Balance
Transaction costs				
15 Dec 2007	Bank	50 000		50 000 Dr
GST receivable				
15 Dec 2007	Bank	5 000		5 000 Dr
Bank				
15 Dec 2007	Balance	452 600		452 600 Dr
	Transaction costs		55 000	397 600 Dr

The balance sheet after the call would show the following accounts and amounts for shareholders' equity:

Clematis Ltd
Balance sheet as at 31 May 2008 (Extract)

	$
Shareholders' equity	
Share capital	
Ordinary shares (100 000 shares with an issue price of $5.00 paid to $4.20)	420 000
less Calls in arrears (5 500 shares called to $1.20)	6 600
	413 400
add Calls in advance	39 200
Total share capital	452 600
less Transaction costs*	50 000
Total shareholders' equity	402 600

* Transaction costs would be matched against unappropriated profits at the end of the period.

Question 2.23

On 1 March 2007 Wentworth Ltd was registered as a public company limited by shares. The application for registration listed five subscribers who had each agreed to take 500 ordinary shares at a nominal value of $1 each.

    Money from subscribers was received on 4 March 2007.

    On 5 March 2007 establishment costs totalling $2 200 including GST were paid.

    On 7 March 2007 the directors issued a prospectus inviting applications for 200 000 preference shares with an issue price of $3 per share payable as follows:
- $2 on application;
- $0.50 on allotment; and
- two calls of $0.25 each.

    On 15 May 2007 applications had been received for 300 000 shares with application money. The prospectus did not allow the directors to retain excess application monies. A full refund had to be made.

    On 25 May 2007 directors allotted shares and made refunds.

    On 30 June 2007 all allotment money had been received.

    On 1 August 2007 transaction costs amounting to $1 650 including GST were paid.

    On 28 October 2007 directors made the first call for $0.25 per share to be received by 20 November.

    On 20 November 2007 all call money on the first call was received.

    On 15 May 2008 directors made the final call for $0.25 per share to be received by 15 June.

On 15 June 2008 call money was received on 180 000 shares.

You are required to prepare:
a   journal entries to account for all share transactions; and
b   the shareholders' equity section of the balance sheet as at 30 June 2008.

Question 2.24

Pokolbin Ltd was registered as a public company limited by shares on 29 January 2007. The application for registration named seven subscribers who had each agreed to take:
- 20 000 ordinary shares at $1 each; and
- 3 000 deferred shares at $2 each.

On 1 February 2007 the seven subscribers paid for all shares taken. In addition, $6 600 in establishment costs were paid.

A prospectus was issued to the public on 19 February 2007 providing for the issue of:
- 100 000 6% cumulative preference shares at a price of $3 per share payable in full on application; and
- 800 000 ordinary shares at a price of $5 per share payable $2 on application, $1 on allotment, and one call of $2 payable as and when required by the directors.

The prospectus indicated that, for the 6% cumulative preference shares, directors were allowed to accept oversubscription to a maximum of 20% above the issued number of 100 000 shares. For ordinary shares, in the event of an oversubscription the directors can make a pro rata issue of shares and excess application money can be applied to allotment and the call.

Costs associated with the share issue totalling $18 500 were paid on 31 March 2007.

Applications for both classes of shares closed on 31 March 2007 and by that date application money had been received for:

Cumulative preference shares:	110 000 shares fully paid to $3 per share
Ordinary shares:	30 000 shares applied for at $5 each
	200 000 shares applied for at $3 each
	650 000 shares applied for at $2 each

Allotment by the directors occurred on 1 April 2007 as follows:

Share type	Shares applied for	Shares allotted
Cumulative preference	110 000	110 000
Ordinary	30 000 shares applied for at $5 each	25 000
	200 000 shares applied for at $3 each	175 000
	650 000 shares applied for at $2 each	600 000

Allotment money owing was received in full by the due date of 7 May 2007.

You are required to prepare:
a   journal entries for all transactions;
b   the general ledger and a trial balance as at 7 May 2007; and
c   an extract balance sheet for the shareholders' equity as at 30 June 2007.

Bookbuilding and stapled securities

Raising capital through an issue of shares may also occur through **bookbuilding** and **stapled securities**.

Bookbuilding

Bookbuilding occurs where an investment banker solicits bids for shares from institutional investors prior to pricing an equity issue.

Investment banks commonly 'build a book' before pricing an equity issue. In the US it has been standard practice for a number of years. In many other countries where fixed-price offerings were traditionally used, the bookbuilding procedure is becoming increasingly common, especially for international equity issues.

Under the formal bookbuilding procedure, the investment banker solicits indications of interest from institutional investors. Such indications consist of a bid for a quantity of shares and might include a maximum price (i.e., a limit price) or other details. The investment banker uses the information to construct a demand curve. The issue price is not set according to any explicit rule, but rather is based on the banker's interpretation of investors' indications of interest. He generally sets the price at a level at which demand exceeds supply, and then allocates shares to the bidders at his discretion. Thus, the bookbuilding procedure resembles an auction, but there are some important differences. The most important difference is that the pricing and allocation rules are not announced, but are left to the discretion of the investment banker. Another difference is that investors' bids do not represent a commitment, but merely an indication of interest. However, because of the repeated nature of the relationship, it is very rare for any investor to renege on a bid.[1]

Stapled securities

The following is quoted from the introduction to ASX Guidance Note 2 issued in September 2001 and was obtained through the Internet.

1. This Guidance Note is published to assist listed entities and entities considering listing to understand Australian Stock Exchange Limited (ASX) policy in relation to stapled securities. Stapling is an arrangement under which different securities are quoted jointly.
2. ASX provides joint quotation of stapled securities issued by different entities (for example, shares issued by a company and units issued by a trust) and of different classes of securities issued by the same entity (for example, shares and debentures). ASX also provides joint quotation of more complex combinations of stapled securities (for example, units issued by a trust stapled to shares and debentures issued by a company). Joint quotation has the effect that the stapled securities cannot be traded separately, as the stapled securities are treated as one unit.
3. Over recent years, ASX has accommodated a wide range of structures that involve stapled securities.

Question 2.25

Mannix Ltd was registered two years ago with a share capital of 10 000 $1 ordinary shares. The directors required capital for expansion purposes and decided to undertake a share issue.

The prospectus, issued on 1 February 2007, sought capital from the issue of 500 000 ordinary shares at a nominal value of $1 each, payable as follows:
- $0.75 on application; and
- $0.25 on allotment.

On 15 April 2007 applications had been received for 550 000 shares with application money. (The prospectus did not allow the directors to retain excess application monies.)

On 25 April 2007 directors allotted shares and made refunds.

On 30 June 2007 all allotment money had been received.

On 1 July 2007 transaction costs amounting to $3 300 including GST were paid.

On 31 December 2007 another prospectus was issued offering 100 000 $5 preference shares payable $3 on application and $2 on allotment.

By 28 February 2008, the closing date for applications, offers for 150 000 preference shares had been received.

On 15 March 2008 the directors issued the preference shares to successful applicants and made appropriate refunds. Allotment money was due by 31 May 2008.

All allotment money was received by the due date.

Prepare:

a journal entries to account for all share transactions; and
b the shareholders' equity section of the balance sheet as at 30 June 2008.

---

1 F. Cornelli and D. Golreich, 2001, 'Bookbuilding and Strategic Allocation', *Journal of Finance*.

Question 2.26

On 15 July 2007 Orbost Ltd, a registered public company limited by shares, issued a prospectus inviting applications for:
- 300 000 7% preference shares at a price of $3.50 per share payable:
  - $1.50 on application; and
  - $2 on allotment.
- 700 000 ordinary shares at a price of $5 per share payable:
  - $2.75 on application;
  - $1 on allotment;
  - $0.75 on call 1 as and when required; and
  - $0.50 on call 2 as and when required.

Under the prospectus, if there is an oversubscription for either the preference or ordinary shares, the directors can make a pro rata issue of shares and excess application money can be applied to allotment and calls. There was no minimum subscription for preference shares, but there was a minimum subscription for 500 000 ordinary shares together with an underwriting agreement for the remaining 200 000 shares if required.

By 31 August 2007, the closing date for both preference and ordinary share applications, the following had been received:
- 7% preference shares: Applications had been received for 270 000 shares:
  - 250 000 shares applied for and paid to $1.50; and
  - 20 000 shares applied for and paid to $3.50.
- Ordinary shares: Applications had been received for 780 000 shares:
  - 5 000 shares applied for and paid to $2;
  - 590 000 shares applied for and paid to $2.75;
  - 150 000 shares applied for and paid to $3.75; and
  - 35 000 shares applied for and paid to $5.

On 3 September 2007 the directors allotted preference shares to all who had made applications. Ordinary shares were allotted as follows:
- 5 000 shares applied for and paid to $2: Directors allotted nil.
- 590 000 shares applied for and paid to $2.75: Directors allotted 540 000 shares.
- 150 000 shares applied for and paid to $3.75: Directors allotted 130 000 shares.
- 35 000 shares applied for and paid to $5: Directors allotted 30 000 shares.

On 10 September 2007 transaction costs for the preference and ordinary shares issued, including underwriting fee, totalled $45 000 and were paid on this date.

On 10 October 2007 all outstanding allotment money was received by this due date for both preference shares and ordinary shares.

On 1 April 2008 the directors made call 1 on the ordinary shares, and by 15 May 2008 all required call money was received except for $11 250 which was still in arrears at 30 June 2008.

You are required to:
a   complete worksheets for the allocation of application monies received for both preference shares and ordinary shares;
b   complete all necessary transactions in general journal format to 15 May 2008;
c   post to the general ledger and extract a trial balance; and
d   prepare an extract of the balance sheet as at 30 June 2008 showing the shareholders' equity.

Issuing debentures

An alternative method to raising finance by issuing shares is to issue debt such as debentures. Unlike the issue of shares which attract ownership entitlement in the company, voting rights and participation in profit distribution, debt attracts interest and the debt must be repaid within a specified period.

Debt is recognised when a **borrower** obtains finance from a **lender** and is liable to repay the money received from the lender, who holds the debt documentation, also called the debt holder.

The amount borrowed is the **principal**, which has to be repaid at an agreed future time, and interest calculated at the agreed set rate is paid by the borrower to the lender on a six-month or annual basis.

Contracts between borrowers and lenders often indicate that a charge or security is held over a part of the company's assets. A **fixed charge** relates to one or more specific assets, such as land or buildings, and if the borrower defaults in interest or principal payment then this fixed charge is used to satisfy the default. A **floating charge** relates to a class or classes of assets, such as inventories, rather than to a particular specific asset.

The principal is repayable by the borrower to the lender at a specific date in the future and this repayment date of the debt is the **maturity date**. This repayment of the debt is the **redemption**.

A **debenture** is basically an acknowledgement of a debt. The Corporations Law says that a debenture is an undertaking to repay a sum of money as a debt by a body corporate, such as a company, which has been deposited with or lent to the body. Documents that are deemed not to be debentures are mainly cheques, money orders, bills of exchange, promissory notes of $50 000 or more and receipts.

The Law requires that a debt can be only described as a debenture if it is fully secured by a charge or security over the borrowing company's assets. Unsecured debts are still deemed to be debentures for complying with certain sections of the Law, but the borrower must describe them as **unsecured notes** or unsecured deposit notes.

Types of debt

The types of debt considered are:
- debenture;
- mortgage debenture;
- unsecured note; and
- convertible note.

Debenture

Although there is not a definite format for a debenture, the document needs to acknowledge that the borrower has received money from the lender and that a specified interest rate will be paid over a definite time period, such as six-monthly or annually.

A public company can issue debentures to the general public through the issue of a prospectus together with an application. A public company can also make a private placement of debentures to one or a few lenders for very large amounts. The Corporations Law requires the company to appoint a trustee who monitors the borrower to safeguard the interests of the debenture holders, and the company must provide appropriate clear disclosure of all matters relating to the debentures as part of half-yearly financial reports.

Mortgage debenture

A mortgage debenture is a debenture that is secured by a first mortgage over land and/or buildings of the borrower. The total of the mortgage debenture may not exceed 60% of the value of the real estate.

A mortgage is a charge and usually limits the borrower's (mortgagor's) rights to sell or transfer the property without the consent of the lender (mortgagee). If this mortgage agreement is broken, then generally the lender, through the trustee, can take possession of the property and sell it to repay the debentures.

Unsecured note

An unsecured note is a debt that is not secured by any charge over the assets of the company and, as a result of the higher risks by the lender, the interest rates are higher than those for a debenture or mortgage debenture.

Convertible note

A convertible note is a debenture that allows the lender, on maturity of the note, to convert the debt into either paid-up share capital in the company or cash, or a combination of the two. Convertible notes were once popular for tax reasons, but their frequency of issue has now declined.

Contrast of funds from equity and debt

To operate effectively a company needs cash for the purchase of assets and payment of expenses. This is initially financed from share capital. As the company trades profitably its finances will be increased, with a positive cash flow being generated.

As a business expands, it needs cash to obtain adequate inventories to produce and sell, and as it sells more its accounts receivable usually increase, which ties up more cash resources. These needed cash resources may be obtained through short-term sources such as accounts payable and obtaining a bank overdraft. Other possibilities are issuing more shares or making remaining calls on shares already issued. However, a company can also obtain cash through incurring a debt, such as a long-term financial institution loan, or by borrowing cash through the issuing of debentures. Each company decides its own appropriate mix of shares and debt.

The advantages and disadvantages of shares and debentures or, as they are sometimes referred to, equity capital and debt capital or debt securities, are as follows:

- Shares give the investor ownership entitlement of the company, as well as voting rights at general meetings.
- Debentures carry no ownership entitlement for the lenders and give no voting rights.
- Issuing more shares can dilute ownership of the company and generate more owners to share in the profits.
- Debentures do not dilute ownership.
- Debenture holders do not share in the profits of the company.
- Debenture holders are entitled to a fixed regular payment of interest irrespective of whether the company has made a profit or not; payment is compulsory.
- Payment of a dividend to shareholders is at the discretion of the directors.
- Share capital does not have to be repaid.
- Debenture debt must be repaid at a specific future date.
- With debentures it is common to impose on the company the requirement to maintain a specific debt to equity ratio, and this can restrict further long-term borrowing.
- There is no formal restriction on the amount of share capital that can be issued; however, earnings per share can readily become a constraining factor for the directors and the company.
- Debenture interest paid to the lenders is an expense in the year it is incurred and an allowable tax-deductible expense.
- Dividends paid on shares are not an allowable outgoing and are paid after tax has been calculated on the assessable net profit of the company.

Question 2.27

From the following clues relating to the topic matters covered above, complete the crossword that follows.

Across

1. The amount borrowed is the ... which has to be repaid to the lender at an agreed future time.
3. Security held over a class or classes of assets such as inventories rather than a particular specific asset is a ... ... (2 words).
7. Repayment of the debt is the ... of that debt.
8. Debentures carry no ownership entitlement to the lender and give no ... ... (2 words).
9. The Corporations Law requires the company to appoint a ... who monitors the borrower to safeguard the interests of the debenture holders.
12. Where one or more specific assets such as land or buildings are used as security between a borrower and a lender, they are referred to as a ... ... (2 words).
19. Each company decides its own appropriate mix of shares and ...
22. A ... ... (2 words) does not exceed more than 60% of the value of the real estate of the borrower that is secured.
23. An ... ... (2 words) is a debt that is not secured by any charge over the assets of the company.
24. Shares are sometimes referred to as ... capital.

25 Interest is calculated at the agreed set rate and is paid by the borrower to the … on a six- or 12-month basis.
26 The borrower repays the debt at a specific future date known as the … … (2 words).
27 When a business expands, it usually puts pressure on the business availability of …

Down

2 When a business expands, it needs to obtain adequate … to produce and sell.
4 A short-term source of cash is to acquire everything on credit which increases the … … (2 words).
5 With debentures it is a common requirement that a specific debt to … ratio must be maintained and this can restrict further long-term borrowing.
6 These give ownership entitlement of the company to the investor.
10 A short-term source of cash is by obtaining a … … (2 words).
11 Debenture debt must be … at a specific future date.
13 Low cash reserves can be increased by making remaining … on shares already issued.
14 A … is the entity that is liable to repay the money received from the lender.
15 Debenture holders do not share in the … of the company.
16 Debenture holders are entitled to a fixed regular payment of interest irrespective of whether the company has made a profit or not; payment is …
17 Although there is no definite format for it, the document needs to acknowledge that the borrower has received money from the lender.
18 Payment of a dividend to shareholders is at the discretion of the …
20 Debenture interest paid to the lenders is an … in the year it is incurred and an allowable deduction.
21 Dividends paid on shares are not an allowable deduction and are paid after … has been calculated.

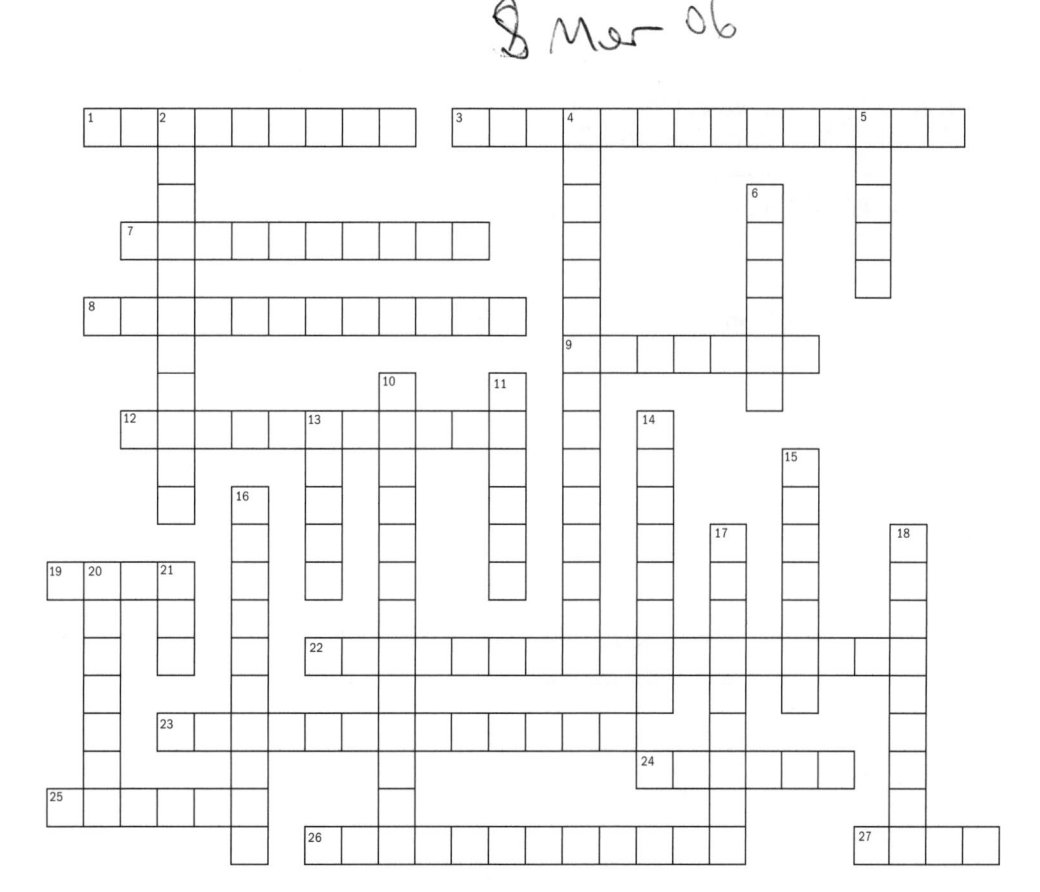

Accounting entries for the issuing and redemption of debentures

When accounting for debentures, there are three distinct phases. These are:
1. issuing a debenture prospectus;
2. making annual interest payments on the debentures; and
3. redeeming (paying out) the debentures.

Issuing a debenture prospectus

The procedure for issuing debentures, mortgage debentures and unsecured notes is similar to, but not as complex as, the procedure for issuing share capital.

Debentures are normally issued at par – that is, the nominal amount of the debenture, often a minimum of $100 each; however, they can be issued at a premium (above par) or at a discount (below par).

A public company will need to prepare a prospectus together with an application form for debentures and appoint a trustee to act on behalf of the debenture holders. Also, a register of the debenture holders must be kept.

During the life of the debenture, interest is paid either six-monthly or annually. At the maturity date for the debentures, payment is usually made for the last interest period together with the payment or redemption of the debenture.

The entries to account for the issue of debentures payable in full on application are as follows:

1. Prospective debenture holders complete the application form contained in the prospectus and forward the appropriate application monies which are held in a trust account.

General journal		
Trust account (debentures)	Dr	
Applications – Debentures		Cr

2. Directors formally allot debentures to successful debenture applicants and refund unsuccessful applicants.

General journal		
Applications – Debentures	Dr	
Debentures		Cr
Trust account (debentures)		Cr

3. Debenture money held in trust is transferred to the normal company account on the allotment of debentures.

General journal		
Bank	Dr	
Trust account (debentures)		Cr

ILLUSTRATION

On 21 August 2007 Grampians Ltd released a prospectus inviting applicants for 1 000 debentures of $1 000 par amount payable in full on application. Terms were an interest rate of 10% p.a. payable six-monthly and a maturity date of 1 October 2010. Oversubscriptions up to $250 000, or 25% of the initial issue, were permissible.

By the closing date of 27 September 2007 Grampians Ltd received applications for 1 700 debentures paid in full. On 1 October 2007 the directors allotted 1 250 debentures, with the balance being refunded.

The journal entries and general ledger postings for this prospectus would be as follows:

1   *Receipt of application monies*

General journal of Grampians Ltd

Date	Particulars	Debit	Credit
2007		$	$
27 Sept	Trust account – Debenture applicants	1 700 000	
	Applications – Debentures		1 700 000
	Receipted money paid by debenture		

General ledger of Grampians Ltd

Date	Particulars	Debit	Credit	Balance
Trust account – Debenture applications				
27 Sept 2007	Applications	1 700 000		1 700 000 Dr
Applications – Debentures				
27 Sept 2007	Trust account		1 700 000	1 700 000 Cr

2   *Allotment of debentures to successful applicants and refunds to unsuccessful applicants*

General journal of Grampians Ltd

Date	Particulars	Debit	Credit
2007		$	$
1 Oct	Applications – Debentures	1 250 000	
	Debentures		1 250 000
	Allotted 1 250 $1 000 debentures		
	Applications – Debentures	450 000	
	Trust account – Debenture applicants		450 000
	Refunds to unsuccessful debenture applicants		

General ledger of Grampians Ltd

Date	Particulars	Debit	Credit	Balance
Applications – Debentures				
27 Sept 2007	Trust account		1 700 000	1 700 000 Cr
1 Oct 2007	Debentures	1 250 000		450 000 Cr
	Trust account	450 000		Nil
Trust account – Debenture applications				
27 Sept 2007	Applications	1 700 000		1 700 000 Dr
1 Oct 2007	Applications – Debentures		450 000	1 250 000 Dr
Debentures				
1 Oct 2007	Applications – Debentures		1 250 000	1 250 000 Cr

3 *Transfer of trust account balance*

General journal of Grampians Ltd

Date	Particulars	Debit	Credit
2007		$	$
1 Oct	Bank	1 250 000	
	Trust account – Debenture applications		1 250 000
	Transfer of money held in trust		

The balance sheet prepared for internal management purposes after these debenture issues transactions could be presented as follows:

Grampians Ltd
Balance sheet as at 1 October 2007

	$
Assets	
Bank	1 250 000
Liabilities	
Debentures (10% p.a. maturing 2010)	1 250 000
Net assets	Nil

Question 2.28

On 1 July 2007 Robertson Ltd issued a prospectus inviting applications for 8 000 debentures at par value of $100 payable in full on application. Terms of issue were 8% p.a. interest payable six-monthly, with a maturity date of 1 August 2011.

Applications for 8 250 debentures, fully paid, had been received by the closing date of 1 August 2007.

On 4 August 2007 the directors allotted 8 000 debentures. Money for the oversubscription was refunded.

You are required to prepare:
a journal entries to record all transactions; and
b the general ledger.

Question 2.29

From the following information provided in respect of Taree Ltd's debenture transactions you are required to prepare:
a   journal entries to record all transactions;
b   the general ledger; and
c   the balance sheet as at 30 November 2007.

Taree Ltd issued a prospectus on 1 October 2007 inviting applications for 3 750 debentures at par of $100 payable in full on application. Terms were 7% p.a. interest payable six-monthly for six years from the closing date. The directors were also permitted to accept oversubscriptions to 4 000 debentures.

The closing date for applications was 10 November 2007, by which date the company had received 4 225 applications together with the correct application amount.

On 14 November 2007 the directors allotted 4 000 debentures to the successful applicants.

Making annual interest payments on the debentures

Debentures are serviced each year through the payment of interest, with the rate and dates of payment being specified in the prospectus.

The payment of interest must occur on the agreed date(s). As the company will be using accrual accounting, the reversal and accrual entries must be made to ensure the correct matching of interest expense with the accounting period.

The entries to record the payment of interest, end-of-period accruals and the closure of interest expense to the profit and loss account are:

1   Payment of interest

General journal		
Interest on debentures	Dr	
Bank		Cr

2   Accrual of interest on debentures incurred but not due for payment at annual balance date

General journal		
Interest on debentures	Dr	
Accrued expense		Cr

3   Closure of interest expense at end of year

General journal		
Profit and loss	Dr	
Interest on debentures		Cr

Where interest was accrued in the previous period a reversal entry will be required in the following period. The reversal entry is as follows:

General journal		
Accrued expense	Dr	
Interest on debentures		Cr

ILLUSTRATION

In the previous illustration, Grampians Ltd allotted $1 250 000 in debentures on 1 October 2007 which attracted interest at a rate of 10% p.a. payable six-monthly and will mature on 1 October 2010.

The annual interest amount payable would be $1 250 000 × 10% = $125 000. This would be paid in two instalments of $62 500 on 1 April and 1 October each year until the debenture matures on 1 October 2010.

The payments and end-of-year accruals for each year are shown in the following table:

	Year ended 30 June							
	2008		2009			2010		2011
	1 Apr	30 Jun	1 Oct	1 Apr	30 Jun	1 Oct	1 Apr	30 Jun	1 Oct
Payment	62 500		62 500	62 500		62 500	62 500		62 500
Accrual (3 months)		31 250			31 250			31 250	

The journal entries for the year ended 30 June 2008 would be as follows:

General journal of Grampians Ltd

Date	Particulars	Debit	Credit
2008		$	$
1 April	Debenture interest	62 500	
	Bank		62 500
	Payment of debenture interest		
30 June	Debenture interest	31 250	
	Accrued interest		31 250
	Adjustment for 3 months' interest on debentures		
	Profit and loss	93 750	
	Debenture interest		93 750
	Closed expense account		

The journal entries for the year ended 30 June 2009 (including the reversal entry for the previous period's adjustment) would be as follows:

General journal of Grampians Ltd

Date	Particulars	Debit	Credit
2008		$	$
1 July	Accrued interest	31 250	
	Debenture interest		31 250
	Reversal entry		
1 Oct	Debenture interest	62 500	
	Bank		62 500
	Payment of debenture interest		
2009	Debenture interest	62 500	
1 April	Bank		62 500
	Payment of debenture interest		

Date	Particulars	Debit	Credit
30 June	Debenture interest	31 250	
	Accrued interest		31 250
	Adjustment for 3 months' interest on debentures		
	Profit and loss	125 000	
	Debenture interest		125 000
	Closed expense account		

The debenture interest account for the year ended 30 June 2009 would appear as follows:

General ledger of Grampians Ltd

Date	Particulars	Debit	Credit	Balance
Debenture interest				
1 July 2008	Accrued interest		31 250	31 250 Cr
1 Oct 2008	Bank	62 500		31 250 Dr
1 April 2009	Bank	62 500		93 750 Dr
30 June 2009	Accrued interest	31 250		125 000 Dr
	Profit and loss		125 000	Nil

Question 2.30

a Calculate the annual interest expense amounts as at 30 June each year associated with the following debentures which commenced in 2007.

	Debenture amount	Annual rate of interest	Interest paid	Date of allotment	Debenture period
Debenture 1	$500 000	9%	Half-yearly	1 September	3 years
Debenture 2	$850 000	6%	Quarterly	1 March	2 years

b For debenture 2 for the year ended 30 June 2009 you are required to:
  i prepare journal entries to account for annual interest calculations; and
  ii show the interest expense account for the year.

Question 2.31

On 15 June 2006 Upwey Ltd issued a prospectus inviting applications for 9 000 debentures at a par price of $100 payable in full on application. Terms of issue were 9% p.a. interest payable six-monthly from the date of allotment, with a maturity date of five years from the date of allotment. Directors were permitted to accept a 10% oversubscription on the original issue number.

Applications closed on 27 July 2007 with applications received for 10 500 debentures paid in full.

The directors allotted debentures on 1 August 2007 to the maximum level permitted by the prospectus and refunded the balance to the unsuccessful applicants.

You are required to prepare:
a journal entries to record the application and allotment of the debentures;
b journal entries to pay and accrue interest on the debentures for the year ended 30 June 2008;
c the general ledger for the year ended 30 June 2008; and
d a trial balance as at 30 June 2008.

Redeeming (paying out) the debentures

When a debenture matures, the borrower is required to pay the lender the amount borrowed. This is called debenture redemption.

The vast majority of redemptions by the borrower occur when the debenture matures – that is, the date due for repayment to the lender.

The borrower may redeem debentures before the maturity date by purchasing its own debentures on the stock exchange. The redemption can be at par, at a discount (an amount less than the par value) or at a premium (an amount greater than the par value).

The entries to account for debenture redemption under various conditions are as set out below.

Redemption at maturity

Redemption at the date of maturity will normally involve a final interest payment in addition to the payment of the amount owing on the debenture. The required journal entries are:

1 The final interest payment

General journal		
Interest on debentures	Dr	
Bank		Cr

2 Payment to the debenture holders on redemption

General journal		
Debentures	Dr	
Bank		Cr

ILLUSTRATION

In our continuing illustration, Grampians Ltd held a debenture of $1 250 000 which attracted interest at a rate of 10% p.a. payable six-monthly and maturing on 1 October 2010.

On the date of maturity the interest owing for the previous six months amounted to $62 500.

The journal entries for the year ended 30 June 2011 would be as follows:

General journal of Grampians Ltd

Date	Particulars	Debit	Credit
2010		$	$
1 Oct	Debenture interest	62 500	
	Bank		62 500
	Final interest payment		
	Debenture	1 250 000	
	Bank		1 250 000
	To record debenture redemption		

The debenture liability account would appear as follows:

General ledger of Grampians Ltd

Date	Particulars	Debit	Credit	Balance
Debenture				
1 July 2010	Balance		1 250 000	1 250 00 Cr
1 Oct 2010	Bank	1 250 000		Nil

Question 2.32

Queenscliff Ltd had allotted 5 000 9% debentures of face value $100 with interest payable six-monthly and a maturity date of 5 March 2010.

Prepare journal entries to record the payment of interest and the redemption of the debenture at 5 March 2010.

Question 2.33

Shepparton Ltd had allotted 975 7% debentures of a face value of $1 000 each with a maturity date of 10 October 2008 and interest payable six-monthly.

Prepare in general journal format the payment of interest and the debenture redemption.

Redemption prior to maturity at par

Redemption prior to maturity on the open market usually means through the stock exchange, but it could also be through negotiation with major financial institutions that may wish to liquidate their debenture lending.

If the redemption was at par, the required journals would be the same as those for redemption at maturity but exclude the first journal for the payment of interest.

Redemption prior to maturity at a premium

When a debenture is redeemed at a premium the price paid is greater than the face value of the debenture. The premium is paid to entice the lender to accept redemption before the maturity date. If a debenture has a face value of $100 the debenture may be redeemed at $102, or a premium of $2.

The premium paid on the debenture redemption is treated as an expense by the borrower.

The entry to record the redemption of the debenture and the premium expense is as follows:

General journal		
Debenture	Dr	
Premium on debenture redemption	Dr	
Bank		Cr

Question 2.34

In August 2007 Robertson Ltd had allotted 8 000 8% debentures of a face value of $100 with a maturity date of 1 August 2011.

On 28 November 2009 it was able to redeem, through the ASX, 2 000 debentures at a premium of $3 per debenture.

On 21 August 2010 it was able to redeem 2 500 debentures through the ASX at $102 per $100.

You are required to record the journal entries associated with each redemption.

Redemption prior to maturity at a discount

When a debenture is redeemed by the borrower below its face value it is redeemed at a discount by the borrower. This may occur where the lender is keen to redeem the debenture before the maturity date and offers the borrower a discount to redeem earlier. If a $100 debenture is redeemed at a $5 discount it will be paid out at $95. The discount taken by the borrower is recorded as a revenue account.

The entry to redeem a debenture at a discount is as follows:

General journal		
Debenture	Dr	
Discount on debenture redemption		Cr
Bank		Cr

Question 2.35

Taree Ltd allotted 4 000 7% debentures at $100 with a maturity date of 10 November 2009.
    On 29 January 2009, it redeemed 1 200 debentures at $96 per $100.
    On 24 May 2011, it redeemed 1 500 debentures at a discount of $6 per debenture.
    You are required to record the journal entries associated with each redemption.

Alternate accounts for different debt issues

Where different types of debt are issued, the following relevant accounts apply depending on the debt document issued.

Debenture	Mortgage debenture	Unsecured note
Debenture applications	Mortgage debenture applications	Unsecured note applications
Debentures	Mortgage debentures	Unsecured notes
Interest on debentures	Interest on mortgage debentures	Interest on unsecured notes
Premium on debenture redemption	Premium on mortgage debenture redemption	Premium on unsecured note redemption
Discount on debenture redemption	Discount on mortgage debenture redemption	Discount on unsecured note redemption

Question 2.36

Balmoral Ltd issued a prospectus on 1 May 2007 inviting applications for 8 500 debentures at par of face value $100, payable in full on application and closing on 1 June 2007. Terms of the issue were 7% p.a. interest payable six-monthly with a maturity date of 1 June 2010.
    By 1 June, application money totalling $750 000 had been received in respect of 7 500 $100 7% debentures.
    On 3 June 2007 the directors met and allotted the debentures.
    You are required to prepare journal entries for:
a the application and allotment of the debentures;
b the final interest payment; and
c redemption of the debentures.

Question 2.37

On 1 November 2007 a prospectus inviting applications for 900 unsecured notes at par of face value $1 000 payable in full on application was issued by Cobargo Ltd. Terms of issue were 10% p.a. interest payable six-monthly with a maturity date of 1 December 2011.

By 1 December 2007, the closing date for applications, a total of 975 applications together with the correct money were received.

On 3 December 2007 the directors made the allotment.

You are required to prepare journal entries for:
a   the application and allotment of the debentures;
b   the final interest payment; and
c   debenture redemption.

Question 2.38

On 10 January 2007 Daylesford Ltd issued a prospectus inviting applications for 7 500 mortgage debentures at par of value $100 payable in full on application. Terms of issue were 6% p.a. interest payable six-monthly on 1 August and 1 February, with a maturity date of 31 July 2008.

On 29 January 2007 applications closed for the mortgage debentures. Applications for the 6% mortgage debentures together with the appropriate money for 7 850 debentures had been received.

On 1 February 2007 the directors allotted 7 500 mortgage debentures.

On 21 August 2010 Daylesford redeemed 1 500 mortgage debentures at $102 per $100.

On 19 February 2011 Daylesford redeemed another 3 200 mortgage debentures at $97 per $100.

You are required to prepare journal entries to record:
a   the application and allotment of debentures;
b   the various redemptions;
c   the interest amounts for the year ended 30 June 2008; and
d   debenture redemption at maturity date.

Note: Questions 2.39, 2.40 and 2.41 include share issues where directors may retain excess application money.

Question 2.39

From the following information for Gulargambone Ltd, you are required to:
a   prepare all relevant journals in general journal format; and
b   show the liabilities and shareholders' equity section of the balance sheet as at 31 August 2007.

Gulargambone Ltd was registered as a public company limited by shares on 17 January 2007.

On 6 February, five subscribers paid for and were issued with a total of 15 000 fully paid deferred shares at a price of $3 per share.

A prospectus was issued to the public on 1 March 2007 providing for the issue of:
• 250 000 7% cumulative preference shares at a price of $4 per share payable in full on application; and
• 600 000 ordinary shares at a price of $6 per share payable $2.50 on application, $2 on allotment, and one call of $1.50 payable as and when required by the directors.

The prospectus indicated that for the 7% cumulative preference shares the directors were allowed to accept oversubscription to a maximum of 5% above the issued number of 250 000 shares. For ordinary shares, in the event of an oversubscription the directors could make a pro rata issue of shares and excess application money could be applied to allotment and the call.

Application for both classes of shares closed on 2 April 2007 and by that date application and money had been received for:
- 7% cumulative preference shares: 270 000 shares fully paid to $4 per share.
- Ordinary shares of $6 as follows:

Shares applied for	Paid to	Shares allotted
550 000	$2.50	390 000
185 000	$4.50	140 000
90 000	$5.00	70 000

Allotment by the directors occurred on 3 April 2007. Preference shares were allotted to the maximum number permitted.

Share issue expenses of $17 300 were paid on 5 April 2007.

Outstanding allotment money was received in full by the due date of 6 May 2007.

On 1 June 2007 a prospectus was issued inviting applications for 12 000 mortgage debentures at par of value $100 payable in full on application. Terms of issue were 8% p.a. interest payable six-monthly from the allotment date with a maturity date of 31 July 2010.

On 14 July 2007 applications closed for the mortgage debentures. Applications for 13 000 debentures together with the appropriate money had been received.

On 1 August 2007 the directors allotted the mortgage debentures.

Question 2.40

On 6 June 2007 Horsham Ltd was registered as a public company limited by shares.

On 20 June 2007 a prospectus was issued inviting applications for:
- 250 000 9% preference shares at a price of $3 per share payable:
  - $1.75 on application; and
  - $1.25 on allotment.
- 600 000 ordinary shares at a price of $7 per share payable:
  - $3 on application;
  - $1.50 on allotment;
  - $1.30 on call 1 as and when required; and
  - $1.20 on call 2 as and when required.

Under the prospectus, if there is an oversubscription for either the preference or ordinary shares then the directors can make a pro rata issue of shares and excess application money can be applied to allotment and calls. There was no minimum number for preference shares, but there was a minimum of 450 000 ordinary shares together with an underwriting agreement for the remaining shares.

On 5 August 2007 the closing date for both preference and ordinary share applications, the following had been received:
- 9% preference shares: Applications had been received for 270 000 shares:
  - 20 000 shares applied for and paid to $3; and
  - 250 000 shares applied for and paid to $1.75.
- Ordinary shares: Applications had been received for 775 000 shares:
  - 35 000 shares applied for and paid to $7;
  - 150 000 shares applied for and paid to $4.50; and
  - 590 000 shares applied for and paid to $3.

On 7 August 2007 the directors allotted the 9% preference shares to all applicants and did not refund any applications received. Ordinary shares were allotted as follows:
  - 35 000 shares applied for and paid to $7: Directors allotted 35 000 shares.
  - 150 000 shares applied for and paid to $4.50: Directors allotted 100 000 shares.

- 590 000 shares applied for and paid to $3: Directors allotted 465 000 shares.

On 14 August 2007 all outstanding allotment money was received by this due date for both 9% preference shares and ordinary shares.

On 16 August 2007 transaction costs for the preference and ordinary shares issued, including underwriting fee, totalled $25 000 and were paid on this date.

On 12 October 2007 a prospectus was issued inviting applications for 6 000 debentures at par of $100 payable in full on application. Terms were 7% p.a. interest payable six-monthly for four years from the closing date on 30 November 2007. The directors were also permitted to accept oversubscriptions to 6 500 debentures.

By the closing date for debenture applications the company had received 6 250 applications together with the correct application amount.

On 1 December 2007 the directors allotted the debentures to the successful applicants.

On 2 April 2008 the directors made call 1 on the ordinary shares.

On 7 May 2008 all required call money was received with the exception of calls on 15 000 shares.

On 30 June 2008 2 000 debentures were redeemed at $94 per $100.

On 12 October 2008 another 1 000 debentures were redeemed at $102 per $100.

You are required to:
a complete worksheets for both 9% preference shares and ordinary shares recording the allotment of applications received;
b record all transactions in the general journal;
c post to the general ledger and extract a trial balance; and
d prepare an extract of the balance sheet as at 30 October 2008 showing liabilities and shareholders' equity.

Question 2.41

On 12 October 2007 Warburton Ltd was registered as a public company limited by shares.

On 14 October 2007 money was received from the five subscribers, each of whom agreed to purchase 3 000 fully paid ordinary shares at a price of $5 per share.

On 20 October 2007 a prospectus was issued to the public inviting applications for:
- 150 000 5% preference shares at a price of $4 per share payable:
  - $3 on application; and
  - $1 on allotment.
- 800 000 ordinary shares at a price of $5 per share payable:
  - $1.75 on application;
  - $1.50 on allotment;
  - $1 on call 1 as and when required; and
  - $0.75 on call 2 as and when required.

Under the prospectus, if there is an oversubscription for either the preference or ordinary shares then the directors can make a pro rata issue of shares and excess application money can be applied to allotment and calls. There was no minimum number for preference shares, but there was a minimum of 550 000 ordinary shares together with an underwriting agreement for the remaining 250 000 shares.

By 28 November 2007, the closing date for both preference and ordinary share applications, the following had been received:
- 5% preference shares: Applications had been received for 200 000 shares:
  - 50 000 shares applied for and paid to $4; and
  - 150 000 shares applied for and paid to $3.
- Ordinary shares: Applications had been received for 950 000 shares:
  - 44 000 shares applied for and paid to $5;
  - 180 000 shares applied for and paid to $3.25;

- 720 000 shares applied for and paid to $1.75; and
- 6 000 shares applied for and paid to $1.50.

On 1 December 2007 the directors allotted the 5% preference shares as follows:
- 50 000 shares applied for: allotted 30 000 shares; and
- 150 000 shares applied for: allotted 120 000 shares

and allotted ordinary shares as follows:
- 44 000 shares applied for: allotted 40 000 shares;
- 180 000 shares applied for: allotted 150 000 shares;
- 720 000 shares applied for: allotted 610 000 shares; and
- 6 000 shares applied for: allotted no shares.

On 5 December 2007 transaction costs for the preference and ordinary shares issued, including underwriting fee, totalled $35 500 and were paid.

On 15 December 2007 all outstanding allotment money was received by this due date for both 5% preference shares and ordinary shares.

On 15 March 2008 the directors made call 1 on ordinary shares. By 30 April 2008 all required call money was received except for 25 000 shares which were still in arrears at 30 June 2008.

On 10 October 2008 the directors issued a prospectus for 10 000 mortgage debentures at par with a face value of $100 payable in full on application. Terms were 6% p.a. interest payable six-monthly by 1 December and 1 June, with a maturity date of 1 December 2008.

On 30 November 2008, the closing date for debentures, applications for 11 300 6% mortgage debentures complete with money had been received.

On 1 December 2008 the directors allotted the 10 000 6% mortgage debentures of $100 to the successful applicants.

You are required to:
a complete worksheets for both 5% preference shares and ordinary shares recording the allotment of applications received;
b enter all transactions to the general journal;
c post to the general ledger and extract a trial balance; and
d prepare a balance sheet as at 31 December 2008.

Note: Questions 2.42, 2.43 and 2.44 include share issues where directors cannot retain excess application money.

Question 2.42

From the following information for Gulargambone Ltd, you are required to:
a prepare all relevant journals in general journal format; and
b show the liabilities and shareholders' equity section of the balance sheet as at 31 August 2007.

Gulargambone Ltd was registered as a public company limited by shares on 17 January 2007.

On 6 February, five subscribers paid for and were issued with a total of 15 000 fully paid deferred shares at a price of $3 per share.

A prospectus was issued to the public on 1 March 2007 providing for the issue of:
- 250 000 7% cumulative preference shares at a price of $4 per share payable in full on application; and
- 600 000 ordinary shares at a price of $6 per share payable:
  - $2.50 on application;
  - $2 on allotment; and
  - one call of $1.50 payable as and when required by the directors.

The prospectus indicated that for the 7% cumulative preference shares the directors were allowed to accept oversubscription to a maximum of 5% above the issued number of 250 000 shares.

For ordinary shares, in the event of an oversubscription the directors were not permitted to retain excess application monies.

Application for both classes of shares closed on 2 April 2007. Application money had been received for:
- 270 000 preference shares; and
- 620 000 ordinary shares.

Allotment of shares occurred on 3 April 2007.

Share issue expenses of $17 300 inclusive of GST were paid on 5 April 2007.

Allotment money was received in full by the due date of 6 May 2007.

On 1 June 2007 a prospectus was issued inviting applications for 12 000 mortgage debentures at par of value $100 payable in full on application. Terms of issue were 8% p.a. interest payable six-monthly from the allotment date with a maturity date of 31 July 2010.

On 14 July 2007 applications closed for the mortgage debentures. Applications for 13 000 debentures together with the appropriate money had been received.

On 1 August 2007 the directors allotted the mortgage debentures.

Question 2.43

On 6 June 2007 Horsham Ltd was registered as a public company limited by shares.

On 20 June 2007 a prospectus was issued inviting applications for:
- 250 000 9% preference shares at a price of $3 per share payable:
  - $1.75 on application; and
  - $1.25 on allotment.
- 600 000 ordinary shares at a price of $7 per share payable:
  - $3 on application;
  - $1.50 on allotment;
  - $1.30 on call 1 as and when required; and
  - $1.20 on call 2 as and when required.

The prospectus conditions included the following:
- Applications to be lodged by 5 August 2007.
- For ordinary shares a minimum subscription level had been set at 450 000 ordinary shares together with an underwriting agreement for the remaining shares not taken.
- Retention of excess application money was not permitted for either prospectus.

By 5 August applications had been received for:
- 270 000 preference shares; and
- 775 000 ordinary shares.

On 7 August 2007 the directors allotted shares to successful applicants and refunded unsuccessful applicants. Allotment money was requested to be paid by 14 August 2007.

On 14 August 2007 allotment money was received.

On 16 August 2007 transaction costs of $25 000 inclusive of GST were paid.

On 12 October 2007 a prospectus was issued inviting applications for 6 000 debentures at par of $100 payable in full on application. Terms were 7% p.a. interest payable six-monthly for four years from the closing date on 30 November 2007. The directors were also permitted to accept oversubscriptions to 6 500 debentures.

By the closing date for debenture applications the company had received 6 250 applications together with the correct application amount.

The directors on 1 December 2007 allotted the debentures to the successful applicants.

On 2 April 2008 the directors made call 1 on the ordinary shares.

On 7 May 2008 all required call money was received with the exception of calls on 15 000 shares.

On 30 June 2008 2 000 debentures were redeemed at $94 per $100.

On 12 October 2008 another 1 000 debentures were redeemed at $102 per $100.

You are required to:
a   record all transactions in the general journal;
b   post to the general ledger and extract a trial balance; and
c   prepare an extract of the balance sheet as at 30 October 2008 showing liabilities and shareholders' equity.

Question 2.44

On 12 October 2007 Warburton Ltd was registered as a public company limited by shares.

On 14 October 2007 money was received from the five subscribers, each of whom agreed to purchase 3 000 fully paid ordinary shares at a price of $5 per share.

On 20 October 2007 a prospectus was issued to the public inviting applications for:
- 150 000 5% preference shares at a price of $4 per share payable:
  - $3 on application; and
  - $1 on allotment.
- 800 000 ordinary shares at a price of $5 per share payable:
  - $1.75 on application;
  - $1.50 on allotment;
  - $1 on call 1 as and when required; and
  - $0.75 on call 2 as and when required.

The directors were not permitted to retain excess application money on either prospectus.

By 28 November 2007, the closing date for both preference and ordinary share applications, the following had been received:
- 200 000 preference shares; and
- 950 000 ordinary shares.

On 1 December 2007 shares were allotted and refunds made with allotment monies requested by 15 December.

On 5 December 2007 transaction costs amounting to $35 500 inclusive of GST were paid.

On 15 December 2007 allotment money was received.

On 15 March 2008 the directors made call 1 on ordinary shares.

By 30 April 2008 all call money was received on 775 000 ordinary shares.

On 10 October 2008 the directors issued a prospectus for 10 000 mortgage debentures at par with a face value of $100 payable in full on application. Terms were 6% p.a. interest payable six-monthly by 1 December and 1 June, with a maturity date of 1 December 2008.

On 30 November 2008, the closing date for debentures, applications for 11 300 6% mortgage debentures complete with money had been received.

On 1 December 2008 the directors allotted the 10 000 6% mortgage debentures of $100 to the successful applicants.

You are required to:
a   record all transactions to the general journal;
b   post to the general ledger and extract a trial balance; and
c   prepare a balance sheet as at 31 December 2008.

CHAPTER 3
ACCOUNTING FOR THE CONVERSION OF A BUSINESS TO A COMPANY

Objectives

Upon satisfactory completion of this chapter you should be able to:

- explain how Accounting Standard AASB 3: Business Combinations values assets and liabilities when businesses are combined;
- explain the requirement of Accounting Standard AASB 3: Business Combinations when a business is purchased above and below its fair value;
- define the term 'vendors' and explain how a vendor's account is used when converting a business to a company;
- complete journal and general ledger entries recording the takeover of an existing sole trader or partnership business by a newly formed company limited by shares; and
- prepare a balance sheet for the company where a company is combined with a sole trader or partnership business.

Introduction

Sole trader and partnership forms of business ownership may convert their existing business into a company limited by shares. When a company is initially established and acquires the net assets of the sole trader or partnership business it is necessary to apply the requirements of the appropriate accounting standards.

Converting a business into a company

Sole trader and partnership types of business ownership may consider a change of business structure to a company form of ownership, be it a proprietary company or a public company (small or large).

Conversion from a non-corporate form of business ownership to a corporate form may be desirable in the following circumstances:

- **To obtain increased capital:** Sole trader and partnership businesses may experience difficulty in obtaining increased capital from the existing owners. Conversion to a company, particularly a public company, will allow the business to issue shares to the public and thereby increase capital contributions.
- **To avoid unlimited liability:** Associated with sole trader and partnership forms of business ownership is the principle of unlimited liability. This principle requires the owners of these business forms of ownership to take personal responsibility for the business debts when the business is unable to meet those debts. When a company is formed it is normal to limit the liability of the owners (shareholders) to the issue price of the shares acquired, thereby giving them limited liability in relation to the debts of the business – that is, the owners are only liable up to the unpaid amount of the shares they hold.

The procedure to convert a sole trader or partnership form of business ownership to a company is the same procedure detailed in Chapter 1. That procedure is summarised as follows:

Step 1 Register the business by obtaining an ABN and consider registering for GST.
Step 2 Adopt the Replaceable Rules or prepare a constitution.
Step 3 Allot shares to founding members.
Step 4 Appoint director(s) and company secretary.
Step 5 Complete and lodge the application form.
Step 6 Commence operating as a company on the granting of the certificate of registration.

Once the company has been registered it is then necessary for it to acquire the appropriate assets and liabilities from the sole trader or partnership business. This will require the company (the purchaser) and the sole trader or partnership (the vendor) to agree on the assets and liabilities that will be taken over by the company and the appropriate values of each.

Where the owner of the sole trader or owners of the partnership are converting their businesses into a company, then the purchaser and vendor (the seller) are physically the same person(s). However, from a business entity point of view, the purchaser and the vendor are separate entities.

The purchase amount agreed to is called the purchase price. The consideration paid by the purchaser to the vendor may be in the form of cash, shares in the company, or both cash and shares.

Approved accounting standards

Accounting Standard AASB 3: Business Combinations became effective on 1 January 2005. This standard identifies when businesses combine and the accounting treatment that must be applied when a business combination is identified.

AASB 3: Business Combinations defines a business combination as follows:

> A business combination is the bringing together of separate entities or businesses into one reporting entity. The result of nearly all business combinations is that one entity, the acquirer, obtains control of one or more other businesses, the acquiree ...

When a business is being acquired the purchaser will buy the net assets (assets less liabilities) of the vendor's business. The values of the assets and liabilities reported on the vendor's balance sheet are reported at their carrying cost. Accounting Standard AASB 116: Property, Plant and Equipment defines carrying cost as 'the amount at which an asset is recognised after deducting any accumulated depreciation and accumulated impairment losses'.

AASB 3: Business Combinations requires the net assets acquired in a business combination to be measured at their fair value. The fair value is defined in AASB 116: Property, Plant and Equipment as 'the amount for which an asset could be exchanged between knowledgeable, willing parties in an arm's length transaction'.

Example

Shown below is a table indicating the carrying amounts of assets of a sole trader and the fair values placed on those assets by the purchaser.

		Carrying amounts	Fair values
	$	$	$
Cash at bank		6 000	6 000
Vehicles – At cost	26 000		
less Accumulated depreciation	3 000	23 000	21 000
Land and buildings		75 000	79 000
Debtors – At cost	36 000		
– Less Allowance for doubtful debts	4 000	32 000	31 000
		136 000	137 000

This reveals that the value of assets being carried on the existing sole trader balance sheet totals $136 000. However, the fair values agreed by the purchaser total $137 000. The fair values are the values that must be brought to account in accordance with AASB 3 and AASB 116.

When acquiring assets from an existing business at fair values the following principles must be applied:

- Never introduce accumulated depreciation on non-current assets. Always introduce the asset at its fair value. In the above example the carrying amounts of vehicles are: cost price $26 000 less accumulated depreciation of $3 000, giving a carrying amount of $23 000. However, the fair value is $21 000. Thus, the vehicle would be introduced at $21 000.
- Always recognise the full value of debtors and use the allowance for doubtful debts account to adjust the carrying amount to the fair value. In the example, debtors are being carried at $32 000 – that is, a full value of $36 000 less the allowance for doubtful debts of $4 000. However, the fair value of the debtors is $31 000. Thus, the following values for the debtors would be recorded:

	$	$
Debtors – At cost	36 000	
less Allowance for doubtful debts	5 000	31 000

Purchase consideration in excess of fair values

When a company acquires another entity it may pay a price in excess of the fair values. This may occur where the purchaser believes that the business being purchased has an extremely profitable future and a higher price might encourage the vendor to sell, or it may be warranted if the vendor is a competitor who needs a little enticement to sell.

Where the purchase price exceeds the fair values of the assets being acquired, the purchaser is entitled to bring to account goodwill in accordance with AASB 3, clause 31, which states:

> Goodwill which is purchased by the company shall be measured as the excess of the cost of acquisition incurred by the company over the fair value of the identifiable net assets acquired.

It should be noted that companies are not permitted to bring to account goodwill that is internally generated. The only way that a company can bring to account goodwill is by purchasing the goodwill from another entity by paying a purchase price in excess of the fair values.

In the previous example the fair value of the net assets of the vendor totalled $137 000. If the purchaser paid $150 000 to acquire these net assets, i.e. $13 000 in excess of the fair values, this amount would represent purchased goodwill and would need to be brought to account in the purchaser's books.

Question 3.1

Drayon Ltd purchased the business belonging to Lance Holt on 1 July 2007. On this date the carrying amounts and the agreed fair values of Lance's net assets were as follows.

		Carrying amounts	Fair values
	$	$	$
Inventory		100 000	110 000
Debtors	40 000		
less Allowance for doubtful debts	5 000	35 000	32 000
Plant and equipment		500 000	450 000
Vehicles	80 000		
less Accumulated depreciation	60 000	20 000	25 000

The price paid by Drayon Ltd was $650 000.

You are required to determine the amount of goodwill (if any) that Drayon Ltd should bring to account in respect of the above purchase.

Accounting entries

When a company is formed to acquire the assets of a sole trader or a partnership, the company becomes the 'purchaser' and the sole trader or partnership becomes the 'vendor(s)'.

The vendor who is disposing of net assets to the company will require payment for the assets. This may take the form of cash, the issue of shares in the company, or both. The amount owing to the vendor may be paid immediately on the sale of the business or over a longer period of time.

To accommodate the consideration owing and subsequently paid to the vendor(s) it is necessary to include a vendor's account when accounting for the acquisition of assets. If a balance remains to be paid to the vendor(s) at balance date, the vendor's account will be classified as a liability in the company's books.

The accounting entries to record the formation of a new proprietary company limited by shares to take over an existing sole trader or partnership business may be summarised into three steps.

1 Record the allotment of shares to the subscribers and the receipt of payment.

Subscribers	Dr	
Share capital – Ordinary shares		Cr

Bank	Dr	
Subscribers		Cr

2. Record the assets and liabilities acquired at fair values, including the purchase consideration owed to the vendor.

Various assets (including goodwill, if any)	Dr	
Various liabilities		Cr
Vendor's account (liability)		Cr

- Debit the accounts of assets acquired at the agreed fair valuation. (*Note:* Fixed assets are recorded at the historical cost to the company and no accumulated depreciation accounts are recorded. Debtors are also brought into the company at the gross amount and the company raises its own allowance for doubtful debts.)
- Credit the appropriate accounts for liabilities assumed at agreed fair valuation.
- Credit the vendor's account to record the full purchase consideration (paid-up amount of shares issued plus cash owing, if any).
- Ascertain and record the value of goodwill purchased (if any) at acquisition.

3. Record the settlement of the purchase consideration. Depending upon the specifications of the sale agreement, the purchase price may be settled in cash, by the issue of shares, or by a combination of cash and shares.

To record the payment of cash:

Vendor's account	Dr	
Bank		Cr

To record the issue of shares:

Vendor's account	Dr	
Share capital – Ordinary shares		Cr
Share capital – Preference shares		Cr

ILLUSTRATION

C. Wood owns and operates a sole proprietorship business trading as Footscray Electrical Services. On 1 February 2007 he makes an agreement with his spouse, P. Wood, to convert the business to a proprietary company limited by shares.

Allotting shares to shareholders

The couple follow the appropriate procedures to incorporate the company and on 1 March 2007 the company is incorporated, trading as Saltway Pty Ltd, with both ordinary and preference share capital. C. Wood and P. Wood as subscribers take one ordinary share each in the company at $1 each.

The resulting journal entries to allocate the shares and receipt the subscribers would be recorded as follows:

Saltway Pty Ltd
General journal

Date	Particulars	Debit	Credit
2007		$	$
1 March	Subscribers	2	
	Share capital – Ordinary shares		2
	Allotment of subscriber shares in accordance with the Corporations Law		
1 March	Bank	2	
	Subscribers		2
	Receipt of subscribers' payment		

Recording the assets and liabilities of the sole trader at fair values

The agreement made by C. Wood and P. Wood stated that the company would:
- purchase all of the assets of Footscray Electrical Services at their current values with the following exceptions:
    - Debtors to be revalued at $29 000
    - Stock to be revalued at $55 000
    - Shop premises to be valued at $50 000
    - Delivery vehicles to be valued at $7 000
- assume all the liabilities of Footscray Electrical Services except the bank overdraft; and
- pay the vendor, C. Wood, $95 000 consisting of:
    - 45 000 fully paid ordinary shares at $1 each;
    - 40 000 fully paid preference shares at $1 each; and
    - $10 000 cash on 30 April 2007.

The balance sheet of Footscray Electrical Services at the date of incorporation was stated as follows:

C. Wood
Trading as Footscray Electrical Services
Balance sheet as at 28 February 2007

Assets	$	$	Liabilities	$	$
Cash in registers		3 000	Creditors control	47 000	
Debtors control	32 000		Bank overdraft	17 000	
less Allowance for doubtful debts	2 000	30 000	Mortgage	25 000	89 000
Stock		60 000			
Shop premises		40 000	Owner's equity		
Furniture and equipment	20 000		Capital – C. Wood		60 000
less Accumulated depreciation	12 000	8 000			
Delivery vehicles	18 000				
less Accumulated depreciation	10 000	8 000			
		149 000			149 000

A comparison of the carrying amounts in the books of Footscray Electrical Services and the fair values as agreed, shows that the assets and liabilities that are being taken over are valued at $80 000 as follows:

	Carrying amounts	Fair values
	$	$
Cash in registers	3 000	3 000
Debtors control – At cost $32 000	30 000	29 000
Stock	60 000	55 000
Shop premises	40 000	50 000
Furniture and equipment	8 000	8 000
Delivery vehicles	8 000	7 000
Creditors control	(47 000)	(47 000)
Mortgage	(25 000)	(25 000)
	77 000	80 000

An analysis of the amount being paid to the vendor, C. Wood (i.e. $95 000), and the net fair values of the net assets being acquired (i.e. $80 000) reveals that the company is paying $15 000 in excess of the fair values. This represents purchased goodwill.

The journal entry is to record:
- the fair values of the assets and liabilities being acquired;
- the recognition of goodwill; and
- the amount owing to the vendor.

The journal would be recorded as follows:

Saltway Pty Ltd
General journal

[Handwritten note: Change debtors with doubtful debts only]

Date	Particulars	Debit	Credit
2007			
1 March	Cash in registers	3 000	
	Debtors control	32 000	
	Stock	55 000	
	Shop premises	50 000	
	Furniture and equipment	8 000	
	Delivery vehicles	7 000	
	Goodwill	15 000	
	Allowance for doubtful debts		3 000
	Creditors control		47 000
	Mortgage on shop premises		25 000
	Vendor – C. Wood		95 000
	Assets and liabilities taken over as per sale agreement dated 1 March 2007		

Note:
1. Debtors are always recorded at their historic value (as they all have the potential to pay), and any adjustments to the fair value are made to the allowance for doubtful debts account.
2. Non-current assets are recorded at their fair value, which represents the new historic cost to the company. Accumulated depreciations that existed in the vendor's books cannot be brought to account.

Recording the allotment of shares to the vendor

The sale agreement stated that the vendor, C. Wood, would receive:
- 45 000 fully paid ordinary shares at $1 each;
- 40 000 fully paid preference shares at $1 each; and
- $10 000 cash on 30 April 2007.

The entry to record the allocation of shares to C. Wood, the vendor, would be as follows:

Saltway Pty Ltd
General journal

Date	Particulars	Debit	Credit
2007		$	$
1 March	Vendor – C. Wood	45 000	
	Share capital – Ordinary shares		45 000
	Allotment to vendor of 45 000 ordinary shares as per sale agreement		
	Vendor – C. Wood	40 000	
	Share capital – Preference shares		40 000
	Allotment to vendor of 40 000 fully paid preference shares as per sale agreement		

Note: The $10 000 cash will be paid in cash on 30 April 2007.

The vendor's liability account, which records the amount owing to C. Wood, would appear in the general ledger as follows:

General ledger

Date	Particulars	Debit	Credit	Balance
	Vendor – C. Wood			
2007				
1 March	Sundries		95 000	95 000 Cr
	Share capital – Ordinary shares	45 000		50 000 Cr
	Share capital – Preference shares	40 000		10 000 Cr

The financial position after the incorporation of the company, the acquisition of the net assets of Footscray Electrical Services, including the purchased goodwill and the amount owing to the vendor, could be prepared as follows:

Saltway Pty Ltd
Balance sheet as at 1 March 2007

	$	$	$
Assets			
Cash in registers		3 000	
Cash at bank (subscriber shares)		2	
Debtors control	32 000		
less Allowance for doubtful debts	3 000	29 000	
Stock		55 000	87 002
Non-current assets			
Shop premises		50 000	
Furniture and equipment		8 000	
Delivery vehicles		7 000	
Goodwill		15 000	80 000
Total assets			167 002
Liabilities			
Creditors control	47 000		
Vendor – C. Wood (due April 2007)	10 000	57 000	
Mortgage on shop premises		25 000	82 000
Net assets			85 002
Shareholders' equity			
Share capital			
45 002 ordinary shares fully paid		45 002	
40 000 fully paid 10% preference shares fully paid		40 000	
Total equity			85 002

Question 3.2

Whim and Julie Arden are converting their existing partnership business into a proprietary company on 1 July 2007. You are required to:

a prepare entries in the general journal of Arden Plumbing Supplies Pty Ltd, recording the acquisition and the allotment of shares as consideration paid to the vendors; and

b complete the vendor's account in the general ledger after posting the entries in (a).

Note: Entries recording the allotment of subscriber shares are not required.

W. & J. Arden, Plumbing Supplies
Balance sheet as at 30 June 2007

	$	$		$	$
Assets			**Liabilities**		
Cash at bank		4 000	Creditors		58 000
Debtors		40 000			
Plumbing supplies		72 000	**Proprietors' equity**		
Shop furniture and equipment	36 000		Capital – W. Arden	40 000	
less Accumulated depreciation	12 000	24 000	Current – W. Arden	4 000	44 000
			Capital – J. Arden	40 000	
			Current – J. Arden	(2 000)	38 000
		140 000			140 000

Additional information

- All the assets were purchased and all the liabilities were assumed by Arden Plumbing Supplies Pty Ltd.
- The directors of the company resolved to allow for doubtful debts of $2 000 and to take over the other assets at the following values:

Plumbing supplies	$70 000
Shop furniture and equipment	$20 000

- The purchase consideration was the immediate allotment of 25 000 ordinary shares at $1 each and 25 000 preference shares at $1 each in the capital of Arden Plumbing Supplies Pty Ltd, plus $36 000 cash repayable to the vendors in two years' time.

Question 3.3

Perfection Sales Pty Ltd was incorporated on 1 May 2007 to acquire the business of You Yang Wholesalers, a business owned in partnership by J. Gown and S. Wide. You are required to:

a prepare journal entries in the books of the new company dated 1 May 2007; and
b prepare a balance sheet for Perfection Sales Pty Ltd as at 1 May 2007 (after all entries in (a) have been recorded).

You Yang Wholesalers
Balance sheet as at 30 April 2007

	$	$		$	$
Assets			**Liabilities**		
Debtors control	50 000		Creditors control		50 000
less Allowance for doubtful debts	1 000	49 000	Bank overdraft		20 000
Stock		100 000	Mortgage on warehouse		40 000
Warehouse		70 000	**Proprietors' equity**		
Fittings and equipment	20 000		Capital – J. Gown	65 000	
less Accumulated depreciation	8 000	12 000	Current – J. Gown	4 000	69 000
Delivery vehicles	25 000		Capital – S. Wide	65 000	
less Accumulated depreciation	14 000	11 000	Current – S. Wide	(2 000)	63 000
		242 000			242 000

Additional information

- To convert You Yang Wholesalers to a proprietary company, J. Gown and S. Wide established Perfection Sales Pty Ltd.
- J. Gown and S. Wide were nominated as subscribers and directors who were allotted one ordinary share each at $1 per share.
- The directors agreed to take over all assets and liabilities of You Yang Wholesalers with the exception of the bank overdraft and the mortgage on the warehouse.
- On takeover the directors revalued the following assets:

	$
Warehouse	80 000
Fittings and equipment	10 000
Debtors	48 000

- The sale agreement made the following considerations:
    - On 1 May 2007 each vendor to be allotted 75 000 ordinary shares and 25 000 preference shares all valued at $1 per share.
    - On 30 September 2007 $5 000 cash to be paid to each vendor.

Purchase consideration below fair values

It may also be possible for a company to purchase the net assets of another entity and pay a price, that is less than the fair value of the entity. This could occur where the vendor entity is experiencing difficult financial times and may be looking for a quick sale and is willing to accept a lower price.

Where the purchaser pays less than the fair values of the net assets acquired, AASB 3: Business Combinations requires the difference to be included in the calculation of profit and loss for the year.

For example, ABC Ltd purchased the business of Paul and Anne for $80 000. The fair values of Paul and Anne's only assets were motor vehicles $40 000 and plant $60 000. Consequently, a discount on acquisition of $20 000 would be recognised by ABC Ltd. This amount would be brought to account as a revenue item in the income statement of the purchaser.

Question 3.4

Smart Ltd acquired the net assets of Gay West on 2 March 2007 by paying $200 000 for the business.
The fair value of the net assets acquired was:

	$	$
Debtors	12 000	
less Allowance for doubtful debts	2 000	10 000
Stock on hand		40 000
Land and buildings		150 000
Equipment	100 000	
less Accumulated depreciation	90 000	10 000

You are required to state the values that would be recorded in the accounts of Smart Ltd on the date of acquisition.

Accounting entries

The accounting procedures to bring to account the net assets of an acquired business where the purchase price is below the fair values of the net assets acquired are the same as those applied when net assets are acquired above fair values. The only difference is that instead of bringing to account goodwill, a revenue amount must be recognised. This can be called 'discount on acquisition'.

ILLUSTRATION

M. Wilson owns and operates a sole trader business trading as Frankston Wholesalers. On 1 March 2007 Wilson established a private company called Wilson's Pty Ltd by issuing 10 000 $10 ordinary shares to register the business.

The company then purchased the net assets of the sole trader for $60 000 cash. The net assets at their fair values consisted of:

Assets	$	$	Liabilities	$	$
Debtors control	25 000		Creditors control	15 000	
less Allowance for doubtful debts	5 000	20 000	Bank loan	25 000	40 000
Stock		40 000			
Vehicle		60 000			
		120 000			40 000

As the net assets total $80 000 ($120 000 – $40 000) and the purchase consideration is $60 000, a discount on acquisition of $20 000 must be brought to account. This would be recorded as follows:

Wilson's Pty Ltd

General journal

Date	Particulars	Debit	Credit
2007		$	$
1 March	Debtors control	25 000	
	Stock	40 000	
	Vehicle	60 000	
	Allowance for doubtful debts		5 000
	Creditors control		15 000
	Bank loan		25 000
	Bank		60 000
	Discount on acquisition		20 000
	Assets and liabilities taken over as per sale agreement dated 1 March 2007		

If a balance sheet was prepared after the acquisition it would include the following amounts:

[Handwritten note:]
Dr Discount on Acquisition (Gain)
Cr Profit & Loss

Wilson's Pty Ltd
Balance sheet as at 1 March 2007

	$	$	$
Assets			
Bank ($100 000 – $60 000)		40 000	
Debtors control	25 000		
less Allowance for doubtful debts	5 000	20 000	
Stock		40 000	
Vehicle		60 000	160 000
Liabilities			
Creditors control		15 000	
Bank loan		25 000	40 000
Net assets			120 000
Shareholders' equity			
Share capital			
10 000 Ordinary shares fully paid		100 000	
Profit and loss (Discount on acquisition)		20 000	120 000

Question 3.5

M. Cash is converting his existing business, Future Furniture, into a proprietary company called Style Pty Ltd, with his brother, on 1 January 2007. You are required to:

a   prepare entries in the general journal of Style Pty Ltd, recording the acquisition and the allotment of shares as consideration paid to the vendor; and

b   complete the vendor's account in the general ledger as at 31 January 2007.

Note: Entries recording the allotment of subscriber shares are not required.

M. Cash, Future Furniture
Balance sheet as at 31 December 2006

	$	$		$	$
Assets			**Liabilities**		
Debtors control		40 000	Creditors control	53 000	
Stock		80 000	Bank overdraft	10 000	63 000
Shop furniture	12 000		**Proprietor's equity**		
less Accumulated depreciation	6 000	6 000	Capital – M. Cash		63 000
		126 000			126 000

Additional information

- All the assets were purchased and all the liabilities, except the bank overdraft, were assumed by Style Pty Ltd.
- The directors of the company resolved to take over the other assets at the following values:

	$
Debtors	36 000
Stock	75 000
Shop furniture	4 000

The purchase consideration was the immediate allotment of 45 000 ordinary shares at $1 per share and 5 000 preference shares at $1 per share in the capital of Style Pty Ltd and a cash payment of $10 000 to be paid on 31 January 2007.

Question 3.6

Harford Traders Pty Ltd was incorporated on 1 July 2007 to acquire the existing partnership of B. Sand and D. Wilton, trading as Donvale Retailers.

From the following information you are required to prepare the balance sheet of Harford Traders Pty Ltd as at 1 July 2007 after the acquisition of the partnership.

Donvale Retailers
Balance sheet as at 1 July 2007

Assets	$	$	Liabilities	$	$
Cash in registers		1 000	Accounts payable		40 000
Accounts receivable		25 000	Bank overdraft		12 000
Stock		40 000	Advance – B. Sand		6 000
Shop premises		50 000	Mortgage on shop premises		14 000
Shop furniture	8 000		Owners' equity		
less Accumulated depreciation	6 000	2 000	Capital – B. Sand	24 000	
Motor vehicles	10 000		Current – B. Sand	3 000	27 000
less Accumulated depreciation	6 000	4 000	Capital – D. Wilton	24 000	
			Current – D. Wilton	(1 000)	23 000
		122 000			122 000

Additional information

- Issued ordinary shares: Subscribers:
  - B. Sand: one share at $1 per share; and
  - D. Wilton: one share at $1 per share.
- It was agreed by the directors that all assets and liabilities of Donvale Retailers be taken over except for the advance to B. Sand of $6 000.
- The directors agreed to revalue the following assets on takeover:

	$
Stock	38 000
Shop premises	70 000
Motor vehicles	3 000

- The sale agreement allowed for the following consideration to each vendor on 1 July 2007:
  - 25 000 ordinary shares at $1 each;
  - 8 500 preference shares at $1 each; and
  - $1 500 cash to be paid to each vendor on 31 August 2007.

CHAPTER 4
FINALISATION OF A COMPANY'S PROFIT AND LOSS ACCOUNT

Objectives

Upon satisfactory completion of this chapter you should be able to:

- write off establishment costs;
- account for the impairment of goodwill;
- account for the revaluation of investment assets;
- account for income tax under the Pay As You Go system; and
- make adjustments to income tax at the end of the year.

Introduction

At the end of the financial year it is necessary for companies to finalise the profit and loss account to include the expensing of intangible assets, the revaluation of investment assets and the calculation of profit (after tax).

These transactions must be performed in accordance with the accounting standards and other statutes. This chapter will examine the finalisation of company accounts in accordance with the accounting standards and acceptable accounting practices.

Finalisation of the profit and loss account

At the end of the accounting period all revenue and expense account balances would be transferred to the profit and loss account. In addition to transferring traditional revenue and expense accounts, companies may need to consider adjustments for:

- the write-off of establishment costs;
- the impairment of goodwill;
- the impairment of investment assets; and
- adjustments to income tax expended.

Writing off establishment costs

Establishment costs (also known as preliminary expenses or formation costs) incurred by a company at its inception must be included in the financial statements at the end of the period. There are two schools of thought in relation to the treatment and classification of establishment costs.

One school of thought is to classify the costs of establishment as an expense and include it in the income statement. This school of thought is supported by Statement of Accounting Concepts (SAC) 4, which defines an expense as:

> consumptions or losses of future economic benefits in the form of reductions in assets or increases in liabilities of the entity ... that result in a decrease in equity during the reporting period.

Accordingly, this school of thought requires the full amount of establishment costs incurred by a company to be included as an expense in the determination of profit in the year in which the expenditure was incurred.

ILLUSTRATION

Jasper Ltd was incorporated on 15 April 2007, incurring $5 000 in establishment costs. The directors required the expenditure to be treated as an expense in the current year. The journal entry transferring the expense to the profit and loss account would be as follows:

General journal of Jasper Ltd

Date	Particulars	Debit	Credit
2007		$	$
30 June	Profit and loss	5 000	
	Costs of establishment		5 000
	Closed account		

Another school of thought is to classify the costs of establishment as an asset and include them as an intangible asset in the balance sheet. The asset is then written off (amortised) against annual profits (in the income statement) until it is extinguished. This accounting treatment is based on the following principles:
1 SAC 4 defines assets as 'a future economic benefit resulting from past transactions or past events'. SAC 4 also states that an asset should only be brought to account if the asset poses a cost and can be measured reliably, and the future economic benefit will eventuate. Supporters of this principle argue that expenditure incurred on establishing the company may be significant and will benefit the company into the future as the company trades and, as such, should be identified as an asset.
2 As the costs of establishment benefit the company as it trades in the future, the asset should be amortised against future profits rather than writing it off against the profits in the company's first year of operation.

ILLUSTRATION

Harvey Ltd incurred $15 000 in establishment costs on 1 January 2007. The directors required that the costs be classified as an asset and be amortised over five years.

The amortisation amount over a whole year would be $3 000 ($15 000 / 5 years). The amount to be included in the first year is $1 500, being for six months. The journal entries to record the expense amount and to close the expense to the profit and loss account are:

General journal of Jasper Ltd

Date	Particulars	Debit	Credit
2007		$	$
30 June	Amortisation of costs of establishment	1 500	
	Accumulated amortisation of establishment costs		1 500
	To record the write-off of establishment costs		
	Profit and loss	1 500	
	Costs of establishment (Amortisation)		1 500
	Closed account		

The balance sheet would show the following amounts in respect of the costs of establishment.

Albert Park Ltd
Balance sheet as at 30 June 2007 (Extract)

	$
Intangible assets	
Costs of establishment	15 000
less Accumulated amortisation of establishment costs	1 500
	13 500

Impairment of goodwill

A company will bring goodwill to account when it purchases another entity and pays a purchase price that exceeds the fair values of the net assets acquired. This accounting treatment is consistent with AASB 3: Business Combinations, which states:

> Goodwill which is purchased by the company shall be measured as the excess of the cost of acquisition incurred by the company over the fair value of the identifiable net assets acquired.

Once goodwill is brought to account by a company it must, in the year of recognising the goodwill, determine if it has been impaired. The impairment of goodwill is described in AASB 136: Impairment of Assets. This standard requires companies to ensure that assets are reported at values that do not exceed their recoverable amount.

The recoverable amount of an asset refers to the asset's fair value or the amount that it could be sold for on the open market. An asset is deemed to be impaired under AASB 136 if the amount appearing in the accounts, i.e. its carrying cost, is greater than its recoverable amount.

Where an asset's value is deemed to be impaired, it is required by the standard to recognise the difference between the carrying cost of the asset and its recoverable amount as an 'impairment loss'.

To determine if purchased goodwill has been impaired the company must first allocate the goodwill against the cash-generating assets that have been acquired in the business combination, i.e. the assets that will benefit from the combination taking place. Examples of cash-generating assets include debtors (as cash is received when payment is made), inventories (as these generate cash when sold) and tangible assets such as plant and equipment (as these can generate cash through sales).

These assets, once identified, must then be tested for impairment, i.e. to determine if their recoverable amount is below their carrying cost. If the carrying cost of the asset exceeds the asset's recoverable amount, then the excess must be brought to account by reducing goodwill and bringing to account an impairment loss. Where the recoverable amount exceeds the carrying cost, goodwill has not been impaired and, as a result, no accounting entries are required.

ILLUSTRATION

Harvey Ltd acquired the net assets of a competitor earlier in the year. The net assets included a motor vehicle with a fair value of $50 000 and inventory with a fair value of $20 000. Harvey has determined that both these assets are considered 'cash-generating assets' for the purpose of testing the impairment of goodwill. Goodwill brought to account at the date of acquisition was $2 000, being the excess paid for the net assets acquired.

At the end of the financial year, 30 June 2007, Harvey determined that the recoverable amount of the vehicle was $47 000 and inventory $21 000. As the recoverable amount of the inventory is greater than its carrying cost, no adjustment is required.

However, as the recoverable amount of the vehicle is $3 000 below its carrying cost ($47 000 − $50 000), goodwill has been impaired and an adjustment is required. As the difference between the asset's carrying cost and recoverable amount ($3 000) is greater than the amount of goodwill ($2 000), an adjustment is required to reduce the value of goodwill and the value of the vehicle. The impairment of goodwill and the reduction in the carrying cost of the vehicle could be recorded as follows:

General journal of Harvey Ltd

Date	Particulars	Debit	Credit
2007		$	$
30 June	Impairment loss – Goodwill	2 000	
	Goodwill		2 000
	To record the impairment of goodwill		
	Impairment loss – Vehicle	1 000	
	Vehicle		1 000
	To record the impairment of vehicles		
	Profit and loss	3 000	
	Impairment loss – Goodwill		2 000
	Impairment loss – Vehicle		1 000
	Closed accounts		

Revaluation of investment assets

When a company purchases shares in another company where it does not either control or influence that other company, it may wish to revalue its investment in that company from time to time in line with market valuations.

Downward revaluations

Where the recoverable or market-value amount of the investment is less than the carrying amount of the investment on the balance sheet, the asset has been impaired in value and an impairment loss can be brought to account in accordance with AASB 136: Impairment of Assets.

ILLUSTRATION

Harvey Ltd purchased shares in Crash Ltd at a cost price of $500 000. During the year Crash Ltd experienced significant trading difficulties and the value of the shares on the stock exchange fell, resulting in the market value of the investment falling to $50 000.

The entry to record the recoverable amount of the investment in the accounts and to bring to account the impairment loss could be recorded as follows:

General journal

Date	Particulars	Debit	Credit
		$	$
30 June	Impairment loss – Investment in Crash Ltd	450 000	
	Accumulated write-down in investments		450 000
	Write-down of investments to market value		
	Profit and loss	450 000	
	Impairment loss – Investment in Crash Ltd		450 000
	Closure of account		

As a result of this adjustment the balance sheet would show the following values for the investment:

Harvey Ltd
Balance sheet as at 30 June (Extract)

Assets	$	$
Investments		
Shares in Crash Ltd	500 000	
less Accumulated write-down in investments	450 000	50 000

Upward revaluations

If the recoverable amount of investments that have been previously impaired rises above the carrying amount of the investments, an adjustment can be made to increase the amount reported on the balance sheet.

When increasing the value of an asset as a result of the carrying cost being below its recoverable amount, the valuation principle of 'lower-of-cost-or-market value' may be applied. This principle takes the conservative view that an asset should not be revalued to an amount that exceeds its original cost price, thereby preserving the practice of recording all transactions at their historical cost.

ILLUSTRATION

In the year following the devaluation of the shares held in Crash Ltd, the market value of the shares increased as a result of better-than-expected trading results and positive financial forecasts.

The market value of the investments held by Harvey Ltd has increased to $600 000. As the carrying cost of the investments is $50 000 and the original cost price was $500 000, Harvey Ltd can adjust the value of the investments back to $500 000.

The entry to increase the value of the investments and to bring to account the gain resulting from the increase could be recorded as follows:

General journal

Date	Particulars	Debit	Credit
		$	$
30 June	Accumulated write-down in investments	450 000	
	Recovery of write-down in investments		450 000
	Upward revaluation of investments to market value		
	Recovery of write-down in investments	450 000	
	Profit and loss		450 000
	Closure of account		

Question 4.1

You are required to prepare the general journal entries to record the following decisions of the directors of Hardy Ltd at the end of the financial year.

- The investment in TNT Ltd is to be revalued from its carrying cost of $600 000 to its recoverable amount of $320 000.

- During the year, goodwill of $100 000 was brought to account as a result of a business combination. This resulted in cash-generating assets being recorded at fair values of $200 000. It has been determined that the recoverable amounts of these assets are now $190 000.
- Costs of establishment totalling $15 000 paid during the year are to be expensed.

Question 4.2

The following trial balance extract reflects some of the accounts of Bidalow Ltd as at 30 June.

Bidalow Ltd
Trial balance as at 30 June (Extract)

	Debit	Credit
	$	$
Goodwill	30 000	
Investment in PHB Ltd	250 000	
Accumulated write-down in investment in PHB Ltd		50 000
Establishment costs	20 000	

You are required to update the general ledger by making the following end-of-year adjustments:
- Goodwill brought to account as a result of a business combination is to be impaired by $25 000 as a result of a fall in related cash-generating assets.
- Establishment costs are to be written off.
- The investment in PHB Ltd is to be revalued at its recoverable amount of $230 000.

Question 4.3

From the following extract of the general ledger of Stinger Ltd you are required to prepare the profit and loss account.

Stinger Ltd
Trial balance as at 30 June (Extract)

	Debit	Credit
	$	$
Accumulated write-down of investment in Ansett Ltd	150 000	150,000
Advertising	25 000	
Vehicles	100 000	
Bad and doubtful debts	8 000	
Cost of goods sold	320 000	
Costs of establishment	22 000	
Discount revenue		2 500
Entertainment costs	14 500	
Goodwill	15 000	
GST clearing		16 000
Investment in Ansett Ltd	850 000	
Profit on sale of equipment		32 000
Sales		750 000
Wages	130 000	

Additional information

- Costs of establishment are to be written off.
- Goodwill was established from a business combination in which vehicles were identified as the only cash-generating asset. The recoverable amount of this asset on 30 June is $80 000.
- Investment in Ansett Ltd is to be revalued at its recoverable amount of $500 000.

Adjustments to income tax

In relation to income tax, Australian companies need to comply with both the Pay As You Go (PAYG) instalment system and the *Income Tax Assessment Act*. In addition, companies will need to adhere to the requirements of the accounting standard AASB 1020: Income Taxes.

The PAYG system requires companies to pay income tax each quarter, while the *Income Tax Assessment Act* requires them to submit at the end of each financial year an income tax return that complies with the Act.

The Pay As You Go instalment system

Under the PAYG taxation system, companies are required to pay a percentage of each quarter's sales to the Australian Taxation Office (ATO) in the form of income tax. That is, as sales income is earned, taxation is paid.

The ATO advises all companies registered under the PAYG system of the required percentage of sales that must be remitted as tax. The percentage is determined from the information supplied by each company for the previous year.

The percentage is calculated by dividing the income tax payable for the year by the assessable income earned in the same year. For example, if a company derived assessable income of $250 000 and had paid $25 000 income tax on that income, the percentage would be equal to 10% ($25 000 / $250 000). If the company then made sales in the quarter ending 30 September totalling $1 000 000 it would be required to pay income tax equal to 10% of this amount, i.e. $100 000.

The PAYG system requires companies to calculate the amount of tax payable at the end of each quarter ending on 30 September, 31 December, 31 March and 30 June. The amounts calculated must be forwarded to the ATO by the 28th day of the month following the end of each quarter (the December quarter can be extended to 28 February), i.e. 28 October, 28 February, 28 April and 28 July.

At the end of the financial year the income tax that has been expensed is closed off to the profit and loss account and the final unpaid amount for the quarter ended 30 June is included in the balance sheet as a current liability, to be paid by 28 July.

ILLUSTRATION

Longer Ltd has been advised by the ATO that it has a PAYG instalment percentage rate of 10%.

For the quarter ended 30 September 2006 the company recorded sales income of $1 000 000, requiring the company to pay $100 000 by 28 October.

The resulting journal entries would be made to record the income tax expense and liability and the payment of that liability.

General journal

Date	Particulars	Debit	Credit
2006		$	$
30 Sept	Income tax expense	100 000	
	Income tax payable		100 000
	To record income tax payable on sales income for the first year		

Cash payments journal

Date	Particulars	Chq. No.	Sundries	Bank
2006			$	$
28 Oct	Income tax payable		100 000	100 000

The resulting ledger accounts would be as follows:

General ledger

Date	Particulars	Debit	Credit	Balance
Income tax expense				
30 Sept 2006	Income tax payable	100 000		100 000 Dr
Income tax payable				
30 Sept 2006	Income tax expense		100 000	100 000 Cr
28 Oct 2006	Bank	100 000		–
Bank				
28 Oct 2006	Income tax payable		100 000	100 000 Cr

If Longer Ltd recorded sales income of $1 200 000, $1 500 000 and $1 300 000 for the next three quarters, the company would have recorded income tax of $120 000, $150 000 and $130 000, respectively.

At the end of the financial year the respective income tax accounts in the general ledger would appear as follows:

General ledger

Date	Particulars	Debit	Credit	Balance
Income tax expense				
30 Sept 2006	Income tax payable	100 000		100 000 Dr
31 Dec 2006	Income tax payable	120 000		220 000 Dr
31 Mar 2007	Income tax payable	150 000		370 000 Dr
30 Jun 2007	Income tax payable	130 000		500 000 Dr
Income tax payable				
30 Sept 2006	Income tax expense		100 000	100 000 Cr
28 Oct 2006	Bank	100 000		–
31 Dec 2006	Income tax expense		120 000	120 000 Cr
28 Jan 2007	Bank	120 000		–
31 Mar 2007	Income tax expense		150 000	150 000 Cr
28 Apr 2007	Bank	150 000		–
30 Jun 2007	Income tax expense		130 000	130 000 Cr

The accounting records at 30 June 2007 would show that the company had:
- earned sales revenue of $5 000 000;
- on which $500 000 had been incurred as income tax expense;
- of which $370 000 had been paid; and
- $130 000 remained owing and was due for payment in the next financial year.

The current liabilities section of the balance sheet at the end of the financial year would include the income tax payable amount. This would be paid by 28 July in the following year.

Longer Ltd
Balance sheet as at 30 June 2007 (Extract)

Current liabilities
Income tax payable $130 000

Question 4.4

Drever Ltd had a PAYG instalment percentage of 20%. Quarterly sales for the year ended 30 June 2006 were as follows:

	$
30 September	700 000
31 December	600 000
31 March	750 000
30 June	800 000

For the year ended 30 June 2006 you are required to show:
a the income tax expense and income tax payable accounts; and
b the current liabilities section of the balance sheet.

Question 4.5

From the following information of Conmar Ltd you are required to prepare:
a journal entries recording the company's quarterly income tax transactions;
b the income tax expense and income tax payable accounts for the year; and
c the current liabilities section of the balance sheet as at 30 June 2007.

On 1 July 2006 the company owed $25 000 in income tax. This was paid on 28 July 2006. The company's PAYG instalment amount is 15%.

Quarterly sales for the year ended 30 June 2007 were:

	$
30 September	150 000
31 December	220 000
31 March	180 000
30 June	190 000

The company paid its PAYG instalment amounts on the due dates.

The *Income Tax Assessment Act*

Australian companies are required to lodge an annual income tax assessment with the ATO that complies with the *Income Tax Assessment Act*. The annual assessment will indicate the company's taxable income, which is calculated by including certain items of revenue as assessable income and including certain items of expenses as allowable deductions. The items and amounts declared as assessable or deductible may vary from those included in the company's profit and loss account.

A rate of company income tax is then applied to the company's taxable income to determine the amount of income tax that the company should have paid in the financial year.

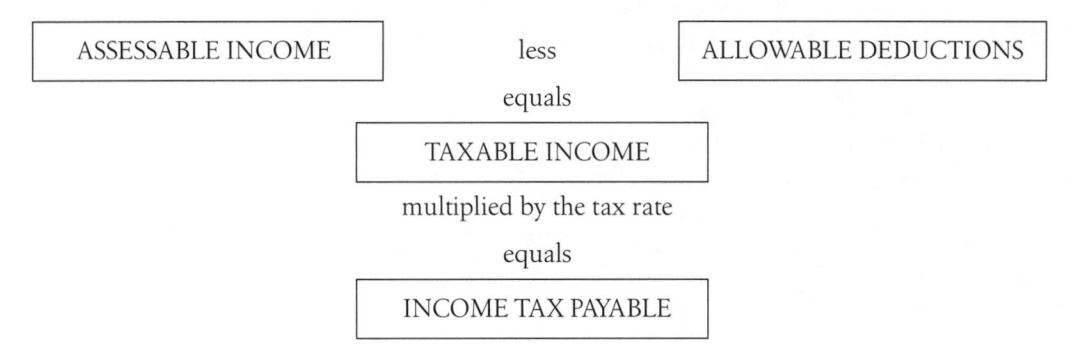

ASSESSABLE INCOME   less   ALLOWABLE DEDUCTIONS

equals

TAXABLE INCOME

multiplied by the tax rate

equals

INCOME TAX PAYABLE

The true value of a company's income tax payable should be based on its taxable income as determined by the *Income Tax Assessment Act*, not on a percentage of sales revenue as is the situation with the PAYG instalment system. Consequently, at the end of the financial year, the company will need to determine its overall income tax liability to the ATO.

If the company has not paid sufficient PAYG taxation instalments, it will owe tax to the ATO. If the company has paid too much tax, the ATO will issue a refund.

The accounting standard

Accounting Standard AASB 1020: Income Taxes sets out the methods a company should follow to calculate annual income tax. This standard requires a company to calculate its income tax expense to be charged against annual profits, on the profit (before income tax) reported in the profit and loss account.

PROFIT

multiplied by the tax rate

equals

INCOME TAX EXPENSE

A company's income tax expense should be based on its profit. Under the PAYG instalment system, income tax expense will have been calculated as a percentage of the company's sales revenue. Thus, at the end of the financial year the company may need to adjust the amount reported as income tax expense.

The end-of-period tax adjustment will depend on two important factors. These are:

1 **The ability of the company to determine its true taxation position at the end of the period:** If the company can calculate its true taxation expense based on its taxable income at the year's end, it will be able to make an adjustment in the current year. However, if the company is not in a position to finalise its taxation position on or around the end of the current period it may have to include the adjustments in the transactions for the next accounting period.
2 **The similarity between the amounts used in the determination of net profit (loss) in the accounting records and the amounts to be included in the calculation of taxable income:** Some companies may have included amounts in the calculation of net profit that may not be deductible or assessable for taxation purposes or may be reported as a different value for taxation purposes.

Taxation adjustments in the current period

If the company is in a position at the end of the period to calculate its taxation outcomes based on taxable income, it will be able to adjust its income tax accounts in the current period.

If the amount of income tax paid during the year under the PAYG system is below the amount that should have been paid based on the company's taxable income, an adjustment must be made to increase the taxation amounts. The adjusting entry to be recorded in the current period's accounts would be as follows:

General journal

Income tax expense   Dr
    Income tax payable   Cr

In the next accounting period the company would settle its PAYG instalment by 28 July and lodge its income tax return with the ATO. During the next accounting period the ATO would forward the company its assessment notice requesting the company to pay the outstanding amount of income tax.

ILLUSTRATION

For the year ended 30 June 2007 Longer Ltd had recorded income tax expense of $400 000 and had yet to meet its final PAYG instalment of $90 000. The company has determined that its taxable income and accounting profit for the year was $1 400 000. The company tax rate is 30%.

The amount of income tax that the company should have paid for the year, based on its taxable income and accounting profit, is $420 000 ($1 400 000 × .30). This is $20 000 more than the company has incurred as income tax expense under the PAYG system. Thus, the company will need to increase both its income tax expense and its income tax payable by $20 000 to $420 000.

The journal entries to account for this adjustment and close the expense account would be as follows:

General journal

Date	Particulars	Debit	Credit
2006		$	$
30 June	Income tax expense	20 000	
	Income tax payable		20 000
	To adjust taxation outcomes		
	Profit and loss	420 000	
	Income tax expense		420 000
	Closed account		

If the company has paid PAYG tax in excess of the amount required, based on the year's taxable income, the tax outcomes would have to be reduced. The entry to reduce the taxation outcomes in the current period would be as follows:

General journal

Income tax payable   Dr
    Income tax expense   Cr

In this case the company would still have to pay its final PAYG instalment by 28 July; however, the ATO, during the year, would forward the company its assessment notice and a refund of the amount of income tax overpaid.

After taxation adjustments have been made, the income tax expense account can be closed to the profit and loss account. The closing entry would be as follows:

General journal		
Profit and loss	Dr	
Income tax expense		Cr

ILLUSTRATION

For the year ended 30 June 2007 Hill Ltd had recorded income tax expense of $350 000 and had yet to meet its final PAYG instalment of $65 000. The company has determined that its taxable income and accounting profit for the year was $1 300 000. The company tax rate is 30%.

The applicable income tax expense and income tax payable should have been $390 000 ($1 300 000 × .30). As the income tax amount incurred during the year of $350 000 is $40 000 below the amount that should be recorded, an adjustment is required to increase both the income tax expense and income tax payable accounts.

The required adjustment would be recorded as follows:

General journal

Date	Particulars	Debit	Credit
2006		$	$
30 June	Income tax payable	40 000	
	Income tax expense		40 000
	To adjust taxation outcomes		
	Profit and loss	390 000	
	Income tax expense		390 000
	Closed account		

Question 4.6

For the year ended 30 June 2007 Hi Flow Ltd had recorded sales of $800 000 and PAYG income tax expense of $120 000 of which the final quarter's amount of $30 000 remained outstanding. The company calculated its accounting profit and taxable income at $370 000. The company taxation rate is 30%.

You are required to:
a prepare the journal entry at 30 June 2007 to adjust the income tax expense and income tax payable ✓ accounts;
b show the income tax expense account, the profit and loss account and the income tax payable account after the adjustment and the closure of the expense account; and
c explain how your answer would differ if taxable income was $420 000.

Question 4.7

From the following information supplied by Tombola Ltd you are required to:
a prepare the journal entry to adjust the taxation accounts at the end of the year; and
b show the income tax expense and income tax payable accounts.

For the year ended 30 June 2007 Tombola Ltd had calculated its PAYG amounts at $190 000. Of this amount $60 000 remained unpaid at the end of the year. The company calculated its taxable income at $600 000. The tax rate was 30%.

Question 4.8

For the year ended 30 June 2007 Travis Ltd reported the following amounts in respect of its PAYG instalments.

The company's PAYG instalment rate is 10%.
Quarterly sales for the year ended 30 June 2007 were:

30 September	$600 000
31 December	$650 000
31 March	$750 000
30 June	$800 000

All PAYG amounts were paid by the required dates.

On 30 June the company calculated its taxable income at $1 000 000. The tax rate is 30%. The company received its Income Tax Assessment Notice on 1 August 2007 and paid the amount owing by 28 August.

You are required to:
a   record all taxation entries for the year ended 30 June 2007 (including the end-of-period adjustment);
b   show the income tax expense and income tax payable accounts for the year ended 30 June 2007; and
c   show the income tax payable account at 28 August 2007.

Question 4.9

From the following information relating to the accounts of Jimbo Ltd for the year ended 30 June 2007 you are required to:
a   record all taxation entries for the year ended 30 June 2007 (including the end-of-period adjustment);
b   show the income tax expense and income tax payable accounts for the year ended 30 June 2007; and
c   show the income tax payable account at 30 September 2007.

Jimbo Ltd's PAYG instalment rate is 15%. Its quarterly sales amounts were:

30 September	$700 000
31 December	$800 000
31 March	$750 000
30 June	$750 000

All PAYG amounts were paid by the due dates.

By 30 June 2007 the company had calculated its taxable income at $1 400 000. The income tax rate was 30%.

The company received its Income Tax Assessment Notice on 30 September 2007 together with a refund cheque.

Taxation adjustments in the next period

If a company is not in a position at the end of the current period to determine its taxable income and adjust its income tax expense account, it will have to make any adjustments to its income tax accounts in the next accounting period.

As the company will not be adjusting its taxation expense account in the current period, it will close the income tax expense account showing the amount expended under the PAYG system to the profit and loss account. The closing journal entry would be as follows:

Chapter 4: Finalisation of a company's profit and loss account

General journal		
Profit and loss	Dr	
Income tax expense		Cr

In the next accounting period the company would determine its taxable income and lodge the appropriate documentation with the ATO. The amount calculated as owing to the ATO will most likely not be the same amount as that paid under the PAYG system in the previous period.

Where the amount paid in the previous period is less than the amount calculated on the company's taxable income, the company will have to record an adjustment in the next accounting period to record the amount of income tax expense underpaid in the previous period and the amount owing.

The adjusting entry to be recorded in the next period's accounts would be as follows:

General journal		
Under-provision of income tax	Dr	
Income tax payable		Cr

When the company receives its Income Tax Assessment Notice during the current period it will be required to make payment for the amount owing. This would be recorded as follows:

General journal		
Income tax payable	Dr	
Bank		Cr

The under-provision of income tax account is classified as an expense account and is closed to the profit and loss account at the end of the next accounting period. This effectively charges the underpaid income tax amount for the previous period against the profits of the next period.

The journal entry recording the closure of the under-provided income tax at the end of the period is as follows:

General journal		
Profit and loss	Dr	
Under-provision of income tax		Cr

Alternatively, the company may determine in the next accounting period that its taxable income and related tax liability was less than the PAYG amounts paid in respect of the previous period's amounts. In this case the company will need to adjust its accounts in the next period to record that it is owed money by the ATO as a result of over-providing for income tax in the previous period. The adjusting entry would be as follows:

General journal		
Income tax receivable	Dr	
Over-provision of income tax		Cr

The company will be forwarded a refund when it receives its Income Tax Assessment Notice, and at the end of the year it will have to close the over-provision of income tax account to the profit and loss account as a revenue account. This will increase the current period's profit as a result of excess income tax paid in the previous period.

The entries recording the refund from the ATO and the closure of the over-provision of income tax account would be as follows:

General journal

Bank	Dr	
Income tax receivable		Cr

General journal

Over-provision of income tax	Dr	
Profit and loss		Cr

ILLUSTRATION

For the year ended 30 June 2006 Gosha Ltd had incurred $70 000 in income tax expense and still owed $15 000 as its final PAYG instalment. The company was not in a position to determine its taxable income for the current period and chose to finalise its accounts without adjusting its income tax calculations.

The journal entries on 30 June 2006 to close the income tax expense account would be as follows:

General journal of Gosha Ltd

Date	Particulars	Debit	Credit
2006		$	$
30 June	Profit and loss	70 000	
	Income tax expense		70 000
	Closed expense account		

The entry recording the final PAYG instalment on 28 July 2006 would be as follows:

General journal of Gosha Ltd

Date	Particulars	Debit	Credit
2006		$	$
28 July	Income tax payable	15 000	
	Bank		15 000
	Paid June quarter PAYG instalment		

By 15 September the company had determined that its taxable income was $300 000 and the tax payable on this amount was $90 000. As the company had already paid PAYG instalments in the previous period of $70 000 it would only be required to pay $20 000.

The journal entry recording the amount owing as a result of the previous period's under-provision would be as follows:

General journal of Gosha Ltd

Date	Particulars	Debit	Credit
2006		$	$
15 Sept	Under-provision of income tax	20 000	
	Income tax payable		20 000
	Income tax adjustment		

On 5 October the company received its Income Tax Assessment Notice confirming the amount owing of $20 000 and requiring payment by 30 November.

The journal entry recording this payment would be as follows:

General journal of Gosha Ltd

Date	Particulars	Debit	Credit
2006		$	$
30 Nov	Income tax payable	20 000	
	Bank		20 000
	Paid income tax owing		

On 30 June 2007 the under-provision for income tax account would be closed to the profit and loss account as follows:

General journal of Gosha Ltd

Date	Particulars	Debit	Credit
2007		$	$
30 June	Profit and loss	20 000	
	Under-provision of income tax		20 000
	Closed account		

Question 4.10

For the year ended 30 June 2006 Carter Ltd had made sales totalling $1 400 000. The company had a PAYG instalment rate of 5% and had recorded $70 000 in income tax expense. Of this amount, $12 000 remained unpaid at 30 June and was paid by the due date.

The company was not in a position to finalise its income tax position at 30 June 2006 and decided to make its adjustments in the following year.

By 20 October 2006 the company had calculated its taxable income at $280 000 and lodged its tax return accordingly. The income tax rate is 30%.

On 30 October 2006 the company received its Income Tax Assessment Notice verifying its tax liability and requiring payment by 12 December 2006. The company paid the amount on this date.

You are required to:
a prepare the journal entries at 30 June 2006 in respect of income tax expense;
b prepare journal entries for the year ended 30 June 2007 for all tax-related transactions; and
c show the general ledger accounts arising from parts a and b.

Question 4.11

From the following information supplied by Carma Ltd you are required to:
a prepare all journal entries arising in respect of the income tax calculations from 30 June 2007 to 30 June 2008; and
b show the income tax expense and income tax payable accounts as they would appear in the general ledger from 30 June 2007 to 30 June 2008.

The trial balance of Carma Ltd on 30 June 2007 showed the following account balances.

Carma Ltd
Trial balance as at 30 June 2007 (Extract)

Date	Debit	Credit
	$	$
Income tax expense	300 000	
Income tax payable		80 000

It was company policy to finalise income tax calculations in the following year.

The company settled its PAYG instalment amount by the due date.

On 30 October the company forwarded its income tax return which recorded a taxable income of $900 000. The company tax rate was 30%.

On 20 November the ATO forwarded the tax assessment to the company with the appropriate refund amount.

Question 4.12

For the year ended 30 June 2007 Parsons Ltd had earned the following quarterly sales income:

30 September	$400 000
31 December	$550 000
31 March	$450 000
30 June	$400 000

The company had a PAYG instalment rate of 20% and paid all instalments by the due dates.

The company was not in a position to finalise its taxation calculations on 30 June 2007 and closed its accounts accordingly.

On 30 September the company lodged its taxation return showing a taxable income of $1 300 000 on which tax payable was $390 000.

You are required to prepare the journal entries to:
a account for quarterly PAYG taxation instalments;
b remit quarterly PAYG instalments;
c close the accounts at 30 June 2007; and
d record adjusting entries for the year ended 30 June 2008.

Question 4.13

The profit and loss account for Challenge Ltd for the year ended 30 June 2007 was as follows:

Challenge Ltd
Trading and profit and loss account

Date	Particulars	Debit	Credit
2007		$	$
30 June	Sales	1 300 000	1 300 000 Cr
	Cost of sales	520 000	780 000 Cr
	Wages	200 000	580 000 Cr
	Advertising	30 000	550 000 Cr

The company had a PAYG instalment rate of 12% and at 30 June 2007 owed PAYG instalments of $48 750.

As the company was not in a position to finalise its income tax position it chose to make its adjustments in the following period.

The company lodged its taxation return on 30 October 2007 on the basis of its profit and loss account. A notice of assessment was received on 30 November 2007 requesting amounts owing to be paid on 31 January 2008.

The company tax rate is 30%. You are required to:

a   prepare journal entries for all taxation-related transactions on 30 June 2007;
b   show the profit and loss account in the general ledger at 30 June 2007;
c   prepare journal entries for all taxation-related transactions for the year ended 30 June 2008; and
d   show the income tax expense and income tax payable accounts for the period 30 June 2007 to 30 June 2008.

CHAPTER 5
ACCOUNTING FOR COMPANY INCOME TAX

Objectives

Upon satisfactory completion of this chapter you should be able to:
+ explain the causes of differences between profit and taxable income;
+ identify permanent differences in the calculation of profit;
+ identify temporary differences in the calculation of profit and taxable income;
+ calculate income tax payable;
+ record adjustments for the recognition of deferred tax assets;
+ record adjustments for the recognition of deferred tax liabilities; and
+ account for taxation on losses.

Introduction

Companies are required to calculate and make payment for income tax under the PAYG instalment system based on sales and other revenue. However, at the end of each year an income tax return declaring the liability for income tax must be lodged in accordance with the *Income Tax Assessment Act* based on the company's taxable income.

As a consequence of the differences in the calculation of income tax based on the PAYG system and the *Income Tax Assessment Act*, a company's income tax expense may not be the same as its income tax payable. Differences between the two may occur where the accounting records include items of revenue or expense that will never be included in the calculation of taxable income, referred to as permanent differences.

In addition, the calculation of profit and of taxable income may include items of revenue and expense of different amounts in different periods. These are referred to as temporary differences.

When accounting for income tax in the accounting records, companies are required to comply with the requirements of AASB 112: Income Taxes which prescribes the adjustments required in relation to permanent and temporary differences.

Permanent differences

Under Australian income tax law, certain items of revenue or expense that a company may identify for accounting purposes may not be assessable or deductible for taxation purposes. Alternatively, the calculation of taxable income may include certain items of revenue or expense that will never be included in the calculation of profit for accounting purposes. Here are some such items of revenue or expense.

- **Non-assessable dividends received by public companies:** In some cases, dividends received by a company and included as revenue in the calculation of profit will not be assessable as income for taxation purposes.
- **The impairment of goodwill:** Companies that purchase an equity share of another business may identify goodwill on the purchase of the business where the amount paid exceeds the net assets acquired. Companies recording purchased goodwill are required to test the cash-generating assets acquired to determine if the goodwill has been impaired. The impairment of goodwill reduces a company's profit, but this expense cannot be claimed as an allowable deduction for taxation purposes to reduce taxable income.
- **Depreciation on buildings:** The annual depreciation of buildings by companies reduces the reported accounting profit. However, for taxation purposes the depreciation on buildings may not be an allowable deduction from assessable income. Generally, buildings that are not capable of producing income cannot be depreciated for taxation purposes.
- **Entertainment expenses:** Many companies incur entertainment expenses in relation to business activities, which are subsequently written off against annual profits. Generally these expenses cannot be claimed as allowable deductions for taxation purposes.
- **Revaluation of investments:** Companies that hold investments in other companies may find it necessary to reduce the value of their investment to reflect a more realistic value on their balance sheet. This may occur when the recoverable amount of the investments falls below their carrying costs.

    Where an investment in another company is devalued, the company incurring the write-down would reduce profits by incurring an expense. The expense, impairment loss in investment, would not be allowed as a taxation deduction.

    Similarly, if a company brings to account a gain from the upward revaluation of investments this will not be included as assessable income for taxation purposes.
- **Establishment costs:** The costs of setting up a company when written off against company profits are generally not allowable as taxation deductions.
- **Investment allowances:** The federal government at times may encourage producers to invest in capital projects by granting businesses a special taxation deduction, known as an investment allowance.

The investment allowance is only an item that reduces taxable income. It is not a payment to the company and, as such, is not recorded in the calculation of profits.

The items listed above are called permanent differences in that they will:

- never be included in the calculation of taxable income, but will be included in the calculation of profit – for example, impairment of goodwill, depreciation on certain buildings, impairment of investments, non-assessable income; or
- never be included in the calculation of profit, but will be included in the calculation of taxable income – for example, investment allowance.

The effect of permanent differences on the calculation of income tax

Permanent differences identified between the calculation of profit (before income tax) and taxable income must be removed or included to determine the company's adjusted accounting profit on which the annual income tax expense is calculated. The term 'accounting profit' is used in this text to describe the result of adjusting the profit (before income tax) with permanent differences.

$$\boxed{\text{Profit (before income tax)}} \pm \boxed{\text{Permanent differences}} = \boxed{\text{Accounting profit}}$$

The calculation of accounting profit is undertaken on a worksheet. The adjustments for permanent differences are *not* made within the profit and loss account.

Once the accounting profit has been calculated it is then multiplied by the rate of company income tax to derive the company's income tax expense for the year. This expense is thus based on the actual items of revenue or expense that will be identified for income tax purposes.

$$\boxed{\text{Accounting profit}} \times \boxed{\text{Tax rate}} = \boxed{\text{Income tax expense}}$$

ILLUSTRATION

Space Ltd has a reported profit of $800 000 and has recorded an income tax expense of $245 000. The profit includes the following items:

	$
Impairment loss – Goodwill	20 000
Depreciation on buildings	50 000

The ATO will allow the following adjustments:

	$
Investment allowance	40 000
Depreciation on buildings	(Not allowable)
Impairment loss – Goodwill	(Not allowable)

These permanent differences will affect profit as follows:

	$	$
Profit		800 000
add back Permanent differences		
Impairment loss – Goodwill	20 000	
Depreciation on buildings	50 000	70 000
		870 000
less Permanent differences		
Investment allowance		40 000
Accounting profit (after permanent differences)		830 000
Multiplied by the tax rate		× .30
Income tax expense		249 000

As income tax has been recorded at $245 000 under the PAYG system, it will need to be increased by $4 000 to derive the $249 000 required by the accounting standard – that is, debit income tax expense $4 000.

The income statement would reveal the following result:

	$
Profit (before income tax)	800 000
less Income tax expense	249 000
Profit (after income tax)	551 000

A company's annual liability for income tax is calculated on taxable income – that is, items of assessable revenue less items of allowable deductions.

Where a company has adjusted its profit to account for permanent differences, and the remaining items of revenue and expense are both assessable and allowable for taxation purposes, then the accounting profit will equal the taxable income. In these circumstances the amount of income tax payable will equal the income tax expense.

ILLUSTRATION

In the previous example, Space Ltd's profit included:

	$
Sales revenue	1 510 000
Wages	600 000
Advertising	40 000

Income tax incurred under the PAYG system was $245 000.

These items were assessable and allowable for taxation purposes. The calculation of taxable income and resulting income tax payable would be as follows:

	$	$
Sales revenue		1 510 000
less Wages	600 000	
Advertising	40 000	640 000
		870 000
less Investment allowance		40 000
Taxable income		830 000
Multiplied by the tax rate		× .30
Income tax payable		249 000

As the company has incurred income tax totalling $245 000 during the year, an adjustment would be required during the year to record the amount owing – i.e. credit income tax payable $4 000.

Question 5.1

The income statement of Brother Ltd for the year ended 30 June 2007 revealed a profit (before income tax) of $650 000. This included the following non-deductible items for income tax purposes:

	$
Entertainment allowance	50 000
Depreciation on buildings	100 000
Impairment loss – Goodwill	10 000
Impairment loss – Investments	440 000

You are required to calculate the amount of income tax expense for the year ended 30 June 2007 using a 40% rate of income tax.

Question 5.2

Explain the difference between the following terms:
a profit (before income tax) and accounting profit;
b profit (before income tax) and taxable income; and
c accounting profit and taxable income.

Question 5.3

From the following information relating to Jolson Pty Ltd you are required to calculate the amounts of income tax expense and income tax payable.

For the year ended 30 June 2007 Jolson Pty Ltd reported a profit (before tax) of $36 000. This included the following items, which are non-assessable or non-deductible tax items.

	$
Impairment loss – Goodwill	50 000
Depreciation on buildings	200 000
Dividends income	72 000

In addition, the company was eligible to claim a $90 000 investment allowance on capital investments. The tax rate is 30%.

Question 5.4

The following information relates to the business of J. & K. Trading Ltd. You are required to:

a prepare a general journal entry at 30 June 2007 to adjust the income tax expense and income tax payable accounts;
b complete the profit and loss account for the year ended 30 June 2007; and
c show the income tax payable account in the balance sheet as at 30 June 2007.

Profit and loss

Date	Particulars	Debit	Credit	Balance
2007		$	$	$
30 June	Trading (gross profit)		380 000	380 000 Cr
	Wages	40 000		340 000 Cr
	Impairment loss – Goodwill	10 000		330 000 Cr
	Depreciation on buildings	15 000		315 000 Cr
	Dividends income		35 000	350 000 Cr
	Entertainment expenses	25 000		325 000 Cr
	Gold mining profits		5 000	330 000 Cr
	Income tax expense	96 500		233 500 Cr

Additional information

- Impairment loss – goodwill, building depreciation of $10 000, dividend income, entertainment expenses and gold mining profits are considered as non-deductible or non-assessable items for the purposes of income tax.
- Income tax payable at 30 June 2007 is $20 000.
- The tax rate is 30%.

Temporary differences

A company may include items of revenue and expense in the calculation of profit that may not be included in the calculation of taxable income in the same year. They may, however, be recognised as assessable income or as allowable deductions for income tax purposes in a future period.

Alternatively, a company may include in its calculation of taxable income certain items of assessable income and allowable deductions that may not be used in the calculation of profit in the same year. These items of revenue or expense may be included in the calculation of profit in a future period.

These differences in the recognition of the timing of revenues or expenses for accounting purposes as opposed to taxation purposes are called temporary differences.

Temporary differences will arise as the calculation of taxable income is derived by applying the rules and regulations of the *Income Tax Assessment Act*, whereas the calculation of profit and loss is determined in accordance with the principles of accrual accounting and applicable accounting standards.

When the amounts included in the calculation of taxable income differ from the amounts included in the calculation of profit and loss, AASB 112: Income Taxes requires temporary differences to be identified and reported as either a deferred tax asset or a deferred tax liability.

To identify a temporary difference, AASB 112 requires a comparison to be made of the values of assets and liabilities reported in the balance sheet (carrying costs), and the values of the same assets and liabilities included in the calculation of taxable income (referred to as the tax base).

The carrying costs of assets and liabilities may differ from the tax base of assets and liabilities as a result of the differences that exist between the *Income Tax Assessment Act* and the accounting standards in reference to the recognition of revenues and expenses and assessable income and allowable deductions.

Carrying costs and tax base of assets and liabilities

To determine the amount of a deferred tax liability or a deferred tax asset, comparisons must be made between the carrying cost of an asset or liability on the balance sheet and the tax base of the liability or asset.

The carrying cost of an asset or a liability refers to the net value of the asset or liability in the books of the company.

Assets are normally reported on the balance sheet showing their cost price, less reductions, and the resulting carrying cost (written-down value). The following balance sheet extract illustrates the carrying cost of selected assets.

Balance sheet		
Assets	$	$
Debtors	50 000	
less Allowance for doubtful debts	5 000	
Carrying cost of debtors		45 000
Equipment	180 000	
less Accumulated depreciation	50 000	
Carrying cost of equipment		**130 000**

Liabilities are also reported on the balance sheet at their carrying cost, as shown below.

Balance sheet	
Liabilities	$
Provision for annual leave	25 000
Provision for long service leave	89 000

The tax base of an asset or a liability may have the same value as the carrying cost on the balance sheet, in which case a temporary difference would not be identified.

However, assets and liabilities may have a different tax base valuation as a result of:

- the company's adopting different methods of valuation for taxation purposes – for example, different methods of depreciating assets; and
- the valuation of assets and liabilities using accrual accounting as opposed to cash accounting principles applied for taxation purposes.

As a result of adopting different valuation methods or different methods of accounting, the carrying cost of an asset or liability will differ from the tax base valuation of the asset or liability. The difference in values represents a temporary difference.

All temporary differences will result in a difference in the amount of profit calculated in the company's accounting records and taxable income in the company's taxation records, which will result in an adjustment to the accounting records by bringing to account either:

- a deferred tax asset; or
- a deferred tax liability.

The resulting deferred tax asset or deferred tax liability means that the company will pay either more or less tax in the future.

Calculating the tax base of an asset

The tax base of an asset is determined by applying the following formula:

Carrying amount of asset
less Future assessable amount
plus Future deductible amount
equals Tax base of asset

The future assessable amount for an asset is equal to any amount that will be assessable under income tax law (to a maximum amount equal to its carrying cost) and is represented by the expected cash flows to be received from the asset either:
- through its use; or
- from its sale.

The future deductible amount refers to the amount that can be claimed as a future tax-deductible item.

Once the tax base of the asset has been determined, the amount can be compared to the carrying cost of the asset and the difference identified as a temporary difference. Each temporary difference must then be analysed to determine if it is giving rise to a deferred tax asset or a deferred tax liability.

Calculating the tax base of a liability

The calculation of the tax base of a liability will vary depending on whether the liability relates to a prepaid amount.

The tax base of a liability not affected by prepaid amounts is calculated as follows:

Carrying amount of liability
plus Future assessable amount
less Future deductible amount
equals Tax base of liability

The future assessable amount equates to the amount that will be paid to the liability in the financial year, while the future deductible amount equates to the amount that can be claimed as a future tax deduction.

Where a liability has been adjusted for prepaid revenue amounts the tax base is calculated as follows:

Carrying amount of liability
less Revenue received in advance
equals Tax base of liability

Temporary differences arising from the comparison of the tax base of a liability and the carrying cost of the liability must be analysed to determine if it is giving rise to a deferred tax asset or a deferred tax liability.

Deductible temporary differences and deferred tax assets

A **deferred tax asset** will eventuate when temporary differences result in:
- the carrying cost of an asset being lower than the tax base of the asset, which will occur when the calculation of profit includes an *expense amount that is higher* than the amount reported in the calculation of taxable income; or
- the carrying cost of a liability being greater than the tax base of the liability, which will occur when the calculation of profit includes an *expense amount that is higher* than the amount reported in the calculation of taxable income.

With higher expenses being reported in the calculation of profit compared to the calculation of taxable income, the company will report a taxable income greater than the reported profit. The understated taxation expense in the current period will allow the company to claim the understated amount in a future period. Hence a future taxation benefit can be identified in the current period and is referred to as a deferred tax asset.

A deferred tax asset will be identified when the accounting records include a larger amount of expense than the tax records. This will occur as a result of the accounting records applying accrual accounting (higher expenses) compared to cash accounting for tax records – for example, bad and doubtful debts, annual leave and long service leave.

A deferred tax asset will also arise if adjustments are made for revenues received in advance and accrued expenses.

Examples

Debtors: The carrying cost of debtors will be smaller than the tax base for debtors when the accounting records include adjustments in the financial year for both bad and doubtful debts. The *Income Tax Assessment Act* does not allow a business to claim doubtful debts as a deductible item in the year in which the adjustment is first made; only actual bad debts written off in a period are deductible. However, in the future the business can claim the doubtful debts as deductible when they eventually turn bad. The future deductibility of doubtful debts brought to account in the accounting books will result in the recognition of a deferred tax asset temporary difference.

Global Ltd on 1 July was owed $50 000 by its debtors. At 30 June a debtor owing $10 000 was written off as a bad debt, thereby reducing the balance of debtors to $40 000. An adjustment was also made to recognise $2 000 in doubtful debts.

The carrying cost of debtors would be calculated as follows:

	$
Cost price at start of year	50 000
less Bad debt written off	10 000
Cost price at end of year	40 000
less Allowance for doubtful debts	2 000
Carrying cost at end of period	38 000

The tax base of debtors would be calculated as follows:

	$
Carrying amount of asset	38 000
less Future assessable amount*	0
plus Future deductible amount	2 000
equals Tax base of asset	40 000

Note: *The assessable amount would be equal to nil, as the amount of $38 000 represents sales to debtors in the past which would have been assessable when the sale was made.

The deferred tax asset temporary difference would be calculated as follows:

	$
Tax base of asset	40 000
less Carrying amount of asset	38 000
equals Temporary difference	2 000

The difference in the carrying cost of debtors and the tax base of debtors results from the different amounts of expenses included for bad and doubtful debts in the calculation of profit in the accounting records and taxable income in the taxation records. This is shown in the following table.

	Accounting records	Taxation records	Temporary amount
Bad and doubtful debts	$12 000	$10 000	$2 000

Provisions for leave: When a business makes adjustments for annual leave or long service leave, the profit and loss account will include the expense for the leave adjustment and the leave payable account will increase. When the business pays employees for their accrued leave, the leave payable account will be reduced.

The *Income Tax Assessment Act* does not allow adjustments for leave expenses to be claimed as a taxation deduction in the year in which they are incurred; only actual leave payments can be claimed. The leave adjustment, however, will be deductible in a future period when it is paid. In the current accounting period it must be recognised as giving rise to a future deductible amount and must be reported as a deferred tax asset temporary difference.

On 1 July Global Ltd had a balance in its long service leave payable account of $100 000. During the year $20 000 was paid from the leave payable account. On 30 June a $25 000 adjustment was made for additional leave accrued to employees.

The carrying cost of the long service leave payable would be calculated as follows:

	$
Carrying amount at start of year	100 000
less Amount paid	20 000
	80 000
plus Long service leave expensed	25 000
Carrying amount at end of period	105 000

The tax base for long service leave payable would be calculated as follows:

	$
Carrying amount of liability	105 000
plus Assessable amount (amount paid)	20 000
	125 000
less Future deductible amount	25 000
equals Tax base of asset	100 000

The deferred tax asset temporary difference would be calculated as follows:

	$
Carrying amount of liability	105 000
less Tax base of liability	100 000
equals Temporary difference	5 000

A deferred tax asset temporary difference will always arise when the accounting records report leave expense adjustments in a period before the leave is paid, or where the amount expensed in a year exceeds the amount paid for leave, which are reported for taxation purposes. This is shown in the following table.

	Accounting records	Taxation records	Temporary amount
Long service leave	$25 000	$20 000	$5 000

Accrued expenses: Adjustments for accrued expenses will result in an increase in the expense amount included in the calculation of annual profit. The same expense amount may be reported for taxation purposes, in which case a temporary difference will not arise. However, if the company reports on the cash amount paid for the expense for taxation purposes, a temporary difference will arise.

At 1 July Global Ltd owed $20 000 for rent. By 30 June the amount had been paid. A further $25 000 had not been paid for the year and was expensed.

The carrying amount for accrued rent would be calculated as follows:

	$
Carrying amount of liability at start of year	20 000
less Amount paid	20 000
	0
plus Amount owing	25 000
equals Carrying amount at end of period	25 000

The tax base of accrued rent would be calculated as follows:

	$
Carrying amount of liability	25 000
plus Assessable amount (amount paid)	20 000
	45 000
less Future deductible amount	25 000
equals Tax base of liability	20 000

The deferred tax asset temporary difference would be calculated as follows:

	$
Carrying amount of liability	25 000
less Tax base of liability	20 000
equals Temporary difference	5 000

Whenever an amount expensed in a year in the accounting records exceeds the amount paid in respect of the expense for taxation records, a deferred tax asset temporary difference will arise. This comparison is shown in the following table.

	Accounting records	Taxation records	Temporary amount
Rent	$25 000	$20 000	$5 000

Question 5.5

For each of the following you are required to calculate the carrying cost, tax base and resulting temporary difference.

Debtors

Balance at 1 July	$60 000
Sales to 30 June	$400 000
Bad debts written off in the year	$30 000
Receipts from debtors	$300 000

Doubtful debts to be provided at 5%.

Long service leave

Balance as at 1 July	$80 000
Amount paid during the year	$20 000
Amount to be expensed	$30 000

Question 5.6

From the following information you are required to determine the amounts for the deferred tax asset or deferred tax liability arising from any temporary differences.

	Balance as at 1 July $	Balance as at 30 June $
Debtors information		
Debtors	50 000	60 000
Bad debts		5 000
Doubtful debts		10 000
Annual leave information		
Annual leave payable	25 000	30 000
Annual leave expense		15 000

Assessable temporary differences and deferred tax liabilities

A **deferred tax liability** will eventuate when a temporary difference causes:
- the carrying cost of an asset to be higher than the tax base of an asset; or
- the carrying cost of a liability to be lower than the tax base of the liability.

Temporary differences which give rise to these differences in carrying costs and tax bases of assets and liabilities will occur when the calculation of profit in the accounting records includes:

a a smaller amount of expense than the tax records – for example:
   - accounting records use the straight-line method of depreciation (lower) and tax records use the reducing balance method (higher); and
   - expenses are prepaid in accounting records (lower) and cash amounts (higher) are included in tax records; and

b a larger amount of revenue (higher) than the tax records (lower) – for example, revenues are accrued in accounting records and cash is included in tax records.

The reporting of higher expenses and lower revenues in the calculation of taxable income will result in the company deferring income tax in the current period and bringing to account a deferred tax liability.

Examples

Machinery: At 1 July Global Ltd had a balance of $100 000 in its machinery account. For the year ended 30 June the asset was to be depreciated at 20% p.a. using the straight-line method for accounting purposes. To reduce income tax payable the company adopted the reducing balance method of depreciation for taxation purpose at 40% p.a.

The carrying cost of the asset would be calculated as follows:

	$
Cost price of asset	100 000
less Accumulated depreciation (20%)	20 000
Carrying cost at end of period	80 000

The tax base of the asset would be calculated as follows:

	$
Carrying amount of asset	80 000
less Future assessable amount[1]	80 000
	0
plus Future deductible amount[2]	70 000
Tax base of asset	70 000

Notes:
1. Future assessable amount is equal to the expected amount to be received from its use (sales revenue) but cannot exceed its carrying amount.
2. Future deductible amounts are equal to allowable tax deductions in future years – that is, $100 000 less $30 000 depreciation (40%) = $70 000.

The deferred tax liability temporary difference would be calculated as follows:

	$
Carrying amount of asset	80 000
less Tax base of asset	70 000
equals Temporary difference	10 000

A deferred tax liability temporary difference will always arise when the accounting records report the initial depreciation expense using the straight-line method and the taxation records report depreciation amounts based on the reducing balance method, which derives a higher depreciation charge. This is shown in the following table.

	Accounting records	Taxation records	Temporary records
Depreciation expense	$20 000	$30 000	$10 000

Prepaid expenses: When a company adjusts expenses in its accounting records to account for prepayments and reports the amount actually paid for taxation purposes, a temporary difference will be identified.

On 30 June Global Ltd had paid $40 000 in advertising expenses. Of this amount $5 000 had been prepaid and an adjustment was made resulting in $35 000 being reported as advertising expense.

The carrying cost of the asset prepaid advertising would be $5 000.

The tax base of the asset would be calculated as follows:

	$
Carrying amount of asset	5 000
less Future assessable amount (amount paid)	5 000
	0
plus Future deductible amount	0
Carrying cost at end of period	0

The deferred tax liability temporary difference would be calculated as follows:

	$
Carrying amount of asset	5 000
less Tax base of asset	0
equals Temporary difference	5 000

A deferred tax liability temporary difference will always arise when the accounting records reduce expenses as a result of prepayments and the amount paid is reported in the taxation records. This is shown in the following table.

	Accounting records	Taxation records	Temporary amount
Advertising	$35 000	$40 000	$5 000

Accrued revenues: If revenues are adjusted to account for amounts yet to be received, the calculation of profit will be higher than the calculation of taxable income if only the cash amount is included in the taxation records resulting in the deferral of income tax.

By 30 June Global Ltd had received $800 000 in sales revenue. An additional $50 000 was yet to be received and an adjustment was made to report sales at $850 000 in the accounting records.

The carrying cost of the asset accrued sales revenue (debtors) would be $50 000. The tax base of the asset would be calculated as follows:

	$
Carrying amount of asset	50 000
less Future assessable amount (sales)	50 000
	0
plus Future deductible amount	0
Carrying cost at end of period	0

This would result in a temporary difference of $50 000, as the carrying cost exceeds the tax base of the asset.

Whenever adjustments are made to accrue revenues in the calculation of profit and the cash amount is included in the calculation of taxable income, a deferred tax liability will be brought to account as understated assessable income will become assessable in a future period. This will be evident in a comparison of the sales amounts in the respective accounting and taxation records as shown:

	Accounting records	Taxation records	Temporary amount
Sales	$850 000	$800 000	$50 000

In summary:

1. A deferred tax asset will arise as a result of a company reporting higher expense amounts in the calculation of profit compared to the calculation of taxable income. This will result from:
   - bad and doubtful debts;
   - annual leave expense; or
   - long service leave expense.

2. A deferred tax liability will arise as a result of a company reporting higher profits than taxable incomes as a result of:
   - adopting straight-line depreciation adjustments for accounting purposes and the reducing balance method for taxation purposes;
   - adjusting expenses for prepayments; or
   - adjusting revenues for accruals.

Question 5.7

For each of the following you are required to calculate the carrying cost, tax base and resulting temporary difference.
- Equipment:
  - Balance at 1 July: $250 000
  - Accounting depreciation to be charged at 10% p.a.
  - Taxation depreciation to be charged at 15% p.a.

- Sales:
  - Sales revenue for the year: $500 000
  - Accrued revenue at 30 June: $30 000
- Advertising:
  - Advertising paid during the year: $85 000
  - Advertising prepaid at end of year: $15 000

Question 5.8

From the following information you are required to determine the amounts for the deferred tax asset or deferred tax liability arising from any temporary differences.

	Balance at 1 July	Balance at 30 June
Equipment information	$	$
Equipment	500 000	500 000
Accumulated depreciation (accounting)	50 000	100 000
Accumulated depreciation (taxation)	75 000	150 000
Wages information		
Wages expense		250 000
Prepaid wages		20 000

Question 5.9

Compare the revenues and expenses and the respective amounts included in the accounting records and taxation records in the following table and:

a calculate the annual profit (loss) and taxable income (loss); and

b indicate if a temporary difference is occurring and whether it is a deferred tax asset or a deferred tax liability.

	Accounting deduction	Taxation deduction
Revenues	$	$
Sales	750 000	700 000
Commission	25 000	20 000
Rent revenue	30 000	30 000
Expenses		
Advertising	60 000	60 000
Annual leave	50 000	45 000
Bad and doubtful debts	15 000	8 000
Depreciation of vehicles	120 000	180 000
Long service leave	40 000	0
Wages	160 000	175 000

Accounting for temporary differences

Where temporary differences are recognised, a difference between accounting profit and taxable income will eventuate. Consequently, the income tax expense amount will be different from the income tax payable.

	When	
ACCOUNTING PROFIT	does not equal	TAXABLE INCOME
	then	
INCOME TAX EXPENSE	will not equal	INCOME TAX PAYABLE

The recognition of initial temporary differences which cause accounting profit and taxable income to be different must be analysed individually to ascertain if they are causing either a deferred tax asset or a deferred tax liability.

Deferred tax asset

A deferred tax asset must be recorded when an initial item of revenue or expense causes the calculation of accounting profit to be less than the calculation of taxable income.

This can arise when:

1. expenses are included in the calculation of accounting profit before they are included in the calculation of taxable income. Examples include annual leave and long service leave expenses, reducing balance depreciation (accounting purposes) compared to straight-line depreciation (taxation purposes) in the initial years, doubtful debts expense and accrued expenses; or
2. revenues are included in the calculation of taxable income before they are included in the calculation of accounting profit – for example, revenue received in advance.

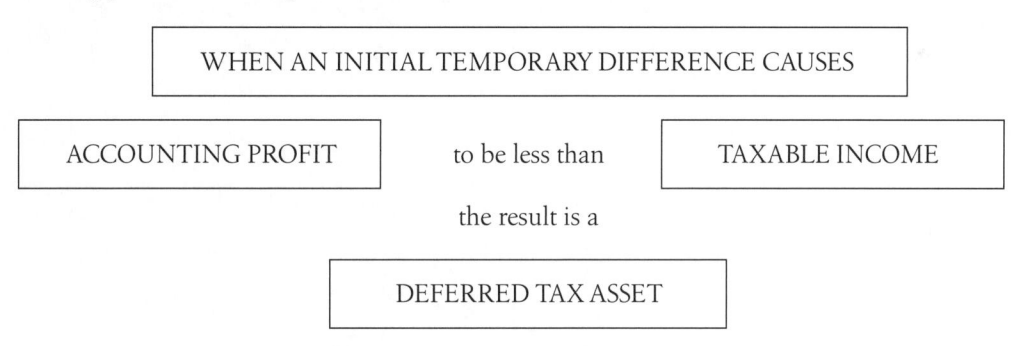

WHEN AN INITIAL TEMPORARY DIFFERENCE CAUSES

ACCOUNTING PROFIT	to be less than	TAXABLE INCOME

the result is a

DEFERRED TAX ASSET

A deferred tax asset is identified because the company will record a taxation liability (income tax payable) which is greater than the recorded income tax expense. The company will, in essence, prepay income tax in the current period. The benefit will be derived in a future period. Consequently, the deferred tax asset account will be classified in the balance sheet as an asset.

In addition to identifying the deferred tax asset, AASB 112 requires an income tax revenue to be identified for the same amount. The standard then permits the income tax revenue account to be offset against the income tax expense account.

ILLUSTRATION

Brat Ltd reported a profit (before tax) of $200 000 for the year ended 30 June 2007 on which $70 000 tax had been expended. Included in this calculation were the following amounts:

	$
Depreciation on buildings	50 000
Bad and doubtful debts	4 000
Annual leave expense	5 000
Long service leave expense	2 000

For the purposes of income tax the following amounts were identified:

	$
Depreciation on buildings	Non-deductible
Bad debts	3 000
Annual leave paid	4 000
Long service leave paid	Nil

The rate of company taxation is 30%.
The calculations of income tax are as follows:

1 *Adjustment to profit (before tax) for permanent differences to determine accounting profit*

	$
Profit (before tax)	200 000
add back Permanent difference	
Depreciation on buildings	50 000
Accounting profit	250 000

2 *Calculation of income tax expense*

	$	
Accounting profit	250 000	
Multiplied by the tax rate	× .30	
Income tax expense	75 000	Dr
less Income tax expended	70 000	
Income tax expense adjustment	5 000	Dr

3   Calculation of taxable income and resulting income tax payable

	$
Accounting profit	250 000
add back Overstated accounting expenses not allowable (claimable) as taxation deductions	
Bad debts	1 000
Annual leave	1 000
Long service leave	2 000
Taxable income	254 000
Multiplied by the tax rate	× .30
Income tax payable	76 200 Cr
less Income tax expended	70 000
Income tax payable adjustment	6 200 Cr

4   Calculation of result of temporaray differences causing a deferred tax asset – that is, causing profit to be less than taxable income:

	$
Bad debts	1 000
Annual leave	1 000
Long service leave	2 000
	4 000
Multiplied by the tax rate	× .30
Deferred tax asset	1 200 Dr

These calculations reveal that income tax payable has to be increased by $6 200 and a deferred tax asset needs to be recognised for $1 200.

The entries to bring to account the increased income tax payable, the deferred tax asset and to offset the income tax revenue adjustment are as follows:

General journal

Date	Particulars	Debit	Credit
2007		$	$
30 June	Income tax expense	5 000	
	Income tax payable		5 000
	Increased income tax owing as arising from calculation of taxable income		
	Deferred tax asset	1 200	
	Income tax payable		1 200
	Adjustment arising from recognition of temporary differences		

Alternative method of calculating and recording adjustments

An alternative method of calculating the taxation adjustments in this illustration is shown in the following table. The table requires a direct comparison to be made of the expenses (or revenues) that give rise to the temporary differences.

The table commences with the profit before temporary differences. This is calculated by adding back the temporary difference amounts included in the calculation of profit to the accounting profit. In this illustration the calculation is as follows:

	$
Accounting profit	250 000
add back Temporary differences	
Bad and doubtful debts	4 000
Annual leave expense	5 000
Long service leave expense	2 000
Profit before temporary differences	261 000

This amount represents items of revenue and expense that would be included in the calculation of profit and in the calculation of taxable income – that is, the calculations of profit and taxable income include the same items and the same amounts.

This amount then needs to be adjusted in both the accounting records and the taxation records for each temporary difference to derive the accounting profit from which the income tax expense adjustment can be determined and the taxable income from which the income tax payable adjustment can be calculated.

Items	Accounting records	Taxation records	Temporary result
	$	$	
Profit (before temporary differences)	261 000	261 000	
less Expenses			
Bad and doubtful debts	4 000	3 000	1 000 deferred asset*
Annual leave	5 000	4 000	1 000 deferred asset*
Long service leave	2 000	–	2 000 deferred asset*
Accounting profit	250 000		
Taxable income		254 000	
Multiplied by tax rate	× .30	× .30	
Income tax expense	75 000 Dr		
Income tax payable		76 200 Cr	
less Tax expended	70 000	70 000	
Adjustments	5 000 Dr	6 200 Cr	

* Deferred tax asset = ($1 000 + $1 000 + $2 000) = $4 000 × .30 = $1 200.

The journal entry to record these adjustments could be combined as follows.

General journal

Date	Particulars	Debit	Credit
2007		$	$
30 June	Income tax expense	5 000	
	Deferred tax asset	1 200	
	Income tax payable		6 200
	Adjustments to tax outcomes arising from temporary differences		

While this entry does not technically conform with the requirements of AASB 112, it has the same effect on the accounts.

Question 5.10

You are provided with the following information about Bongo Ltd for the year ended 30 June 2007. You are required to:
a calculate income tax expense, income tax payable and result of temporary differences; and
b calculate profit (after tax).
Profit (before tax) was $720 000. This included:

	$
Entertainment expenses	5 000
Impairment loss – Goodwill	2 500
Annual and long service leave expense	4 200
Bad and doubtful debts	1 500

For income tax purposes the following were identified:
- Bad debts totalled $500.
- Entertainment expenses and impairment loss – goodwill are not allowable as deductions.
- Income tax expended totalled $210 000.
- The tax rate is 30%.

Question 5.11

Pine Ltd provides you with the following information from which you are required to calculate income tax in accordance with AASB 112 for the year ended 30 June and journalise the results.
- Profit (before tax) $550 000
- Income tax expensed $190 000
- Permanent differences:

	$
Impairment loss – Investments	150 000
Exempt dividends income	30 000

- Temporary differences:

	Accounting records $	Taxation records $
Annual leave	20 000	15 000
Long service leave	14 900	3 700
Bad and doubtful debts	5 100	2 600

- The tax rate is 30%.

Deferred tax liability

A deferred tax liability will arise when an item of revenue or expense causes the calculation of accounting profit to be greater than the calculation of taxable income.
This can be brought about by:
1 expenses being included in the calculation of taxable income before being included in the calculation of accounting profit. Examples include straight-line depreciation (accounting purposes) compared to reducing balance depreciation (taxation purposes) in the initial years and prepaid expenses; or
2 revenues being included in the calculation of accounting profit before being included in the calculation of taxable income – for example, revenues accrued.

Company accounting and financial statements

```
WHEN AN INITIAL TEMPORARY DIFFERENCE CAUSES

ACCOUNTING PROFIT    to be greater than    TAXABLE INCOME

                      the result is a

                   DEFERRED TAX LIABILITY
```

When accounting profit is greater than taxable income the company will record an income tax expense that is greater than its income tax liability. As the liability for tax is less than the expense for income tax, the company has deferred the payment of tax; hence a deferred tax liability is created. This account will be treated as a liability in the balance sheet.

When a temporary difference results in the recognition of a deferred tax liability, AASB 112 requires the adjustment to be made against income tax expense.

ILLUSTRATION

Argle Ltd reported a profit (before tax) of $600 000 for the year ended 30 June 2007. This included:

	$
Impairment loss – Goodwill	20 000
Depreciation on equipment	40 000
Interest expense	100 000
Commission received	36 000

For taxation purposes the following were identified:

	$
Impairment loss – Goodwill	Non-deductible
Depreciation on equipment	60 000
Interest paid	120 000
Commission received	24 000

Income tax expended was $190 000, of which $130 000 had been paid. Income tax payable is $60 000. The income tax calculations required would be as follows:

1 *Adjustment to profit (before tax) for permanent differences to determine accounting profit*

	$
Profit (before tax)	600 000
add back Permanent difference	
Impairment loss – Goodwill	20 000
Accounting profit	620 000

2   *Calculation of income tax expense*

	$	
Accounting profit	620 000	
Multiplied by the tax rate	× .30	
Income tax expense	186 000	Dr
less Income tax expended	190 000	
Income tax expense adjustment	4 000	Cr

3   *Calculation of taxable income and resulting deferred tax liability*

	$	
Accounting profit	620 000	
less Understated accounting expenses allowable as taxation deductions		
Depreciation equipment	20 000	
Interest expense	20 000	
	580 000	
less Overstated income		
Commission received	12 000	
Taxable income	568 000	
Multiplied by the tax rate	× .30	
Income tax payable	170 400	Cr
less Income tax expended	190 000	
Income tax payable adjustment	19 600	Dr

4   *Calculation of result of temporary differences causing a deferred tax liability – that is, causing profit to be greater than taxable income*

	$	
Depreciation on equipment	20 000	
Interest expense	20 000	
Commission received	12 000	
	52 000	
Multiplied by the tax rate	× .30	
Deferred tax liability	15 600	Cr

These calculations reveal that income tax has been overpaid under the PAYG system by $19 600 and must be reduced. Temporary differences require a deferred income tax liability to be brought to account at $15 600.

The journal entries to record these adjustments are:

General journal

Date	Particulars	Debit	Credit
		$	$
2007 30 June	Income tax payable	19 600	
	Income tax expense		19 600
	Adjustment to income tax payable based on taxable income		
	Income tax expense	15 600	
	Deferred tax liability		15 600
	Adjustment to income tax arising from temporary differences		

Alternative method of calculating and recording adjustments

The calculation and recording of tax adjustments could be made as follows. The profit before temporary differences is:

	$
Accounting profit	620 000
add back Temporary differences	
Depreciation on equipment	40 000
Interest expense	100 000
Commission received	(36 000)
Profit before temporary differences	724 000

The comparison of the calculation of accounting profit and taxable income and resulting taxation outcomes is shown in the following table.

Items	Accounting records	Taxation records	Temporary result
	$	$	$
Profit (before temporary differences)	724 000	724 000	
add Commission received	36 000	24 000	12 000 deferred liability
	760 000	748 000	
less Expenses			
Depreciation on equipment	40 000	60 000	20 000 deferred liability
Interest expense	100 000	120 000	20 000 deferred liability
Accounting profit	620 000		
Taxable income		568 000	
Multiplied by the tax rate	× .30	× .30	
Income tax expense	186 000 Dr		
Income tax payable		170 400 Cr	
less Income tax expended/payable	190 000	190 000	
Income tax expense adjustment	(4 000)		
Income tax payable adjustment		19 600*	

* As the income tax payable account currently has a balance of $60 000, it must be reduced by $19 600 to derive $40 400, while income tax expense must be reduced by $4 000. These adjustments have resulted from temporary differences of ($12 000 + $20 000 + $20 000) = $52 000 × .30 = $15 600.

The general journal arising from these calculations would be:

General journal

Date	Particulars	Debit	Credit
2007		$	$
30 June	Income tax payable	19 600	
	Income tax expense		4 000
	Deferred tax liability		15 600
	Being for income tax expense, income tax payable adjustments and temporary differences		

Question 5.12

Banksia Ltd's income statement revealed the following details for the year ended 30 June.

	$
Profit (before tax)	90 000
Income tax expensed	26 000
Depreciation on buildings	5 000
Depreciation on computers	15 000
Interest received	6 000

For income tax purposes the following were recognised:

	$
Depreciation on computers	22 500
Interest received	3 000
Depreciation on buildings	Nil (not allowable)

The tax rate is 30%.

You are required to complete the general journal entry to determine income tax at 30 June, in accordance with AASB 112.

Question 5.13

From the following information for Erica Ltd for the year ended 30 June you are required to complete the general journal entry that records income tax in accordance with accounting standard AASB 112.
- Profit (before tax): $126 000
- Expenses and revenues:

	Accounting records $	Taxation records $
Entertainment expenses	14 000	Nil
Establishment costs	2 000	Nil
Dividends received	5 200	Nil (exempt)
Depreciation on lathes	50 000	100 000
Promotion expenses	120 000	122 000
Commission received	33 000	21 000

- The tax rate is 30%.
- Income tax of $42 000 had been expended during the year.
- Income tax payable at 30 June was $10 000.

Combining deferred tax assets and liabilities

In any one financial year a company may identify temporary differences, that result in both a deferred tax asset and a deferred tax liability. Each item of revenue and expense must be analysed separately to ascertain its effect on income tax. When all temporary differences have been accounted for they can be added together to record a final outcome in the respective deferral accounts.

Where a deferred tax asset and a deferred tax liability are recognised in the same reporting period, AASB 112 permits a company to offset one account against the other.

ILLUSTRATION

For the year ended 30 June 2007 Big Tree Ltd provided the following information in relation to its accounting and taxation records.

Profit (before income tax) was $596 000 on which $165 000 had been recorded as an income tax expense under the PAYG instalment system.

There were no permanent differences; however, the following temporary differences were identified.

Temporary difference	Accounting records	Taxation records	Temporary difference	Deferred tax
	$	$	$	
Interest revenue	50 000	40 000	10 000	Liability
Depreciation on equipment	40 000	60 000	20 000	Liability
Bad and doubtful debts	15 000	12 000	3 000	Asset
Annual leave	32 000	28 000	4 000	Asset

The calculations of the required taxation amounts would be as follows:

1 *Income tax payable adjustment*

	$
Profit (before income tax)	596 000
add back Overstated expenses	
Bad and doubtful debts	3 000
Annual leave	4 000
	603 000
less Understated expenses	
Depreciation on equipment	20 000
	583 000
less Overstated revenue	10 000
Taxable income	573 000
Multiplied by the tax rate	× .30
Income tax payable	171 900
less Income tax expensed	165 000
Income tax payable adjustment	6 900 Cr

2 *Calculation of deferred tax liability*

	$
Interest revenue	10 000
Depreciation on equipment	20 000
	30 000
Multiplied by the tax rate	× .30
Deferred tax liability adjustment	9 000 Cr

3 *Calculation of deferred tax asset*

	$
Bad and doubtful debts	3 000
Annual leave	4 000
	7 000
Multiplied by the tax rate	× .30
Deferred tax asset adjustment	2 100 Dr

The journal entries to record these adjustments are as follows:

Date	Particulars	Debit	Credit
2007		$	$
30 June	Income tax expense	6 900	
	Income tax payable		6 900
	Adjustment to income tax payable based on taxable income		
	Income tax expense	9 000	
	Deferred tax liability		9 000
	Adjustment to income tax arising from temporary differences		
	Deferred tax asset	2 100	
	Income tax revenue		2 100
	Adjustment to income tax arising from temporary differences		

Additional entries may be recorded to offset income tax revenue against income tax expense and the deferred tax accounts against each other. These entries would be as follows:

General journal

Date	Particulars	Debit	Credit
2007		$	$
30 June	Income tax revenue	2 100	
	Income tax expense		2 100
	To record offset of income tax revenue		
	Deferred tax liability	2 100	
	Deferred tax asset		2 100
	To record offset of deferred tax liability		

Alternative method of calculating and reporting

An alternative method of determining the required taxation adjustments is presented in the following table.

The profit before temporary differences would be calculated as follows:

	$
Profit (before income tax)	596 000
Adjustments	
Interest revenue	(50 000)
Depreciation on equipment	40 000
Bad and doubtful debts	15 000
Annual leave	32 000
Profit before temporary differences	**633 000**

Temporary difference	Accounting records	Taxation records	Temporary difference	Deferred tax
	$	$	$	
Profit before temporary differences	633 000	633 000		
Interest revenue	50 000	40 000	10 000	Liability
	683 000	673 000		
Depreciation on equipment	40 000	60 000	20 000	Liability
Bad and doubtful debts	15 000	12 000	3 000	Asset
Annual leave	32 000	28 000	4 000	Asset
Profit (before income tax)	596 000			
Taxable income		573 000		
Multiplied by the tax rate	× .30	× .30		
Income tax expense	178 800			
Income tax payable		171 900		
less Income tax expensed	165 000	165 000		
Income tax expense adjustment	13 800			
Income tax payable adjustment		6 900		

Deferred tax asset adjustment	($3 000 + $4 000) × .30	= $2 100 Dr
Deferred tax liability adjustment	($10 000 + $20 000) × .30	= $9 000 Cr

The journal entry to record these adjustments could be combined as follows:

General journal

Date	Particulars	Debit	Credit
2007		$	$
30 June	Income tax expense	13 800	
	Deferred tax asset	2 100	
	Income tax payable		6 900
	Deferred tax liability		9 000
	Taxation adjustments arising from temporary differences		
	Deferred tax liability	2 100	
	Deferred tax asset		2 100
	To record offset of deferred tax liability		

Question 5.14

AZ Ltd provides the following information from which you are required to calculate the taxation outcomes in line with AASB 112.
- Profit (before tax): $400 000
- Permanent differences:

	$
Impairment loss – Goodwill	20 000
Exempt income	30 000

- The tax rate is 30%.
- Temporary differences:

	Accounting records	Taxation records
	$	$
Repairs and maintenance	110 000	65 000
Depreciation	100 000	190 000
Bad and doubtful debts	50 000	25 000
Long service leave	5 000	–
Interest income	30 000	120 000

- Income tax expensed was $115 000.
- Income tax payable is $35 000.

Question 5.15

Able Ltd calculates income tax using tax-effect accounting. Using the information provided below you are required to:

a calculate the income tax expense for the year ended 30 June (assume the company tax rate is $0.30 in the dollar);
b calculate the deferred tax liability;
c calculate the deferred tax asset; and
d show the general journal entry required to adjust income tax for the year ended 30 June.

Additional information

The profit (before income tax) for Able Ltd at 30 June was $280 000. This figure was arrived at after charging the following:

	$
Depreciation of furniture (straight-line)	20 000
Annual leave	15 000
Depreciation of buildings	5 000
Bad and doubtful debts	10 000
Long service leave expense	21 000

The following occurred for income tax purposes for the year ended 30 June:

	$
Actual bad debts written off	6 000
Actual long service leave paid	15 000
Depreciation of furniture (reducing balance)	40 000
Annual leave	10 000

- Depreciation of buildings (not an allowable deduction).
- Income tax expended during the year was $85 500.

Question 5.16

From the following data pertaining to Spur Ltd you are required to:
a show the deferred income tax accounts for the two years;
b show the journal entries for each year to adjust income tax; and
c calculate the company's profit (after tax) for each of the two years.

	30 June 2007	30 June 2008
	$	$
Profit (before deductions below and taxation expense)	300 000	400 000
Accounting deductions		
Impairment loss – Goodwill	5 000	5 000
Bad and doubtful debts	9 000	7 500
Long service leave expense	25 000	25 000
Depreciation (straight-line)	4 000	4 000
Annual leave expense	5 000	7 000
Other related taxation data		
Long service leave paid	–	20 000
Annual leave paid	4 000	6 500
Depreciation (reducing balance)	6 000	4 000
Bad debts	6 000	4 500
Income tax expensed	75 000	110 000

Note: The tax rate is 30%.

Reversal of temporary differences

When a temporary difference is initially recognised, a deferred tax asset or deferred tax liability is brought to account, depending on the differences in the carrying amount of the asset or liability compared to the tax base of the asset or liability.

The differences in carrying amounts and tax bases is generally caused by different amounts of revenue or expense being recognised in the calculation of profit, compared to the amounts included as assessable income or deductible expenses in the calculation of taxable income.

With the passing of subsequent years, the differences in amounts that gave rise to the recognition of the deferred tax asset or deferred tax liability will be recognised as either tax-assessable or tax-deductible items in the calculation of taxable income. Examples include the following:

- Doubtful debts previously recorded as an expense but not allowed as tax deductions may be written off and be allowable as a tax deduction.
- Annual leave and long service leave previously expensed but not allowed as a tax deduction will be paid and be allowed as tax deductible.
- Prepaid expenses not claimed as a tax-deductible expense in a previous year will become deductible in the following year.
- Adjustments for accrued revenues in the previous year which were not included as assessable income in that year will become assessable in the following year.

When items of revenue or expense previously included in the calculation of profit and not taxable income are included in the calculation of taxable income in a future period, this is referred to as the reversal of a temporary difference.

Reversals of temporary differences will also occur when amounts that were included as a tax deduction in a year but not as an expense in the calculation of profit in the same year are eventually included in the calculation of profit in a later year. A typical item is depreciation.

Reversal of deferred tax assets

A deferred tax asset resulted when:

- the carrying amount of an asset was lower than the tax base of the asset (as was the case with debtors caused by the relationship between doubtful debts and bad debts); and
- the carrying amount of a liability was greater than the tax base of the liability (as was the case with leave expenses compared to leave paid).

A reversal of a deferred tax asset will occur when the temporary differences that initially gave rise to the deferred tax asset are identified as tax-deductible items in the calculation of taxable income.

Examples

Debtors: When debtors are initially adjusted for doubtful debts the carrying amount of debtors will be lower than the tax base of debtors, as doubtful debts are not recognised as a tax deduction. If the debtor is written off in a future period, the amount can be claimed as tax deductible in that period. This will result in the tax base of debtors equalling the carrying amount of debtors in that period, thus reversing the temporary difference which gave rise to the deferred tax asset in the previous period.

The following example shows that in year 1 the accounting records recorded a reduction to debtors of $5 000 for doubtful debts which was not allowed as a tax deduction, thereby causing the carrying amount of debtors to be lower than the tax base of debtors.

In the next year, when the debtor is written off, the amount can be claimed as tax deductible but cannot be expensed as it was claimed in year 1. This causes the carrying amount and the tax base of debtors to become equal.

	Year 1		Year 2	
	Carrying amount	Tax base	Carrying amount	Tax base
	$	$	$	$
Debtors balance at start	25 000	25 000	20 000	25 000
less Bad and doubtful debts	5 000	0	0	5 000
Debtors balance at end	20 000	25 000	20 000	20 000

A comparison of the amounts of bad and doubtful debts included in the calculation of profit and taxable income over the two years reveals how the temporary difference was reversed in year 2.

Year		Accounting records	Tax records	Temporary result
		$	$	
1	Bad and doubtful debts	5 000	0	$5 000 deferred tax asset
2	Bad and doubtful debts	0	5 000	$5 000 deferred tax asset reversal

Leave provisions: When a business accrues annual leave and long service leave, the amount expensed will reduce profit and increase the leave provision account. The amount expensed cannot be claimed as a tax-deductible item until it is paid, which would normally be in a future period.

In the following example, $10 000 is expensed to the provision for annual leave liability account in year 1 but no leave is paid. Hence the carrying amount of the liability is greater than the tax base of the liability. In year 2, annual leave of $10 000 is paid and no amount is expensed, resulting in the carrying amount being lower than the tax base; hence there is a reversal of the temporary difference.

Carrying amounts	Year 1	Year 2
	$	$
Annual leave liability at start	0	10 000
plus Annual leave expensed	10 000	0
less Annual leave paid	0	10 000
Annual leave liability at end	10 000	0

Tax bases	Year 1	Year 2
	$	$
Carrying amount	10 000	0
plus Assessable amount	0	10 000
less Future deductible amount	10 000	0
Tax base	0	10 000

A comparison of the amounts of annual leave included in the calculation of profit and taxable income over the two years reveals how the temporary difference was reversed in year 2.

Year		Accounting records	Tax records	Temporary result
		$	$	
1	Annual leave	10 000	0	$10 000 deferred tax asset
2	Annual leave	0	10 000	$10 000 deferred tax asset reversal

ILLUSTRATION

Gamble Ltd for the year ended 30 June reported a profit (before income tax) of $750 000 on which $250 000 had been reported as income tax expense under the PAYG system.

The profit included the following differences in the accounting and taxation records.

Item	Accounting records	Taxation records	Temporary difference
	$	$	
Impairment loss – Goodwill	50 000	Not deductible	Nil
Annual leave	40 000	48 000	8 000
Long service leave	30 000	20 000	10 000
Bad and doubtful debts	12 000	18 000	6 000

Calculation of accounting profit

	$
Profit (before income tax)	750 000
add back Permanent difference	
Impairment loss – Goodwill	50 000
Accounting profit	800 000

Calculation of taxable income and income tax payable adjustment

	$
Accounting profit	800 000
add back Overstated expenses	
Long service leave	10 000
less Understated expenses	
Annual leave	(8 000)
Bad and doubtful debts	(6 000)
Taxable income	796 000
Multiplied by tax rate	× .30
Income tax payable	238 800
less Income tax expensed	250 000
Income tax payable adjustment	**11 200** Cr

Calculation of deferred tax asset

Temporary differences causing a deferred tax asset are as follows:

	$
Increasing the deferred tax asset	
Long service leave	10 000
Reversing the deferred tax asset	
Annual leave	(8 000)
Bad and doubtful debts	(6 000)
Net temporary differences	(4 000)
Multiplied by tax rate	× .30
Deferred tax asset	**1 200** Cr

The journal entries to record these adjustments would be as follows:

Date	Particulars	Debit	Credit
2007		$	$
30 June	Income tax expense	11 200	
	Income tax payable		11 200
	Adjustment to income tax payable based on taxable income		
	Income tax revenue	1 200	
	Deferred tax asset		1 200
	Adjustment to income tax arising from temporary differences		
	Income tax expense	1 200	
	Income tax revenue		1 200
	Offset of income tax revenue		

Alternative method of calculating and recording adjustments

Calculation of profit before temporary differences

	$
Accounting profit	800 000
add back Temporary differences	
Annual leave	40 000
Long service leave	30 000
Bad and doubtful debts	12 000
Profit before temporary differences	**882 000**

Item	Accounting records	Taxation records	Temporary difference
	$	$	$
Profit before temporary differences	882 000	882 000	
less Temporary differences			
Annual leave	40 000	48 000	(8 000) Reversal
Long service leave	30 000	20 000	10 000
Bad and doubtful debts	12 000	18 000	(6 000) Reversal
Accounting profit	800 000		
Taxable income		796 000	
Multiplied by tax rate	× .30	× .30	
Income tax expense/payable	240 000	238 800	
less Income tax expensed	250 000	250 000	
Income tax expense adjustment	**10 000**		
Income tax payable adjustment		**11 200**	

Deferred tax asset adjustment (− 8 000 + 10 000 − 6 000) × .30 = **$1 200 Cr**

General journal

Date	Particulars	Debit	Credit
2007		$	$
30 June	Income tax payable	11 200	
	Income tax expense		10 000
	Deferred tax asset		1 200
	Taxation adjustments arising from temporary differences		

Question 5.17

Scott Ltd calculates income tax using tax-effect accounting. Using the information provided below, you are required to:

a calculate income tax expense for the year ended 30 June;
b calculate the deferred tax asset;
c calculate the deferred tax liability;

d show the general journal entry required to adjust the income tax expense, tax payable and any temporary differences that may have arisen for the year ended 30 June; and

e calculate profit after tax for the year ended 30 June.

Additional information

- Scott Ltd's profit before income tax for the year ended 30 June was $82 000. This figure was arrived at after the following revenue and expenses were included in the calculation of profit.

	$
Depreciation of buildings	8 000
Impairment loss – Goodwill	2 000
Depreciation of motor vehicles	10 000
Long service leave expense	8 000
Bad and doubtful debts	9 000
Annual leave	15 000

- The following occurred for income tax purposes (depreciation of buildings and impairment of goodwill are not allowable tax deductions):

	$
Depreciation of motor vehicles	15 000
Long service leave paid	12 000
Bad debts	3 000
Annual leave paid	16 000

- The company uses the straight-line method of depreciation for accounting purposes and the reducing balance method for taxation purposes.
- The company provides for leave accruals.
- The tax rate is 30%.
- Income tax expensed during the year was $25 000.

Reversal of deferred tax liabilities

A deferred tax liability resulted when the carrying amount of an asset was greater than the tax base of the asset and can be caused by different depreciation methods adopted in the calculation of profit and taxable income, adjustments for prepaid expenses and accrued revenues.

All temporary differences will eventually reverse over time when depreciation amounts change and adjustments are reversed. Consequently, the deferred tax liability must also reverse. The following are examples of the reversal of deferred tax liabilities.

Non-current assets

When a company adopts the straight-line method of depreciation in the calculation of profit but uses the reducing balance method for tax purposes, the value of the tax base of the asset in the early years of the asset's life will be lower than its carrying amount, resulting in the recognition of a deferred tax liability.

In the later years of the asset's life the amounts of depreciation charged under the reducing balance method of depreciation will be lower than the amounts applied under the straight-line method, resulting in the tax base of the asset equalling the carrying cost of the asset over time, thereby reversing the temporary difference created in the early years.

The following table compares the differences in the carrying cost and tax base of a $100 000 asset which has a life of four years and a residual of $15 260. The straight-line method of depreciation is applied for accounting purposes at 25% p.a. and the reducing balance method is applied for taxation purposes at 37.5% p.a.

	Accounting records			Taxation records		
	Balance at start	Annual depreciation	Balance at end	Balance at start	Annual depreciation	Balance at end
	$	$	$	$	$	$
Year 1	100 000	21 185	78 815	100 000	37 500	62 500
Year 2	78 815	21 185	57 630	62 500	23 437	39 063
Year 3	57 630	21 185	36 445	39 063	14 648	24 415
Year 4	36 445	21 185	15 260	24 415	9 155	15 260

The following table compares the amounts of depreciation included in the calculation of profit and taxable income over the four years. In years 1 and 2, tax depreciation was greater than accounting depreciation, causing a deferred tax liability to be recognised. In years 3 and 4, accounting depreciation is greater than tax depreciation, thereby reversing the deferred tax liability.

Year		Accounting records	Taxation records	Temporary difference
		$	$	
1	Depreciation	21 185	< 37 500	$16 315 deferred tax liability
2	Depreciation	21 185	< 23 437	$2 252 deferred tax liability
3	Depreciation	21 185	> 14 648	$6 537 deferred tax liability reversal
4	Depreciation	21 185	> 9 155	$12 030 deferred tax liability reversal

Prepaid expenses

A deferred tax asset is brought to account when the expenses included in the calculation of profit are adjusted for prepayments, whereas the calculation of taxable income is based on the actual amount paid for the expense. However, in the next period, the accounting records will include the amount prepaid in the previous period; whereas the calculation of taxable income will not include the amount as it was included in the previous period. Hence the expense causing the deferred tax liability is reversed in the next period.

Example

For the year ended 30 June 2007 Holt Ltd paid $18 000 in rent of which $3 000 was prepaid. An adjustment was made for the prepaid amount which resulted in rent expense of $15 000 and an asset, prepaid rent, of $3 000. The rent amount included in the calculation of taxable income in that year was $18 000, the actual amount paid.

At 30 June 2007 the carrying amount of the asset would be greater than the tax base of the asset, resulting in the recognition of a deferred tax liability. However, at 30 June 2008 the carrying amount of prepaid rent and its tax base would both be equal to zero, thereby reversing the deferral created in the previous year.

A comparison of the amounts of rent included in the calculation of profit and taxable income in the two years illustrates how the rent amounts become equal.

Year		Accounting records	Taxation records	Temporary result
		$	$	
2007	Rent	15 000	18 000	$3 000 deferred tax liability
2008	Rent	3 000	0	$3 000 deferred tax liability reversal

Accrued revenues

Similar in philosophy to prepaid expenses, a deferred tax liability will result when revenues are adjusted for amounts owing and included in the calculation of profit, whereas the calculation of taxable income includes the actual amount received. This causes the carrying amount of the liability to be lower than the tax base of the liability and requires a deferred tax liability to be brought to account.

In the following year, when the accrual is reversed in the accounting records, the deferred tax liability will also be reversed.

Example

In the year ended 30 June 2007 sales income was $125 000. An adjustment was made to record an amount owing of $15 000. The calculation of profit in that year therefore recorded an amount of $140 000 for sales, whereas the calculation of taxable income recorded sales at $125 000. In the following year the amount owing of $15 000 would be recorded in the calculation of taxable income but would not be included in the calculation of profit.

A comparison of the sales amounts included in the calculations of profit and taxable income over the two years shows how the creation of the deferred tax liability on 30 June 2007 is reversed in 2008.

Year		Accounting records	Taxation records	Temporary result
		$	$	
2007	Sales	140 000	125 000	$15 000 deferred tax liability
2008	Sales	0	15 000	$15 000 deferred tax liability reversal

ILLUSTRATION

On 30 June, Harding Ltd reported a profit (before income tax) of $100 000 on which $30 000 income tax expense had been calculated.

There were no permanent differences included in the calculation of profit; however, the following temporary differences were identified.

Item	Accounting records	Taxation records	Temporary difference
Commission revenue	20 000	15 000	5 000
Depreciation on machinery*	40 000	60 000	20 000
Wages	90 000	100 000	10 000
Depreciation on equipment*	130 000	80 000	50 000

* Assets are depreciated based on the straight-line method for accounting purposes and on the reducing balance method for taxation purposes.

Calculation of taxable income and income tax payable adjustment

	$
Profit	100 000
less Back overstated revenue Commission	(5 000)
less Understated expenses	
Depreciation on machinery	(20 000)
Wages	(10 000)
add Overstated expense	
Depreciation on equipment	50 000
Taxable income	115 000
Multiplied by the tax rate	× .30
Income tax payable	34 500
less Income tax expensed	30 000
Income tax payable adjustment	4 500 Dr

Calculation of deferred tax asset

Temporary differences causing a deferred tax liability are as follows:

	$
Increasing the deferred tax liability	
Commission revenue	5 000
Depreciation on machinery	20 000
Wages	10 000
Reversing the deferred tax liability	
Depreciation on equipment	(50 000)
Net temporary differences	(15 000)
Multiplied by the tax rate	× .30
Deferred tax liability	**4 500 Dr**

Alternatively, the calculations of the taxation adjustments could be made as follows:

	$
Accounting profit	100 000
add back Temporary differences	
Commission revenue	(20 000)
Depreciation on machinery	40 000
Depreciation on equipment	30 000
Wages	190 000
Profit before temporary differences	**340 000**

Item	Accounting records	Taxation records	Temporary difference
	$	$	$
Profit before temporary differences	340 000	340 000	
add Commission	20 000	15 000	5 000
	360 000	355 000	
less			
Depreciation on machinery	40 000	60 000	20 000
Depreciation on equipment	130 000	80 000	(50 000) Reversal
Wages	90 000	100 000	10 000
Accounting profit	100 000		
Taxable income		115 000	
Multiplied by the tax rate	× .30	× .30	
Income tax expense/payable	30 000	34 500	
less Income tax expensed	30 000	30 000	
Income tax expense adjustment	**Nil**		
Income tax payable adjustment		**4 500**	

Deferred tax liability adjustment (+ 5 000 + 20 000 − 50 000 + 10 000) × .30 = **$4 500 Dr**

The journal entry to record these adjustments would be presented as follows:

General journal

Date	Particulars	Debit	Credit
		$	$
2007 30 June	Deferred tax liability	4 500	
	Income tax payable		4 500
	Taxation adjustments arising from temporary differences		

Question 5.18

From the following information provided by Jay Jay Ltd you are required to prepare the general journal to record the adjustments to income tax for the year ended 30 June.

The company reported a profit (before income tax) of $200 000 on which $50 000 income tax expense had been recorded.

Profit included the following permanent differences:

	$
Entertainment expense	50 000
Impairment loss – Goodwill	25 000
Dividends income	100 000

Temporary differences included in the calculation of profit were:

Item	Accounting records $	Taxation records $
Advertising	60 000	70 000
Depreciation on furniture	60 000	45 000
Depreciation on vehicles	50 000	75 000
Interest revenue	30 000	20 000

Additional information

- All assets are depreciated based on the straight-line method for accounting purposes and on the reducing balance method for taxation purposes.
- The tax rate is 30%.

Combined deferrals of tax assets and tax liabilities

Complex applications of tax-effect accounting require adjustments for both permanent and temporary differences.

Permanent differences are items of revenue and expense that are included in the calculation of profit but will never be included in the calculation of taxable income. These items include:

- non-assessable dividend income;
- depreciation on some buildings;

- entertainment expenses; and
- impairment loss – goodwill.

Temporary differences are items of revenue or expense that cause the calculation of the carrying amount of an asset or liability to be different in value from the calculation of the tax base of the asset or liability.

Temporary differences relate to items of revenue or expense that cause the calculation of profit to differ from the calculation of taxable income in the same year. However, these differences will reverse over future periods.

Temporary differences require adjustments to be made to the calculation of income tax payable and income tax expense, and also require the accounts to recognise either a deferred tax asset or a deferred tax liability.

A deferred tax asset will normally occur in the recognition of different amounts in the calculation of profit and taxable income for the following:

- bad and doubtful debts;
- annual leave; and
- long service leave.

A deferred tax liability will normally occur when the accounting records and the taxation records include different amounts in respect of:

- depreciation of assets;
- prepaid expense adjustments; and
- accrued revenue adjustments.

ILLUSTRATION

On 30 June, Tora Ltd reported a profit (before income tax expense) of $90 000. Income tax expense had been recorded at $28 000.

The calculation of profit included permanent differences for the amortisation of goodwill and entertainment expenses.

All assets are depreciated using the straight-line method for accounting purposes and the reducing balance method for taxation purposes.

The calculations of profit and taxable income were as follows:

Item	Accounting records	Taxation records
	$	$
Sales	565 000	520 000
less Purchases	250 000	250 000
Gross profit	315 000	270 000
less Expenses		
Bad and doubtful debts	20 000	25 000
Annual leave	32 000	30 000
Impairment loss – Goodwill	10 000	0
Long service leave	15 000	20 000
Depreciation on machinery	20 000	30 000
Entertainment expenses	8 000	0
Depreciation on equipment	70 000	40 000
Repairs	50 000	70 000
Profit/taxable income	90 000	55 000

Calculation of accounting profit and income tax expense

	$	
Profit (before income tax)	90 000	
add back Permanent difference		
Entertainment expenses	8 000	
Impairment loss – Goodwill	10 000	
Accounting profit	108 000	
Multiplied by the tax rate	× .30	
Income tax expense	32 400	
less Income tax expensed	28 000	
Income tax expense adjustment	4 400	Dr

Calculation of adjustment to income tax payable

	$	
Taxable income	55 000	
Multiplied by the tax rate	× .30	
Income tax payable	16 500	
less Income tax expensed	28 000	
Income tax payable adjustment	11 500	Dr

Calculation of deferred tax asset

	$	
Increasing the deferred tax asset		
Annual leave	2 000	
Reversing the deferred tax asset		
Bad and doubtful debts	(5 000)	
Long service leave	(5 000)	
Net temporary differences	(8 000)	
Multiplied by the tax rate	× .30	
Deferred tax asset	2 400	Cr

Calculation of deferred tax liability

	$	
Increasing the deferred tax liability		
Sales	45 000	
Depreciation on machinery	10 000	
Repairs	20 000	
Reversing the deferred tax liability		
Depreciation on equipment	(30 000)	
Net temporary differences	45 000	
Multiplied by the tax rate	× .30	
Deferred tax liability	13 500	Cr

The journal entries to record these adjustments could be recorded as follows:

General journal

Date	Particulars	Debit	Credit
		$	$
2007			
30 June	Income tax expense	4 400	
	Income tax payable	11 500	
	Deferred tax asset		2 400
	Deferred tax liability		13 500
	Taxation adjustments arising from temporary differences		
	Deferred tax asset	2 400	
	Deferred tax liability		2 400
	Offset of deferred tax asset		

Question 5.19

Holt Ltd calculates income tax using tax-effect accounting. Using the information below, you are required to:

a calculate income tax expense for the year ended 30 June;
b calculate the deferred tax liability;
c calculate the deferred tax asset;
d show the general journal entry required to adjust the income tax expense, tax payable and any temporary differences that may have arisen for the year ended 30 June; and
e calculate profit after tax for the year ended 30 June.

Additional information

- Holt Ltd reported a profit of $400 000 before the inclusion of the following items:

	$
Depreciation of buildings	15 000
Depreciation of vehicles	10 000
Long service leave	5 000
Annual leave	4 000

- The following differences were recognised for taxation purposes:

	$
Depreciation of buildings	(not allowable)
Depreciation of vehicles	7 500
Long service leave paid	4 000
Annual leave paid	4 500

- The company uses the reducing balance depreciation method for taxation purposes.
- The tax rate is 30%.
- Income tax expensed is $120 000.

Question 5.20

Using the following data relating to Holdings Ltd, you are required to record the general journal entries applicable to the company's taxation position as at 30 June each year, using tax-effect accounting.

	2006	2007	2008
	$	$	$
Profit (before tax)		500 000	600 000
Deductions included in determination of profit			
Long service leave expense		7 000	7 000
Annual leave expense		12 000	15 000
Depreciation		8 000	8 000
Bad debts		200	600
Doubtful debts		500	400
Other related data			
Provision for long service leave	37 000	44 000	43 000
Provision for annual leave	2 000	3 000	5 000
Income tax expensed		150 000	170 000

Additional information
- Depreciation for taxation purposes: 2007 $12 000, 2008 $Nil.
- The tax rate is 30%.

Question 5.21

From the following information relating to State Ltd, you are required to:
a record the general journal entry for the year ending 30 June 2007 which records income tax in accordance with the accounting standards; and
b show the profit (before and after tax) calculations at 30 June 2007.
    The company reported the following amounts for the calculation of profit and taxable income.

	Accounting records	Taxation records
	$	$
Sales	1 000 000	800 000
Purchases	400 000	400 000
Wages	160 000	160 000
Building depreciation	60 000	15 000
Vehicle depreciation	12 000	18 000
Annual leave	7 000	9 000
Bad and doubtful debts	3 000	3 200
Entertainment expenses	10 000	Nil
Long service leave	9 000	1 000

Additional information

- Depreciation on buildings includes an amount of $20 000 which is tax deductible. The remainder is a permanent difference.
- Vehicles are depreciated based on the reducing balance method for taxation purposes.
- Entertainment expenses are not an allowable deduction.
- The company provides for leave accruals.
- Sales income and wages expense were adjusted for accruals on 30 June 2007.
- The rate of income tax is 30% and tax had been expensed at $110 000.

Accounting for taxation on losses

In some years companies may incur a taxation loss. This is the result of allowable taxation deductions exceeding assessable income. Under Australian income tax law, companies are permitted to write a taxation loss off against assessable income in future years. This can only be allowed if the company can satisfy the ATO of specific **continuity of ownership** and **continuity of business** tests.

Where a company is permitted to apportion taxation losses against future years' assessable income it effectively reduces the amount of income tax that would fall due in the future. As a result of the taxation loss the company therefore derives a future benefit (deferred tax asset).

In addition, a company may record an accounting loss, as accounting expenses exceed accounting revenues. When tax-effect accounting is applied to an accounting loss the company will record an income tax credit (revenue item) which will result in a reduced accounting loss.

ILLUSTRATION

XYZ Ltd reported a loss (before tax) and a taxation loss of $60 000 for the year ended 30 June 2006. At a taxation rate of 30% the company would obtain a future income tax benefit (deferred tax asset) of $18 000.

The journal entry arising from this transaction would be as follows:

General journal

Date	Particulars	Debit	Credit
		$	$
2006			
30 June	Deferred tax asset	18 000	
	Income tax revenue (credit)		18 000
	Being income tax on losses		

The company can, in future years, offset the $60 000 taxation loss against assessable income to the extent of $60 000. This will reduce future income tax payable by $18 000.

In the year ended 30 June 2006 the income statement would reveal the following loss (before and after tax).

	$
Loss (before income tax)	60 000
less Income tax revenue (credit)	18 000
Loss (after income tax)	42 000

In the year ended 30 June 2007 the company reported a profit (before tax) of $40 000. At a 30% tax rate the company would bring to account $12 000 as income tax expense; however, as

$18 000 of income tax has been deferred in the previous year, this can be offset (reversed) against the deferred tax asset. There were no permanent or temporary differences. This would result in the following journal entry:

General journal

Date	Particulars	Debit	Credit
2007		$	$
30 June	Income tax expense	12 000	
	Deferred tax asset		12 000
	Being for offset of previous year's tax loss		

For the year ended 30 June 2007 the income statement would report the following amounts.

	$
Profit (before income tax)	40 000
less Income tax expense	12 000
Profit (after income tax)	28 000

The balance sheet would show the deferred tax asset at $12 000 at 30 June 2007. In future years, if profits are reported, the deferred tax asset would continue to be reduced until income tax becomes payable.

In the year ended 30 June 2008 the company reported a profit (before tax) of $50 000. There were no permanent or temporary differences.

As the balance of the tax loss being carried forward is $20 000 (on which a deferred tax asset of $6 000 has accumulated), this amount can be offset against the profit of $50 000, leaving $30 000 on which tax will be paid.

The entry to offset the remainder of the tax loss would be as follows:

General journal

Date	Particulars	Debit	Credit
2008		$	$
30 June	Income tax expense	6 000	
	Deferred tax asset		6 000
	Offset of the balance of the tax loss of $20 000		

In addition, entries would be required to record the tax payable on the remaining profit of $30 000 and to offset the respective income tax accounts.

General journal

Date	Particulars	Debit	Credit
2008		$	$
30 June	Income tax expense	9 000	
	Income tax payable		9 000
	To record income tax on taxable income of $30 000		

For the year ended 30 June 2008 the income statement would show the following amounts in relation to profit and income tax.

	$
Profit (before income tax)	50 000
less Income tax expense	15 000
Profit (after income tax)	35 000

The balance sheet at 30 June 2008 would show a $9 000 liability for income tax payable.

Summary of taxation outcomes

The following information summarises the taxation outcomes that will result from accounting profits (losses) and taxable incomes (losses).

Accounting results:
    An **accounting profit** will result in the recognition of **income tax expense**.
    An **accounting loss** will result in the recognition of **income tax revenue**.

Taxation results:
    A **taxable income** will result in the incursion of **income tax payable**. A **taxation loss** will result in the recognition of a **deferred tax asset**.

Question 5.22

The following information relates to the business of Jongo Ltd. You are required to prepare general journal entries to record income tax in each year. The tax rate is 30%.

	2005	2006	2007	2008
	$	$	$	$
Profit (loss) before tax	(100 000)	20 000	40 000	275 000
Accounting depreciation	120 000	120 000	120 000	120 000
Taxation depreciation	180 000	155 000	130 000	110 000
Taxation income (loss)	(160 000)	(15 000)	30 000	285 000

Question 5.23

Blake Ltd reported a loss (before tax) of $25 000 for the year ended 30 June. This included the following permanent differences.

	$
Impairment loss – Goodwill	5 000
Depreciation on buildings	7 500
Entertainment expenses	10 000
Impairment loss – Investments	20 000
Exempt dividends	8 000

The following temporary differences were also identified.

	Accounting records $	Taxation records $
Annual leave	12 000	10 000
Bad and doubtful debts	4 000	1 000
Depreciation equipment	100 000	150 000

The tax rate is 30%. The company had expended $10 000 in income tax.

You are required to prepare a general journal entry on 30 June to record income tax in accordance with the accounting standards.

CHAPTER 6
APPROPRIATION OF COMPANY PROFITS AND CHANGING SHAREHOLDERS' WEALTH

Objectives

Upon satisfactory completion of this chapter you should be able to:

- transfer profit (loss) after income tax to the retained profits account;
- account for interim and final dividends;
- transfer profits to and from revenue reserves;
- close transaction costs;
- account for the revaluation of property, plant and equipment;
- account for the issue of bonus share dividends; and
- prepare the shareholders' equity section of a balance sheet.

Introduction

At the end of the financial year the profit (after income tax) must be transferred to an account called the retained profits account where it is appropriated to the company's shareholders as dividends, transferred to reserve accounts or retained for future use.

In addition, a company may make adjustments to increase the wealth of the shareholders by revaluing tangible assets and issuing bonus shares to shareholders.

This chapter illustrates the entries required to:

- transfer profits to the retained profits account;
- account for dividends;
- transfer profits to and from reserve accounts;
- transfer transaction costs;
- revalue tangible assets; and
- issue bonus share dividends.

Transfer of profit (loss) after income tax

After adjustments have been made to the profit and loss account for the inclusion of intangible write-downs, the revaluation of investment assets and the inclusion of income tax expense, it is necessary to transfer the balance of the account to the retained profits account (where it can be appropriated).

ILLUSTRATION

The profit and loss account of Solochin Ltd is shown below for the year ended 30 June 2007. The company also held $400 000 in retained profits which were unappropriated at the end of the previous year, 2006.

Profit and loss

Date	Particulars	Debit	Credit	Balance
2007		$	$	$
30 June	Trading		600 000	600 000 Cr
	Dividends revenue		7 000	607 000 Cr
	Wages	316 000		291 000 Cr
	Amortised goodwill	20 000		271 000 Cr
	Establishment costs	5 000		266 000 Cr
	Diminution of investments	150 000		116 000 Cr
	Income tax expense	87 300		28 700 Cr
	Retained profits	28 700		Nil

Retained profits

Date	Particulars	Debit	Credit	Balance
2006		$	$	$
1 July	Balance		400 000	400 000 Cr
2007				
30 June	Profit and loss		28 700	428 700 Cr

The general journal entry to transfer the profit (after tax) would be as follows:

General journal

Date	Particulars	Debit	Credit
2007		$	$
30 June	Profit and loss	28 700	
	Retained profits		28 700
	Transfer of profit (after tax)		

Appropriation of profits

The retained profits account is used to appropriate or distribute the profits of a company. The balance of this account represents undistributed profits or retained earnings and is shown in the balance sheet under shareholders' equity. The following are common appropriations to and from the retained profits account:

- dividends; and
- reserve transfers.

Dividends – interim and final

In return for their investment in the company, shareholders receive a distribution of profit in the form of dividends. The constitution of a company may specify the dividend rights of each class of shareholder, together with the basis of payment of dividends – that is, whether payment is based on the nominal value of shares or on the amount paid up per share.

The constitution may also give directors the power to declare and pay a dividend for the year, rather than waiting until the annual accounts are prepared. Such a dividend is termed an interim dividend and must be distinguished from a final or proposed dividend.

Normally, the directors' recommendation regarding a final dividend is considered by the shareholders at the annual general meeting. Shareholders are normally required to accept or reduce the directors' recommendations. They are not, however, permitted to increase the recommendation of the directors.

The accounting standards do not permit a dividend to be brought to account until the shareholders have ratified or agreed to the dividend. Consequently, when a dividend that is subject to ratification at the annual general meeting in the following accounting period is proposed before the end of year accounts have been prepared, it cannot be brought to account until it is ratified.

Where a company's constitution does not require shareholder ratification of dividends, they can be brought to account when declared by the directors.

ILLUSTRATION

Interim dividends

On 10 January 2007 the directors of Solochin Ltd resolved to pay an interim dividend of 4% on share capital of $1 000 000. The dividend was paid on 1 March 2007.

The following entries would be made in the books of Solochin Ltd.

General journal

Date	Particulars	Debit	Credit
2007		$	$
10 Jan	Interim dividend	40 000	
	Dividends payable		40 000
	Declaration of interim dividend		

Cash payments journal

Date	Particulars	Cheque no.	Sundries	Bank
2007			$	$
1 Mar	Dividends payable		40 000	40 000

At the end of the financial year (30 June 2007) an entry must be made transferring the balance of the interim dividend account to the retained profits account. This is shown as follows:

General journal

Date	Particulars	Debit	Credit
2007		$	$
30 June	Retained profits	40 000	
	Interim dividends		40 000
	Transfer of account		

General ledger
Retained profits

Date	Particulars	Debit	Credit	Balance
2006		$	$	$
1 July	Balance			
			400 000	400 000 Cr
2007				
30 June	Profit and loss		28 700	428 700 Cr
	Interim dividend	40 000		388 700 Cr

Interim dividend

Date	Particulars	Debit	Credit	Balance
2007		$	$	$
10 Jan	Dividends payable	40 000		40 000 Dr
30 June	Retained profits		40 000	Nil

Final dividends

On 20 June 2007 the directors of Solochin Ltd recommended a final dividend of $50 000. This dividend was not subject to shareholder approval and was subsequently paid on 3 August 2007. The following entries would be made in the books of Solochin Ltd.

General journal

Date	Particulars	Debit	Credit
2007		$	$
20 June	Final dividend	50 000	
	Dividends payable		50 000
	Declaration of final dividend		
30 June	Retained profits	50 000	
	Final dividend		50 000
	Transfer of account		

The resulting general ledger appears below.

Retained profits

Date	Particulars	Debit	Credit	Balance
2006			$	$
1 July	Balance		400 000	400 000 Cr
2007				
30 June	Profit and loss		28 700	428 700 Cr
	Interim dividends	40 000		388 700 Cr
	Final dividends	50 000		338 700 Cr

Final dividends

Date	Particulars	Debit	Credit	Balance
2007		$	$	$
30 June	Dividends payable	50 000		50 000 Dr
	Retained profits		50 000	Nil

Dividends payable

Date	Particulars	Debit	Credit	Balance
2007		$	$	$
10 Jan	Interim dividends		40 000	40 000 Cr
1 Mar	Bank	40 000		Nil
30 June	Final dividends		50 000	50 000 Cr

The dividends payable account at the end of the financial year would be included as a current liability in the balance sheet.

Solochin Ltd
Balance sheet as at 30 June 2007 (Extract)

Liabilities	$
Current: Dividends payable	50 000

When the final dividend is paid during the next financial year, the following entries will be made.

Cash payments journal

Date	Particulars	Cheque no.	Sundries	Bank
2007			$	$
3 Aug	Dividends payable		50 000	50 000

Question 6.1

You are required to prepare general ledger accounts arising from the following decisions affecting Sharp Ltd for the year ended 30 June:
- Profit and loss account balance after all adjustments: $218 000 Cr
- An interim dividend of $32 000 was declared on all ordinary shares on 31 December. This was paid on 1 February.
- A further dividend of $16 000 is to be provided on 30 June and will be paid on 1 September.
  Note: The company's constitution does not require shareholder approval for dividend declarations.

Question 6.2

You are required to prepare general journal entries arising from the following decisions and information relating to Live-It-Up Ltd at 30 June:
- Final balance in the profit and loss account (after adjustments): $76 000 Cr.
- Interim dividends declared on 31 March of $16 000 and paid on 1 May.
- Final dividends of 10% on $300 000 issued and paid-up capital to be allowed for as at 30 June.
  Note: The company's constitution does not require shareholder approval for dividend declarations.

Revenue reserve transfers

Profit may be 'earmarked' for special purposes by transferring retained earnings to special reserve accounts such as a dividend equalisation reserve. Retained earnings are also often transferred to a general reserve that has not been set up for any specific purpose. Moreover, reserves that have already been created by debiting the retained profits account may at some later stage be transferred back to the retained profits account for the payment of dividends. Reserve accounts that are formed by appropriating profits are called revenue reserves.

Note that the balances of the retained profits account and all reserve accounts are classified as shareholders' equity items. Accordingly, they are included with share capital in the balance sheet.

ILLUSTRATION

On 30 June 2007 the directors of Solochin Ltd resolved to create a stock replacement reserve of $20 000 and to reduce the general reserve from $30 000 to $15 000. The following entries would be required to record the directors' resolution.

General journal

Date	Particulars	Debit	Credit
2007		$	$
30 June	Retained profits	20 000	
	Stock replacement reserve		20 000
	Creation of stock replacement reserve		
	General reserve	15 000	
	Retained profits		15 000
	Reduction in general reserve		

The finalised retained profits account of Solochin Ltd would be as follows:

Retained profits

Date	Particulars	Debit	Credit	Balance
2006		$	$	$
1 July	Balance		400 000	400 000 Cr
2007				
30 June	Profit and loss		28 710	428 700 Cr
	Interim dividends	40 000		388 700 Cr
	Final dividends	50 000		338 700 Cr
	Stock replacement reserve	20 000		318 700 Cr
	General reserve		15 000	333 700 Cr

Question 6.3

From the following information relating to Jumbuck Ltd you are required to prepare:
a general journal entries as at 30 June; and
b general ledger accounts as at 30 June.
- Profit and loss account closing balance: $845 000 Cr
- Retained profits account balance at start of period: $50 000 Cr
- A general reserve of $40 000 is to be created.
- Dividends declared on 1 December of $150 000 and paid on 4 April.
- A proposed final dividend to be made of $71 000.
- Funds to be set aside in a dividend equalisation reserve of $16 000 to cover future dividend shortfalls.

Transaction costs

Transaction costs, being costs associated with an issue of shares, are required to be recorded directly against equity in accordance with accounting standard AASB 132: Financial Instruments. This can be achieved by closing the transaction costs account off to the retained profits account at the end of the period.

ILLUSTRATION

On 15 May 2007 Solochin Ltd had incurred transaction costs totalling $25 000 as a result of issuing shares to the public. The entry to close the transactions account to retained profits would be recorded in the general journal as follows:

General journal

Date	Particulars	Debit	Credit
2007		$	$
30 June	Retained profits	25 000	
	Transaction costs		25 000
	Closed account		

The retained profits account showing the inclusion of transaction costs would be as follows:

Retained profits

Date	Particulars	Debit	Credit	Balance
		$	$	$
2006 1 July	Balance		400 000	400 000 Cr
2007 30 June	Profit and loss		22 280	428 700 Cr
	Interim dividends	40 000		388 700 Cr
	Final dividends	50 000		338 700 Cr
	Stock replacement reserve	20 000		318 700 Cr
	General reserve		15 000	333 700 Cr
	Transaction costs	25 000		308 700 Cr

Question 6.4

The following information has been supplied by Rocket Ltd for the year ended 30 June 2007.

For the year ended 30 June 2007 you are required to prepare:

a the journal entries to finalise the profit and loss account and the retained profits account; and

b the profit and loss account and the retained profits account.

Rocket Ltd
Trial balance as at 30 June 2007 (Extract)

Particulars	Debit	Credit
	$	$
Calls in arrears – Preference shares	5 000	
General reserve		45 000
Interim dividends	26 000	
Profit and loss (after income tax)		265 000
Retained profits (1 July 2006)		120 000
Share capital – Ordinary shares		400 000
Share capital – Preference shares		100 000
Stock replacement reserve		18 000
Transaction costs	6 500	

Additional information as at 30 June 2007

- The general reserve is to be reduced by $25 000.
- The stock replacement reserve is to be increased by $2 000.
- Ordinary shares consist of 800 000 shares issued at $0.50 each. A final dividend of $0.05 per share is to be made on all ordinary shares.
- Preference shares consist of 20 000 shares issued at $5 each. Holders of 5 000 preference shares have not paid the final call. A final dividend of $0.15 per share is to be made on all fully paid preference shares.
- Final dividend declarations have been approved by shareholders.

Question 6.5

From the following information relating to the accounts of Down Yonder Ltd you are required to finalise the profit and loss account and the retained profits account for the year ended 30 June 2007 in accordance with the following directors' recommendations.

- Any income tax adjustments are to be recorded in the accounts of the current year. The income tax rate is 30%.
- A final dividend (approved by shareholders) is to be made at 6% of ordinary shares.
- The general reserve is to be increased to $25 000.

Down Yonder Ltd
Trial balance as at 30 June 2007

Particulars	Debit	Credit
	$	$
Accounts payable		30 000
Accounts receivable	100 000	
Advertising	25 000	
Bad debts	8 000	
Bank	190 000	
Buildings	280 000	
Cost of sales	260 000	
General reserve		20 000
Income tax expense	30 000	
Income tax payable		15 000
Interim dividend	30 000	
Other costs	12 000	
Retained profits (1 July 2006)		30 000
Sales		480 000
Share capital – Ordinary shares		550 000
Stock	120 000	
Transaction costs	10 000	
Wages	60 000	
	1 125 000	1 125 000

Revaluation of property, plant and equipment

The accounting standard AASB 116: Property, Plant and Equipment, clause 15, requires items identified as property, plant and equipment to be measured at their purchase price (cost of purchase). After the initial recording of the cost price of the asset a company is then required to value the asset using either the cost price or the revaluation model (clause 29).

Where the cost model is adopted the asset is valued at its cost price less depreciation. The cost price less accumulated depreciation is called the 'carrying amount' of the asset.

If a company chooses to adopt the revaluation model the asset must be valued at its fair value, commonly referred to as its market value.

Upward revaluations

To revalue an asset upwards from its carrying cost to its fair value involves the creation of a 'capital reserve' by the name of 'asset revaluation reserve'. This reserve will represent an increase in the value of the shareholders' equity of the company.

ILLUSTRATION

The directors of Solochin Ltd resolved on 30 June 2007 to revalue freehold land and buildings at $1 000 000 as per an independent valuer's assessment. Freehold land and buildings were purchased originally in July 2006 for $200 000.

The following entries would be made in the records of Solochin Ltd.

General journal

Particulars		Debit	Credit
2007		$	$
30 June	Freehold land and buildings	800 000	
	Asset revaluation reserve		800 000
	Revaluation of freehold land and buildings at independent valuation as per recommendation of directors		

General ledger
Freehold land and buildings

Date	Particulars	Debit	Credit	Balance
2006		$	$	$
1 July	Balance	200 000		200 000 Dr
2007				
30 June	Asset valuation reserve	800 000		1 000 000 Dr

Asset revaluation reserve

2007		$	$	$
30 June	Land and buildings		800 000	800 000 Cr

Downward revaluations

A downward revaluation of property, plant and equipment to its fair value will result in the impairment of the value of the asset and can be brought about in the following ways:
1 where an asset has been previously revalued upwards and an asset revaluation reserve created, the devaluation shall be debited to the reserve account; or
2 where an asset revaluation reserve has been reversed due to a downward revaluation or a reserve account had not been created, the decrement shall be recorded as a debit to the profit and loss account.

ILLUSTRATION

The directors of Tribal Ltd on 30 June 2007 decided to devalue their land and buildings to $550 000. In the previous year the value of the land and buildings had been increased from $600 000 to $900 000.

The general journal entries to record this decrement would be as follows:

General journal

Particulars		Debit	Credit
2007		$	$
30 June	Asset revaluation reserve	300 000	
	Impairment loss – Land and buildings	50 000	
	Land and buildings		350 000
	Downward revaluation of land and buildings which reverses a previous revaluation and charges the difference against profit		
	Profit and loss	50 000	
	Impairment loss – Land and buildings		50 000
	Closure of account		

Bonus share dividends

The company constitution may permit the directors to make a bonus share dividend issue. This is usually done to avoid paying cash dividends. Instead, dividends are paid in the form of a bonus share issue. Bonus shares are issued from a capital reserve such as the asset revaluation reserve. (Bonus share dividends are not an appropriation of profits and cannot be sourced from the retained profits account.)

ILLUSTRATION

The directors of Frederick Ltd resolved on 1 June to make a bonus share issue of one $1 ordinary share for every 10 ordinary shares held in the company. At this date the company had share capital consisting of 1 000 000 $1 fully paid ordinary shares and an asset revaluation reserve of $200 000. The dividend was to be paid on 10 September.

The following entries would be made in the general journal of Frederick Ltd.

General journal

Particulars		Debit	Credit
		$	$
1 June	Bonus dividend	100 000	
	Dividends payable		100 000
	Declaration of bonus share dividend		
30 June	Asset revaluation reserve	100 000	
	Bonus dividend		100 000
	Allocation of bonus share dividend from capital reserve		
10 Sept	Dividends payable	100 000	
	Ordinary shares		100 000
	Issue of bonus share dividend		

Question 6.6

From the following trial balance extract of Blight Ltd you are required to show the ledger accounts arising from the transactions listed.

Trial balance as at 30 June 2007 (Extract)

Particulars	Debit	Credit
	$	$
Land and buildings – At cost	600 000	
Share capital – 500 000 ordinary shares		1 000 000
Asset revaluation reserve		50 000
Equipment	850 000	

Adjustments

1. Revalue land and buildings at the fair value of $700 000.
2. Revalue equipment at its recoverable amount of $1 100 000.
3. Issue bonus shares at the rate of one for every five shares held.

The balance sheet and shareholders' equity

The shareholders' equity section of a company balance sheet, after appropriation of profits, movements to and from reserves and the revaluation of non-current assets, will show the value of share capital and the reserves to which shareholders may be entitled.

Example

Shown below is the shareholders' equity section of the balance sheet of Jones Ltd as at 30 June 2007.

Jones Ltd
Balance sheet as at 30 June 2007 (Extract)

	$	$
Shareholders' equity		
Contributed equity		
Share capital – 500 000 ordinary shares	500 000	
Calls in arrears 100 000 @ $0.20 per share	20 000	
		480 000
Reserves		
Retained profits		130 000
Stock replacement reserve		20 000
General reserve		30 000
Asset revaluation reserve		500 000
		1 160 000

Question 6.7

The following information relates to Coonawarra Trading Company Ltd. You are required to complete the profit and loss and retained profits accounts as they would appear in the general ledger from 1 July 2006 to 30 June 2007.

Trial balance (after preparation of trading account and profit and loss account) as at 30 June 2007

Account	Debit	Credit
	$	$
Income tax payable		20 000
Ordinary shares		400 000
Retained profits 1 July 2006		25 000
Sundry reserve		15 000
Shares in unrelated company – At cost	200 000	
Unsecured debenture stock		150 000
Long-term loan from unrelated corporation – Fully secured		170 000
Freehold land – At directors' 2001 valuation	300 000	
Premises – At directors' 2001 valuation	200 000	
Leasehold land and premises – At cost	200 000	
Accumulated amortisation – Leasehold land and premises		80 000
Fixtures and fittings – At cost	40 000	
Accumulated depreciation – Fixtures and fittings		16 000
Computer – At cost	60 000	
Accumulated depreciation – Computer		24 000
Asset revaluation reserve		100 000
Debtors	90 000	
Creditors		129 000
Bank	20 000	
Stock – At cost	145 000	
Long service leave payable		28 000
Allowance for doubtful debts		12 000
Goodwill	20 000	
Interim dividend	12 000	
Profit and loss		118 000
	1 287 000	1 287 000

Additional information and directors' recommendations

- Goodwill is to be reduced by $10 000 due to the impaired value of assets.
- Provide for income tax expense for the year ended 30 June 2007 at a rate of 30%. There are no temporary differences.
- The sundry reserve is no longer required and is to be removed from the accounts.
- Freehold land and premises are to be revalued at $400 000 and $250 000, respectively, in accordance with an independent valuation.
- An interim dividend of $12 000 was paid on 1 November 2006. Another $20 000 is to be proposed. Dividend declarations do not require shareholder ratification.
- Share capital consists of 400 000 ordinary shares issued at $1 per share.

Profit and loss account

Date	Particulars	Debit	Credit	Balance
2007		$	$	$
30 June	Trading – Gross profit		343 500	343 500 Cr
	Dividends received		20 000	363 500 Cr
	Wages and salaries	18 000		345 500 Cr
	Insurances	2 000		343 500 Cr
	Loss on sale of computer	40 000		303 500 Cr
	Repairs	5 000		298 500 Cr
	Bad debts	11 000		287 500 Cr
	General expenses	4 000		283 500 Cr
	Accountancy fees	8 000		275 500 Cr
	Discount allowed	500		275 000 Cr
	Rates	4 000		271 000 Cr
	Long service leave expense	5 000		266 000 Cr
	Audit fees	3 000		263 000 Cr
	Amortisation – Land and premises	20 000		243 000 Cr
	Depreciation – Fixtures and fittings	4 000		239 000 Cr
	Depreciation – Motor vehicles	5 000		234 000 Cr
	Interest	32 000		202 000 Cr
	Directors' fees	24 000		178 000 Cr
	Income tax expense	60 000		118 000 Cr

Question 6.8

The following information relates to Lonsdale Traders Ltd. You are required to complete the profit and loss and retained profits accounts as they appear in the general ledger from 1 July 2006 to 30 June 2007.

Trial balance (after preparation of trading account and profit and loss account)
as at 30 June 2007

Account	Debit	Credit
	$	$
Income tax payable		15 000
Share capital – 600 000 ordinary shares		600 000
General reserve		50 000
Retained profits 1 July 2006		20 000
Transaction costs	4 000	
Bank		60 500
Debenture in unrelated corporation (maturing 30 June 2010)	40 000	
Debtors	40 000	
Creditors		23 000
Asset revaluation reserve		20 000
Stock replacement reserve		10 000
Freehold land	480 000	
Premises – At cost	129 000	
Goodwill	20 000	
Stock – At cost	108 000	
Fixtures and fittings – At cost	80 000	
Accumulated depreciation – Fixtures and fittings		16 000
Interim dividend	24 000	
Allowance for doubtful debts		2 000
Profit and loss		108 500
	925 000	925 000

Additional information and directors' recommendations

- Goodwill is to be impaired by $20 000.
- Allow income tax for the year ended 30 June 2007 at 30%.
- The profit on sale of land is non-assessable income.
- Freehold land is to be revalued as per directors' valuation at $530 000.
- General reserve is to be reduced to $30 000.
- An interim dividend of 4% on paid-up capital was paid on 31 October 2006. Another 6% is to be proposed. Dividends do not require shareholder approval.

Profit and loss account

Date	Particulars	Debit	Credit	Balance
2007		$	$	$
30 June	Gross profit – Trading		295 500	295 500 Cr
	Profit on sale of land		10 000	305 500 Cr
	Debenture interest		4 000	309 500 Cr
	Audit fees	3 100		306 400 Cr
	Interest on overdraft	1 500		304 900 Cr
	Directors' emoluments	5 000		299 900 Cr
	Accountancy fees	20 000		279 900 Cr
	Insurance	1 900		278 000 Cr
	Salaries	80 600		197 400 Cr
	Bad debts	3 400		194 000 Cr
	Repairs and maintenance	7 000		187 000 Cr
	General expenses	8 000		179 000 Cr
	Debt collection	500		178 500 Cr
	Rent	2 000		176 500 Cr
	Depreciation – Fixtures	28 000		148 500 Cr
	Income tax expense	40 000		108 500 Cr

CHAPTER 7
CORPORATE REPORTING

Objectives

Upon satisfactory completion of this chapter you should be able to:

+ list the reporting responsibilities of company directors;
+ prepare a company income statement and statement of changes in equity that comply with the accounting standards;
+ prepare a company balance sheet that conforms to the requirements of the accounting standards; and
+ explain the reporting requirements of the accounting standards on company financial statements.

Introduction

All Australian companies that are reporting entities – that is, that must report their financial performance, financial position and cash position to shareholders at large – must comply with the legal provisions of the Corporations Law.

The Law requires company directors to present to an annual general meeting of shareholders financial reports that give a true and fair view. These financial statements and their notes of disclosure are prescribed in the accounting standards developed by the accounting profession.

This chapter examines the reporting of the income statement and the balance sheet as required by the accounting standards and the notes required by the accounting standards in support of these statements.

Corporate reporting requirements

The Corporations Law requires companies to comply with specific reporting requirements in reference to the company's financial reports. When preparing and presenting the financial reports, companies must be cognisant of the following aspects of the Law.

Financial reports are to consist of:

- the financial statements;
- the notes to the financial statements (comprising regulatory disclosures, notes required by the accounting standards and other information necessary to give a true and fair view); and
- the directors' declaration in respect of the statements and notes (stating that the statements comply with the accounting standards, that they give a true and fair view, and that the company can pay its debts when they become due and payable).

Companies must report annually to members either by sending members copies of the financial report, directors' report and auditor's report, or a copy of a concise report of the financial report.

A company must report to its members at least 21 days before the next annual general meeting after the end of the financial year, or four months after the end of the financial year, whichever is the earliest. The directors of a company holding an AGM must present to the AGM the financial report, the directors' report and the auditor's report.

Note: Small proprietary companies will only need to report if shareholders with 5% of the share capital require a report or a direction is made by ASIC. If such a direction is made, the company must report by the later of two months after the date on which the direction was given or four months after the end of the financial year.

A company must lodge its financial report with ASIC within four months after the end of the financial year. Small proprietary companies are excluded from this requirement.

It is also important to note that companies which are defined as disclosing entities under the Law will also need to comply with the provisions of preparing, presenting and lodging half-yearly financial reports.

The accounting standards

Accounting Standard AASB 101: Presentation of Financial Statements requires reporting entities to present the following annual financial statements:

- an income statement;
- a statement of changes in equity;
- a balance sheet;
- a cash flow statement; and
- notes to the accounts describing significant accounting policies and detailing material amounts included in the statements.

The accounting and auditing standards also require reporting entities to state in the notes to the financial statements presented to shareholders:
- whether the financial reports have been prepared in accordance with the Australian Accounting Standards; and
- if the statements presented are general-purpose financial reports or special-purpose financial reports.

Where a shareholder requires reports to be presented in a manner that meets the special information needs of the shareholder and the shareholder is able to obtain such a report from the company, the report is considered a special-purpose report. A bank, for example, may require the balance sheet to be presented in a way that suits the particular financial modelling tools of the bank.

General-purpose financial reports, on the other hand, are reports that meet the information needs of users who do not require information to be presented in a special way.

The income statement

Accounting Standard AASB 101: Presentation of Financial Statements sets out the reporting requirements of an income statement. The standard does not specify a specific format for the presentation of the income statement; however, in clause 81 it gives the minimum items to be shown on the face of the statement. These include:
- *revenue;*
- finance costs;
- tax expense; and
- *profit or loss.*

The standard provides examples of income statements that users could adopt. The examples range from a simple format to formats based on functions or the nature of expenses.

Simple format

The simple format of the income statement that meets the requirements of clause 81 requires the face of the statement to show revenues minus expenses, with both finance expenses and taxation expense shown separately. This income statement can be presented as follows:

Income statement for the financial year ended 30 June	
	$
Revenue	XX
less Expenses (excluding finance costs)	
less Finance costs	XX
Profit (loss) before income tax expense	XX
less Income tax expense	XX
Net profit (loss)	XX

This format does not include 'line items' on the face of the report that disclose the amounts that make up the items revenues or expenses.

Functional expenses format

The income statement using the functional expenses format is also referred to as the 'cost of sales' format as it shows the cost of goods sold expense separately from other expenses. In addition, expenses other than cost of sales can be classified by function, such as distribution (selling and marketing) and administration expenses. This income statement can be presented as follows:

Income statement for the financial year ended 30 June	
	$
Revenue	XX
less Cost of sales	XX
Gross profit	XX
Other income	XX
Distribution expenses	XX
Administration expenses	XX
Other expenses	XX
Profit (loss) before income tax expense	**XX**
less Income tax expense	XX
Net profit (loss)	**XX**

Nature of expenses format

An alternative to the simple or functional expenses income statement format is the nature of expenses format. This format groups expenses by their nature, such as depreciation, purchases of materials, transport costs, employee benefits and advertising costs. This income statement can be presented as follows:

Income statement for the financial year ended 30 June	
	$
Revenue	XX
Other income	XX
less Expenses	XX
Purchases and raw materials	XX
Employee benefits	XX
Depreciation and impairment expenses	XX
Other expenses	XX
Profit (loss) before income tax expense	**XX**
less Income tax expense	XX
Net profit (loss)	**XX**

As with the simple format, the functional expenses and nature of expenses formats do not include 'line items' on the face of the report that disclose the amounts that make up the items, revenues or expenses.

To provide users of the income statement with more information about the amounts included on the face of the income statement, companies are required to attach notes of disclosure to the statement. The disclosure notes required are set out in AASB 101: Presentation of Financial Statements and other accounting standards.

Some of the disclosure notes included in the accounting standards are examined below.

Material items

AASB 101: Presentation of Financial Statements, clause 86 states: 'When items of income and expense are material, their nature and amount shall be disclosed separately.' The decision to specifically disclose or not to disclose an item of revenue or expense may depend on the amount of the item, the regularity of the transactions that give rise to the amount, and the effect that it has on the accounts of the business.

The decision to disclose or not to disclose specific items of revenue or expense in the accounts based on materiality of the amount will vary from entity to entity. Bad debts of $50 000, for example, may be considered material if the sales revenue of the business is $250 000 and the bad debt relates to one debtor. On the other hand, $50 000 in bad debts may be considered immaterial if sales revenue is $2 500 000.

Generally, an item should be disclosed if its individual reporting will assist the user of the reports to obtain more information, from which they will be able to make an informed decision.

AASB 101, clause 87 details items of revenue or expense that may warrant separate disclosure. These include:

a write-downs of inventories to net realisable value or of property, plant and equipment to recoverable amount, as well as reversals of such write-downs;
b disposals of items of property, plant and equipment;
c disposals of investments; and
d litigation settlements.

Consequently the following items, if considered material, should be disclosed:

- profit on sale of property, plant and equipment;
- profit on sale of investments;
- loss on sale of property, plant and equipment;
- loss on sale of investments;
- impairment losses of assets (property, plant and equipment and intangibles);
- legal costs; and
- damages from law suits.

Extraordinary items

AASB 101: Presentation of Financial Statements, clause 85 prevents the disclosure of revenue and expense items as 'extraordinary'. Prior to the introduction of AASB 101: Presentation of Financial Statements, Australian companies were required to indicate when items of revenue or expense were classified as significant (abnormal) or extraordinary. Companies are now banned from continuing this practice.

Items that a company considers to be of interest to the reader of the statements should be included in the notes with other material amounts or on the face of the statement; however, they cannot be referred to as significant or extraordinary.

Revenues

AASB 118: Revenues requires the disclosure of material revenue items derived from sale of goods, provision of services, interest revenue, dividends revenue and income from royalties.

Employee entitlements

AASB 101: Presentation of Financial Statements, clause 93 requires the disclosure of amounts expensed to the profit and loss account as employee benefits. This would include amounts accrued for annual leave, long service leave and sick leave.

AASB 119: Employee Benefits also prescribes amounts that have been set aside as employee benefits expense in the profit and loss account to be disclosed in the financial statements.

Lease expenses

AASB 117: Leases requires the detailed disclosure of amounts relating to both operating and finance leases. Where a company has included lease payments as an expense in the calculation of profit, the amount expensed must be disclosed.

Interest

AASB 132: Financial Instruments requires a comprehensive range of disclosures related to financial assets and financial liabilities. Interest associated with financial instruments that have been included, as either an expense or revenue, in the profit and loss account must be disclosed.

Research and development costs

AASB 138: Intangible Assets requires the disclosure of amount of research and development costs expensed to the profit and loss account.

Income tax expense

AASB 112: Income Taxes requires the disclosure of a range of tax-related information and reconciliations relating to the calculation of income tax. In reference to income tax expense, the standard requires the disclosure of a reconciliation of income tax on net profit and accounting profit.

Intangible asset write-offs

AASB 138: Intangible Assets requires amounts expensed to the profit and loss account as impairment losses, or amortisation of intangible assets such as goodwill, copyrights, franchises and licences, to be disclosed in the income statement or disclosure notes.

Depreciation and impairment losses of property, plant and equipment

AASB 116: Property, Plant and Equipment requires the disclosure of depreciation expenses and impairment losses associated with property, plant and equipment that have been expensed to the profit and loss account.

Payments to auditors

AASB 101: Presentation of Financial Statements requires the disclosure of amounts paid to a company's external auditors.

Payments to directors and executives

AASB 1046: Director and Executives Disclosure requires the disclosure of amounts paid to directors and executive officers. The standard requires that each director and each executive officer be named and the amount received by each person to be individually disclosed.

Reconciliation of revenues and expenses

AASB 101: Presentation of Financial Statements also requires that amounts appearing on the face of the income statement be reconciled to the disclosure notes applicable to each line item on the face of the statement. This requirement will necessitate items not specifically disclosed in the notes to be aggregated as 'Other revenues' and 'Other expenses'.

Summary of the accounting standards relating to the income statement

Statement format:	AASB 101
Note of disclosure	
Sales and other revenue	AASB 118
Amortisation of intangibles	AASB 101
Depreciation of assets	AASB 116
Impairment of assets	AASB 101 and 116
Employee entitlements	AASB 101 and 119
Income tax expense	AASB 112
Finance expense	AASB 132

Profit (loss) on sale of property, plant and equipment	AASB 101
Profit (loss) on sale of investments	AASB 101
Legal and litigation costs	AASB 101
Lease rental expenses	AASB 117
Profit (loss) on asset disposals	AASB 101
Remuneration of auditors	AASB 101
Remuneration of executive officers	AASB 1046
Research and development expenses	AASB 138

Question 7.1

From the following list of accounts, specify if they need to be disclosed in the company income statement and if so state the relevant accounting standard.

- Advertising
- Bad and doubtful debts
- Wages
- Interest expense
- Discount expense
- Commission received
- Sales
- Delivery expenses
- Annual leave expense
- Rates
- Depreciation expense
- Impairment loss – Goodwill
- Selling expenses
- Audit fees
- Directors' fees
- Debt collection expenses
- Cost of goods sold expenses
- Research and development expenses
- Long service leave expense
- Impairment loss – Investments
- Income tax expense
- Interest revenue
- Accountancy fees
- Amortised establishment expenses
- Loss on disposal of non-current assets
- Repair and maintenance expenses
- Profit on sale of non-current assets
- Insurance
- Discount received
- Lease expenses

Question 7.2

From the following profit determination accounts of Bomber Ltd make a list of the accounts that must be disclosed in the company financial statements. (Also show the reason why they must be disclosed.)

Trading

Date	Particulars	Debit	Credit	Balance
2007		$	$	$
30 June	Sales		5 000 000	5 000 000 Cr
	Stock 30 June 2007		1 000 000	6 000 000 Cr
	Stock 1 July 2006	500 000		5 500 000 Cr
	Buying expenses	200 000		5 300 000 Cr
	Insurance of stock	15 000		5 285 000 Cr
	Customs duty and wharfage	215 000		5 070 000 Cr
	Purchases	2 070 000		3 000 000 Cr
	Profit and loss	3 000 000		Nil

Profit and loss

Date	Particulars	Debit	Credit	Balance
2007		$	$	$
30 June	Trading – Gross profit		3 000 000	3 000 000 Cr
	Dividend received		400 000	3 400 000 Cr
	Profit on sale of land		675 000	4 075 000 Cr
	Discount received		16 000	4 091 000 Cr
	Delivery expenses	125 000		3 966 000 Cr
	Loss on asset disposal	100 000		3 866 000 Cr
	Wages and salaries	642 000		3 224 000 Cr
	Printing and stationery	5 000		3 219000 Cr
	Insurance	46 000		3 173 000 Cr
	Interest expense	281 000		2 892 000 Cr
	Bad and doubtful debts	314 000		2 578 000 Cr
	Rental of equipment	5 000		2 573 000 Cr
	Employee entitlements	10 000		2 563 000 Cr
	Repairs and maintenance	20 000		2 543 000 Cr
	Discount allowed	15 000		2 528 000 Cr
	Audit fees	50 000		2 478 000 Cr
	Accountancy fees	40 000		2 438 000 Cr
	Directors' emoluments	486 000		1 952 000 Cr
	Depreciation	330 000		1 622 000 Cr
	Amortisation – Patents	7 000		1 615 000 Cr
	Impairment loss – Goodwill	50 000		1 565 000 Cr
	Power and heating	14 000		1 551 000 Cr
	Telephone	1 000		1 550 000 Cr
	Rates and taxes	100 000		1 450 000 Cr
	Income tax expense	337 500		1 112 500 Cr
	Retained profits	1 112 500		Nil

Retained profits

Date	Particulars	Debit	Credit	Balance
2006		$	$	$
1 July	Balance		200 000	200 000 Cr
2007				
30 June	Profit and loss		1 112 500	1 312 500 Cr
	Interim dividend	360 000		952 500 Cr
	General reserve	50 000		902 500 Cr
	Final dividend	540 000		362 500 Cr

Reconciliation of income tax

AASB 112: Income Taxes requires the disclosure of how the income tax expense recorded in the income statement reconciles to the income tax on the pre-tax net profit. The pre-tax net profit refers to the profit before tax figure reported in the profit and loss account – that is, after the inclusion of all revenue and expense items.

Where permanent differences have been recorded in the calculation of the profit before tax figure – that is, the pre-tax net profit – the resulting income tax expense calculation will not be based on the pre-tax net profit but instead on the accounting profit – that is, the profit before income tax adjusted for permanent differences. Thus, the reconciliation of income tax requires the disclosure of how the taxation calculation was affected by permanent differences.

ILLUSTRATION

Ark Ltd, for the year ended 30 June 2007, recorded a profit before tax of $100 000. This included the following permanent differences:
- *As expenses:* Impairment loss – Goodwill $20 000
- *As revenues:* Profit on land sale $30 000

The tax rate is 30%.

The pre-tax net profit is $100 000 (that is, inclusive of the permanent differences). If income tax was calculated on this figure, income tax expense would be $30 000.

If the income tax calculation is based on the pre-tax net profit figure this would mean that the resulting income tax expense calculation includes the tax deduction of $6 000 for the $20 000 goodwill impairment loss and that the $30 000 profit on land sale attracted $9 000 income tax.

However, as income tax expense is calculated on the profit adjusted for permanent differences, the income tax expense calculation would be as follows:

	$
Profit before income tax	100 000
add (subtract) Adjustments for permanent differences	
Amortisation of goodwill	20 000
Profit on land sale	(30 000)
Accounting profit	**90 000**
Multiplied by the tax rate	× .30
Income tax expense	**27 000**

The required reconciliation note could reconcile the differences in tax calculations as follows:

	$
Income tax on pre-tax net profit	30 000
add (subtract) Tax effect of permanent differences	
Amortisation of goodwill	6 000
Profit on land sale	(9 000)
Income tax expense	**27 000**

Question 7.3

In question 7.2 the company recorded a profit before income tax of $1 450 000 on which income tax expense of $337 500 was reported. This included the following permanent differences:

	$
Profit on sale of land	675 000
Impairment loss – Goodwill	50 000
Depreciation on land and buildings	300 000

The tax rate is 30%.
You are required to reconcile income tax in accordance with the accounting standard.

Completing an income statement

Langhorne Traders Ltd has provided the following accounts. They will be used to illustrate the completion of an income statement and disclosure notes.

ILLUSTRATION

The trading, profit and loss, and retained profits accounts for the year are as follows:

Trading

Date	Particulars	Debit	Credit	Balance
		$	$	$
2007 30 June	Sales		5 000 000	5 000 000 Cr
	Cost of sales	2 000 000		3 000 000 Cr
	Profit and loss	3 000 000		Nil

Profit and loss

Date	Particulars	Debit	Credit	Balance
		$	$	$
2007 30 June	Trading – Gross profit		3 000 000	3 000 000 Cr
	Dividend received		400 000	3 400 000 Cr
	Profit on sale of land		675 000	4 075 000 Cr
	Discount received		16 000	4 091 000 Cr
	Delivery expenses	125 000		3 966 000 Cr
	Loss on asset disposal	100 000		3 866 000 Cr
	Wages and salaries	642 000		3 224 000 Cr
	Printing and stationery	5 000		3 219 000 Cr
	Insurance	46 000		3 173 000 Cr
	Interest expense	281 000		2 892 000 Cr
	Bad and doubtful debts	314 000		2 578 000 Cr
	Rental of equipment	5 000		2 573 000 Cr
	Employee entitlements	10 000		2 563 000 Cr
	Repairs and maintenance	20 000		2 543 000 Cr
	Discount allowed	15 000		2 528 000 Cr
	Audit fees	50 000		2 478 000 Cr
	Accountancy fees	40 000		2 438 000 Cr
	Directors' remuneration	486 000		1 952 000 Cr
	Depreciation	330 000		1 622 000 Cr
	Amortisation – Patents	7 000		1 615 000 Cr
	Impairment loss – Goodwill	50 000		1 565 000 Cr
	Power and heating	14 000		1 551 000 Cr
	Telephone	1 000		1 550 000 Cr
	Rates and taxes	100 000		1 450 000 Cr
	Income tax expense	337 500		1 112 500 Cr
	Retained profits	1 112 500		Nil

Retained profits

Date	Particulars	Debit	Credit	Balance
2006		$	$	$
1 July	Balance		200 000	200 000 Cr
2007				
30 June	Profit and loss		1 112 500	1 312 500 Cr
	General reserve	50 000		1 262 500 Cr
	Interim dividend	360 000		952 500 Cr
	Final dividend	540 000		362 500 Cr

Determine items for disclosure

1 Analyse the accounts and identify the items that must be disclosed in the notes to the report. These items are:

	$
Revenues	
Sales	5 000 000
Dividends received	400 000
Profit on sale of land	675 000
Other revenues	16 000
Expenses	
Cost of sales (considered material)	2 000 000
Loss on asset disposal	100 000
Interest	281 000
Bad and doubtful debts (considered material)	314 000
Rental of equipment	5 000
Employee entitlements	10 000
Depreciations	330 000
Amortisation – Patents	7 000
Impairment loss – Goodwill	50 000
Income tax expense	337 500
Remuneration of auditors	50 000
Remuneration of directors	486 000
Other expenses	1 008 000

2 **a** Calculate total revenue shown in the profit and loss account. This includes:

	$
Sales	5 000 000
Dividends received	400 000
Profit on sale of land	675 000
Other revenue	16 000
Total revenues	**6 091 000**

b Calculate total expenses (excluding interest costs and income tax expense). This can be calculated as follows:

	$	$
Total revenue	6 091 000	
less Profit (after tax)	1 112 500	
Total expenses		4 978 500
less: Interest expense	281 000	
Income tax expense	337 500	618 500
Total expenses		**4 360 000**

3 Identify and calculate the pre-tax net profit, permanent differences and the tax effect of each at the tax rate of 30%

	Gross $	Tax effect $
Pre-tax net profit	1 450 000	435 000
Permanent differences:		
Revenue item: Profit on sale of land	675 000	202 500
Expense items:		
Depreciation on land and buildings	300 000	90 000
Impairment loss – Goodwill	50 000	15 000

Preparing the income statement and disclosure notes

1 Prepare the statement.

Langhorne Traders Ltd
Income statement for the year ended 30 June 2007

	Note	$
Revenues	1	6 091 000
less Expenses (excluding finance costs)	1,2	4 360 000
less Finance costs		281 000
Profit (loss) before income tax expense		1 450 000
less Income tax expense	3	337 500
Net profit (loss)		**1 112 500**

2   Prepare the disclosure notes.

   Notes to the financial report

   Note 1 Profit before income tax includes the following:

	$
Revenues	
Sales	5 000 000
Dividends received	400 000
Profit on sale of land	675 000
Other	16 000
Expenses	
Cost of sales	2 000 000
Loss on asset disposal	100 000
Bad and doubtful debts	314 000
Lease rental	5 000
Employee entitlements	10 000
Depreciations	330 000
Amortisation – Patents	7 000
Impairment loss – Goodwill	50 000
Remuneration of auditors	50 000
Other expenses	1 008 000
Note 2 Remuneration of directors	$486 000
Note 3 Income tax expense	
Income tax on pre-tax net profit	435 000
add (subtract) Tax effect of permanent differences	
Depreciation on land and buildings	90 000
Impairment loss – Goodwill	15 000
Profit on sale of land	(202 500)
Income tax on operating profit	337 500

Question 7.4

The following information relates to Melbourne Ltd. You are required to prepare an income statement for the year ended 30 June 2007 in accordance with the accounting standards.

Trading

Date	Particulars	Debit	Credit	Balance
2007		$	$	$
30 June	Sales		890 000	890 000 Cr
	Cost of sales	594 500		295 500 Cr
	Profit and loss	295 500		Nil

Profit and loss

Date	Particulars	Debit	Credit	Balance
2007		$	$	$
30 June	Gross profit – Trading		295 500	295 500 Cr
	Profit on sale of land		10 000	305 500 Cr
	Debenture interest		4 000	309 500 Cr
	Audit fees	3 100		306 400 Cr
	Interest on overdraft	1 500		304 900 Cr
	Directors' remunerations	20 000		284 900 Cr
	Accountancy fees	5 000		279 900 Cr
	Insurance	1 900		278 000 Cr
	Salaries	50 600		227 400 Cr
	Bad and doubtful debts	33 400		194 000 Cr
	Repairs and maintenance	7 000		187 000 Cr
	General expenses	1 000		186 000 Cr
	Lease expenses	9 500		176 500 Cr
	Depreciations	10 500		166 000 Cr
	Impairment loss – Goodwill	8 500		157 500 Cr
	Income tax expense	46 800		110 700 Cr
	Retained profits	110 700		Nil

Retained profits

Date	Particulars	Debit	Credit	Balance
2006		$	$	$
1 July	Balance		50 000	50 000 Cr
2007				
30 June	Profit and loss		110 700	160 700 Cr
	Dividend reserve		10 000	170 700 Cr
	General reserve	20 000		150 700 Cr
	Interim dividend	75 000		75 700 Cr
	Final dividend	50 000		25 700 Cr
	Transaction costs	5 700		20 000 Cr

Additional information

- The calculation of income tax is made at a rate of 30% after recognising the following permanent differences:
  - profit on sale of land; and
  - impairment loss – goodwill.
- The directors have deemed that cost of sales and bad and doubtful debts are material amounts and should be disclosed.

The statement of changes in equity

AASB 101: Presentation of Financial Statements requires reporting entities to issue a statement of changes in equity when presenting the financial statements. The accounting standard provides an illustration, which is recommended, unless an alternative presentation provides more information. The format of the statement in changes in equity adopted for use in this text is as follows:

Statement of changes in equity for the year ended…		
	$	$
Share capital		
Balance at start of period	XX	
Share capital issued	XX	
Total share capital		XX
Reserves		
Asset revaluation reserve		
Balance at start of period	XX	
Asset revaluation changes	XX	
Balance at end of period	XX	
Revenue reserves[1]		
Balance at start of period	XX	
Transfers to/from retained profits	XX	
Balance at end of period	XX	
Total reserves		XX
Retained profits		
Balance at start of period	XX	
Profit for the period	XX	
Transfers from reserves	XX	
Total for appropriation		
Transfers to reserves	(XX)	
Dividends (interim and final)	(XX)	
Share issue costs	(XX)	
Balance at end of period		XX
Total shareholders' equity		XX

The intention of the statement of changes in equity is to disclose how the amount comprising shareholders' equity changed between the beginning and end of a reporting period. Consequently, it is necessary to know the balances of equity accounts at the start of each period.

In addition to preparing a statement of changes in equity, the accounting standard requires a disclosure note to be included in the accounts stating the dividends that were brought to account during the year. This includes dividends paid during the year (interim dividends) and dividends proposed at the end of the year that did not require shareholder ratification.

ILLUSTRATION

In the previous illustration showing the preparation of an income statement for Langhorne Traders Ltd the company reported a net profit for the year ended 30 June 2007 of $1 112 500.

For the purposes of completing the statement of changes in equity the following information is also provided:

Account balances at 1 July 2006:	$
Share capital	500 000
Asset revaluation reserve	120 000
General reserve	10 000
Dividend reserve	30 000
Retained profits	200 000

Additional information:

- The company issued 300 000 shares at $2 each during the year.
- Land and buildings were revalued upwards during the year by $250 000.
- The retained profits account used in the previous illustration was as follows:

Retained profits

Date	Particulars	Debit	Credit	Balance
		$	$	$
2006				
1 July	Balance		200 000	200 000 Cr
2007				
30 June	Profit and loss		1 112 500	1 312 500 Cr
	General reserve	50 000		1 262 500 Cr
	Interim dividend	360 000		952 500 Cr
	Final dividend	540 000		362 500 Cr

The completed statement of changes in equity arising from this information would be as follows:

Langhorne Traders Ltd
Statement of changes in equity for the year ended 30 June 2007

	Note	$	$
Share capital			
Balance at start of period		500 000	
Share capital issued		600 000	
Total share capital			1 100 000
Reserves			
Asset revaluation reserve			
Balance at start of period		120 000	
Asset revaluation changes		250 000	
Balance at end of period		370 000	
Revenue reserves			
Balance at start of period		40 000	
Transfers to/from retained profits		50 000	
Balance at end of period		90 000	
Total reserves			460 000
Retained profits			
Balance at start of period		200 000	
Profit for the period		1 112 500	
Transfers from reserves		0	
Total for appropriation		1 312 500	
Transfers to reserves		(50 000)	
Dividends	4	900 000	
Balance at end of period			362 500
Total shareholders' equity			1 922 500

Note disclosure
Note 4: Dividends:
- During the year an interim dividend was made totalling $360 000.
- A final dividend was declared at the end of the year amounting to $540 000.

Question 7.5

In question 7.4, you prepared the income statement for Melbourne Ltd. Using the information in question 7.4 and the additional information that follows you are required to prepare the statement of changes in equity for the year ended 30 June 2007.

Account balances at 1 July 2006	$
Share capital	50 000
Asset revaluation reserve	100 000
Dividend reserve	40 000

Additional information

- The company issued 200 000 shares at $1 each during the year.
- Property, plant and equipment was increased from its cost price of $300 000 to $500 000 during the year.

Question 7.6

The following information relates to Watervale Ltd. You are required to prepare the following statements for the year ended 30 June 2007 in accordance with the accounting standards:
a   an income statement; and
b   a statement of changes in equity.

Date	Particulars	Debit	Credit	Balance
	Trading			
2007		$	$	$
30 June	Sales		1 510 000	1 510 000 Cr
	Cost of goods sold	510 000		1 000 000 Cr
	Profit and loss	1 000 000		Nil

Profit and loss

		$	$	$
2007 30 June	Trading – Gross profit		1 000 000	1 000 000 Cr
	Interest – Bank deposits		12 000	1 012 000 Cr
	Profit – Sale of Clare Store		320 000	1 332 000 Cr
	Rent revenue		3 000	1 335 000 Cr
	Interest – Loan	18 200		1 316 800 Cr
	Depreciation – Furniture	15 000		1 301 800 Cr
	Donations	10 000		1 291 800 Cr
	Bad debts	59 600		1 232 200 Cr
	Entertainment expenses	80 000		1 152 200 Cr
	Wages	370 000		782 200 Cr
	Directors' emoluments	100 000		682 200 Cr
	Audit fees	23 000		659 200 Cr
	Accountancy fees	56 200		3 603 000 Cr
	Long service leave	5 000		598 000 Cr
	Insurance	25 000		573 000 Cr
	Rates and taxes	3 000		570 000 Cr
	Delivery expenses	31 000		539 000 Cr
	Loss on equipment sale	25 000		514 000 Cr
	Impairment loss – Goodwill	10 000		504 000 Cr
	Impairment loss – Investments	154 000		350 000 Cr
	Income tax expense	82 200		267 800 Cr
	Retained profits	267 800		Nil

Retained profits

		$	$	$
2006 1 July	Balance		10 000	10 000 Cr
2007 30 June	Profit and loss		267 800	277 800 Cr
	General reserve	60 000		217 800 Cr
	Transaction costs	5 000		212 800 Cr
	Interim dividend	30 000		182 800 Cr
	Final dividend	40 000		142 800 Cr

Additional information

- Income tax is to be applied at 30%. Permanent differences are the profit on sale of Clare Store, impairment losses for goodwill and investments, and entertainment expenses.
- The company issued 200 000 shares at $1 each during the year.
- Property, plant and equipment was increased from its cost price of $300 000 to $500 000 during the year.
- Bad debts, donations, entertainment expenses and cost of sales are considered material amounts.

Account balances at 1 July 2006	$
Share capital	50 000
Asset revaluation reserve	100 000
General reserve	40 000

Question 7.7

The following information relates to Coonawarra Trading Company Ltd. You are required to prepare:
a an income statement; and
b a statement of changes in equity
for the year ended 30 June 2007 in accordance with the accounting standards.

Date	Particulars	Debit	Credit	Balance
	Profit and loss			
		$	$	$
2007 30 June	Trading		343 500	343 500 Cr
	Dividends received		20 000	363 500 Cr
	Wages and salaries	20 000		343 500 Cr
	Loss on sale of premises	40 000		303 500 Cr
	Bad debts	20 000		283 500 Cr
	Accountancy fees	8 500		275 000 Cr
	Rates	4 000		271 000 Cr
	Long service leave	5 000		266 000 Cr
	Audit fees	3 000		263 000 Cr
	Amortisation – Premises	10 000		253 000 Cr
	Depreciation	9 000		244 000 Cr
	Interest	12 000		232 000 Cr
	Directors' remunerations	32 000		200 000 Cr
	Impairment loss – Goodwill	10 000		190 000 Cr
	Income tax expense	60 000		130 000 Cr
	Retained profits	130 000		Nil
	Retained profits			
2007 1 July	Balance		25 000	25 000 Cr
30 June	Profit and loss		130 000	155 000 Cr
	Sundry reserve		15 000	170 000 Cr
	Interim dividend	12 000		158 000 Cr
	Final dividend	20 000		138 000 Cr
	Transaction costs	5 000		133 000 Cr

Additional information

- Income tax was applied at 30%. Impaired goodwill was classified as a permanent difference.
- Bad debts and cost of sales are considered material.
- Sales revenue was $5 000 000.

Account balances at 1 July 2006	$
Share capital	100 000
Asset revaluation reserve	20 000
Sundry reserve	65 000

- The company issued 50 000 shares at $5 each during the year.
- Plant was increased from its cost price of $200 000 to $300 000 during the year.

Question 7.8

The following information relates to Sparkle Ltd. You are required to:
a complete the profit and loss account for the year ended 30 June 2007;
b prepare the retained profits account from 1 July 2006 to 30 June 2007;
c prepare an income statement for the year ended 30 June 2007 that complies with accounting standards; and
d prepare a statement of changes in equity for the year ended 30 June 2007 that complies with accounting standards.

Account balances at 1 July 2006 (Extract)

Account	$
Assets	
Establishment costs	20 000
Freehold land and buildings (revalued 2005)	490 000
Goodwill	40 000
Investments	50 000
Shareholders' equity	
Share capital – $1 ordinary shares	200 000
Asset revaluation reserve	200 000
General reserve	60 000
Retained profits	20 000

Date	Particulars	Debit	Credit	Balance
		Trading		
2007		$	$	$
30 June	Sales		1 750 000	1 750 000 Cr
	Cost of sales	1 371 300		378 700 Cr
	Profit and loss		378 700	Nil

Profit and loss (before adjustments)

2007		$	$	$
30 June	Trading		378 700	378 700 Cr
	Interest received		8 100	386 800 Cr
	Profit on sale of land		43 000	429 800 Cr
	Condemnation of warehouse	60 000		369 800 Cr
	Advertising and insurance	18 000		351 800 Cr
	Depreciations	14 000		337 800 Cr
	Rates and taxes	7 000		330 800 Cr
	Bad debts	25 000		305 800 Cr
	Auditors' fees	12 000		293 800 Cr
	Salaries	70 000		223 800 Cr
	Directors' fees	40 000		183 800 Cr
	Administration expenses	5 000		178 800 Cr
	Lease payments	12 000		166 800 Cr
	Interest expenses	17 800		149 000 Cr
	Vehicle expenses	28 000		121 000 Cr
	Office rent	15 000		106 000 Cr
	Office expenses	6 000		100 000 Cr
	Employee benefits	26 000		74 000 Cr
	Income tax expense (before adjustment)	12 000		62 000 Cr

Additional information and directors' recommendations

Adjustments to profit and loss
- Write $5 000 off establishment costs.
- Impair the full balance of goodwill.
- Revalue the investments at their recoverable amount of $30 000.
- Provide for income tax expense at 30%. Permanent differences are impaired goodwill, profit on sale of land, amortised establishment costs and impaired investments.

Adjustments to retained profits
- General reserve to be reduced by $20 000.
- Create a dividend equalisation reserve of $5 000.
- An interim dividend of $12 000 on share capital was paid on 1 December 2006.
- Establish a final dividend of $0.05 per share on issued shares at 30 June 2007. This is not subject to shareholder approval.
- Transaction costs of $1 700 to be accounted for.

Other adjustments and information
- Freehold land and buildings are to be revalued at 30 June 2007 at $600 000.
- The company issued 100 000 shares on 1 May 2007 at $1 each.
- Bad debts and cost of sales are considered material.

The balance sheet

AASB 101: Preparation of Financial Statements makes specific requirements of the presentation and disclosure of a balance sheet. The accounting standard requires reporting entities to disclose current and non-current assets and liabilities on the face value of the balance sheet.

The standard defines current assets and liabilities and non-current assets and liabilities as set out below.

Current assets

AASB 101: Presentation of Financial Statements, clause 57 states:

> An asset shall be classified as current when it satisfies any of the following criteria:
>
> a   it is expected to be realised in, or is intended for sale or consumption in, the entity's normal operating cycle;
> b   it is held primarily for the purpose of being traded;
> c   it is expected to be realised within twelve months after the reporting date; or
> d   it is cash or a cash equivalent.
>
> All other assets shall be classified as non-current.

Current liabilities

AASB 101: Presentation of Financial Statements, clause 60 states:

> A liability shall be classified as current when it satisfies any of the following criteria:
>
> a   it is expected to be settled in the entity's normal operating cycle;
> b   it is held primarily for the purpose of being traded;
> c   it is due to be settled within twelve months after the reporting date; or
> d   the entity does not have an unconditional right to defer settlement of the liability for at least twelve months after the reporting date.
>
> All other liabilities shall be classified as non-current.

The accounting standard specifies that the face of the balance sheet should include at least the following:
- Assets:
  - Cash and cash equivalents
  - Trade and other receivables
  - Inventories
  - Investment property
  - Property, plant and equipment
  - Intangible assets
  - Financial assets
  - Investments
  - Biological assets
  - Deferred tax assets
- Liabilities:
  - Financial liabilities
  - Trade and other payables
  - Provisions
  - Liabilities for current tax
  - Deferred tax liabilities
- Shareholders' equity:
  - Issued capital

- Reserves
- Retained profits

AASB 101 provides an example of a balance sheet that complies with the requirements of the accounting standard. This example is as follows:

Balance sheet as at

Assets
Current assets
- Cash and cash equivalents
- Trade receivables
- Inventories
- Other current assets
- Total current assets

Non-current assets
- Available-for-sale investments
- Other financial assets
- Deferred tax assets
- Property, plant and equipment
- Goodwill
- Other intangible assets
- Other non-current assets
- Total non-current assets

Total assets

Liabilities
Current liabilities
- Trade and other payables
- Short-term borrowings
- Current tax payable
- Short-term provisions
- Current portion of long-term borrowings
- Other current liabilities
- Total current liabilities

Non-current liabilities
- Long-term borrowings
- Deferred tax liabilities
- Long-term provisions
- Other non-current liabilities
- Total non-current liabilities

Total liabilities

Net assets

Equity
- Share capital
- Reserves
- Retained profits

Total equity

Reporting and disclosure of assets

When classifying, presenting and disclosing assets to comply with AASB 101: Presentation of Financial Statements the following examples may prove useful.

Current assets	
Cash and cash equivalents	Cash at bank, petty cash, cash in registers, cash on hand and deposits at call and short-term deposits
Trade receivables	Debtors, accounts receivable and allowances (provisions) for doubtful debts
Inventories	Stocks of finished goods, raw materials, work in progress
Other current assets	Prepaid expenses, accrued revenues
Non-current assets	
Available-for-sale investments	Short-term investments in shares and other assets purchased with the intention of selling the asset
Other financial assets	Long-term investments, such as shares in other companies, bonds and securities, long-term deposits
Deferred tax assets	Arising from differences in the calculation of income tax expense and income tax payable
Property, plant and equipment	Representing land and buildings, vehicles, machinery and equipment, and other income-generating assets, less any accumulations (provisions) for depreciation
Goodwill	Goodwill purchased during a business combination
Other intangible assets	Patents, franchises and copyrights less any accumulated amortisations of these assets

Notes of disclosure would support the detail of each category of asset included within the report.

In relation to property, plant and equipment, AASB 116: Property, Plant and Equipment also requires the following information to be disclosed:

a the measurement bases used for determining the gross carrying amount;
b the depreciation methods used;
c the useful lives or the depreciation rates used;
d the gross carrying amount and the accumulated depreciation (aggregated with accumulated impairment losses) at the beginning and end of the period; and
e a reconciliation of the carrying amount at the beginning and end of the period showing:
   i additions;
   ii assets classified as held for sale or included in a disposal group classified as held for sale in accordance with AASB 5 and other disposals;
   iii acquisitions through business combinations;
   iv increases or decreases resulting from revaluations;
   v impairment losses recognised in profit or loss;
   vi impairment losses reversed in profit or loss; and
   vii depreciation.

ILLUSTRATION

The trial balance of Barton Ltd for the year ended 30 June 2007 included the following assets:

Trial balance as at 30 June 2007

Account	Debit	Credit
	$	$
Accrued revenues	10 000	
Equipment	120 000	
Accumulated depreciation – Equipment		72 000
Franchise	200 000	
Cash at bank	15 000	
Cash on hand	2 000	
Debtors	50 000	
Allowance for doubtful debts		2 500
Deposits at call	100 000	
Deferred tax assets	6 000	
Goodwill	25 000	
Government bonds (due 1 December 2007)	30 000	
Land and buildings (independent valuation)	200 000	
Motor vehicles	80 000	
Accumulated depreciation – Motor vehicles		48 000
Patents	100 000	
Petty cash	1 000	
Prepaid expenses	3 500	
Investment in shares in Gold Ltd (held for resale)	60 000	
Accumulated impairment losses – Shares in Gold Ltd		6 000
Stock of finished goods	35 000	
Stock of materials	40 000	

Additional information

Land and buildings were revalued upwards on 1 May as per an independent valuer's valuation (Right Estate Agency).

The balance sheet prepared from these accounts to conform to AASB 101 could be presented as follows:

Barton Ltd
Balance sheet as at 30 June 2007

Assets	Note	$	$
Current assets			
Cash	5	118 000	
Trade receivables	6	47 500	
Inventories	7	75 000	
Other	8	13 500	
Total current assets			254 000
Non-current assets			
Available for sale investments	9	54 000	
Other financial assets	10	30 000	
Deferred tax assets	11	6 000	
Property, plant and equipment	12	280 000	
Goodwill	13	25 000	
Other intangibles	14	300 000	
Total non-current assets			695 000
Total assets			**949 000**

Notes to and forming part of the accounts

			$	$
5	Cash			
	Cash at bank		15 000	
	Cash on hand		2 000	
	Petty cash		1 000	
	Deposits at call		100 000	118 000
6	Trade receivables			
	Debtors		50 000	
	Allowance for doubtful debts		2 500	47 500
7	Inventories			
	Stock of finished goods		35 000	
	Stock of materials		40 000	75 000
8	Other			
	Accrued revenues		10 000	
	Prepaid expenses		3 500	13 500
9	Available for sale investments			
	Shares in Gold Ltd		60 000	
	Accumulated impairment loss in investments		6 000	54 000
10	Other financial assets			
	Government bonds (due 1 December 2007)			30 000
11	Deferred tax assets			6 000

12	Property, plant and equipment		
	Equipment	120 000	
	Accumulated depreciation – Equipment	72 000	48 000
	Motor vehicles	80 000	
	Accumulated depreciation – Motor vehicles	48 000	32 000
	Land and buildings (independent valuation)		200 000
			280 000

Land and buildings were revalued upwards on 1 May by Right Estate Agency in line with market prices. It is intended to review the valuation of land and buildings annually.

13	Goodwill		25 000
14	Intangibles		
	Franchise	200 000	
	Patents	100 000	300 000

Question 7.9

From the following extract of the trial balance of Asean Ltd for the year ended 30 June 2007 you are required to prepare a balance sheet and disclosure notes that conform to the requirements of AASB 101.

Trial balance as at 30 June 2007 (Extract)

Account	Debit	Credit
	$	$
Accounts receivable	65 000	
Allowance for doubtful debts		1 000
Furniture and equipment	400 000	
Accumulated depreciation – Furniture and equipment		72 000
Machinery	120 000	
Accumulated depreciation – Machinery		19 200
Cash at bank	30 000	
Cash in registers	5 000	
Deposits at call	20 000	
Deferred tax asset	10 500	
Goodwill	9 500	
Investment shares in Laker Ltd	90 000	
Accumulated impairment loss – Shares in Laker Ltd		1 200
Land and buildings (directors' valuation)	500 000	
Petty cash	500	
Prepaid wages	1 800	
Stock on hand	12 000	
Term investment (maturing in nine months)	20 000	

Additional information
- Land and buildings were revalued upwards on 10 December by the directors.
- The investment shares in Laker Ltd were purchased with the intention of obtaining a gain in the short term.

Reporting and disclosure of liabilities

When classifying, presenting and disclosing liabilities to comply with AASB 101: Presentation of Financial Statements the following examples may prove useful.

Current liabilities	
Trade and other payables	Creditors, accounts payable
Short-term borrowings	Bank overdrafts and other short-term loans
Current tax payable	Income tax payable, GST payable
Short-term provisions	Provisions for annual leave, long service leave, employee entitlements and dividends payable within 12 months
Current portion of long-term borrowings	Mortgage, long-term debts payable within 12 months
Other current liabilities	Accrued expenses, prepaid revenues
Non-current liabilities	
Long-term borrowings	Mortgage, long-term loans, debentures
Deferred tax liabilities	Arising from differences in the calculation of income tax expense and income tax payable
Long-term provisions	Provisions for long service leave, employee entitlements and dividends payable later than 12 months

Notes of disclosure would support the detail of each category of liability included within the report.

ILLUSTRATION

The following is an extract of the trial balance of Mega Ltd as at 30 June 2007.

Trial balance as at 30 June 2007 (Extract)

Account	Debit	Credit
	$	$
Accrued wages		5 000
Bank loan (unsecured and due in nine months)		25 000
Bank overdraft		15 000
Creditors		8 000
Dividends payable		30 000
Mortgage (secured over buildings)		150 000
Prepaid interest revenue		2 500
Annual leave payable		35 000
Deferred tax liability		3 000
Income tax payable		55 000
Long service leave payable		85 000
GST payable		18 000
Sundry creditors		1 000
Term loan (unsecured and due in five years)		20 000

Additional information
- It is company policy that annual leave is taken within 12 months of accrual.
- Ten per cent of the long service leave is due within the next 12 months.
- The mortgage is being paid over 10 years in equal instalments.

The balance sheet prepared from these accounts to conform to AASB 101 could be presented as follows:

Mega Ltd
Balance sheet as at 30 June 2007

Liabilities	Note	$	$
Current liabilities			
Trade payables	15	9 000	
Short-term borrowings	16	40 000	
Current tax payable	17	73 000	
Short-term provisions	18	73 500	
Current portion of long-term borrowings	19	15 000	
Other	20	7 500	
Total current liabilities			218 000
Non-current liabilities			
Long-term borrowings	21	155 000	
Deferred tax liabilities	22	3 000	
Long-term provisions	23	76 500	
Total non-current liabilities			234 500
Total liabilities			**452 500**

Notes to and forming part of the accounts

			$	$
15	Trade payables			
	Creditors		8 000	
	Sundry creditors		1 000	
				9 000
16	Borrowings			
	Bank overdraft		15 000	
	Bank loan (unsecured and due in nine months)		25 000	
				40 000
17	Current tax payable			
	GST payable		18 000	
	Income tax payable		55 000	
				73 000
18	Short-term provisions			
	Dividends payable		30 000	
	Annual leave payable		35 000	
	Long service leave payable		8 500	
				73 500

19	Current portion of long-term borrowings		
	Mortgage (secured over buildings)		15 000
20	Other		
	Accrued wages	5 000	
	Prepaid interest revenue	2 500	7 500
21	Long-term borrowings		
	Mortgage (secured over buildings)	135 000	
	Term loan (unsecured and due in five years)	20 000	155 000
22	Deferred tax liabilities		3 000
23	Long-term provisions		
	Long service leave payable		76 500

Reporting and disclosure of equity

AASB 101 requires shareholders' equity to be classified and reported as follows:

Equity	
Share capital	Issued capital
	Less calls in arrears.
	Note: AASB 101 requires each class of share to be disclosed separately and that the number and issue price of all shares be disclosed
Reserves	Reserves include: • revenue reserves: general reserve, dividend reserve, etc. • capital reserves: asset revaluation reserve
Retained profits	Represented by the closing balance of retained profits

ILLUSTRATION

The shareholders' equity accounts of Casey Ltd as at 30 June 2007 are shown in the trial balance extract below.

Trial balance as at 30 June 2007 (Extract)

Account	Debit	Credit
	$	$
Asset revaluation reserve		250 000
Calls in arrears – Ordinary shares	2 500	
Dividend reserve		15 000
General reserve		5 000
Share capital – Ordinary shares		100 000
Share capital – Preference shares		100 000
Retained profits		120 000

Additional information
- Share capital consists of:
  - 100 000 ordinary shares; and
  - 50 000 preference shares.
- During the year the company issued 20 000 ordinary shares.
- A call was made on ordinary shares during the year with the holders of 5 000 shares failing to meet the call.
- During the year, assets were revalued upwards by $100 000.

The balance sheet prepared from these accounts to conform with AASB 1040 could be presented as follows:

Casey Ltd
Balance sheet as at 30 June 2007

	Note	$	$
Equity			
Share capital	24	197 500	
Reserves	25	270 000	
Retained profits		120 000	
Total equity			587 500

Notes to and forming part of the accounts

		$	$
24	**Share capital**		
	Ordinary shares issued total (100 000 at $1)	100 000	
	(20 000 ordinary shares were issued in the year)		
	Preference shares total (50 000 at $2)	100 000	
			200 000
	Calls in arrears (5 000 ordinary shares at $0.50)		2 500
			197 500
25	**Reserves**		
	Revenue reserves		
	Dividend reserve	15 000	
	General reserve	5 000	20 000
	Capital reserve		
	Asset revaluation reserve		250 000
			270 000

Question 7.10

From the following trial balance extract of Hope Ltd you are required to prepare a balance sheet and disclosure notes that would meet the requirements of AASB 101.

Trial balance as at 30 June 2007

Account	Debit	Credit
	$	$
Accounts payable		10 000
Accrued expenses		15 000
Asset revaluation reserve		300 000
Bank loan (unsecured and due in six months)		20 000
Bank overdraft		5 000
Calls in arrears	5 000	
Dividends payable		40 000
General reserve		15 000
Mortgage (secured over plant)		130 000
Share capital – Ordinary shares		200 000
Share capital – Preference shares		100 000
Prepaid interest revenue		3 000
Annual leave payable		12 000
Deferred tax liability		5 500
Income tax payable		28 000
Long service leave payable		80 000
Retained profits		33 000
GST payable		2 500
Stock replacement reserve		25 000
Term loan (unsecured and due in 2011)		25 000

Additional information
- Total assets amount to $1 044 000.
- It is company policy that annual leave is taken within 12 months of accrual. Half of the long service leave is due within the next 12 months.
- The mortgage is being paid over 20 years in equal instalments.
- Share capital consists of 200 000 ordinary shares and 50 000 preference shares. During the year the company issued 20 000 ordinary shares.
- A call was made on ordinary shares during the year with the holders of 10 000 shares failing to meet the call.

Question 7.11

Glen Ltd has prepared its 30 June 2007 balance sheet for internal purposes. You are required to present the statement so as to meet the requirements of the accounting standards.

Glen Ltd
Balance sheet as at 30 June 2007

	$	$	$
Current assets			
Cash in hand		12 000	
Cash at bank		30 000	
Trade debtors	150 000		
less Allowance for doubtful debts	5 000	145 000	
Stock at cost		380 000	
Deferred tax asset		7 000	574 000
Current liabilities			
Trade creditors		90 000	
Income tax payable		100 000	
Dividends payable		20 000	
Deferred tax liability		5 000	215 000
Working capital			359 000
Fixed assets			
Land and premises		1 000 000	
Furniture and fittings – At cost	150 000		
less Accumulated depreciation	30 000	120 000	1 120 000
Intangible assets			
Goodwill		70 000	
Trade marks		50 000	120 000
Investments			
Shares in ABC Ltd (long term)	200 000		
less Accumulated impairment loss of shares	150 000	50 000	
Government bonds (due December 2009)		250 000	300 000
			1 899 000
Non-current liabilities			
Loan from unrelated company – Fully secured		260 000	
Long service leave payable		15 000	275 000
Shareholders' equity			
Share capital – 500 000 ordinary shares		500 000	
Reserves and unappropriated profits			
Asset revaluation reserve	385 000		
General reserve	30 000		
Retained profits	709 000	1 124 000	1 624 000
			1 899 000

Question 7.12

From the following trial balance of Tafe Ltd you are required to prepare a balance sheet as at 30 June 2007 which conforms to the accounting standards.

Tafe Ltd
Trial balance as at 30 June 2007

Account	Debit	Credit
	$	$
Share capital – Ordinary shares		500 000
Retained profits		296 000
Bank	969 000	
Dividends payable		64 000
Income tax payable		135 000
Calls in arrears	25 000	
Long service leave payable		230 000
Stock	185 000	
Plant and equipment – At directors' valuation 2006	2 200 000	
Accumulated depreciation – Plant and equipment		980 000
Deposits at call	160 000	
Shares in Langer Ltd	220 000	
Accumulated impairment loss – Shares in Langer Ltd		20 000
Term deposits (maturing in 2009)	180 000	
Deferred tax asset	20 000	
Deferred tax liability		45 000
Debtors	102 000	
Allowance for doubtful debts		12 000
Creditors		78 000
Asset revaluation reserve		1 200 000
General reserve		52 000
Mortgage (maturing in 2014, secured)		460 000
Prepaid expenses	16 000	
Accrued expenses		5 000
	4 077 000	4 077 000

Additional information

- Shares in Langer Ltd were purchased for resale.
- Long service leave of $30 000 falls due in the next 12 months.
- The mortgage will be reduced by $40 000 in the forthcoming period.
- Share capital: 500 000 ordinary shares have been issued and called to $1 each. Calls are outstanding on 125 000 shares at $0.20 each.

Question 7.13

The following information relates to Space Manufacturing Ltd. For the year ended 30 June 2007 you are required to prepare:
a an income statement;
b a statement of changes in equity;
c a balance sheet; and
d appropriate disclosure notes to the accounts.

Trial balance as at 30 June 2007

Account	Debit	Credit
	$	$
Prepaid revenue		300 000
Allowance for doubtful debts		10 000
Share capital – Ordinary shares (at $1 per share)		3 000 000
Bank		300 000
Deposits – At call	250 000	
Asset revaluation reserve		1 400 000
General reserve		80 000
Dividend equalisation reserve		300 000
Stock replacement reserve		500 000
Retained profits		967 000
Dividends payable		210 000
Fully secured debentures – 14% maturing 30 June 2010		100 000
Goodwill	155 000	
Land and buildings – At cost	1 500 000	
Land and buildings – At directors' valuation 30 June 1999	3 000 000	
Mortgage loan		1 000 000
Motor vehicles	100 000	
Accumulated depreciation – Motor vehicles		40 000
Plant and machinery	2 600 000	
Accumulated depreciation – Plant and machinery		1 100 000
Prepaid expenses	160 000	
Long service leave payable		80 000
Shares in Galaxy Ltd	100 000	
Accumulated impairment loss – Shares in Galaxy Ltd		50 000
Stock	1 550 000	
Trade creditors		328 000
Trade debtors	400 000	
Income tax payable		50 000
	9 815 000	9 815 000

Date	Particulars	Debit	Credit	Balance
	Profit and loss			
2007		$	$	$
30 June	Trading		2 693 000	2 693 000 Cr
	Profit on sale of franchise		100 000	2 793 000 Cr
	Profit on sale of factory		20 000	2 813 000 Cr
	Interest on deposits		38 000	2 851 000 Cr
	Dividends from Galaxy Ltd		5 000	2 856 000 Cr
	Lease expense	7 000		2 849 000 Cr
	Wages and salaries	900 000		1 949 000 Cr
	Payroll tax	20 000		1 929 000 Cr
	Other taxes and rates	20 000		1 909 000 Cr
	Advertising	100 000		1 809 000 Cr
	Directors' fees	220 000		1 589 000 Cr
	Auditor's fees	50 000		1 539 000 Cr
	Long service leave	33 000		1 506 000 Cr
	Postage and stationery	30 000		1 476 000 Cr
	Maintenance	50 000		1 426 000 Cr
	Debenture interest	14 000		1 412 000 Cr
	Bad debts	40 000		1 372 000 Cr
	Interest on mortgage loan	18 000		1 354 000 Cr
	Depreciations	424 000		930 000 Cr
	Repairs	40 000		890 000 Cr
	Interest on overdraft	10 000		880 000 Cr
	Insurances	20 000		860 000 Cr
	Impairment loss – Goodwill	25 000		835 000 Cr
	Impairment loss – Investments	50 000		785 000 Cr
	Income tax expense	228 000		557 000 Cr
	Retained profits	557 000		Nil
	Retained profits			
1 July	Balance			800 000 Cr
30 June	Profit and loss		557 000	1 357 000 Cr
	General reserve		20 000	1 377 000 Cr
	Interim dividend	200 000		1 177 000 Cr
	Final dividend	210 000		967 000 Cr

Adjustments

- Land and buildings at cost are to be revalued at their fair value of $1 750 000 as per directors' valuation at 30 June 2007.

Classification requirements

- Sales for the year totalled $10 500 000.
- Income tax is applied at 30%. The following permanent differences exist: Impairment losses of goodwill and in shares in Galaxy Ltd and the profit on the sale of franchise. There are no temporary differences.

- $30 000 will be paid to employees for long service leave during the year ended 30 June 2008.
- Bad debts incurred during the year are larger than normal and considered material.
- The mortgage loan is being repaid at $200 000 per year.
- Shares in Galaxy Ltd have been acquired as a long-term investment.

Question 7.14

The following information relates to Smart Enterprises Ltd. You are required to prepare an income statement, a statement of changes in equity, a balance sheet and suitable disclosure notes in accordance with the accounting standards for the year ended 30 June 2007.

Trial balance as at 30 June 2007

Account	Debit	Credit
	$	$
Share capital – Ordinary shares ($1 each)		7 000 000
Retained profits 30 June 2007		415 000
Dividend reserve		500 000
General reserve		250 000
Asset revaluation reserve		1 430 000
Trade debtors	1 590 000	
Allowance for doubtful debts		150 000
Stock – At cost	2 000 000	
Prepaid expenses	52 000	
Deferred tax asset	204 000	
Shares in Wire Ltd	900 000	
Accumulated impairment loss in shares in Wire Ltd		880 000
Bank		46 000
Prepaid income		16 000
Trade creditors		1 000 000
Accrued expenses		25 000
Mortgage loan – Bank of Upper Gully		900 000
GST payable		50 000
Motor vehicles	600 000	
Accumulated depreciation – Motor vehicles		240 000
Land and buildings – Directors' valuation 30 June 2007	3 000 000	
Land and buildings – At directors' 2006 valuation	4 300 000	
Deferred tax liability		4 000
Equipment	1 300 000	
Accumulated depreciation – Equipment		320 000
Employee benefits payable		300 000
Debentures (15% maturing June 2008)		1 000 000
Debentures (16% maturing June 2009)		2 000 000
Franchises	3 000 000	
Dividends payable		420 000
	16 946 000	16 946 000

Date	Details	Debit $	Credit $	Balance $
	Profit and loss			
30 June	Trading		3 190 000	3 190 000 Cr
	Rent of premises		10 000	3 200 000 Cr
	Bad debts recovered		800 000	4 000 000 Cr
	Profit on sale of store		2 000 000	6 000 000 Cr
	Repairs	60 000		5 940 000 Cr
	Depreciation – Equipment	80 000		5 860 000 Cr
	Plant write-off	500 000		5 360 000 Cr
	Directors' fees	230 000		5 130 000 Cr
	Auditor's fees	100 000		5 030 000 Cr
	Employee benefits	60 000		4 970 000 Cr
	Interest on overdraft	10 000		4 960 000 Cr
	Lease costs	90 000		4 870 000 Cr
	Payroll tax expense	40 000		4 830 000 Cr
	Insurances	50 000		4 780 000 Cr
	Rates	20 000		4 760 000 Cr
	Interest on debentures	470 000		4 290 000 Cr
	Depreciation – Vehicles	30 000		4 260 000 Cr
	Advertising	160 000		4 100 000 Cr
	Loss on disposal of vehicles	200 000		3 900 000 Cr
	Bad debts	300 000		3 600 000 Cr
	Interest on mortgage	480 000		3 120 000 Cr
	Wages	1 620 000		1 500 000 Cr
	Impairment loss – Goodwill	505 000		995 000 Cr
	Impairment loss – Investments	880 000		115 000 Cr
	Income tax credit		150 000	265 000 Cr
	Retained profits	265 000		Nil
	Retained profits			
1 July	Balance		900 000	900 000 Cr
30 June	Profit and loss		265 000	1 165 000 Cr
	Dividend reserve		100 000	1 265 000 Cr
	General reserve	150 000		1 115 000 Cr
	Interim dividend	280 000		835 000 Cr
	Final dividend	420 000		415 000 Cr

Additional information

- Sales for the year totalled $12 000 000.
- Taxation was calculated at 30%. Permanent differences exist in the profit on sale of the store and impairment losses.
- During the year 1 000 000 ordinary shares were issued at a nominal value of $1 each.
- Land and buildings were revalued by the directors during the year from $2 000 000 to $3 000 000.
- Shares in Wire Ltd have been purchased as a long-term asset that will assist the company in restructuring its future operations.

Classification requirements

- Employees will be paid $90 000 for long service leave during the year ended 30 June 2008.
- Bad debts are normally around $30 000 per year. In this year bad debts are considerably larger than normal due to the write-off of a major client.

Question 7.15

The following information relates to Monday Bar Supplies Ltd. For the year ended 30 June 2007 you are required to:

a complete the profit and loss account;
b prepare the retained profits account;
c prepare an income statement;
d prepare a statement of changes in equity;
e prepare a balance sheet; and
f prepare appropriate disclosure notes.

Monday Bar Supplies Ltd
Trial balance as at 30 June 2007 (before finalisation of net profit)

Account	Debit	Credit
	$	$
Income tax payable		80 000
Land and buildings (directors' valuation 30 June 2004)	5 000 000	
Land and buildings (at cost 2007)	6 074 000	
Bank		199 000
Asset revaluation reserve		1 500 000
Stock replacement reserve		400 000
General reserve		350 000
Profit and loss		971 000
Retained profits 1 July 2006		580 000
Transaction costs	20 000	
Interim dividend	500 000	
Trade debtors	245 000	
Allowance for doubtful debts		6 000
Cash in hand	5 000	
Share capital – Ordinary shares ($1 each)		10 000 000
First and final call	250 000	
Deposits at call	700 000	
Plant and machinery	2 200 000	
Accumulated depreciation – Plant and machinery		900 000
Investment in Clive Ltd	320 000	
Accumulated impairment loss – Investments in Clive Ltd		200 000
Goodwill	200 000	
Accrued expenses		20 000
Stocks on hand	550 000	
Mortgage loan – Keysborough Lending		200 000
Trade creditors		58 000
Debentures (maturing 31 December 2007)		200 000
Employee benefits payable		400 000
	16 064 000	16 064 000

Profit and loss (before end of year adjustments)

Date	Details	Debit	Credit	Balance
		$	$	$
30 June	Trading		3 069 000	3 069 000 Cr
	Interest revenue		110 000	3 179 000 Cr
	Profit on disposal of property		600 000	3 779 000 Cr
	Debenture interest	20 000		3 759 000 Cr
	Wages	900 000		2 859 000 Cr
	Audit fees	50 000		2 809 000 Cr
	Rates and insurances	95 000		2 714 000 Cr
	Bad debts	118 000		2 596 000 Cr
	Rent of premises	42 000		2 554 000 Cr
	Employee benefits	70 000		2 484 000 Cr
	Legal expenses	30 000		2 454 000 Cr
	Bank interest	4 000		2 450 000 Cr
	Dep'n – Plant and machinery	360 000		2 090 000 Cr
	Interest on mortgage loan	20 000		2 070 000 Cr
	Lease costs	160 000		1 910 000 Cr
	Directors' fees	500 000		1 410 000 Cr
	Impairment loss – Investments	200 000		1 210 000 Cr
	Income tax expense (before adjustments)	239 000		971 000 Cr

Additional information and directors' recommendations

Profit adjustments and information
- Goodwill is to be impaired by $200 000.
- The investment in Clive Ltd (purchased as a long-term investment) was impaired in December by $200 000. Due to further falls in its recoverable amount it is to be revalued at $20 000 at 30 June.
- The current taxation rate is 30%. Permanent differences exist in the form of impairment losses and the profit on the sale of the property. There are no temporary differences.

Retained profit adjustments and information
- The general reserve is to be increased to $400 000.
- An interim dividend of 5% was paid on 28 February.
- A final dividend is to be provided at 6% on fully paid share capital.
- The holders of 500 000 ordinary shares failed to meet the first and final call of $0.50 per share by the due date of 30 June and under the company's constitution they do not qualify for the proposed dividend declared.

Other adjustments and information
- Sales revenue was $9 000 000.
- $10 000 will be paid to employees for long service leave during the next 12 months.
- Land and buildings at directors' valuation at 30 June 2004 are to be revalued at $6 000 000.
- In February a final call of $0.50 per share was made on the 10 000 000 issued shares. By 30 June the holders of 500 000 ordinary shares had failed to meet the call.

CHAPTER 8
THE CASH FLOW STATEMENT

Objectives

Upon satisfactory completion of this chapter you should be able to:

- describe the inclusions of a cash flow statement;
- define cash and cash equivalents;
- list the cash flow activities and transactions;
- identify the cash flow statement format;
- prepare a basic cash flow statement;
- prepare a cash flow statement adjusted for accruals;
- complete a cash flow statement adjusted for non-cash transactions;
- identify the effect of the appropriation of profits on a cash flow statement;
- explain the effect of asset revaluations on cash flow movements; and
- prepare a cash flow statement after recognising cash flows from the issue of shares.

Introduction

In addition to preparing an income statement and a balance sheet, companies are required to prepare a cash flow statement in accordance with AASB 1026: Cash Flow Statement.

Essentially the cash flow statement indicates where a company obtained cash and how that cash was applied. As a consequence the statement reveals the changes to the company's short-term liquidity position, the ability of the company to generate future cash flows, to meet dividend and taxation commitments, and to service debt, and the methods used to finance the business.

The cash flow statement

The accounting standard requires the cash flow statement to be presented as follows:

1. The presentation of the cash flow statement must disclose separately the cash flows relating to operating activities and other activities such as investing and financing activities. These classifications may be defined as follows:
   - **Operating activities:** activities associated with the provision of goods and services.
   - **Investing activities:** activities related to the purchase or disposal of non-current assets.
   - **Financing activities:** activities which predominantly involve the financing of the structure of the business.

2. The cash flows to be included within these activities must be shown at their gross flows rather than net flows. This method, referred to as the direct reporting method, will show the amounts of cash that were received and issued for a particular activity. For example, the trial balances of XYZ Ltd revealed the following:

	30 June 2006	30 June 2007
Mortgage	$50 000	$60 000

Under the net method of comparison the difference of $10 000 in the mortgage would indicate an increase in cash. However, this may have consisted of a $45 000 payment on 31 December and a $55 000 increase on 31 March. The mortgage account would appear as follows:

Mortgage

		Debit	Credit	Balance
2006		$	$	$
1 July	Balance			50 000 Cr
31 Dec	Bank (repayment)	45 000		5 000 Cr
2007				
31 Mar	Bank		55 000	60 000 Cr

Under the direct reporting method the individual gross flows would be:

	$
Increase in mortgage	55 000
Decrease in mortgage	45 000

3. Within the classification of activities there is no mandatory layout required. A business may choose to detail all cash flows that took place; other companies may reveal a sequence of headings showing groupings of cash flow movements. The accounting standard does, however, make reference to the inclusion of the following items if they occur:
   - interest and similar items received;
   - dividends received;

- interest and other finance expenses paid; and
- income tax paid.

4 Included with the statement of cash flow must be a note of reconciliation of cash flows from operating activities with net profit.

Cash defined

Cash is defined as 'cash on hand' – that is, cash held in the bank, cash in registers, petty cash, cash received from debtors, cash paid to suppliers, etc. – and 'cash equivalents', which are items used in daily cash management dealings. Cash equivalents include 'highly liquid investments which are readily convertible to cash on hand' and borrowings.

Examples of cash equivalents include:
- bank overdrafts;
- borrowings (repayable on demand);
- at-call deposits;
- bank investments; and
- deposits on the money market.

Items which may not be classified as cash equivalents would include:
- receivables;
- investments in share portfolios;
- deposits with a fixed maturity date; and
- borrowings with a fixed date of repayment.

Cash flow activities

Shown below are the three distinct activities that derive cash flows. Below each activity is a list of transactions that comprise the activity. Also noted is the relationship of the activity to either the income statement or the balance sheet.

Operating activities

| Receipts from customers |
| Payments to suppliers and employees |
| Interest received |
| Interest paid |
| Dividends received |
| Income tax paid |

Note: Operating activities generally relate to activities associated with the profit and loss account.

Investing activities

| Purchase of non-current assets |
| Proceeds from the disposal of non-current assets |
| Purchase of investments |
| Proceeds from disposal of investments |
| Loans given |
| Loans repaid |

Note: Investing activities generally relate to activities associated with movements in non-current assets on the balance sheet.

Financing activities

Proceeds from share issues
Borrowings acquired
Borrowing repaid
Dividends paid

Note: Financing activities generally relate to activities associated with movements in non-current liabilities and shareholders' funds on the balance sheet.

Question 8.1

Classify the following items into either operating, investing or financing activities:

- a Cash sales [O]
- b Paying damages in a law suit [O]
- c Income from investments [O]
- d Purchasing investments [I]
- e Sale of non-current assets [I]
- f Purchasing non-current assets [I]
- g Receipts from customers [O]
- h Payments to suppliers [O]
- i Increased mortgage [F]
- j Repaying borrowings [F]
- k New share capital [F]
- l Interest paid [O]
- m Rent paid [O]
- n Wages paid [O]
- o Interest received [O]
- p Sale of investments [I]
- q Loans given to employees. [I]

Cash flow statement format

The following format is included as a guide to the setting out of a cash flow statement.

XYZ Ltd
Cash flow statement for the year ended ...

	$	$
Cash flows related to operating activities		
Receipts from customers	XX	
Payments to suppliers and employees	(XX)	
Dividends received	XX	
Interest received	XX	
Interest paid	(XX)	
Income taxes paid	(XX)	
Other	XX	
Net operating cash flows		XX

Cash flows related to investing activities		
Cash paid for purchases of property, plant and equipment	(XX)	
Cash proceeds from sale of property, plant and equipment	XX	
Cash paid for purchases of equity investments	(XX)	
Cash proceeds from sale of equity investments	XX	
Loans to other entities	(XX)	
Loans repaid by other entities	XX	
Other	XX	
Net investing cash flows		XX
Cash flows related to financing activities		
Cash proceeds from issues of shares, options, etc.	XX	
Borrowings	XX	
Repayment of borrowings	(XX)	
Dividends paid	(XX)	
Other	XX	
Net financing cash flows		XX
Net increase (decrease) in cash held		XX
Cash at beginning of year		XX
Cash at end of year		XX

Completing a cash flow statement

The following illustration is included to show the presentation of a cash flow statement without inclusion of adjustments for accruals, non-cash transactions, appropriation of profits, asset revaluation or share issues.

ILLUSTRATION

Lee Ltd
Balance sheets as at 30 June

	2006	2007
	$	$
Assets		
Bank	20 000	16 000
Buildings	10 000	30 000
	30 000	46 000
Equities		
Loan from Attco Finances	8 000	18 000
Ordinary shares ($1 each)	22 000	28 000
	30 000	46 000

Lee Ltd
Income statement for the year ended 30 June 2007

	$	$
Fees income		78 000
Miscellaneous operating revenue		
Interest		1 000
		79 000
less Operating expenses		
Wages	36 000	
Telephone	6 000	
Lease payments – Motor vehicle	13 000	
Rent	3 000	
Advertising	6 000	
Condemnation of building	10 000	
Miscellaneous	5 000	79 000
Net profit		Nil

Notes:
1. The company issued an additional 6 000 fully paid shares during the year.
2. The company replaced buildings during the year which had been condemned by the local council.
3. The loan from Attco Finances was repaid on 1 December 2006. A new loan was acquired on 2 May 2007.

To determine the true cash flows relating to buildings it is necessary to reconstruct the account.

Buildings

Date	Details	$	Date	Details	$
2006			2007		
1 July	Balance	10 000	30 June	Profit and loss (condemnation)	10 000
2007					
30 June	Purchases*	30 000		Balance	30 000
		40 000			40 000

* Cash flow arising from acquisition of new building: $30 000.

Loan – Attco Finances

Date	Details	$	Date	Details	$
2006			2006		
1 Dec	Bank no. 1	8 000	1 June	Balance	8 000
2007			2007		
30 June	Balance	18 000	2 May	Bank no. 2	18 000
		26 000			26 000

No. 1 – Cash flow to repay loan: $8 000.
No. 2 – Cash flow to acquire loan: $18 000.

In addition to these calculations the income statement reveals the following payments to suppliers and employees.

	$
Wages	36 000
Telephone	6 000
Lease payments	13 000
Rent	3 000
Advertising	6 000
Miscellaneous	5 000
Total	69 000

Analysis of the financial statements indicates that cash was obtained (or used) from:
- operations (trading);
- investing (new buildings); and
- financing (loan – Attco Finances).

The cash flow statement for Lee Ltd would appear as follows:

Lee Ltd
Cash flow statement for the year ended 30 June 2007

	$	$
Cash flows related to operating activities		
Receipts from customers	78 000	
Payments to suppliers and employees	(69 000)	
Interest received	1 000	
Net operating cash flow		10 000
Cash flows related to investing activities		
Purchase of building	(30 000)	
Net investing cash flow		(30 000)
Cash flows related to financing activities		
Proceeds from share issue	6 000	
Borrowings paid (Attco Finances)	(8 000)	
Borrowings received (Attco Finances)	18 000	
Net financing cash flow		16 000
Net decrease in cash held		(4 000)
Cash at 1 July 2006		20 000
Cash at 30 June 2007		16 000

The notes supporting the statement would be as follows:

1 *Reconciliation of cash*

	30 June 2006	30 June 2007
	$	$
Cash balances – bank	20 000	16 000

2 Reconciliation of net profit with cash flows from operating activities

	$
Net profit	10 000
add (subtract) Non-cash items appearing in the income statement	Nil
add (subtract) Operating flows on the balance sheet	Nil
Cash flows from operating activities	10 000

Analysis of the cash flow statement

An analysis of the cash flow statement of Lee Ltd indicates the company obtained cash and cash equivalents of $26 000, being $10 000 from operating activities and $16 000 from financing activities. These funds were used to assist in the purchase of a new building (investing activities) costing $30 000, with the shortfall of $4 000 being taken from the cash at bank account, which fell from $20 000 at the start of the period to $16 000 at the end of the period.

Question 8.2

You are required to use the following financial statements of Hart Ltd to prepare a cash flow statement for the year ended 30 June 2007 in accordance with the accounting standards.

Hart Ltd
Income statement for the year ended 30 June 2007

	$	$
Sales		700 000
less Purchases		420 000
Gross profit		280 000
add Other income		
Interest received		10 000
		290 000
less Expenses		
Advertising	35 000	
Rates	20 000	
Motor vehicle expenses	18 400	
Interest expense	6 600	
Wages	200 000	280 000
Net profit		10 000

Hart Ltd
Balance sheets as at 30 June

	2006	2007
	$	$
Equities		
Ordinary shares	100 000	150 000
Retained profits	20 000	30 000
Bank loans	15 000	20 000
Mortgage	50 000	48 000
	185 000	248 000
Assets		
Bank	10 000	33 000
Motor vehicles	55 000	55 000
Equipment	120 000	160 000
	185 000	248 000

Additional information
- The company was not liable for income tax.
- Additional equipment was purchased during the year.
- On 1 August the bank loan was reduced by $5 000. An additional bank loan was acquired on 1 June.

Question 8.3

From the following financial statements of Long Ltd you are required to prepare a cash flow statement (including reconciliation) for the year ended 30 June 2007 in accordance with accounting standards.

Long Ltd
Income statement for the year ended 30 June 2007

	$	$
Sales – Cash		882 000
less Purchase – Cash		680 000
Gross profit		202 000
add Other income		
Interest received	22 000	
Commission received	3 000	
Damages – Law suit	30 000	55 000
		257 000
less Expenses		
Wages	150 000	
Advertising	32 000	
Rent	40 000	
Interest	5 000	227 000
Net profit		30 000

Long Ltd
Balance sheets as at 30 June

	2006	2007
	$	$
Equities		
Ordinary shares ($1 each)	260 000	390 000
Retained profits	60 000	90 000
Mortgage	100 000	150 000
Debentures	400 000	600 000
Bank overdraft	–	6 000
	820 000	1 236 000
Assets		
Bank	35 000	–
Property, plant and equipment	750 000	1 000 000
Shares in ABC Ltd	–	200 000
Deposits at call	10 000	15 000
Loan to Bell Company	25 000	21 000
	820 000	1 236 000

Additional information
- Damages from the law suit were treated as a permanent difference resulting in no income tax.
- On 31 December 2006 debentures of $300 000 matured and were repaid.

Adjustments for accruals

Some amounts appearing in the income statement may not represent the actual operating cash flow for the account. This will be so in the following cases:

- Sales made on invoice to debtors will be shown as credit sales. This does not represent the amount paid by debtors.
- Where a company purchases stock on credit, the cost of sales will not reveal the actual payment made to creditors.
- Revenue and expense accounts adjusted due to accruals and prepayments will not reveal the actual amount received or paid.
- Annual leave, long service leave and other employee entitlements appearing in the income statement do not represent the amounts paid to employees for these items.
- Income tax expense is calculated on the company's accounting profit and loss and does not necessarily represent the amount paid, which is calculated on the company's taxable income.

Where an amount appearing in the income statement does not represent the actual operating cash flow for the account it may be necessary to reconstruct the account to determine the true cash flow. The cash amount is then used to represent the account in the statement of cash flow.

The account reconstructions will involve a related balance sheet account. These normally relate to current asset or current liability accounts, which derive their existence due to transactions in the income statement.

Examples are as follows:
- Debtors will need to be reconstructed where credit sales are reported.
- Creditors reconstruction is required where credit purchases have been recorded under a physical stock recording system.
- Creditors and possibly stock reconstructions are necessary under a perpetual stock recording system.
- Prepaid and accrued expenses and revenues will require reconstruction where related expenses and revenues have been adjusted.
- Annual leave payable, long service leave payable and employee entitlements payable reconstructions will result when leave expenses exist.
- The income tax payable account may need reconstruction to identify the previous year's liability which was paid in the current year.

For the purposes of reconciliation of the net profit (after income tax) to operating cash flows, the annual movements in the associated balance sheet accounts are included under the heading 'Operating flows on the balance sheet'. Thus, annual movement in debtors, stock, creditors, GST payable, accrued and prepaid revenues and expenses, accruals for leave, income tax payable, deferred tax liability and deferred tax asset must be included in the reconciliation.

ILLUSTRATION

The financial statements of Brask Ltd appear as follows:

Brask Ltd
Income statement for the year ended 30 June 2007

	$	$
Sales – Cash	390 000	
– Credit	100 000	490 000
less Cost of goods sold		330 000
		160 000
less Expenses		
Wages	60 000	
Rent expense	4 000	
Annual leave expense	10 000	
Bad debts	6 500	
Discount allowed	500	81 000
Profit (before income tax)		79 000
less Income tax		23 700
Net profit		55 300

Brask Ltd
Balance sheets as at 30 June

	2006	2007
	$	$
Equities		
Ordinary shares	75 000	75 000
Retained profits	–	55 300
Creditors	7 000	6 000
Annual leave payable	25 000	23 000
Income tax payable	4 000	7 530
Deferred tax liability	–	2 810
	111 000	169 640
Assets		
Bank	52 700	99 800
Debtors	5 000	9 000
Stock	35 000	38 000
Prepaid rent	600	400
Vehicles	16 500	16 500
Deferred tax asset	1 200	5 940
	111 000	169 640

Reconstructions (in 'T' account format)

Debtors

Date	Details	$	Date	Details	$
1 July	Balance	5 000	30 June	Bad debts	6 500
30 June	Credit sales	100 000		Discount allowed	500
				Bank*	89 000
				Balance	9 000
		105 000			105 000

*Amount received from debtors: $89 000.

Stock

Date	Details	$	Date	Details	$
1 July	Balance	35 000	30 June	Cost of sales	330 000
30 June	Creditors (purchases)	333 000		Balance	38 000
		368 000			368 000

Creditors

Date	Details	$	Date	Details	$
30 June	Bank*	334 000	1 July	Balance	7 000
	Balance	6 000	30 June	Stock (purchases)	333 000
		340 000			340 000

* Amount paid to creditors: $334 000.

Rent expense

Date	Details	$	Date	Details	$
1 July	Prepaid rent	600	30 June	Profit and loss	4 000
30 June	Bank *	3 800		Prepaid rent	400
		4 400			4 400

* Amount paid for rent expense: $3 800.

Annual leave payable

Date	Details	$	Date	Details	$
30 June	Bank *	12 000	1 July	Balance	25 000
	Balance	23 000	30 June	Annual leave	10 000
		35 000			35 000

* Amount paid for annual leave: $12 000.

Income tax payable

Date	Details	$	Date	Details	$
2006			2006		
21 July	Bank*	4 000	1 July	Balance	4 000
2007			2007		
30 June	Bank*	18 100	30 June	Income tax expense	23 700
	Balance	7 530		Adjustment	1 930
		29 630			29 630

* Amount paid for income tax: $22 100. (Adjustment = Deferred tax asset Dr $4 740 – Deferred tax liability Cr $2 810)

Brask Ltd
Cash flow statement for the year ended 30 June 2007

	$
Cash flows related to operating activities	
Receipts from customers [Note 1]	479 000
Payments to suppliers and employees [Note 2]	(409 800)
Income tax paid	(22 100)
Net operating cash flows	47 100
Cash at 1 July 2006	52 700
Cash at 30 June 2007	99 800

Reconciliation of cash

	30 June 2006 $	30 June 2007 $
Cash balances – Bank	52 700	99 800

Reconciliation of net profit with cash flows from operating activities

	$
Profit (after tax)	55 300
add (subtract) Non-cash flows appearing in the income statement	Nil
add (subtract) Operating flows appearing on the balance sheet	
Debtors ↑	(4 000)
Stock ↑	(3 000)
Prepaid rent ↓	200
Creditors ↓	(1 000)
Annual leave payable ↓	(2 000)
Income tax payable ↑	3 530
Deferred tax asset ↑	(4 740)
Deferred tax liability ↑	2 810
Cash flows from operating activities	47 100

	$
Note 1 Receipts from customers	
Cash sales	390 000
Debtors	89 000
	479 000
Note 2 Payments to suppliers and employees	
Creditors	334 000
Wages	60 000
Rent paid	3 800
Annual leave paid	12 000
	409 800

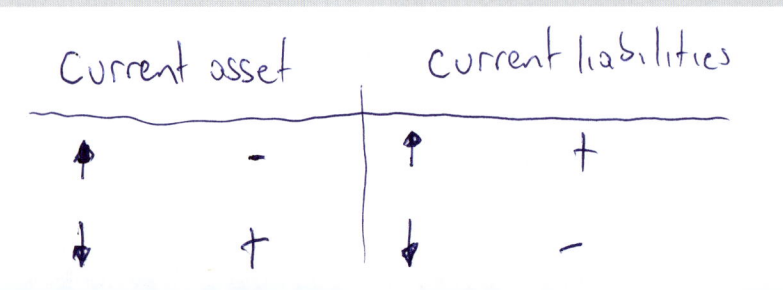

Question 8.4

Using the financial statements of HiLite Ltd for the year ending 30 June 2007 shown below, you are required to prepare a statement of cash flows in accordance with AASB 1026.

Hilite Ltd

Income statement for the year ended 30 June 2007

	$	$
Cash sales		900 000
less Cost of sales		470 000
Gross profit		430 000
add Other revenue		
Discount revenue		1 000
		431 000
less Expenses		
Wages	160 000	
Advertising	30 000	
Rent	5 000	
Long service leave	14 000	
Interest	6 000	215 000
Profit (before income tax)		216 000
Income tax expense		64 800
Net profit		151 200
Retained profits 1 July 2006		56 000
Retained profits 30 June 2007		207 200

Hilite Ltd

Balance sheets as at 30 June

	2006	2007
	$	$
Equities		
Ordinary shares	1 219 000	1 260 000
Retained profits	56 000	207 200
Creditors	12 000	15 000
Accrued wages	4 000	2 500
Bank overdraft	82 800	100 700
Income tax payable	16 000	18 779
Deferred tax liability	3 200	406
Long service leave payable	42 000	50 000
	1 435 000	1 654 585
Assets		
Cash in registers		21 600
Equipment	560 000	560 000
Prepaid advertising	2 000	2 400
Buildings	800 000	1 000 000
Stock	72 000	70 000
Deferred tax asset	1 000	585
	1 435 000	1 654 585

Question 8.5

You are required to use the following financial statements of Accrual Ltd to prepare a cash flow statement for the year ended 30 June 2007 in accordance with the accounting standards.

Accrual Ltd
Income statement for the year ended 30 June 2007

	$	$
Credit sales		800 000
less Cash purchases		500 000
Gross profit		300 000
add Other income		
Interest received		7 500
		307 500
less Expenses		
Advertising	26 000	
Rent	14 000	
Annual leave	32 000	
Interest	5 000	
Wages	150 000	227 000
Profit (before income tax)		80 500
Income tax expense		24 150
Profit (after income tax)		56 350

Accrual Ltd
Balance sheets as at 30 June

	2006	2007
	$	$
Equities		
Ordinary shares	500 000	600 000
Retained profits	50 000	106 350
Prepaid interest revenue	–	1 000
Annual leave payable	6 000	4 000
Income tax payable	10 000	8 200
Deferred tax liability	–	3 000
Mortgage	62 000	40 000
	628 000	762 550
Assets		
Bank	27 000	(3 950)
Deposits at call	150 000	180 000
Debtors	65 000	72 000
Prepaid wages	6 000	4 500
Loan to director	50 000	30 000
Fittings	80 000	80 000
Equipment	250 000	400 000
	628 000	762 550

Non-cash transactions

When calculating the cash flow items from the income statements for operating activities it is necessary to analyse each item to determine the true cash flow. Certain items such as depreciation expense, doubtful debts, amortised intangible assets, profits and losses on disposal of non-current assets and the impairment of assets are considered 'book entries', not involving a flow of cash. Such items are not included in the cash flow statements and are used as items of reconciliation of net profit with cash flow from operating activities – that is, non-cash items appearing in the income statement.

ILLUSTRATION

Shown below are the financial statements of Peel Ltd.

Peel Ltd
Income statement for the year ended 30 June 2007

	$	$
Sales (credit)	674 100	
less Cost of sales	596 000	
Gross profit		78 100
add Other revenue		
Profit on sale of equipment		5 000
		83 100
less Expenses		
Depreciation of equipment	6 000	
Wages	84 000	
Doubtful debts	600	
Impairment loss – Goodwill	4 000	
Impairment loss – Investments	20 000	114 600
Net loss		(31 500)

Peel Ltd
Balance sheets as at 30 June

	2006	2007
	$	$
Equities		
Ordinary shares	200 000	200 000
Retained profits	100 000	68 500
	300 000	268 500
Assets		
Stock	10 400	11 600
Bank	30 000	29 000
Debtors	20 600	22 500
less Allowance for doubtful debts	(1 000)	(1 600)
Equipment	50 000	40 000
less Accumulated depreciation	(15 000)	(14 000)
Goodwill (less impairment losses)	25 000	21 000
Investments	200 000	200 000
Accumulated impairment loss – Investments	(20 000)	(40 000)
	300 000	268 500

Reconstructions

Debtors

Date	Details	$	Date	Details	$
1 July	Balance	20 600	30 June	Bank*	672 200
30 June	Sales	674 100		Balance	22 500
		694 700			694 700

* Amounts received from customers: $672 200.

Stock

Date	Details	$	Date	Details	$
1 July	Balance	10 400	30 June	Cost of sales	596 000
30 June	Bank*	597 200		Balance	11 600
		607 600			607 600

* Amounts paid to suppliers: $597 200.

Equipment

Date	Details	$	Date	Details	$
1 July	Balance	50 000	30 June	Disposal	10 000
				Balance	40 000
		50 000			50 000

Accumulated depreciation – Equipment

Date	Details	$	Date	Details	$
30 June	Disposal	7 000	1 July	Balance	15 000
	Balance	14 000	30 June	Depreciation	6 000
		21 000			21 000

Disposal of equipment

Date	Details	$	Date	Details	$
30 June	Equipment	10 000	30 June	Accumulated depreciation	7 000
	Profit and loss	5 000		Bank*	8 000
		15 000			15 000

* Proceeds from disposal of equipment: $8 000.

Peel Ltd
Cash flow statement for the year ended 30 June 2007

	$	$
Cash flows related to operating activities		
Receipts from customers	672 200	
Payments to suppliers and employees [Note 1]	(681 200)	
Net operating cash flows		(9 000)
Cash flows related to investing activities		
Proceeds from disposal of equipment	8 000	
Net investing cash flows		8 000
Net decrease in cash held		(1 000)
Cash at 1 July 2006		30 000
Cash at 30 June 2007		29 000

Reconciliation of cash

	30 June 2006	30 June 2007
	$	$
Cash balances – Bank	30 000	29 000

Reconciliation of net profit with cash flows from operating activities

	$
Net loss	(31 500)
add (subtract) Non-cash items appearing in the income statement	
Profit on disposal of equipment	(5 000)
Depreciation of equipment	6 000
Doubtful debts	600
Impairment loss – Goodwill	4 000
Impairment loss – Investments	20 000
	(5 900)
add (subtract) Operating flows on the balance sheet	
Stock	(1 200)
Debtors	(1 900)
Cash flows from operating activities	(9 000)
Note 1 Payments to suppliers and employees	
Wages	84 000
Purchases	597 200
	681 200

Question 8.6

Complete the worksheet below by identifying the treatment of each item listed.

	Item	Activity Operating	Investing	Financing	Reconciliation Non-cash item	Operating item
1	Cash sales	X				
2	Interest paid	X				
3	New share capital			X		
4	Debentures repaid			X		
5	Increase in debtors					X
6	Income tax paid	X				
7	Annual leave paid	X				
8	Income tax payable increase					X
9	Dividends received	X				
10	Doubtful debts expense				X	
11	Purchase of plant		X			
12	Depreciation expense				X	
13	Increase in borrowings			X		
14	Decrease in creditors					X
15	Increase in accruals					X
16	Wages paid	X				
17	Impairment losses				X	
18	Increase in inventory					X
19	Receipts from receivables	X				
20	Interest income	X				
21	Loan from finance company			X		
22	Loan to supplier		X			
23	Proceeds from asset sale		X			
24	Profit on asset disposal				X	
25	Decrease in GST payable					X
26	Advertising paid	X				

Question 8.7

You are required to prepare a cash flow statement in accordance with AASB 1026, from the following financial statements of Ross Ltd, for the year ended 30 June 2007.

Ross Ltd
Income statement for the year ended 30 June 2007

	$	$
Fees received (credit)		350 000
less Expenses		
Loss on sale of plant	48 000	
Doubtful debts	2 000	
Interest expense	5 000	
Depreciation of plant	20 000	
Bad debts	4 000	
Wages	256 000	
Rent expense	15 000	
Impairment loss – Investments	40 000	390 000
Net loss		(40 000)

Ross Ltd
Balance sheets as at 30 June

	2006	2007
	$	$
Equities		
Ordinary shares ($1 each)	500 000	560 000
Retained profits	50 000	10 000
Debentures	100 000	140 000
	650 000	710 000
Assets		
Bank	16 000	8 000
Deposits at call	30 000	45 000
Accounts receivable	28 000	38 000
less Allowance for doubtful debts	(4 000)	(6 000)
Plant	150 000	200 000
less Accumulated depreciation	(60 000)	(75 000)
Investments in shares	500 000	550 000
less Accumulated impairment loss	(10 000)	(50 000)
	650 000	710 000

Additional information

- Bad debts were written off against accounts receivable.
- Additional plant of $160 000 was purchased on 1 February 2007.
- Shares were issued on 1 April 2007.
- Debentures of $30 000 were repaid on 1 December 2006.

Question 8.8

You are required to use the following financial statements of Cashless Ltd to prepare a cash flow statement for the year ended 30 June 2007 in accordance with the accounting standards.

Cashless Ltd
Income statement for the year ended 30 June 2007

	$	$
Cash sales		800 000
less Cash purchases		500 000
Gross profit		300 000
add Other income		
Profit on sale of equipment		2 500
Interest received		7 500
		310 000
less Expenses		
Advertising	26 000	
Impairment loss – Goodwill	8 000	
Long service leave	32 000	
Depreciation of equipment	35 000	
Wages	150 000	251 000
Profit (before income tax)		59 000
Income tax expense		15 300
Profit (after income tax)		43 700

Cashless Ltd
Balance sheets as at 30 June

	2006	2007
	$	$
Equities		
Ordinary shares	20 000	26 000
Retained profits	25 000	68 700
Bank overdraft	34 500	4 100
Long service leave payable	12 000	10 000
Income tax payable	3 500	6 800
Debentures	50 000	20 000
	145 000	135 600
Assets		
Cash in registers	4 000	6 000
Prepaid advertising	1 000	600
Goodwill (less impairment losses)	60 000	52 000
Equipment	180 000	200 000
less Accumulated depreciation	(100 000)	(123 000)
	145 000	135 600

Additional information

- Equipment costing $30 000 and depreciated by $12 000 was sold during the year.

Appropriation of profits

The operating activities section of the cash flow statement reveals the cash flows relating solely to activities associated with the provision of goods and services. The related reconciliation statement reconciles the net profit (after tax) shown in the income statement with the cash flows related to operating activities shown in the cash flow statement.

The appropriation of profits, an event that occurs after the calculation of net profit, does not have an effect on operating cash flows. The appropriation of profits normally involves the distribution of profits in the following ways:
- distribution by way of interim and final dividends; and
- transfer to a revenue reserve such as a general reserve, stock replacement reserve, dividend equalisation reserve, etc.

Of these appropriations the only movements involving a cash flow are those involving the payment of dividends. The payment of dividends, being a return to shareholders who financed the business, is identified in the cash flow statement as a reduction to cash flows related to financing activities.

The dividends paid within a year will be the interim dividends within the current year and the dividends proposed in the previous year. Dividends that are proposed at the end of the current year will not involve a cash flow until the next accounting period.

ILLUSTRATION

The financial statements of Dacron Ltd appear below.

Dacron Ltd
Income statement for the year ended 30 June 2007

	$	$
Sales (cash)		396 000
less Purchases (cash)		146 000
Gross profit		250 000
less Expenses		
Wages	120 000	
Depreciation	10 000	130 000
Operating profit (before taxation)		120 000
less Income tax expense		36 000
Net profit (after taxation)		84 000
Retained profits 1 July 2006		50 000
Total available for appropriation		134 000
Transfers to general reserve	20 000	
Dividends – Interim	9 000	
– Final	6 000	35 000
Retained profits 30 June 2007		99 000

Dacron Ltd
Balance sheets as at 30 June

	2006	2007
	$	$
Equities		
Ordinary shares ($1)	400 000	400 000
Retained profits	50 000	99 000
General reserve	15 000	35 000
Dividends payable	10 000	6 000
Income tax payable	10 000	12 000
	485 000	552 000
Assets		
Bank	25 000	105 000
Prepaid wages	10 000	7 000
Equipment	500 000	500 000
less Accumulated depreciation	(50 000)	(60 000)
	485 000	552 000

Additional information
- The interim dividend was declared on 1 December 2006 and paid on 20 December 2006.
- The proposed dividend of 30 June 2006 was paid on 1 August 2006.
- The final dividend proposed on 30 June 2007 is to be paid on 1 September 2007.

Reconstructions

Wages

Date	Details	$	Date	Details	$
1 July	Prepaid wages	10 000	30 June	Prepaid wages	7 000
30 June	Bank*	117 000		Profit and loss	120 000
		127 000			127 000

* Amount paid to employees as wages: $117 000.

Income tax payable

Date	Details	$	Date	Details	$
30 June	Bank*	34 000	1 July	Balance	10 000
	Balance	12 000	30 June	Income tax expense	36 000
		46 000			46 000

* Amount paid for taxation: $34 000.

Dividends payable

Date	Details	$	Date	Details	$
2006			2006		
1 Aug	Bank*	10 000	1 July	Balance	10 000
20 Dec	Bank*	9 000	1 Dec	Interim	9 000
2007			2007		
30 June	Balance	6 000	30 June	Final	6 000
		25 000			25 000

* Amounts paid for dividends: $19 000.

Dacron Ltd
Cash flow statement for the year ended 30 June 2007

	$	$
Cash flows related to operating activities		
Receipts from customers	396 000	
Payments to suppliers and employees [Note 1]	(263 000)	
Income tax paid	(34 000)	
Net operating cash flows		99 000
Cash flows related to financing activities		
Dividends paid	(19 000)	
Net financing cash flows		(19 000)
Net increase in cash held		80 000
Cash at 1 July 2006		25 000
Cash at 30 June 2007		105 000

Reconciliation of cash	30 June 2006	30 June 2007
	$	$
Cash balances – Bank	25 000	105 000

Reconciliation of net profit with cash flows from operating activities		$
Net profit (after income tax)		84 000
add (subtract) Non-cash flows appearing in the income statement		
Depreciation		10 000
		94 000
add (subtract) Operating flows on the balance sheet		
Prepaid wages		3 000
Income tax payable		2 000
Cash flows from operating activities		99 000
Note 1 Payments to suppliers and employees		
Purchases		146 000
Wages paid		117 000
		263 000

Question 8.9

You are required to prepare a cash flow statement in accordance with the accounting standards from the following information relating to Bromley Ltd for the year ended 30 June 2007.

Bromley Ltd
Income statement for the year ended 30 June 2007

	$	$
Sales (credit)		290 000
less Cost of goods sold		
Stock 1 July 2006	39 000	
Purchases (cash)	91 000	
	130 000	
less Stock 30 June 2007	40 000	90 000
Gross profit		200 000
add Other revenue		
Interest received		5 000
		205 000
less Expenses		
Wages	86 000	
Interest expense	4 000	
Depreciation	25 000	
Annual leave expense	6 000	121 000
Operating profit (before income tax)		84 000
less Income tax expense		25 200
Net profit		58 800
add Retained profits 1 July 2006		20 000
		78 800
less Transfer to sundry reserve	6 000	
Dividends – Interim	14 000	
– Final	16 000	36 000
Retained profits 30 June 2007		42 800

Bromley Ltd
Balance sheets as at 30 June

	2006	2007
	$	$
Equities		
Ordinary shares	5	5
Sundry reserve	–	6 000
Retained profits	20 000	42 800
Income tax payable	11 500	6 240
Dividends payable	15 000	16 000
Annual leave payable	60 000	42 000
Loan – Ajax Finance	50 000	55 000
	156 505	168 045

Assets		
Bank	(21 695)	15 005
Stock	39 000	40 000
Debtors	62 000	70 000
Vehicles	80 000	80 000
less Accumulated depreciation	(15 000)	(40 000)
Accrued interest revenue	200	400
Deferred tax asset	12 000	2 640
	156 505	168 045

Additional information

- Ajax Finance was repaid $30 000 on 30 September 2006.
- The final dividend declared on 30 June 2006 was paid on 1 October 2006.
- The interim dividend was declared on 1 February 2007 and paid on 1 March 2007.
- A final dividend was proposed on 24 June 2007. This will be paid on 2 October 2007.

Asset revaluations

Where a company revalues non-current assets, the revaluation does not constitute a flow of funds. As a result an upward or downward change in an asset, and the corresponding change in the asset revaluation reserve, would be ignored in the statement of cash flow.

Where the revaluation was either 'credited to' or 'debited to' the profit and loss account, the amount would be ignored in the calculation of cash flow; however, it would need to be disclosed in the reconciliation of net profit to operating cash flows as a non-cash item appearing in the income statement.

In some circumstances an asset account may include the purchase of additional assets, disposal of an asset and a revaluation. Where this occurs it may be necessary to reconstruct the asset account to determine the actual cash flow associated with the purchase of the asset, this being a cash flow associated with investing activities.

ILLUSTRATION

Trask Ltd's opening balance of the plant and equipment account on 1 July 2006 was $200 000. On 31 July plant costing $60 000 was sold. Additional plant was purchased on this date. On 31 December 2006 all assets in the plant and equipment category were revalued upwards by $100 000. The balance of plant and equipment on 30 June 2007 was $400 000.

The reconstruction of the plant and equipment account would be as follows:

Plant and equipment

Date	Details	$	Date	Details	$
2006			2006		
1 July	Balance	200 000	31 July	Disposal of asset	60 000
31 July	Purchases*	160 000			
2007			2007		
31 Dec	Asset revaluation reserve	100 000	30 June	Balance	400 000
		460 000			460 000

* The reconstruction reveals that $160 000 of additional plant and equipment was purchased on 31 July 2006. This constitutes an outgoing of cash under investing activities in the cash flow statement.

Question 8.10

The following information relates to Danone Ltd. You are required to prepare a cash flow statement for the year ended 30 June 2007 in accordance with the accounting standards.

Danone Ltd

Income statement for the year ended 30 June 2007

	$	$
Sales – Cash	231 000	
– Credit	400 000	631 000
less Cost of goods sold		
Stock 1 July 2006	89 400	
Purchases – Credit	406 080	
	495 480	
less Stock 30 June 2007	70 300	425 180
Gross profit		205 820
add Other revenue		
Profit on sale of plant		1 000
		206 820
less Expenses		
Rent	15 000	
Wages	60 000	
Depreciation of plant	7 920	
Impairment loss – Goodwill	6 000	
Doubtful debts	3 000	91 920
Profit (before income tax)		114 900
less Income tax expense		36 270
Net profit		78 630

Danone Ltd

Balance sheets as at 30 June

	2006	2007
	$	$
Equities		
Ordinary shares	410 000	440 000
Retained profit	30 600	14 230
Asset revaluation reserve	–	30 000
General reserve	–	15 000
Dividends payable	40 000	60 000
Creditors	45 000	56 000
Accrued rent	3 400	2 350
Income tax payable	12 000	15 000
Debentures	–	50 000
Bank overdraft	–	57 560
	541 000	740 140

Assets		
Bank	12 440	–
Debtors	91 000	117 460
Allowance for doubtful debts	(8 000)	(11 000)
Stock	89 400	70 300
Prepaid wages	2 860	2 000
Investments in shares	40 000	70 000
Deposits at call	20 000	10 000
Plant	112 000	250 000
Accumulated depreciation	(18 700)	(20 620)
Premises	182 000	240 000
Goodwill (less impairment losses)	18 000	12 000
	541 000	740 140

Additional information

- Premises were revalued upward by $30 000 on 30 June 2007.
- Plant costing $8 000 was sold.
- The proposed dividend declared on 30 June 2006 was paid on 1 November 2006.
- An interim dividend of $20 000 was declared on 1 December 2006 and paid on 30 January 2007.
- The final dividend of 30 June 2007 will be paid on 1 October 2007.

Issuing shares

Companies can obtain funds by issuing shares. Shares may be issued at nominal value and subject to future calls. Companies may also issue shares as a bonus dividend. Where cash is received from the issue of shares, the amount must be disclosed in the statement of cash flow as a financing activity.

Shares issued

Where shares are issued via a prospectus the amount received from the share issue will be revealed as an increase in the ordinary shares account on the balance sheet. For example:

Extracts of financial position

	2006	2007
	$	$
Equities		
Ordinary shares	10 000	60 000

A comparison of the respective balance sheet amounts indicates that $50 000 was received from the issue of shares.

Shares issued (below nominal value) and subject to calls

Where shares are issued below nominal value and subject to future calls it is necessary to compare the value of ordinary shares on the balance sheet and adjust the value of the increase by the amount of unpaid calls. For example:

Extracts of financial position

	2006	2007
	$	$
Equities		
Ordinary shares	10 000	150 000
Calls in arrears	–	(10 000)

This example shows a $50 000 increase in ordinary shares issued. However, the calls in arrears account reveals $10 000 in calls have not been received. In this illustration the amount of cash received from the call on ordinary shares is $40 000.

Bonus share dividend

Companies may issue a bonus share dividend financed from a reserve account such as the asset revaluation reserve. Where bonus share dividends are issued there is no cash flow. Consequently, the increase in the ordinary shares account must be ignored as a cash flow where it is a result of a bonus share dividend. For example:

The XYZ Ltd company issued a 1 for 5 bonus share dividend to all existing shareholders at 1 July 2006. The bonus share issue was funded from the asset revaluation reserve.

Extracts of financial position

	2006	2007
	$	$
Equities		
Ordinary shares	100 000	120 000
Asset revaluation reserve	40 000	20 000

In this example the increase in the ordinary shares account of $20 000 does not constitute a flow of cash as it was financed by a $20 000 reduction in the asset revaluation reserve.

Other information to be disclosed

In addition to the cash flow statement and associated reconciliations, companies are required to disclose information about external financing arrangements that exist at the end of a financial year. The company must disclose the details of the financing arrangement, including the amount of the credit facility and the amount of the facility used. Examples would include the extent of a bank overdraft facility and the actual amount used, details of financial leasing arrangements, etc.

ILLUSTRATION

The financial statements of Risky Ltd appear below.

Balance sheets as at 30 June

	2006	2007
	$	$
Equities		
Ordinary shares ($1)	500 000	600 000
Calls in arrears	–	(20 000)
Retained profits	60 000	60 000
Asset revaluation reserve	10 000	200 000
	570 000	840 000
Assets		
Bank	50 000	20 000
Land and buildings	520 000	820 000
	570 000	840 000

Additional information
- In December 2006, land and buildings were revalued upwards by $200 000. Additional land was purchased on this date for $100 000.
- In January 2007, a call of $40 000 was made on shares. By June 2007, only $20 000 had been received.
- In March 2007, 50 000 shares were issued at $1 each.
- In June 2007, $10 000 in shares were issued as a bonus dividend from the asset revaluation reserve.

Reconstructions

Ordinary shares

Date	Details	$	Date	Details	$
			2006		
			1 July	Opening balance	500 000
			Jan	Call*	40 000
			March	Applications*	50 000
2007			2007		
June	Closing balance	600 000	June	Dividend payable	10 000
		600 000			600 000

		$
* Cash amounts	– Calls	40 000
	– Applications	50 000
		90 000
less	– Calls in arrears	20 000
		70 000

Risky Ltd
Cash flow statement for the year ended 30 June 2007

	$	$
Cash flows related to investing activities		
Acquisition of land	(100 000)	
Net investing cash flow		(100 000)
Cash flows related to financing activities		
Issue of shares	70 000	
Increase in shares premium reserve	10 000	
Net financing cash flow		80 000
Net decrease in cash held		(20 000)
Cash at 1 July 2006		50 000
Cash at 30 June 2007		30 000
Reconciliation of cash	30 June 2006	30 June 2007
Cash balance – Bank	50 000	30 000

Question 8.11

The following information relates to Wood Ltd. You are required to prepare a cash flow statement for the year ended 30 June 2007 in accordance with the accounting standards.

Wood Ltd

Balance sheets as at 30 June

	2006		2007	
	$	$	$	$
Current assets				
Cash on hand		4 150		16 800
Debtors	40 000		69 750	
less Allowance for doubtful debts	4 000	36 000	9 750	60 000
Stock		103 000		129 500
Prepaid advertising		3 850		3 000
		147 000		209 300
Non-current assets				
Land and buildings		240 000		540 000
Furniture	80 000		80 000	
less Accumulated depreciation	20 000	60 000	30 000	50 000
Motor vehicles	25 000		25 000	
less Accumulated depreciation	4 000	21 000	5 000	20 000
Goodwill (less impairment losses)		32 000		17 000
Total assets		500 000		836 300
Current liabilities				
Bank overdraft	5 000		12 000	
Creditors	79 000		84 400	
Annual leave payable	2 000		1 000	
Income tax payable	15 000		16 000	
Deferred tax liability	–		13 800	
Dividends payable	4 000	105 000	3 000	130 200
Deferred liabilities				
Loan from Beneficial Finance	50 000		70 000	
Debentures – Maturing 2009	–		100 000	
		50 000		170 000
Total liabilities		155 000		300 200
Shareholders' equity				
Share capital				
50 000 $1 ordinary shares fully paid			50 000	
200 000 $1 ordinary shares paid to $0.50	100 000		100 000	
General reserve	–		10 000	
Dividend reserve	50 000		30 000	
Asset revaluation reserve	150 000		200 000	
Retained profits	45 000	345 000	146 100	536 100
Total equities		500 000		836 300

Extract from general ledger as at 30 June 2007

Date	Particulars	Debit	Credit	Balance
	Trading			
		$	$	$
30 June	Sales (credit)		593 500	593 500 Cr
	Stock		129 500	723 000 Cr
	Stock	103 000		620 000 Cr
	Purchases (credit)	296 250		323 750 Cr
	Profit and loss	323 750		Nil
	Profit and loss account			
		$	$	$
30 June	Trading		323 750	323 750 Cr
	Insurance recovery		20 000	343 750 Cr
	Interest		5 000	348 750 Cr
	Wages and salaries	100 000		248 750 Cr
	Advertising	38 500		210 250 Cr
	Annual leave	9 500		200 750 Cr
	Doubtful debts	5 750		195 000 Cr
	Depreciation of furniture	10 000		185 000 Cr
	Depreciation of motor vehicles	1 000		184 000 Cr
	Legal damages	21 000		163 000 Cr
	Impairment loss – Goodwill	15 000		148 000 Cr
	Income tax expense	48 900		99 100 Cr
	Retained profits	99 100		Nil
	Retained profits account			
		$	$	$
1 July	Balance			45 000 Cr
30 June	Profit and loss		99 100	144 100 Cr
	Interim dividend	5 000		139 100 Cr
	Final dividend	3 000		136 100 Cr
	General reserve	10 000		126 100 Cr
	Dividend reserve		20 000	146 100 Cr

Additional information
- The final dividend declared on 30 June 2006 was paid on 1 October 2006.
- A bonus share dividend of 1 for 4 ordinary shares was made on 1 March 2007 and paid on 30 March from the asset revaluation reserve. Land was revalued during the year.
- $20 000 of the loan from Beneficial Finance was repaid on 30 November 2006. On 1 June 2007 the loan was increased to $70 000.

Question 8.12

The following data relates to Video Ltd. You are required to prepare a cash flow statement for the year ended 30 June 2007 in accordance with AASB 1026.

Balance sheets as at 30 June

	2006 $	2006 $	2007 $	2007 $
Shareholders' equity				
Share capital – $1 ordinary shares	130 000		185 000	
General reserve	20 000		30 000	
Dividend reserve	10 000		15 000	
Asset revaluation reserve	70 000		100 000	
Retained profits	40 000	270 000	100 300	430 300
Current liabilities				
Bank overdraft	60 000		54 700	
Loan – Video Rentals	65 000		63 000	
Accrued wages	15 000		12 000	
Dividends payable	20 000		25 000	
Income tax payable	10 000	170 000	5 000	159 700
Deferred liabilities				
Loan – Maturing 2010	40 000		70 000	
Debentures – Maturing 2009	50 000	90 000	50 000	120 000
Total equities		530 000		710 000
Current assets				
Cash in registers		28 000		16 000
Accounts receivable	52 000		64 000	
less Allowance for doubtful debts	6 000	46 000	7 000	57 000
Loan to employee		75 000		68 000
Prepayments – Rent		6 000		4 000
		155 000		145 000
Non-current assets				
Motor vehicles – At cost	135 000		146 000	
less Accumulated depreciation	15 000	120 000	20 000	126 000
Machinery – At cost	96 000		96 000	
less Accumulated depreciation	26 000	70 000	42 000	54 000
Land and buildings		180 000		380 000
Intangible assets				
Goodwill		5 000		5 000
Total assets		530 000		710 000

Video Ltd

Date	Particulars	Debit	Credit	Balance
	Profit and loss account			
		$	$	$
30 June	Rental revenue		420 000	420 000 Cr
	Dividends received		30 000	450 000 Cr
	Profit on sale of land		80 000	530 000 Cr
	Salaries and wages	240 000		290 000 Cr
	Rent	54 000		236 000 Cr
	Loss on sale of motor vehicle	2 000		234 000 Cr
	Depreciation of motor vehicle	11 000		223 000 Cr
	Depreciation of machinery	16 000		207 000 Cr
	Maintenance	65 000		142 000 Cr
	Advertising	5 000		137 000 Cr
	Interest	7 000		130 000 Cr
	Doubtful debts	1 000		129 000 Cr
	Income tax expense	14 700		114 300 Cr
	Retained profits	114 300		Nil
	Retained profits account			
		$	$	$
1 July	Balance			40 000 Cr
30 June	Profit and loss		114 300	154 300 Cr
	Interim dividend	14 000		140 300 Cr
	Final dividend	25 000		115 300 Cr
	General reserve	10 000		105 300 Cr
	Dividend reserve	5 000		100 300 Cr

Additional information

- Motor vehicles costing $20 000 were sold on 30 April 2007.
- Land which cost $100 000 was sold on 1 June 2007. This was considered to be an extraordinary transaction.
- Land and buildings were revalued upwards by $60 000 on 1 September 2006. Additional land was purchased on 1 February 2007.
- The final dividend on 30 June 2006 was paid on 1 August 2006.
- The bonus issue of 1 for 4 ordinary shares was declared from the asset revaluation reserve on 1 November 2006.
- In March 2007 there was an issue of 10 000 ordinary shares at $1 per share in full on application. The share issue was fully subscribed.

Question 8.13

The information presented below relates to Grand Ltd. You are required to prepare a cash flow statement for the year ended 30 June 2007 in accordance with the accounting standards.

Grand Ltd

Income statement for the year ended 30 June 2007

	$	$
Sales – Cash	172 000	
– Credit	400 000	572 000
less Cost of sales		312 000
Gross profit		260 000
add Other revenue		
Discount revenue	9 000	
Dividends received	4 000	13 000
		273 000
less Expenses		
Discount expense	400	
Bad debts	600	
Interest	2 500	
Wages	145 000	
Impairment loss – Goodwill	10 000	
Loss on vehicle disposal	4 000	
Depreciation – Vehicles	15 000	
Depreciation – Plant	40 500	
Employees' benefits	14 000	
Condemnation of buildings	76 000	308 000
Profit (loss) (before tax)		(35 000)
less Income tax expense		15 300
Net profit (loss)		(50 300)

Grand Ltd
Balance sheets as at 30 June

	2006		2007	
	$	$	$	$
Equities				
Ordinary shares		500 000		1 560 000
Calls in arrears		–		(50 000)
General reserve		35 000		30 000
Asset revaluation reserve		100 000		100 000
Retained profits		75 000		11 700
		710 000		1 651 700
Creditors control	70 000		54 000	
Income tax payable	6 000		8 000	
Employee benefits payable	35 000		40 000	
Dividends payable	10 000		12 000	
Mortgage – Land and buildings	400 000		250 000	
Debentures	–	521 000	200 000	564 000
		1 231 000		2 215 700
Assets				
Bank		133 100		(200 050)
Debtors control		9 000		21 000
Stock control		5 000		16 500
Deferred tax asset		12 150		15 750
Prepaid interest expense		250		500
Land and buildings		600 000		1 550 000
Plant and equipment	160 000		160 000	
less Accumulated depreciation	60 500	99 500	101 000	59 000
Motor vehicles	50 000		65 000	
less Accumulated depreciation	8 000	42 000	2 000	53 000
Goodwill		10 000		Nil
Shares in Adlib Ltd		320 000		700 000
		1 231 000		2 215 700

Additional information

- All stock is purchased on credit and controlled using a perpetual inventory system.
- Proposed final dividends at 30 June 2006 were paid on 1 August 2006.
- An interim dividend of $6 000 was declared on 30 November 2006 and paid on 23 December 2006.
- A final dividend, declared on 30 June 2007, will be paid on 1 December 2007.
- At 1 July 2006 ordinary shares consisted of 1 000 000 $1 ordinary shares paid to $0.50 each. On 1 August 2006 a final call was made on these shares. At 30 June 2007 calls were outstanding on 100 000 shares.
- On 1 March 2007, 200 000 ordinary shares were issued by way of a bonus dividend to shareholders. This was declared on 1 February 2007 and issued from the asset revaluation reserve.
- On 1 June 2007 additional shares were issued to the public.
- Buildings with a cost of $76 000 were condemned on 3 October 2006. Additional buildings were purchased on 10 November 2006. All land and buildings were revalued upwards by $200 000 on 1 June 2007.
- Vehicles costing $18 000 were sold on 20 March 2007 and replaced.

CHAPTER 9
CONSOLIDATED ACCOUNTS

Objectives

Upon satisfactory completion of this chapter you should be able to:

- explain why corporate reporting entities need to present consolidated accounts;
- identify when a company has the capacity to control other companies;
- prepare a consolidated worksheet to eliminate acquisition values of another company, at fair values, and above and below fair values;
- complete consolidated worksheets which eliminate intercompany indebtedness and servicing and amortise goodwill on acquisition;
- eliminate intercompany sales and purchases and unrealised profits in shares held in consolidated worksheets;
- eliminate in consolidated worksheets unrealised profits (losses) on non-current asset disposals; and
- prepare consolidated worksheets which eliminate intercompany dividends from pre- and post-acquisition profits.

Introduction

Companies may expand their operations by purchasing all or some of the share capital of other companies. Expansion in this way creates an economic entity comprising the investing company, commonly referred to as the parent entity, and the investee companies, which may be classified as either controlled entities (subsidiaries) or non-controlled entities.

Where an economic entity comprises the parent entity and controlled entities (subsidiaries), it is necessary to provide financial reports that consolidate the financial position and activities of the companies within the group. This is achieved by applying the fundamentals of **consolidated accounting**.

Where the economic entity includes the parent entity and non-controlled entities, the financial reports should comply with the fundamentals of **equity accounting**, which is beyond the scope of this book.

Obligation to present group accounts

The Corporations Law requires the directors of a company to present the income statement for the year and the balance sheet as at the end of the year to the shareholders at each annual general meeting. The Law also states that where a company is a parent entity the directors of that company must present at its annual general meeting group accounts comprising:

- the group's profit or loss; and
- the group's state of affairs as at the end of the financial year.

As the Corporations Law requires companies to comply with the accounting standards, directors will need to ensure that the accounting standard AASB 127: Consolidated and Separate Financial Statements is applied when presenting group accounts.

Consolidated accounts

The principal accounting standard that regulates the preparation and presentation of consolidated accounts is AASB 127: Consolidated and Separate Financial Statements.

The purpose of the standard is to identify both parent entities and subsidiary entities, prescribe the circumstances in which consolidated accounts are to be prepared, and detail the information that is to be included in the accounts, so that the consolidated accounts reflect the activities of a single economic entity.

The commentary within the standard makes reference to the use of consolidated accounts, stating that users of the financial reports who have an interest in the performance, financial position, financing and investing of the economic entity will find it much more useful to have one set of accounts rather than relying solely on the individual accounts prepared by the parent and each of its subsidiaries.

The standard gives the following definitions of consolidated financial statements, parent entity and subsidiary:

- **Consolidated financial statements** means financial statements of a group of companies presented as a single economic entity.
- **Parent entity** means an entity that has one or more subsidiaries.
- **Subsidiary** means an entity that is controlled by another entity known as the parent entity.

Companies that are both reporting entities and parent entities are required by the standard to consolidate the accounts of the parent and its subsidiaries. The consolidated reporting is prepared by combining the accounts of each of the entities comprising the economic entity, and the aggregated information is then presented as one set of accounts. This is illustrated as follows:

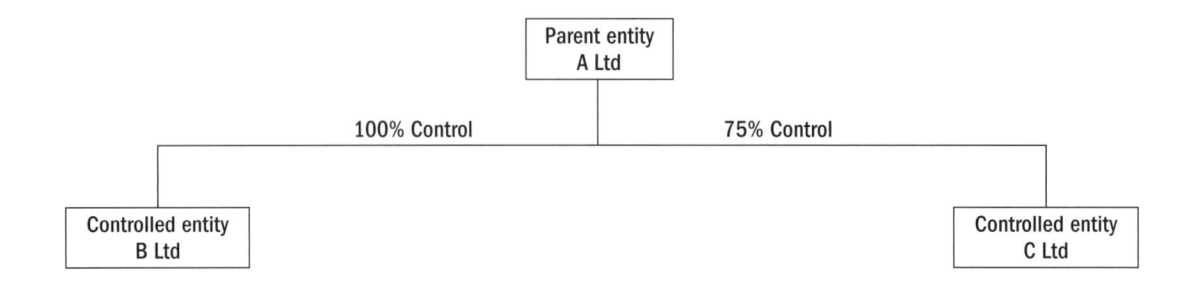

```
                    Parent entity
                       A Ltd
         100% Control          75% Control
    Controlled entity       Controlled entity
         B Ltd                    C Ltd
```

The individual companies (A Ltd, B Ltd and C Ltd) would be required by the Corporations Law and the accounting standards to present separate financial statements as separate entities. In addition, the parent entity, A Ltd, would be required to aggregate the accounts of all companies in the group and present one set of consolidated accounts reflecting the activities of the economic entity, which comprises A Ltd, B Ltd and C Ltd.

In practice, most parent entities present the consolidated accounts of the economic entity alongside the accounts of the parent.

Capacity to control

The existence of an economic entity (which must also be a reporting entity) depends on the ability of a parent to control a subsidiary. Control is defined in AASB 127: Consolidated and Separate Financial Statements as follows:

> Control is the power to govern the financial and operating policies of an entity so as to obtain benefits from its activities.

The accounting standard notes that the capacity to control an entity is a matter of judgement, dependent on a range of factors and circumstances. This includes the capacity of the parent company to:

- dominate the subsidiary company's board of directors;
- appoint or remove a majority of a board of directors of the subsidiary company;
- control casting of a majority of votes at a subsidiary's board meeting;
- control casting of a majority of votes at a general meeting of the subsidiary; and
- hold a legal instrument giving one entity the capacity to enjoy a majority of the benefits and be exposed to a majority of the risks of another entity, even though control apparently lies elsewhere.

'Capacity' can refer to the ability or power to exercise control through a trust, an agreement or practices, but that agreement or arrangement, however defined, does not have to be enforced. The accounting standard refers to ownership as an indicator of control, stating that control may (but need not) be indicated by majority ownership. However, ownership is only an indicator of control to the extent that it is complemented by an equivalent interest in voting rights of the entity that is controlled. AASB 127 takes the view that control may not be reflected in ownership and states that a board of directors may be dominated by the voting rights of one entity, even though that entity can command less than 50% of all voting rights that exist.

Capacity to control is the relevant indicator for determining a parent entity–subsidiary relationship, but that capacity as a matter of principle does not need to be exercised. It can, for example, be achieved by demanding the supply of various types of financial information.

In summary, AASB 127 has identified the requirement to consolidate as the basis of one entity's capacity to control another entity. The primary purpose of consolidated statements is to provide accounts that reflect a true and fair view of the earnings and position of a single economic unit.

Elimination adjustments

The consolidated accounts of the companies in the economic entity can be achieved by aggregating the accounts of the parent and subsidiaries on a single worksheet, from which financial reports can be prepared.

Consolidated accounts comprise a consolidated income statement and a consolidated balance sheet. The standard also requires adjustments to be made to the consolidated accounts to ensure that the financial statements of the economic entity reflect the activities of a single reporting entity.

The adjustments required fall into two categories. These are:

1. the elimination of the investment by the parent entity in the subsidiaries; and
2. the elimination of the transactions between the parent entity and the subsidiaries (intercompany transactions).

Elimination of an investment in a subsidiary

Where a company purchases a controlling interest in another entity it is required to record the value of assets acquired at their cost of acquisition. This is equivalent to the purchase consideration and other costs relating to the acquisition. Purchase consideration could encompass the issue of share capital, the exchanging of assets, the undertaking of liabilities or the giving of other securities by the purchaser in exchange for the net assets or shares of the other entity at fair values.

In order for the consolidated accounts to reflect the values of a single reporting entity the consolidation process must eliminate the carrying amount of the parent company's investment in each subsidiary.

Eliminations of an investment purchased at fair values

It is vital that the elimination of the investment in a subsidiary occurs at the values as at the date of acquisition. These values represent the historical value of the investment in the subsidiary. As accounting periods pass, it would be anticipated that the subsidiary would trade profitably, which would be reflected in the values on the balance sheet. On consolidation, the increase in wealth derived by the subsidiary since the date of acquisition is added to the value of the economic entity.

ILLUSTRATION

On 1 July 1982 Take Ltd purchased a 100% controlling interest in Over Ltd. On this date the balance sheet of Over Ltd was as follows:

Over Ltd

Balance sheet as at 1 July 1982

Assets	$	Equities	$
Bank	50 000	Ordinary shares	100 000
Debtors	20 000	General reserve	30 000
Vehicles	60 000	Retained profits	40 000
Equipment	40 000		
	170 000		170 000

To acquire the business, Take Ltd paid $1.70 for each share. This amounted to a total of $170 000. On 30 June 2007 the balance sheets of both companies were as follows:

Over Ltd *Subsidiary*
Balance sheet as at 30 June 2007

Assets	$	Equities	$
Bank	70 000	Ordinary shares	100 000
Debtors	40 000	General reserve	20 000
Equipment	200 000	Retained profits	140 000
Plant	90 000	Asset revaluation reserve	140 000
	400 000		400 000

Take Ltd *Parent*
Balance sheet as at 30 June 2007

Assets	$	Equities	$
Bank	200 000	Ordinary shares	500 000
Debtors	100 000	General reserve	50 000
Equipment	200 000	Retained profits	120 000
Investment in Over Ltd	170 000		
	670 000		670 000

An evaluation of the respective balance sheets of Over Ltd indicates an increase in wealth over the 25-year period of $230 000. This is summarised as follows:

	1982	2007	Increase (Decrease)
	$	$	$
Assets	170 000	400 000	230 000
Represented by:			
Ordinary shares	100 000	100 000	
General reserve	30 000	20 000	(10 000)
Retained profits	40 000	140 000	100 000
Asset revaluation reserve		140 000	140 000
			230 000

The increase in value upon consolidation of the accounts will add to the value of the economic entity. The resulting consolidated worksheet would be as follows:

Consolidated worksheet as at 30 June 2007

	Take Ltd	Over Ltd	Eliminations Debit	Eliminations Credit	Economic entity
	$	$	$	$	$
Assets					
Bank	200 000	70 000			270 000
Debtors	100 000	40 000			140 000
Equipment	200 000	200 000			400 000
Investment in Over Ltd	170 000			170 000 (1)	
Plant		90 000			90 000
	670 000	400 000			900 000
Equities					
Ordinary shares	500 000	100 000	100 000 (1)		500 000
General reserve	50 000	20 000	30 000 (1)		40 000
Retained profits	120 000	140 000	40 000 (1)		220 000
Asset revaluation reserve		140 000			140 000
	670 000	400 000	170 000	170 000	900 000

Elimination

1 Elimination of investment at date of acquisition at fair values.

The elimination removes the investment in the subsidiary by eliminating the ownership interest in the subsidiary – that is, ordinary shares, general reserve and retained profits. Since the date of acquisition Over Ltd has added profit to the consolidated accounts as reflected by the increase in the retained profits account and the reduction in the general reserve. In addition, value has been added by the inclusion of the asset revaluation reserve to the accounts since acquisition date.

The consolidated balance sheet on 30 June 2007 would be as follows:

Consolidated balance sheet as at 30 June 2007

	$	$
Assets		
Bank	270 000	
Debtors	140 000	
Equipment	400 000	
Plant	90 000	900 000
Equities		
Ordinary shares	500 000	
General reserve	40 000	
Retained profits	220 000	
Asset revaluation reserve	140 000	900 000

Note: The consolidated balance sheet should be prepared in a manner consistent with the requirements of AASB 1040: Balance Sheet. In this chapter, balance sheets will be prepared in a form suitable for internal management purposes.

In summary, the elimination entry required to eliminate the investment in a subsidiary at values applicable at the date of acquisition is as follows:

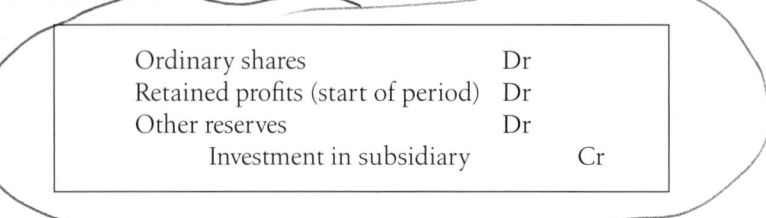

Ordinary shares	Dr	
Retained profits (start of period)	Dr	
Other reserves	Dr	
Investment in subsidiary		Cr

Question 9.1

From the following information you are required to prepare:

a the consolidated worksheet at 30 June 2007; and
b the consolidated balance sheet as at 30 June 2007.

Big Ltd purchased a 100% interest in Little Ltd on 1 January 2007 by paying $2.50 for each ordinary share issued at that date.

Little Ltd
Balance sheet as at 1 January 2007

Assets	$	Equities	$
Bank	250 000	Ordinary shares	
Vehicles	150 000	(200 000 at $1)	200 000
Stock	100 000	Reserves	300 000
	500 000		500 000

The respective company balance sheets as at 30 June 2007 are as follows:

Big Ltd
Balance sheet as at 30 June 2007

Assets	$	Equities	$
Bank	600 000	Creditors	100 000
Vehicles	100 000	Ordinary shares	
Stock	400 000	(1 000 000 at $1)	1 000 000
Equipment	50 000	Reserves	550 000
Shares in Little Ltd	500 000		
	1 650 000		1 650 000

Little Ltd
Balance sheet as at 30 June 2007

Assets	$	Equities	$
Bank	300 000	Creditors	50 000
Vehicles	150 000	Ordinary shares	200 000
Stock	120 000	Reserves	350 000
Debtors	30 000		
	600 000		600 000

Elimination of an investment purchased above fair values

A parent entity may pay a purchase price that is in excess of the fair values expressed in the balance sheet of a subsidiary, to gain a controlling interest. This may occur where the parent believes the subsidiary's balance sheet is undervalued or the parent is keen on acquiring the entity to obtain a greater market share, a diversified industry or a technical process.

Where the purchase consideration exceeds the fair values of the subsidiary at the date of acquisition the process of consolidation will bring to account goodwill on acquisition in accordance with AASB 3: Business Combinations.

ILLUSTRATION

On 30 June 2003, Cabernet Ltd acquired a 100% controlling interest in Shiraz Ltd by paying $3.50 to all Shiraz Ltd shareholders, the amount totalling $875 000.

Shiraz Ltd's balance sheet at this date was as follows:

Balance sheet as at 30 June

	$	$
Shareholders' equity		
Ordinary shares		250 000
Retained profits		400 000
General reserve		50 000
		700 000
Assets	800 000	
less Liabilities	100 000	
		700 000

In this illustration, the parent, Cabernet Ltd, has paid $875 000 for net assets of Shiraz Ltd of only $700 000 (assets of $800 000 minus liabilities of $100 000). In the consolidated worksheets that would follow the date of acquisition the investment of $875 000 would be eliminated, as would the following date of acquisition values: ordinary shares, $250 000; retained profits, $400 000; and general reserve, $50 000. The difference of $175 000 will represent the balancing item, goodwill, on acquisition.

Shown overleaf is the consolidated worksheet for the year ended 30 June 2007. It is four years since the date of acquisition.

Consolidated worksheet as at 30 June 2007

	Cabernet Ltd	Shiraz Ltd	Eliminations Debit	Eliminations Credit	Economic entity
	$	$	$	$	$
Assets					
Cash at bank	620 000	50 000			670 000
Debtors	150 000	40 000			190 000
Freehold land and premises	1 400 000	700 000			2 100 000
Motor vehicles	100 000	40 000			140 000
Fixtures and fittings	25 000	5 000			30 000
Investment in Shiraz Ltd	875 000			875 000 (1)	
Goodwill on acquisition			175 000 (1)		175 000
	3 170 000	835 000			3 305 000
Equities					
Creditors	275 000	32 000			307 000
Mortgage loan	500 000				500 000
Debentures	900 000				900 000
Ordinary shares	800 000	250 000	250 000 (1)		800 000
General reserve	20 000	60 000	50 000 (1)		30 000
Asset revaluation reserve	400 000				400 000
Retained profits	275 000	493 000	400 000 (1)		368 000
	3 170 000	835 000	875 000	875 000	3 305 000

Elimination

1 Elimination of investments at date of acquisition, above fair values.

The consolidated balance sheet for the economic entity is as follows:

Cabernet Ltd
Consolidated balance sheet as at 30 June 2007

	$	$
Shareholders' equity		
Paid-up capital – 800 000 ordinary	800 000	
General reserve	30 000	
Asset revaluation reserve	400 000	
Retained profits	368 000	1 598 000
Current liabilities		
Creditors		307 000
Non-current liabilities		
Mortgage loan	500 000	
Debentures	900 000	1 400 000
Total equities		3 305 000
Current assets		
Cash at bank	670 000	
Debtors	190 000	860 000
Non-current assets		
Freehold land and premises	2 100 000	
Motor vehicles	140 000	
Fixtures and fittings	30 000	
Goodwill on acquisition	175 000	2 445 000
Total assets		3 305 000

The goodwill recognised at the date of acquisition in normal circumstances would be amortised systematically over a number of years against profits. The amortisation of goodwill will be covered in the section dealing with the elimination of intercompany transactions.

In summary, the elimination entry required to eliminate the investment in a subsidiary where the purchase consideration is in excess of fair values of the subsidiary at the date of acquisition is as follows:

Ordinary shares	Dr	
Retained profits (start of period)	Dr	
Other reserves	Dr	
Goodwill on acquisition	Dr	
Investment in subsidiary		Cr

Question 9.2

On 30 June 2006 Low Ltd acquired a 100% interest in High Ltd by paying $3.95 for each issued ordinary share, thus gaining full control. On this date High Ltd held the following: ordinary shares, $300 000; retained profits, $400 000; and asset revaluation reserve, $200 000.

Shown below are the respective balance sheets at 30 June 2007 in the consolidated worksheet. You are required to complete the worksheet and then prepare a consolidated balance sheet as at 30 June 2007.

Consolidated worksheet as at 30 June 2007

	Low Ltd	High Ltd	Eliminations		Economic entity
			Debit	Credit	
	$	$	$	$	$
Assets					
Bank	100 000				
Debtors	150 000	60 000			
Stock	520 000	50 000			
Buildings	1 000 000	800 000			
Vehicles	300 000	100 000			
Equipment	125 000	140 000			
Investment in High Ltd	1 185 000				
	3 380 000	1 150 000			
Equities					
Bank overdraft		20 000			
Creditors	200 000	80 000			
Mortgage	300 000				
Paid-up capital ($1 shares)	1000 000	300 000			
General reserve	900 000	50 000			
Asset revaluation reserve	500 000	200 000			
Retained profits	480 000	500 000			
	3 380 000	1 150 000			

Elimination of an investment purchased below fair values

In contrast to the previous illustration, a subsidiary may be purchased at less than the fair value of the equity acquired; in this case the difference gives rise to a discount on acquisition. The recognition of a discount on acquisition is consistent with the requirements of AASB 3: Business Combinations.

A company may consider paying a value that is less than the fair value where the company being acquired has suffered losses in previous periods or the values on the vendor's balance sheet are in excess of market values.

The accounting standard requires a discount on acquisition to be accounted for by including the discount brought to account in the calculation of profits.

ILLUSTRATION

Elgers Ltd purchased all the issued capital in Forex Ltd on 1 July 2006 for $145 000 at which time Forex's balance sheet revealed ordinary shares of $100 000, retained profits of $20 000 and other reserves of $30 000.

In this illustration the purchase consideration of $145 000 is below the fair value by $5 000 — that is:

	$	$
Purchase consideration		145 000
less Equity acquired		
Ordinary shares	100 000	
Retained profits	20 000	
Other reserves	30 000	150 000
Discount on acquisition		(5 000)

The consolidated worksheet as at 30 June 2007 would appear as follows:

Consolidated worksheet as at 30 June 2007

	Elgers Ltd	Forex Ltd	Eliminations		Economic entity
			Debit	Credit	
	$	$	$	$	$
Assets					
Bank	3 000	27 000			30 000
Stock	40 000	30 000			70 000
Vehicles	17 000	30 000			47 000
Buildings	100 000	140 000			240 000
Shares in Forex Ltd	145 000			145 000 (1)	
	305 000	227 000			387 000
Equities					
Current liabilities	38 000	40 000			78 000
Non-current liabilities	30 000	12 000			42 000
Paid-up capital	200 000	100 000	100 000 (1)		200 000
Retained profits	15 000	40 000	20 000 (1)		35 000
Other reserves	22 000	35 000	30 000 (1)		27 000
Profit and loss (Discount on acquisition)				5 000 (1)	5 000
	305 000	227 000	150 000	150 000	387 000

Eliminations

1   Cost of acquisition and recognition of discount on acquisition.

In summary, the elimination entries required to eliminate the investment in a subsidiary where the purchase consideration is below the fair values of the subsidiary at the date of acquisition are as follows:

Ordinary shares	Dr
Retained profits (start of period)	Dr
Other reserves	Dr
Goodwill on acquisition	Dr
Investment in subsidiary	Cr
Profit and loss (discount on acquisition)	Cr

Question 9.3

On 1 January 2007 Dam Ltd purchased all of the issued shares of Bass Ltd by paying $4 for each share. Bass Ltd's balance sheet at this date was as follows:

Bass Ltd
Balance sheet as at 1 January 2007

Assets	$	Equities	$
Stock	100 000	Mortgage	50 000
Bank	100 000	Ordinary shares	
Patents	400 000	(200 000 × $2)	400 000
Vehicles	300 000	Reserves	450 000
	900 000		900 000

The respective company balance sheets at 31 December were as follows:

Dam Ltd
Balance sheet as at 30 June 2007

Assets	$	Equities	$
Stock	300 000	Creditors	100 000
Bank	250 000	Ordinary shares	1 000 000
Vehicles	600 000	Reserves	850 000
Investment in Bass Ltd	800 000		
	1 950 000		1 950 000

Bass Ltd
Balance sheet as at 30 June 2007

Assets	$	Equities	$
Stock	200 000	Mortgage	40 000
Bank	150 000	Ordinary shares	400 000
Patents	400 000	Reserves	960 000
Vehicles	600 000		
Debtors	50 000		
	1 400 000		1 400 000

You are required to prepare:
a the consolidated worksheet as at 30 June 2007; and
b the consolidated balance sheet as at 30 June 2007.

Elimination of intercompany transactions

The purpose of consolidated financial statements is to present the activities of the parent entity and its subsidiaries as one economic unit – that is, to present a true and fair view of the profit or loss and the state of affairs of the group with its dealings with parties outside the group.

As groups of companies have close associations within the group it is normal practice to 'trade' or 'deal' within the group. As many intercompany transactions do not alter the economic financial position of the group, those transactions must be eliminated.

AASB 127: Consolidated and Separate Financial Statements requires the elimination, in full, of the effects of all transactions between entities within the economic entity. Intercompany transactions that require annual eliminations on consolidation are:
- impairment of goodwill on acquisition;
- intercompany indebtedness and servicing;
- intercompany stock transactions;
- intercompany disposal of non-current assets; and
- intercompany dividends.

Impairment of goodwill

Where a parent entity has acquired the assets of a subsidiary by paying a purchase consideration above fair values, goodwill on acquisition will be identified at the time of consolidating the accounts. In accordance with the accounting standards it is necessary to regularly assess the fair values of the cash-generating assets acquired in a business combination and compare the fair values against the acquisition values.

Where the fair values of the cash-generating assets are less than the carrying amounts of these assets, their values have been impaired and must be included as an impairment loss in the calculation of profits.

Where the consolidated accounts include goodwill on acquisition and the goodwill has been impaired since the date of acquisition, the impairment losses will need to be identified and recorded as follows:

1. the impairment amount relating to the period covering the *date of acquisition* to the *beginning of the current reporting* period; and
2. the impairment amount relating to the *current period*.

To accommodate the impairment of goodwill it is necessary to incorporate the income statement and the balance sheet of the parent entity and the subsidiary into the consolidated worksheet. With the income statement incorporated with the balance sheet it is then possible to write off the components of impaired goodwill against previous periods' profits (retained profits) and the current period's profit as follows:

1. Impaired goodwill that has been recognised since the *date of acquisition* to the *beginning of the current reporting period* is to be written off against the retained profits of the subsidiary at the *start of the period*. This is justified on the basis that in each previous period the consolidated worksheets would have reduced annual profits by the amount of impairment loss of goodwill in that year. Consequently, the retained profits at the start of the period, as stated in the subsidiary's income statement, would be overstated by the amount of accumulated impairment losses of goodwill on acquisition since the date of acquisition.
2. Goodwill impairment losses recognised in the *current period* are to be expensed in the current period's profit by including the item as an expense within the period.

ILLUSTRATION

Journal Entry

On 1 January 2004, Banana Ltd purchased a 100% controlling interest in Republic Ltd by paying $300 000. On this date the shareholders' equity of Republic Ltd consisted of:

Investment in republic Cr $ 300,000

	$
Ordinary shares *Dr*	100 000
Retained profits *Dr*	50 000
Asset revaluation reserve *Dr*	50 000
Goodwill *Dr* *100,000*	200 000

The goodwill on acquisition in this purchase is $100 000. For the period 1 January 2004 to the start of the current reporting year 1 July 2006, Banana Ltd determined that the assets acquired had been impaired by $50 000.

They also determined that the same assets had been impaired by a further $20 000 in the current period ending 30 June 2007.

On 30 June 2007 the consolidated worksheet that incorporates the financial reports of both entities appears as follows. Included are the elimination entries to eliminate the purchase consideration at the date of acquisition and the amortisation of goodwill over the three-and-a-half-year period.

Consolidated worksheet as at 30 June 2007

	Banana Ltd	Republic Ltd	Eliminations Debit	Eliminations Credit	Economic entity
	$	$	$	$	$
Sales	400 000	200 000			600 000
Cost of sales	160 000	60 000			220 000
Gross profit	240 000	140 000			380 000
Interest received	20 000	10 000			30 000
Rental income	10 000				10 000
	270 000	150 000			420 000
Wages expenses	170 000	50 000			220 000
Other expenses	45 000	25 000	20 000 (3)		90 000
Profit before tax	55 000	75 000			110 000
Income tax expense	22 000	30 000			52 000
Profit after tax	33 000	45 000			58 000
Retained profits 1 July 2006	76 000	60 000	50 000 (1)		
			50 000 (2)		36 000
	109 000	105 000			94 000
Transfer to general reserve	–	15 000			15 000
Retained profits 30 June 2007	109 000	90 000			79 000
Ordinary shares	300 000	100 000	100 000 (1)		300 000
General reserve	35 000	20 000			55 000
Asset revaluation reserve	80 000	50 000	50 000 (1)		80 000
Current liabilities	20 000	15 000			35 000
Non-current liabilities	50 000	20 000			70 000
	594 000	295 000			619 000
Current assets	50 000	20 000			70 000
Fixed assets	244 000	275 000			519 000
Investment in Republic Ltd	300 000			300 000 (1)	
Goodwill on acquisition			100 000 (1)	50 000 (2)	
				20 000 (3)	30 000
	594 000	295 000	370 000	370 000	619 000

Eliminations

1 Elimination of investment at date of acquisition and recognition of goodwill on acquisition.
2 Impairment losses of goodwill from the date of acquisition to the beginning of the current reporting year.
3 Impairment loss of goodwill for the current reporting year.

In summary, the elimination entry required to eliminate successive years' goodwill impairment losses is as follows:

Expenses (impairment loss – goodwill)	Dr	20,000
Retained profits (start of period)	Dr	50,000
Goodwill on acquisition	Cr	70,000

Intercompany indebtedness and servicing

The provision of loans by one company to one or more companies within the group is a normal part of group transactions. While these transactions are represented in the final reports of those entities involved, they do not alter the overall financial position of group activities, and for this reason intercompany loans must be eliminated.

In addition, where a company within the group makes a payment to another company within the group for expenses, this will also need to be eliminated. This may occur where a company pays interest on its debts, pays for the use of assets by way of rent or pays for expenses for management services rendered.

The elimination entry required to eliminate intercompany indebtedness is as follows:

Debt acquired (liability)	Dr	
Debt provided (asset)	Cr	cancelling.

The elimination entry required to eliminate intercompany servicing is as follows:

Revenue item	Dr	
Expense item	Cr	reversed.

ILLUSTRATION

On 1 July 2002, Far Ltd purchased all of the issued capital of Away Ltd. The price paid per share was $2.25. At this date Away Ltd held the following shareholders' equity:

	$
Ordinary shares	20 000
General reserve	10 000
Retained profits	5 000

Additional information

During the year ended 30 June 2007 the following intercompany transactions occurred:
- Far Ltd paid interest of $2 000 to Away Ltd on its $10 000 long-term loan.
- Away Ltd paid Far Ltd $8 000 for factory rental.
- Goodwill has been impaired by $5 000 since the date of acquisition, consisting of $4 000 from the date of acquisition to the start of the current period and $1 000 in the current year.

Consolidated worksheet as at 30 June 2007

	Far Ltd	Away Ltd	Eliminations Debit	Eliminations Credit	Economic entity
	$	$	$	$	$
Sales	400 000	200 000			600 000
Cost of sales	160 000	60 000			220 000
Gross profit	240 000	140 000			380 000
Interest received	22 000	10 000	2 000 (3)		30 000
Rental income	8 000		8 000 (5)		
	270 000	150 000			410 000
Wages expense	170 000	50 000			220 000
Interest expense	15 000	5 000		2 000 (3)	18 000
Rental expense	8 000			8 000 (5)	
Other expenses	45 000	27 000	1 000 (2)		73 000
Profit (before tax)	40 000	60 000			99 000
Income tax expense	16 000	24 000			40 000
Profit (after tax)	24 000	36 000			59 000
Retained profits 1 July 2006	76 000	14 000	5 000 (1)		81 000
			4 000 (2)		
Retained profits 30 June 2007	100 000	50 000			140 000
Ordinary shares	100 000	20 000	20 000 (1)		100 000
General reserve	20 000	20 000	10 000 (1)		30 000
Asset revaluation reserve	80 000	10 000			90 000
Current liabilities	20 000	15 000			35 000
Non-current liabilities	50 000	20 000	10 000 (4)		60 000
	370 000	135 000			455 000
Current assets	50 000	20 000			70 000
Non-current assets	275 000	115 000		10 000 (4)	380 000
Investment in Away Ltd	45 000			45 000 (1)	
Goodwill on acquisition			10 000 (1)	5 000 (2)	5 000
	370 000	135 000	70 000	70 000	455 000

Eliminations

1. Investment in Away Ltd at date of acquisition values and creation of goodwill on acquisition.
2. Impairment loss of goodwill on acquisition from date of acquisition to date of reporting:
   - $4 000 from 1 July 2002 to 30 June 2006
   - $1 000 from 1 July 2006 to 30 June 2007.
3. Elimination of interest on loan.
4. Elimination of loan.
5. Elimination of rental servicing.

Question 9.4

On 1 July 1989, Bond Ltd purchased all of the issued capital of Wells Ltd for $55 000 to gain control. On this date Wells Ltd's shareholders' equity consisted of:

	$
Ordinary shares	20 000
General reserve	10 000
Retained profits	5 000

Additional information

During the year ended 30 June 2007 the following transactions occurred:
- Wells Ltd paid $20 000 interest to Bond Ltd on its $100 000 long-term loan.
- Wells Ltd paid Bond Ltd $40 000 for management services rendered.
- Goodwill has been impaired by $18 000 since the date of acquisition, consisting of $1 000 for the current year and $17 000 for previous years.

You are required to complete the consolidated worksheet for the year ended 30 June 2007.

Consolidated worksheet as at 30 June 2007

	Bond Ltd	Wells Ltd	Eliminations Debit	Eliminations Credit	Economic entity
	$	$	$	$	$
Gross profit	540 000	850 000			1,390,000
Interest received	40 000	20 000	20,000		40,000
Management fees income	60 000		40,000		20,000
	640 000	870 000			1,450,000
Interest expense	5 000	20 000		20,000	5,000
Management fees	40 000			40,000	0
Other expenses	250 000	530 000	1000		781,000
Profit (before tax)	385 000	280 000			664,000
Income tax expense	154 000	112 000			266,000
Profit (after tax)	231 000	168 000			398,000
Retained profits 1 July 2006	180 000	60 000	5000+17000		218,000
Retained profits 30 June 2007	411 000	228 000	17000		616,000
Ordinary shares	500 000	20 000	20 000		500,000
General reserve	100 000	40 000	10000		130,000
Current liabilities	45 000	70 000			115,000
Non-current liabilities	250 000	400 000	100000		550,000
	1 306 000	758 000			1,911,000
Current assets	150 000	220 000			370,000
Non-current assets	1 101 000	538 000		100,000	1,539,000
Investment in Wells Ltd	55 000			55,000	0
					20000
	1 306 000	758 000			1,911,000

Intercompany stock transactions

Where companies within the group participate in the exchange of products it is necessary to eliminate the effect of intercompany profits associated with stock transactions to ensure that the consolidated reports represent a true and fair view of a single economic entity. This will therefore necessitate the eliminations of:

- intercompany sales and purchases;
- unrealised profits in closing stocks; and
- unrealised profits in opening stocks.

Intercompany sales and purchases

Intercompany sales and purchases are eliminated to avoid 'double counting'. This elimination is necessary as it is only the profit (loss) made between the economic entity and external parties that alters the financial status of the economic entity, not sales and purchases between economic entity members. Thus, the sales between economic entity members are eliminated on the basis that the sale by one economic entity member is the purchase of the other.

ILLUSTRATION

Assume that Big Ltd has purchased goods for $40 000, and in turn sells them to Small Ltd, a subsidiary, for $50 000. Small in turn sells them to outside parties for a total of $60 000. Both companies would record the above transactions in the 'normal' way as they are both individual economic units.

The extract of the income statements of Big Ltd and Small Ltd is as follows:

Consolidated worksheet (profit and loss section)

	Big Ltd	Small Ltd	Total	Adjustments	Economic entity
	$	$	$	$	$
Sales	50 000 Cr	60 000 Cr	110 000 Cr	50 000 Dr	60 000
less Cost of goods sold	40 000 Dr	50 000 Dr	90 000 Dr	50 000 Cr	40 000
Gross profit	10 000	10 000	20 000		20 000

Without adjustment, sales for the group would total $110 000. However, sales to outsiders only amounted to $60 000, and so sales would have been overstated by $50 000, the price at which the merchandise was exchanged within the economic entity. Similarly, cost of goods sold would have totalled $90 000. However, the cost to the economic entity was only $40 000; again, cost of goods sold would have been overstated by $50 000. The adjustment required is for the amount the merchandise was exchanged for within the economic entity.

The total profit is the same to the economic entity whether the adjustment has taken place or not – that is, $20 000. Without adjustment the directors of Big Ltd could not present economic entity accounts reflecting a true and fair view of the state of affairs, as both sales and cost of sales would be overstated.

Question 9.5

You are required to complete the consolidated worksheet for the parent entity, ABC Ltd, and its wholly controlled subsidiary, XYZ Ltd, by incorporating the following transaction.

The XYZ company sold stock to ABC Ltd at 20% mark-up on its cost price of $20 000. ABC Ltd subsequently sold these goods with a sales mark-up of 30%.

Consolidated worksheet

	ABC Ltd	XYZ Ltd	Eliminations		Economic entity
			Debit	Credit	
	$	$	$	$	$
Sales	300 000	200 000	24,000		476,000
Cost of goods sold					
Stock (beginning)	50 000	40 000			90 000
Purchases	140 000	80 000		24,000	196,000
	190 000	120 000			286,000
less					
Stock (end)	30 000	50 000			80 000
Cost of goods sold	160 000	70 000			206,000
Gross profit	140 000	130 000	24,000	24,000	270,000

Unrealised profits in closing stocks

In conjunction with intercompany sales and purchases may be the related problem of unrealised profits retained in stock on hand at the end of the period. The stock figures in the respective balance sheets will be overstated by the amount of profit that is unrealised (unearned) with parties outside the group. The procedure adopted to deal with unrealised profit in stock on hand is to eliminate the profit element in the stock.

Another effect of making adjustments for intercompany transactions is the effect of the adjustment on income tax expense. Where an adjustment alters profit, there will be an effect on the calculation of income tax expense. If the adjustment reduces profit, income tax expense will fall and a deferred tax asset will be brought to account. As the adjusting entry only affects the calculation of net profit and not taxable income, income tax payable liability will not be affected.

ILLUSTRATION

In the previous illustration, Big Ltd sold Small Ltd $50 000 worth of merchandise which cost the group $40 000. This is a mark-up of $10 000 (20% of selling price). If at balance date Small Ltd had $12 000 of this stock on hand, clearly then $2 400 (20% of the selling price) has not been realised. This amount is overstating both balance sheet stock on hand and its counterpart stock at end in the trading statement. The tax rate is 40%.

Adjusting entries on consolidation to eliminate the unrealised profit are therefore:

> Stock at end (trading)   Dr $2 400
>   Stock on hand (balance sheet)   Cr $2 400

The effect on profit of this elimination is shown in the table below.

	Profit before adjustment	Profit after adjustment
	$	$
Sales (group)	60 000	60 000
less Cost of sales		
Purchases (group)	40 000	40 000
less Stock at end	12 000	9 600
Cost of sales	28 000	30 400
Gross profit	32 000	29 600
Income tax expense @ 30%	9 600	8 880
Profit after tax	22 400	20 720

By reducing stock at end by $2 400, cost of sales is increased from $28 000 to $30 400. This reduces profit from $32 000 to $29 600.

As a result of reducing the profit of the economic entity it is necessary to reduce the group's income tax expense and create a deferred tax asset. Profit has been reduced by $2 400 and thus income tax expense will need to be reduced by $720 ($2 400 × .30). The adjusting entry would be:

Deferred tax asset	Dr $720
Income tax expense	Cr $720

Question 9.6

Complete the consolidated worksheet for the Black and White group for the year ended 30 June 2006 from the following information.

On 1 October 2002, Black Ltd purchased all of the issued capital of White Ltd. The price paid per share was $2.50.

At this date White Ltd held the following shareholders' equity:

	$
Ordinary shares	40 000
Retained profits	60 000

Additional information

- During the year ended 30 June 2007 Black Ltd sold White Ltd $100 000 of stock on credit.
- At 30 June 2007 White Ltd's closing stock included unrealised profits of $20 000.
- The tax rate is 30%.

Consolidated worksheet as at 30 June 2007

Account	Bond Ltd	Wells Ltd	Eliminations Debit	Eliminations Credit	Economic entity
	$	$	$	$	$
Sales	900 000	400 000	100,000		1,200,000
less Cost of sales					
Stock at start	180 000	80 000			260,000
Purchases	540 000	240 000			680,000
	720 000	320 000		100,000	940,000
Stock at end	144 000	65 000	20,000		189,000
	576 000	255 000			
Gross profit	324 000	145 000			
Other expenses	154 000	80 000			
Profit before tax	170 000	65 000			
Income tax expense	51 000	19 500			
Profit after tax	119 000	45 500			
Retained profits 1 July 2006	50 000	90 000	60,000		
Retained profits 30 June 2007	169 000	135 500			
Ordinary shares	200 000	40 000	40,000		
Liabilities	150 000	240 000			
	519 000	415 500			
Stock on hand	144 000	65 000		20,000	
Deferred tax asset	12 000	4 000			
Other assets	263 000	346 500			
Investment in White Ltd	100 000			100,000	
	519 000	415 500			791,000

Unrealised profits in opening stock

The stock at the end of a period becomes the opening stock in the next period. As elimination only occurs on consolidation, the opening stocks of a company that had unrealised profits in the previous year's closing stocks must again be amended. Adjustments must also be made to recognise the tax effect of the transaction, as profit is brought to account.

The problem here is that last year's closing stocks affected last year's profits, and not only is opening stock overstated but so too is opening retained profits (after tax). Both of these amounts must be reduced and the income tax recognised.

In the previous illustration the stock at the end of the year was reduced by $2 400 as a result of an unrealised profit. The stock adjustment reduced profits and income tax was also reduced by $720. These two entries resulted in profit (after tax) falling by $1 680 ($2 400 − $720).

In the following period the adjustments from the previous year will impact on the consolidated worksheet as follows:

- The opening retained profits reported on the balance sheets will be overstated by the amount of after-tax profits not realised in the previous year, i.e. $1 680. Consequently the opening retained profits amounts will need to be reduced by $1 680.
- As the closing stock of the previous period was overstated by $2 400, the opening stock of the following period will also need to be reduced on the consolidated worksheet by $2 400.
- The reduction to opening stock will result in lower costs and a higher profit. Consequently, the income tax expense for the period will be increased by $720 ($2 400 × .30).

The entries required to eliminate the unrealised profits in the opening stocks of the previous illustration in the next accounting period would be:

Retained profits (start of period)	Dr $1 680	
Income tax expense	Dr $720	
Stock at beginning		Cr $2 400

The adjustment to stock at beginning effectively records the profit that was unrealised in the previous period – that is, it is recognised in the group accounts. As a result of recognising the profit in the current period, income tax expense must be increased. This analysis can be evaluated as follows:

	Profit before adjustment	Profit after adjustment
	$	$
Sales (budgeted)	100 000	100 000
less Cost of sales		
Stock at beginning	12 000	9 600
Gross profit	88 000	90 400
Income tax expense at 30%	26 400	27 120
Profit after tax	61 600	63 280
Retained profits (start) (assumed)	10 000	8 320
Retained profits (end)	71 600	71 600

These calculations indicate that due to the reduction in stock at beginning, profit before tax has risen from $88 000 to $90 400. At an income tax rate of 30% this results in an after-tax profit of $61 600, compared to $63 280 – an increase of $1 680.

After adjusting the retained profits (at start) downward by $1 680 from $10 000 to $8 320 the result is a retained profits figure of $71 600 before and after the adjustments. While there is no change to retained profits (at end) before and after the adjustments, the directors can be assured that they have reported a true and fair view of the respective profit calculations for the economic entity.

In summary, the adjusting entries to eliminate intercompany sales, unrealised profits in closing stocks and unrealised profits in opening stocks are as follows:

- Elimination of intercompany sales

Sales	Dr	
Purchases		Cr

- Elimination of unrealised profits in closing stocks

Stock at end (trading)	Dr	
Stock on hand (balance sheet)		Cr
Deferred tax asset	Dr	
Income tax expense		Cr

- Elimination of unrealised profits in opening stocks

Retained profits (start)	Dr	
Income tax expense	Dr	
Stock at beginning		Cr

Question 9.7

You are required to complete the consolidated worksheet from the information given below.

On 1 January 2005, Trouble Ltd purchased all of the issued capital of Shooter Ltd and gained control. At this date Shooter Ltd held the following shareholders' equity:

	$
Ordinary shares	100 000
Retained profits	40 000

Additional information

- Intercompany annual sales for the year ended 30 June 2007 were:

	$
Trouble Ltd to Shooter Ltd	150 000
Shooter Ltd to Trouble Ltd	50 000

- The opening stock of Shooter Ltd includes $10 000 unrealised profit.
- The tax rate is 30%.

Consolidated worksheet as at 30 June 2007

	Trouble Ltd	Shooter Ltd	Eliminations Debit	Eliminations Credit	Economic entity
	$	$	$	$	$
Sales	620 000	550 000			
less Cost of sales					
Stock at start	100 000	180 000			
Purchases	340 000	330 000			
	440 000	510 000			
Stock at end	120 000	90 000			
	320 000	420 000			
Gross profit	300 000	130 000			
Other expenses	110 000	90 000			
Profit before tax	190 000	40 000			
Income tax expense	76 000	16 000			
Profit after tax	114 000	24 000			
Retained profits 1 July 2006	180 000	60 000			
Retained profits 30 June 2007	294 000	84 000			
Ordinary shares	500 000	100 000			
Liabilities	250 000	400 000			
	1 044 000	584 000			
Current assets	150 000	220 000			
Non-current assets	754 000	364 000			
Investment in Shooter Ltd	140 000				
	1 044 000	584 000			

Question 9.8

You are required to complete the consolidated worksheet for the year ended 30 June 2007 for the Hill and Dale group from the following information.

On 1 January 2005, Hill Ltd purchased all of the issued capital of Dale Ltd and gained control. At this date Dale Ltd held the following shareholders' equity:

	$
Ordinary shares	100 000
Retained profits	15 000

Additional information for the year ended 30 June 2007

- Intercompany sales totalled $300 000 for the year.
- Hill Ltd's opening stock includes $5 000 of unrealised profits.
- Dale Ltd's closing stock includes an unrealised profit of $20 000.
- Dale Ltd owes Hill Ltd $40 000 for stock purchased during the year.
- Goodwill is to be impaired by $4 000, consisting of $2 000 for the year ended 30 June 2006 and $2 000 for the current year.
- The tax rate is 30%.

Consolidated worksheet as at 30 June 2007

	Hill Ltd	Dale Ltd	Eliminations Debit	Eliminations Credit	Economic entity
	$	$	$	$	$
Sales	900 000	386 000			
less Cost of sales					
Stock at start	26 000	16 000			
Purchases	600 000	250 000			
	626 000	266 000			
Stock at end	26 000	25 000			
	600 000	241 000			
Gross profit	300 000	145 000			
Other expenses	200 000	70 000			
Profit before tax	100 000	75 000			
Income tax expense	40 000	30 000			
Profit after tax	60 000	45 000			
Retained profits 1 July 2006	20 000	45 000			
Retained profits 30 June 2007	80 000	90 000			
Ordinary shares	30 000	100 000			
Liabilities	250 000	250 000			
	360 000	440 000			
Bank	60 000	42 000			
Stock on hand	26 000	25 000			
Deferred tax asset	4 000	12 000			
Other assets	145 000	361 000			
Investment in Dale Ltd	125 000				
	360 000	440 000			

Intercompany disposal of non-current assets

Companies may periodically dispose of non-current assets to other entities, some of which may be companies, which are part of the economic entity. These assets may be sold at cost price, at a profit or at a loss.

Disposal at cost price

Where assets are sold to companies within the economic entity at cost price this will result in the transfer of ownership from one company to another. The value of the asset on sale by the vendor company will be the same as the purchase price paid by the purchasing company. There is no need for an adjustment to be made on consolidation as, from the economic entity's viewpoint, the asset is still owned by the economic entity and it is recorded at its cost price. Ownership of the asset between companies within the economic entity has merely changed hands.

Disposal above cost price

Non-current assets exchanged between a parent and a controlled entity, above the cost price of the asset, will result in a profit being reported by the selling company, with the purchasing company recording the asset above its original cost price.

When eliminating an unrealised profit on the sale of an asset there are three entries required in the consolidated accounts in the year in which the asset was sold. These are:

1. elimination of the unrealised profit;
2. elimination of overstated depreciation; and
3. adjustment to income tax.

Elimination of the unrealised profit. When an asset is sold at a profit between two companies where one company has a controlling interest over the other, the respective company accounts will record a profit on the sale of the asset in the accounts of the selling company and an asset in the purchasing company accounts recorded above its cost price.

To eliminate an unrealised profit on the sale of an asset on consolidating the accounts the following adjusting entry is required.

Profit on sale of asset	Dr	
Asset		Cr

Example: AD Ltd has a 100% controlling interest of YZ Ltd. On 1 July 2006 YZ Ltd sold equipment costing $500 000 to AD Ltd for $650 000 and brought to account a profit of $150 000.

In respective company accounts the following would have been recorded:

AD Ltd			YZ Ltd		
Equipment	$650 000 Dr		Bank	$650 000 Dr	
Bank		$650 000 Cr	Equipment		$500 000 Cr
			Profit on sale of asset		$150 000 Cr

As the asset is overstated by the amount of profit, the asset value must be reduced and the profit must be eliminated from the consolidated accounts. The required elimination entry is as follows:

Profit on sale of asset	Dr $150 000
Equipment	Cr $150 000

Elimination of overstated depreciation. If the asset has been depreciated, the consolidated accounts would be showing a higher amount of depreciation based on the inflated value of the asset. Hence the annual depreciation amounts would need to be adjusted.

To reduce the depreciation charge on the consolidation worksheet the following adjusting entry is required.

Accumulated depreciation of asset	Dr	
Depreciation expense		Cr

Example: Using the previous example, AD Ltd depreciated the asset at 10% for the year which resulted in an annual depreciation charge of $65 000. As the true cost of the asset to the economic entity is $500 000, the true depreciation charge should have been $50 000. Thus, depreciation is overstated by $15 000. The elimination entry to adjust the annual depreciation charge would be:

Accumulated depreciation of equipment	Dr $15 000	
Depreciation of equipment		Cr $15 000

Adjustment of income tax. Finally, an adjustment will be required to the company's income tax expense account as a result of the removal of the profit on the sale of the asset and depreciation expense. Where the consolidated accounts report a reduced profit arising from the elimination of an unrealised profit on the sale of an asset, the income tax expense account must be reduced and the deferred tax asset account increased. The income tax payable account will not be affected, as the unrealised profit is only an internal book entry.

The entry to adjust income tax on an unrealised profit on the sale of an asset is as follows:

Deferred tax asset	Dr	
Income tax expense		Cr

Example: The adjusting entries in the two previous examples eliminated the profit on the sale of the asset of $150 000 and depreciation expense of $15 000. Hence profit has been reduced by $135 000. If an income tax rate of 30% was applied, then income tax would be overstated by $40 500.

The entry to eliminate the overstated income tax amount would be:

Deferred tax asset	Dr $40 500	
Income tax expense		Cr $40 500

Adjustment of subsequent consolidated accounts. The consolidation worksheets in the financial periods following the sale of the asset between the two companies will need to adjust the respective account balances until the asset is sold to an outside entity whereby the profit or loss on the sale will be realised. Until that event occurs the following entry will be required in successive consolidated worksheets to reduce the value of the equipment and the amount of retained profits (profit after income tax).

Retained profits (at start of period)	Dr	
Deferred tax asset	Dr	
Accumulated depreciation	Dr	
Equipment		Cr

Example: The value of equipment in the previous examples was reduced by $150 000 and accumulated depreciation was reduced by $15 000. Profit was reduced by $135 000 and income tax reduced by $40 500. Hence the after-tax adjustment was $94 500 ($135 000 less $40 500).

The adjusting entry resulting from the elimination entries in the year of sale in subsequent consolidated accounts would be as follows:

Retained profits (at start of period)	Dr $94 500	
Deferred tax asset	Dr $40 500	
Accumulated depreciation	Dr $15 000	
Equipment		Cr $150 000

Question 9.9

On 1 July 2006 Growth Ltd purchased a vehicle from its controlled subsidiary Hall Ltd at a cost price of $800 000. Hall Ltd purchased the asset in a previous year for $600 000. Depreciation is charged at 15% p.a. on the straight-line method and the income tax rate is 30%.

You are required to prepare the elimination entries for the consolidated accounts at:
a 30 June 2007; and
b 1 July 2007.

Disposal below cost price

When companies in an economic entity exchange assets below cost price the asset will result in a loss being reported by the selling company, with the purchasing company recording the asset below its original cost price.

When eliminating an unrealised loss on the sale of an asset there are three entries required in the consolidated accounts in the year in which the asset was sold. These are:
1 elimination of the unrealised loss;
2 elimination of overstated depreciation; and
3 adjustment to income tax.

Elimination of the unrealised loss. When a loss on the sale of an asset between companies in an economic entity occurs, the consolidated accounts must be adjusted to eliminate the loss and bring the asset back up in value to its original cost.

To eliminate an unrealised loss on the sale of an asset on consolidating the accounts the following adjusting entry is required.

Asset	Dr	
Loss on sale of asset		Cr

Example: G Ltd has a 100% controlling interest in D Ltd. On 1 July 2007 G Ltd sold machinery costing $700 000 to G Ltd for $600 000 and brought to account a loss of $100 000.

In respective company accounts the following would have been recorded:

G Ltd			D Ltd		
Bank	$600 000 Dr		Machinery	$600 000 Dr	
Loss on sale of asset	$100 000 Dr		Bank		$600 000 Cr
Machinery		$700 000 Cr			

As the asset is understated by the amount of the loss, the asset value must be increased and the loss must be eliminated from the consolidated accounts. The required elimination entry is as follows:

Machinery	Dr $100 000	
Loss on sale of machinery		Cr $100 000

Elimination of understated depreciation. As the asset has been recorded at a value below its original cost price, any depreciation adjustments would be understated compared to the depreciation that would have been recorded if calculated on its cost price. Hence the annual depreciation amounts would need to be adjusted.

To reduce the depreciation charge on the consolidation worksheet the following adjusting entry is required.

Depreciation expense	Dr	
Accumulated depreciation of asset		Cr

Example: Using the previous example, if D Ltd depreciated the asset at 10% for the year calculated on the purchase price of $600 000, this would result in an annual depreciation charge of $60 000. As the true cost of the asset to the economic entity is $700 000, the true depreciation charge should have been $70 000. Thus, depreciation is understated by $10 000. The entry to adjust the annual depreciation charge would be as follows:

Depreciation of equipment	Dr $10 000
Accumulated depreciation of equipment	Cr $10 000

Adjustment of income tax. The adjustments to eliminate the loss on the sale of the asset and increase the amount of depreciation would effectively increase profits and, as a consequence, income tax would need to be adjusted.

The entry to adjust income tax on an unrealised loss on the sale of an asset is as follows:

Income tax expense	Dr
Deferred tax liability	Cr

Example: The adjusting entries in the two previous examples eliminated the loss on the sale of the machinery of $100 000 and depreciation expense of $10 000. Hence profit has been increased by $90 000. If an income tax rate of 30% is applied, then income tax would be understated by $27 000.

The elimination entry to eliminate the overstated income tax amount would be:

Income tax expense	Dr $27 000
Deferred tax liability	Cr $27 000

Adjustment of subsequent consolidated accounts. If the asset that was exchanged between the two companies is not sold to a company external to the economic entity, subsequent consolidations will need to eliminate the unrealised loss brought to account in the year of the sale. The required entry is as follows:

Asset	Dr
Retained profits (at start)	Cr
Accumulated depreciation	Cr
Deferred tax liability	Cr

Example: The value of equipment in the previous examples was reduced by $100 000 and accumulated depreciation was increased by $10 000. Profit was increased by $90 000 and income tax increased by $27 000. Hence the after-tax adjustment was $63 000.

The adjusting entry resulting from the elimination entries in the year of sale in subsequent consolidated accounts would be as follows:

Machinery	Dr $100 000
Retained profits (at start)	Cr $63 000
Accumulated depreciation	Cr $10 000
Provision for deferred tax liability	Cr $27 000

Question 9.10

Rocket Ltd sold equipment to its parent company Mars Ltd on 1 January 2007 for $750 000. The original cost of the asset was $1 000 000. Depreciation is charged at 20% on the straight-line method and the income tax rate is 30%.

You are required to prepare the elimination entries for the consolidated accounts at:
a 30 June 2007; and
b 1 July 2007.

Question 9.11

Star Ltd purchased all of the issued capital of Trek Ltd on 1 August 2005 and gained control. On this date Trek Ltd held $50 000 in ordinary shares, $2 000 in a general reserve and $40 000 in retained profits.

On 1 October 2006 Trek Ltd sold a vehicle which had a historical cost of $100 000 to Star Ltd for $120 000.

On 1 January 2007 Star Ltd brought to account a loss on the disposal of equipment, which it had sold to Trek Ltd. The equipment originally cost $260 000.

All assets are depreciated at 20% p.a. and the rate of income tax is 30%.

You are required to complete the consolidated worksheet for the year ended 30 June 2007.

Consolidated worksheet as at 30 June 2007

	Star Ltd	Trek Ltd	Eliminations Debit	Eliminations Credit	Economic entity
	$	$	$	$	$
Gross profit	300 000	900 000			
Profit on vehicle sale	–	20 000			
	300 000	920 000			
Loss on equipment sale	60 000				
Other expenses	160 000	200 000			
Profit (before tax)	80 000	720 000			
Income tax expense	56 000	280 000			
Profit (after tax)	24 000	440 000			
Retained profits 1 July 2006	50 000	100 000			
Retained profits 30 June 2007	74 000	540 000			
Ordinary shares	180 000	50 000			
General reserve	50 000	10 000			
Current liabilities (including deferred tax)	40 000	70 000			
Non-current liabilities	80 000	50 000			
	424 000	720 000			
Current assets (including deferred tax)	70 000	340 000			
Vehicle	120 000	60 000			
Accumulated depreciation	(40 000)	(20 000)			
Plant	80 000	150 000			
Equipment	120 000	200 000			
Accumulated depreciation	(18 000)	(10 000)			
Investment in Trek Ltd	92 000	–			
	424 000	720 000			

Question 9.12

From the following information you are required to complete the consolidated worksheet for the year ended 30 June 2007.

On 1 July 2004, Future Ltd purchased all of the issued capital of Past Ltd. The price paid per share was $2.12. At this date Past Ltd held the following shareholders' equity:

	$
Ordinary shares	25 000
Retained profits	10 000
General reserve	8 000

Additional information

During the year ended 30 June 2007 the following intercompany transactions occurred:
- Future Ltd paid interest of $1 000 to Past Ltd on its $10 000 long-term loan.
- Past Ltd paid Future Ltd $10 000 for rental.
- Goodwill has been impaired by $6 000, $2 000 in the current period and $4 000 for previous periods.
- The opening stock of Future Ltd included $10 000 in unrealised profit.
- Intercompany sales:
  - Future to Past $50 000
  - Past to Future $10 000.
- The closing stock of Past Ltd includes an unrealised profit of $5 000.
- On 1 April, Future Ltd sold a building which had a historical cost of $80 000 for $72 000 cash to Past Ltd. The transaction was not affected by income tax.
- The tax rate is 30%.

Consolidated worksheet as at 30 June 2007

	Star Ltd	Trek Ltd	Eliminations		Economic entity
			Debit	Credit	
	$	$	$	$	$
Sales	400 000	200 000			
less Cost of sales					
Stock at start	20 000	8 000			
Purchases	150 000	70 000			
	170 000	78 000			
Stock at end	15 000	6 000			
Cost of sales	155 000	72 000			
Gross profit	245 000	128 000			
Interest received	20 000	10 000			
Rental income	10 000				
	275 000	138 000			
Wages expense	162 000	50 000			
Loss on building sale	8 000				
Interest expense	15 000	5 000			
Rental expense	10 000				
Other expenses	45 000	23 000			
Profit before tax	45 000	50 000			
Income tax expense	21 000	20 000			
Profit after tax	24 000	30 000			
Retained profits 1 July 2006	79 000	15 000			
	103 000	45 000			
Transfer to general reserve	10 000	2 000			
Retained profits 30 June 2007	93 000	43 000			
Ordinary shares	100 000	25 000			
General reserve	20 000	15 000			
Asset revaluation reserve	50 000	10 000			
Current liabilities	20 000	15 000			
Non-current liabilities	77 000	20 000			
	360 000	128 000			
Current assets					
Stock	15 000	6 000			
Other	50 000	20 000			
Non-current assets	242 000	102 000			
Investment in Past Ltd	53 000				
	360 000	128 000			

Intercompany dividends (from pre-acquisition profits)

When a company purchases a controlling interest in another company it acquires a proportion of the subsidiary's shareholders' funds. The shareholders' funds at the date of acquisition will include share capital and may include reserves from which dividends can be paid.

If the subsidiary pays a dividend from reserves that existed prior to the date of acquisition (pre-acquisition profits) the parent company is required to reduce the carrying amount of the investment in the subsidiary.

Dividends arising from pre-acquisition profits may be:

- payable at the date of acquisition;
- an interim dividend paid after acquisition; or
- a final dividend declared after acquisition.

Dividends payable at the date of acquisition

If at the date of acquisition the subsidiary has already declared a dividend it will have reduced its reserves. The parent company will pay a purchase price that reflects the fair values of the assets and liabilities which includes the dividend that is payable. Thus, the carrying amount of the investment in the subsidiary, in the parent company's books, will reflect the ownership of the subsidiary's share capital, remaining reserves and dividend payable.

Accordingly, when the dividend is received the parent company will offset the dividend against the carrying amount of the investment – that is, it has received part of its original investment in the subsidiary.

ILLUSTRATION

On 1 July 2007 A Ltd paid $170 000 for a 100% controlling interest in B Ltd. On this date B Ltd's balance sheet revealed:

	$
Ordinary shares	100 000
Retained profits	30 000
General reserve	20 000
Dividends payable	20 000

If the accounts were consolidated on this date the elimination entry would be as follows:

		$	$
Ordinary shares	Dr	100 000	
Retained profits	Dr	30 000	
General reserve	Dr	20 000	
Dividends payable	Dr	20 000	
Investment in B Ltd	Cr		170 000

The dividend payable is eliminated as it does not represent a liability to an entity that is external to the economic entity.

The payment of the dividend by B Ltd and its receipt by A Ltd would be recorded as follows:

A Ltd		B Ltd	
Bank	$20 000 Dr	Dividends payable	$20 000 Dr
Investment in B Ltd	$20 000 Cr	Bank	$20 000 Cr

These entries effectively eliminate the dividend payable and reduce the investment by the same amount. In future periods the consolidation entry to eliminate the investment at the date of acquisition would be as follows:

		$	$
Ordinary shares	Dr	100 000	
Retained profits	Dr	30 000	
General reserve	Dr	20 000	
Investment in B Ltd			Cr 150 000

Interim dividends

If the subsidiary declares and pays a dividend from pre-acquisition profits in a period after the acquisition date, it will reduce the amount of pre-acquisition reserves owing to the parent company. If the dividends are brought to account by the parent company they must be offset against the investment in the subsidiary.

The consolidated accounts for the period in which the dividend is declared and paid will need to reflect the fact that the dividend has been offset against the investment and that the reserves attributable at the date of acquisition have been reduced.

This will require two consolidation entries in the period in which the dividend was declared and received. The first is to eliminate the amounts applicable at the date of acquisition:

Ordinary shares	Dr	
Retained profits	Dr	
Investment in subsidiary		Cr

The second is to eliminate the interim dividend declared by the subsidiary and to offset the amount against the investment:

Investment in subsidiary	Dr	
Interim dividend		Cr
(in the retained profits account)		

ILLUSTRATION

On 1 July 2006 Try Ltd purchased all of the issued capital of Me Ltd for $70 000 and gained control. On this date Me Ltd's shareholders' equity included:

	$
Ordinary shares	60 000
Retained profits	10 000

In the following year, on 1 May 2007, Me Ltd declared an interim dividend of $10 000 from the retained profits available from the date of acquisition. The interim dividend was paid on 1 June 2007.

The respective company books would record the interim dividend as follows:

Try Ltd			Me Ltd		
Bank	$10 000 Dr		Interim dividend	$10 000 Dr	
Investment in Me Ltd		$10 000 Cr	Dividends payable		$10 000 Cr
			Dividends payable	$10 000 Dr	
			Bank		$10 000 Cr

On the assumption that Me Ltd did not derive any profits for the year ended 30 June 2007 the retained profits account would show:

	$
Retained profits 1 July 2006	10 000
less Interim dividend	10 000
Retained profits 30 June 2007	Nil

Thus, the elimination entry in the consolidated worksheet for the year ended 30 June 2007 would be:

| Investment in Me Ltd | Dr $10 000 | |
| Interim dividend | | Cr $10 000 |

The consolidated worksheet for the year ended 30 June 2007 might appear as follows:

Consolidated worksheet as at 30 June 2007

	Try Ltd	Me Ltd	Eliminations		Economic entity
			Debit	Credit	
	$	$	$	$	$
Retained profits 1 July 2006	50 000	10 000	10 000 (1)		50 000
Interim dividend		10 000		10 000 (2)	
Retained profits 30 June 2007	50 000	Nil			50 000
Ordinary shares	200 000	60 000	60 000 (1)		200 000
	250 000	60 000			250 000
Bank	190 000	60 000			250 000
Investment in Me Ltd	60 000		10 000 (2)	70 000 (1)	
	250 000	60 000	80 000	80 000	250 000

Eliminations

1 This eliminates the date of acquisition values of Me Ltd's shareholders' funds and the investment in the subsidiary.
2 This ensures that the investment in the subsidiary is brought to a nil balance in line with the treatment of the dividend received by Try Ltd (that is, offset against the investment) and eliminates the retained profits that were attributable at the date of acquisition.

Note: In the period following the receipt of the dividend it would only be necessary to eliminate on consolidation the book value of the investment in the subsidiary against the remaining values of shareholders' funds of the subsidiary. In the above illustration the retained profits of $10 000 attributable to the parent company have now been paid and the original cost of the investment of $70 000 reduced to $60 000. This is the equivalent of the subsidiary's ordinary shares. Thus, for the year ending 30 June 2008 and onwards the consolidation entry to eliminate the date of acquisition values of the investment would be as follows:

| Ordinary shares | Dr $60 000 | |
| Investment in Me Ltd | | Cr $60 000 |

Question 9.13

From the following information you are required to complete the consolidated worksheet for the year ended 30 June 2007.

North Ltd paid $300 000 to obtain all of the share capital of South Ltd on 1 October 2006 and gained control. South Ltd's balance sheet included the following:

	$
Ordinary shares	250 000
Retained profits	40 000
Dividends payable	10 000

The dividend payable on the date of acquisition was paid on 30 October 2006.

On 5 May 2007 South Ltd declared an interim dividend from the pre-acquisition retained profits. This was paid on 1 June 2007.

Consolidated worksheet as at 30 June 2007

	North Ltd	South Ltd	Eliminations Debit	Eliminations Credit	Economic entity
	$	$	$	$	$
Retained profits 1 July 2006	100 000	40 000			
Interim dividend		10 000			
Retained profits 30 June 2007	100 000	30 000			
Ordinary shares	400 000	250 000			
	500 000	280 000			
Current assets	50 000	100 000			
Non-current assets	170 000	180 000			
Investment in South Ltd	280 000				
	500 000	280 000			

Final dividends

The subsidiary may declare a final dividend from pre-acquisition profits in a period subsequent to acquisition. The final dividend may be brought to account by the parent in the same period or it may be accounted for in the following period. We will discuss final dividends recognised in the same period first.

When the subsidiary declares a final dividend from pre-acquisition profits after the acquisition date, it may reduce its reserves in that period but not pay the dividend until the next period. If the parent brings the dividend account into the same period it will do so in accordance with AASB 1015, clause 30. The journal entries in the respective companies would be as follows:

Parent entity			Subsidiary		
Dividends receivable	Dr		Final dividends	Dr	
Investment in subsidiary		Cr	Dividends payable		Cr
			Retained profits	Dr	
			Final dividends		Cr

These entries create an intercompany indebtedness in the form of dividends receivable and payable, reduce the subsidiary's retained profits and offset the amount against the investment in the subsidiary. The consolidation entries at the end of the period to eliminate these entries are as follows:

Dividends payable	Dr	
Dividends receivable		Cr
Investment in subsidiary	Dr	
Final dividends		Cr
(in the retained profits account)		

ILLUSTRATION

Brake Ltd purchased a 100% controlling interest in Fast Ltd on 1 December 2006 for $100 000. On this date Fast Ltd held:

	$
Ordinary shares	70 000
Retained profits	30 000

At the end of the period 30 June 2007 Fast Ltd declared a $20 000 final dividend from its pre-acquisition profits, to be paid on 1 August 2007. Brake Ltd recognises dividends when declared.

Shown below is the consolidated worksheet as at 30 June 2007 which eliminates the investment and the final dividend.

Consolidated worksheet as at 30 June 2007

	Brake Ltd	Fast Ltd	Eliminations		Economic entity
			Debit	Credit	
	$	$	$	$	$
Retained profits 1 July 2006	200 000	30 000	30 000 (1)		200 000
Final dividend		20 000		20 000 (3)	
Retained profits 30 June 2007	200 000	10 000			200 000
Ordinary shares	400 000	70 000	70 000 (1)		400 000
Dividends payable		20 000	20 000 (2)		
	600 000	100 000			600 000
Current assets	500 000	100 000			600 000
Dividends receivable	20 000			20 000 (2)	
Investment in Fast Ltd	80 000		20 000 (3)	100 000 (1)	
	600 000	100 000	140 000	140 000	600 000

Eliminations

1. Eliminates the investment at date of acquisition.
2. Eliminates the intercompany indebtedness.
3. Returns the final dividend to the retained profits account and reduces the investment to a nil balance.

Notes:
1. In subsequent periods the consolidation entry would eliminate the remainder of the pre-acquisition retained profits. The retained profits at date of acquisition were $30 000, of which $20 000 has been accounted for, leaving $10 000 to be brought to account in future consolidations. The future consolidations entry would be as follows:

		$	$
Ordinary shares		Dr 70 000	
Retained profits		Dr 10 000	
	Investment in Fast Ltd		Cr 80 000

2 In the next period ending 30 June 2008 the dividend would be paid by the subsidiary and received by the parent company. This would remove the company indebtedness for dividends receivable and dividends payable, thus not making them an issue on consolidation.

We will now turn to final dividends not recognised in the same period. If the parent entity does not bring to account a final dividend declared by the subsidiary in the period in which it was declared, the parent entity will bring it to account in the next period when it is received. When this occurs a consolidation elimination entry is only required in the period in which the dividend was declared. When the subsidiary declares the final dividend from its pre-acquisition profits it will reduce its retained profits and declare a dividend payable to the parent company. The entries to declare the dividend by the subsidiary are as follows:

Final dividend	Dr	
Dividends payable		Cr
Retained profits	Dr	
Final dividends		Cr

As the dividend is owed to the parent company, it does not constitute a liability to an entity outside of the group. Thus, on consolidation it must be eliminated and returned to retained profits. The elimination entry to achieve this is as follows:

Dividends payable	Dr	
Final dividends		Cr
(in retained profits account)		

As the parent company has yet to account for the dividend it will not be offset against the investment in the subsidiary until the next period when it is actually received. The consolidation entry in the subsequent periods would be the same as those indicated in previous pages where the retained profits amount is reduced by the dividend brought to account matched by a corresponding reduction in the investment in the subsidiary.

ILLUSTRATION

On 1 July 2006 Twin Ltd purchased all of the issued capital in Bays Ltd for $200 000 to gain control. On this date, Bays Ltd held:

	$
Ordinary shares	150 000
Retained profits	50 000

At the end of the period 30 June 2007 Bays Ltd declared a final dividend of $10 000 from the pre-acquisition profits. Twin Ltd did not bring the dividend to account.

The consolidated worksheet as at 30 June 2007 would show the following balances and eliminations (assuming no profits were derived in the period):

Consolidated worksheet as at 30 June 2007

	Twin Ltd	Bays Ltd	Eliminations Debit	Eliminations Credit	Economic entity
	$	$	$	$	$
Retained profits 1 July 2006	80 000	50 000	50 000 (1)		80 000
Final dividend		10 000		10 000 (2)	
Retained profits 30 June 2007	80 000	40 000			80 000
Ordinary shares	220 000	150 000	150 000 (1)		220 000
Dividends payable		10 000	10 000 (2)		
	300 000	200 000			300 000
Current assets	100 000	200 000			300 000
Investment in Bays Ltd	200 000			200 000 (1)	
	300 000	200 000	210 000	210 000	300 000

Eliminations

1. Eliminates the investment at the date of acquisition.
2. Eliminates the final dividend by removing the dividend payable and returning the dividend to retained profits.

In the following year ending 30 June 2008 Bays Ltd would pay the dividend, thereby eliminating the dividend payable. Twin Ltd would receive the dividend and reduce the value of the investment in Bays Ltd in accordance with AASB 1015, clause 30.

For the year ending 30 June 2008 and onwards the entry on consolidation to eliminate the values at the date of acquisition would be:

	$	$
Ordinary shares	Dr 150 000	
Retained profits (start)	Dr 40 000	
Investment in Bays Ltd		Cr 190 000

Question 9.14

Laker Ltd paid $500 000 to obtain 100% control over Ava Ltd on 1 July 2006. On this date Ava Ltd's balance sheet included the following:

	$
Ordinary shares	400 000
Retained profits	60 000
Dividends payable	40 000

Additional information

- The dividend payable on the date of acquisition was paid on 1 August 2006.
- On 1 February 2007 Ava Ltd declared an interim dividend of $20 000 from the pre-acquisition retained profits. This was paid on 1 March 2007.
- On 1 June 2007 Ava Ltd declared a final dividend of $15 000 from the pre-acquisition profits. This was to be paid on 1 August 2007.
- Laker Ltd recognises dividends when they have been declared.

You are required to:
a complete the following consolidated worksheet from the above information; and
b prepare the consolidation elimination entry to eliminate the investment in Ava Ltd for the year ending 30 June 2007.

Consolidated worksheet as at 30 June 2007

	Laker Ltd	Ava Ltd	Eliminations		Economic entity
			Debit	Credit	
	$	$	$	$	$
Retained profits 1 July 2006	235 000	60 000			
Interim dividend	10 000	20 000			
Final dividend	10 000	15 000			
Retained profits 30 June 2007	215 000	25 000			
Ordinary shares	350 000	400 000			
Dividends payable		15 000			
	565 000	440 000			
Current assets	45 000	100 000			
Non-current assets	80 000	340 000			
Dividends receivable	15 000				
Investment in Ava Ltd	425 000				
	565 000	440 000			

Intercompany dividends (from post-acquisition profits)

Dividends paid or proposed by a subsidiary to the parent entity do not constitute a flow of funds to an external party. If the directors are to ensure that a true and fair view of the group accounts is to be reported, the dividends paid or proposed between a subsidiary and its parents must be eliminated.

The elimination of dividends from post-acquisition profits falls into two categories. These are the interim dividends and the final dividends.

Interim dividends

Where the subsidiary has paid an interim dividend during the current period it will have reduced its after-tax profits by appropriating the dividend from retained profits. The parent entity on receipt of the dividend will have recorded dividend income in its annual accounts.

The appropriation of the interim dividend by the subsidiary and the receipt by the parent entity is illustrated as follows:

Parent entity income statement (Extract)		Subsidiary income statement (Extract)	
	$		$
Sales	1 000 000	Profit (after tax)	180 000
Cost of sales	400 000	Retained profits (start)	120 000
Gross profit	600 000	Funds for appropriation	300 000
add Other revenue		less Interim dividend	20 000
Dividend income	20 000		
	620 000	Retained profits (end)	280 000

The illustration shows that the subsidiary has reduced its retained profits by appropriating an interim dividend of $20 000 and the parent entity has included dividend income (as other revenue) of $20 000.

To eliminate this transaction it is necessary to reduce the revenue of the group and return the dividend to retained profits. The entry to eliminate interim dividends paid by the subsidiary is as follows:

> Dividends income (profit and loss)   Dr
> Interim dividends   Cr
> (in retained profits account)

Final dividends

The declaration of a final dividend at the end of the current reporting period by the subsidiary reduces the subsidiary's retained profits and creates a liability to the parent entity in the form of dividends payable. The parent entity, in the same period, may choose to either:

a disregard the final dividend in the current period, choosing to recognise it in the next period when it is actually received; or
b bring the dividend to account, recognising the dividend income and the fact that it is accrued by the subsidiary.

In all cases the dividend declared by the subsidiary and where it has been recognised by the parent entity must be eliminated.

a **Elimination of a final dividend not recognised in the current period by the parent entity.** The illustration that follows reveals the actions taken by both the parent entity and the subsidiary when the subsidiary declares a final dividend but the parent does not recognise the dividend.

Parent entity income statement (Extract)	Subsidiary income statement (Extract)	
		$
No entries made as final dividend has not yet been received.	Profit (after tax)	600 000
	Retained profits (start)	400 000
	Funds for appropriation	1 000 000
	less Final dividend	300 000
	Retained profits (end)	700 000
	Balance sheet extract	
	Current liabilities	
	Dividends payable	300 000

The illustration reveals that the subsidiary has reduced its retained profits by appropriating a final dividend of $300 000, which it reports as a current liability on the balance sheet. The parent entity takes no action as the dividend has not been received.

To eliminate the dividend declared by the subsidiary the following entry is required:

> Dividends payable   Dr
> Final dividends   Cr
> (in retained profits account)

This entry has the effect of eliminating the debt owed by the subsidiary and returns the dividend to the retained profits account.

ILLUSTRATION

On 1 July 1998, Go Ltd purchased 100% of the issued capital of Fast Ltd to gain control. At this date Fast Ltd held the following shareholders' funds:

	$
Ordinary shares	30 000
General reserve	18 000
Retained profits	2 000

For the year ended 30 June 2007 Fast Ltd had paid an interim dividend of $15 000 and declared a final dividend of $10 000. Go Ltd only recognises dividends when received. The resulting worksheet would be as follows:

Consolidated worksheet as at 30 June 2007

	Go Ltd	Fast Ltd	Eliminations Debit	Eliminations Credit	Economic entity
	$	$	$	$	$
Profit	80 000	46 000			126 000
Dividend income	15 000		15 000 (2)		
	95 000	46 000			126 000
Expenses	15 000	6 000			21 000
Profit before tax	80 000	40 000			105 000
Income tax expense	32 000	16 000			48 000
Profit after tax	48 000	24 000			57 000
Retained profits 1 July 2006	76 000	14 000	2 000 (1)		88 000
	124 000	38 000			145 000
Interim dividend	20 000	15 000		15 000 (2)	20 000
Final dividend	20 000	10 000		10 000 (3)	20 000
Transfer to general reserve	4 000	8 000			12 000
Retained profits 30 June 2007	80 000	5 000			93 000
Ordinary shares	100 000	30 000	30 000 (1)		100 000
General reserve	20 000	20 000	18 000 (1)		22 000
Asset revaluation reserve	80 000	10 000			90 000
Dividends payable	20 000	10 000	10 000 (3)		20 000
Current liabilities	20 000	15 000			35 000
Non-current liabilities	50 000	20 000			70 000
	370 000	110 000			430 000
Current assets	50 000	20 000			70 000
Fixed assets	270 000	90 000			360 000
Investment in Fast Ltd	50 000			50 000 (1)	
	370 000	110 000	75 000	75 000	430 000

Eliminations

1. Investment in Fast Ltd at date of acquisition values.
2. Interim dividend.
3. Final dividend.

Question 9.15

You are required to complete the consolidated worksheet for the year ended 30 June 2007 from the following information.

On 1 June 1998, Stop Ltd purchased all of the issued capital of Gap Ltd and obtained control. At this date Gap Ltd held the following shareholders' funds:

		$
Ordinary shares		40 000
Retained profits		10 000
General reserve		10 000

Additional information

During the year ended 30 June 2007 Gap Ltd paid an interim dividend and declared a final dividend.

Consolidated worksheet as at 30 June 2007

	Stop Ltd	Gap Ltd	Eliminations Debit	Eliminations Credit	Economic entity
	$	$	$	$	$
Profit	180 000	40 000			220,000
Dividend income	5 000		5,000 (2)		
	185 000	40 000			220,000
Expenses	25 000	10 000			35,000
Profit before tax	160 000	30 000			185,000
Income tax expense	64 000	12 000			76,000
Profit after tax	96 000	18 000			109,000
Retained profits 1 July 2006	74 000	12 000	10,000 (1)		76,000
	170 000	30 000			185,000
Interim dividend	20 000	5 000		5,000 (2)	20,000
Final dividend	20 000	10 000		10,000 (3)	20,000
Transfer to general reserve	4 000	5 000			9,000
Retained profits 30 June 2007	126 000	10 000			136,000
Ordinary shares	200 000	40 000	40,000 (1)		200,000
General reserve	20 000	15 000	10,000 (1)		25,000
Asset revaluation reserve	60 000	20 000			80,000
Dividends payable	20 000	10 000	10,000 (3)		20,000
Current liabilities	40 000	25 000			65,000
Non-current liabilities	34 000	80 000			114,000
	500 000	200 000			640,000
Current assets	100 000	50 000			150,000
Fixed assets	340 000	150 000			490,000
Investment in Gap Ltd	60 000			60,000 (1)	
	500 000	200 000			640,000

Eliminate
1. Investment at date of acquisition.
2. Interim dividend.
3. Final dividend.

b **Elimination of a final dividend recognised in the next reporting period by the parent entity.** Where a parent entity does not recognise a final dividend in the period in which it was declared but waits until it is received in the next reporting period, the economic entity's income will be overstated in the period after the dividend was declared.

As the dividend was declared in the previous period by the subsidiary, the subsidiary's retained profits at the start of the period will be understated from the group's viewpoint. Thus the elimination will need to remove the dividend income from the consolidated accounts and return the amount to the group's retained profits at the start of the reporting period.

Using the details of the previous illustration, the receipt of the final dividend in the next reporting period by the parent entity is shown below where the parent has increased its revenue by $300 000. This is illustrated as follows:

Parent entity income statement (Extract)		Subsidiary income statement (Extract)
	$	
Sales	900 000	No entries made as the final dividend
Cost of sales	500 000	was declared in the previous period.
Gross profit	400 000	
add Other revenue		
Dividend income	300 000	
	700 000	

The elimination entry to return a dividend not recognised by the parent until received in the next accounting period is as follows:

Dividend income	Dr	
Retained profits (at start)		Cr

ILLUSTRATION

On 1 June 2006 Emp Ltd purchased 100% of the issued capital of Athy Ltd. This gave Emp Ltd full control. At this date Athy Ltd held the following shareholders' equity:

	$
Ordinary shares	50 000
General reserve	15 000
Retained profits	5 000

Additional information

In the year ended 30 June 2006 Athy Ltd declared a final dividend of $10 000. This was not recognised by Emp Ltd until received on 1 October 2006.

The consolidated worksheet on 30 June 2007 would be as follows:

Consolidated worksheet as at 30 June 2007

	Emp Ltd	Athy Ltd	Eliminations Debit	Eliminations Credit	Economic entity
	$	$	$	$	$
Profit	400 000	96 000			496 000
Dividend income	25 000		15 000 (2)		
			10 000 (3)		
	425 000	96 000			496 000
Expenses	15 000	6 000			21 000
Profit before tax	410 000	90 000			475 000
Income tax expense	164 000	36 000			200 000
Profit after tax	246 000	54 000			275 000
Retained profits 1 July 2006	76 000	25 000	5 000 (1)	10 000 (3)	106 000
	322 000	79 000			381 000
Interim dividend	20 000	15 000		15 000 (2)	20 000
Transfer to general reserve	4 000	10 000			14 000
Retained profits 30 June 2007	298 000	54 000			347 000
Ordinary shares	200 000	50 000	50 000 (1)		20 000
General reserve	15 000	20 000	15 000 (1)		20 000
Asset revaluation reserve	80 000	10 000			90 000
Current liabilities	20 000	15 000			35 000
Non-current liabilities	90 000	20 000			110 000
	703 000	169 000			802 000
Current assets	50 000	20 000			70 000
Fixed assets	583 000	149 000			732 000
Investment in Athy Ltd	70 000			70 000 (1)	
	703 000	169 000	95 000	95 000	802 000

Eliminations

1. Investments in subsidiary at fair values.
2. Interim dividend paid during period.
3. Final dividend declared in year ending 30 June 2006 and received in current period.

Elimination of a final dividend recognised in the current period by the parent entity

The declaration of a final dividend by the subsidiary will create a debt in the form of dividends payable through the appropriation of retained profits. If the parent entity recognises the final dividend in the same period, it will bring to account dividend income and recognise an asset in the name of dividends receivable.

This is illustrated as follows:

Parent entity income statement (Extract)		Subsidiary income statement (Extract)	
	$		$
Gross profit	280 000	Profit (after tax)	120 000
add Other revenue		Retained profits (start)	180 000
Dividends income	50 000	Funds for appropriation	300 000
Profit	330 000	less Final dividend	50 000
		Retained profits (end)	250 000
Balance sheet (Extract)		**Balance sheet (Extract)**	
Current assets:		Current liabilities:	
Dividends receivable	50 000	Dividends payable	50 000

This illustration reveals that:
- the subsidiary has declared a $50 000 final dividend by appropriating profits and has created a current liability, dividends payable; and
- the parent entity has included $50 000 dividend income in its calculation of profit and identified dividends receivable.

To eliminate the declaration of the dividend by the subsidiary and its recognition by the parent the following elimination entries are required:

Dividends payable	Dr	
Final dividends		Cr
(retained profits account)		
Dividends income	Dr	
Dividends receivable		Cr

ILLUSTRATION

On 1 July 1974, Big Ltd purchased a 100% controlling interest in Apple Ltd. On this date Apple Ltd held the following shareholders' equity:

	$
Ordinary shares	20 000
General reserve	9 000
Retained profits	6 000
Asset revaluation reserve	5 000

During the year ended 30 June 2007 Apple Ltd paid an interim dividend of $10 000 and declared a final dividend of $12 000. Big Ltd recognises dividends when declared.

Consolidated worksheet as at 30 June 2007

	Big Ltd	Apple Ltd	Eliminations Debit	Eliminations Credit	Economic entity
	$	$	$	$	$
Gross profit	88 000	216 000			304 000
Dividend income	22 000		10 000 (2)		
			12 000 (4)		
	110 000	216 000			304 000
Wages expense	40 000	50 000			90 000
Other expenses	15 000	6 000			21 000
Profit before tax	55 000	160 000			193 000
Income tax expense	22 000	64 000			86 000
Profit after tax	33 000	96 000			107 000
Retained profits 1 July 2006	76 000	14 000	6 000 (1)		84 000
	109 000	110 000			191 000
Interim dividend	20 000	10 000		10 000 (2)	20 000
Final dividend	20 000	12 000		12 000 (3)	20 000
Transfer to general reserve	5 000	2 000			7 000
Retained profits 30 June 2007	64 000	86 000			144 000
Ordinary shares	200 000	20 000	20 000 (1)		200 000
General reserve	20 000	20 000	9 000 (1)		31 000
Asset revaluation reserve	60 000	8 000	5 000 (1)		63 000
Dividends payable	20 000	12 000	12 000 (3)		20 000
Current liabilities	30 000	15 000			45 000
Non-current liabilities	40 000	30 000			70 000
	434 000	191 000			573 000
Current assets	50 000	20 000			70 000
Fixed assets	332 000	171 000			503 000
Dividends receivable	12 000			12 000 (4)	
Investment in Apple Ltd	40 000			40 000 (1)	
	434 000	191 000	74 000	74 000	573 000

Eliminations

1 Investment in Apple Ltd at fair values at date of acquisition.
2 Interim dividend paid by Apple Ltd.
3 Final dividend declared by Apple Ltd.
4 Final dividend recognised by Big Ltd.

Question 9.16

You are required to complete the consolidated worksheet for the year ended 30 June 2007 from the following information.

On 1 June 1998, Bag Ltd purchased all of the issued capital of Limit Ltd. At this date Limit Ltd held the following shareholders' equity:

	$
Ordinary shares	20 000
Retained profits	6 000
General reserve	14 000

Additional information

- Limit Ltd paid and declared interim dividends during the year.
- Bag Ltd recognises dividends when declared.

Consolidated worksheet as at 30 June 2007

	Bag Ltd	Limit Ltd	Eliminations Debit	Eliminations Credit	Economic entity
	$	$	$	$	$
Gross profit	100 000	216 000			
Dividend income	20 000				
	120 000	216 000			
Wages expense	40 000	50 000			
Other expenses	15 000	6 000			
Profit before tax	65 000	160 000			
Income tax expense	26 000	64 000			
Profit after tax	39 000	96 000			
Retained profits 1 July 2006	76 000	14 000			
	115 000	110 000			
Interim dividend	20 000	10 000			
Final dividend	20 000	10 000			
Transfer to general reserve	5 000	2 000			
Retained profits 30 June 2007	70 000	88 000			
Ordinary shares	200 000	20 000			
General reserve	20 000	20 000			
Asset revaluation reserve	60 000	8 000			
Dividends payable	20 000	10 000			
Current liabilities	30 000	15 000			
Non-current liabilities	40 000	30 000			
	440 000	191 000			
Current assets	60 000	20 000			
Fixed assets	330 000	171 000			
Dividends receivable	10 000				
Investment in Limit Ltd	40 000				
	440 000	191 000			

Summary of elimination entries on consolidation

1. Elimination of investment above fair values at acquisition date:

Ordinary shares	Dr
Reserves	Dr
Retained profits (start)	Dr
Goodwill on acquisition	Dr
Investment	Cr

2. Elimination of investment below fair values at acquisition date:

Ordinary shares	Dr
Reserves	Dr
Retained profits	Dr
Investment	Cr
Profit and loss (discount on acquisition)	Cr

3. Impairment of goodwill on acquisition:

Impairment loss expense – Goodwill	Dr
Retained profits (start)	Dr
Goodwill on acquisition	Cr

4. Elimination of intercompany indebtedness:

Loan from company	Dr
Loan to company	Cr

5. Elimination of intercompany servicing:

Revenue item	Dr
Expense item	Cr

6. Elimination of stock-related transactions:

   a. Unrealised profit in opening stock

Income tax expense	Dr
Retained profits (start)	Dr
Stock at start (trading)	Cr

   b. Yearly sales and purchases:

Sales	Dr
Purchases	Cr

   c. i. Unrealised profit in closing stock:

Stock at end (trading)	Dr
Stock on hand (balance sheet)	Cr

      ii. Tax effect on closing stock:

Deferred tax asset	Dr
Income tax expense	Cr

   d. Related debtors and creditors:

Creditors	Dr
Debtors	Cr

7   Elimination of unrealised profits (losses) on non-current asset sales:
    a   Unrealised profits in current period
            Profit on asset sale   Dr
                Asset   Cr
            Accumulated depreciation   Dr
                Depreciation expense   Cr
            Deferred tax asset   Dr
                Income tax expense   Cr
    b   Unrealised profits in previous periods
            Accumulated depreciation   Dr
            Deferred tax asset   Dr
            Retained profits (start of period)   Dr
                Asset   Cr
    c   Unrealised loss in current period
            Asset   Dr
                Loss on asset sale   Cr
            Depreciation expense   Dr
                Accumulated depreciation   Cr
            Income tax expense   Dr
                Deferred tax liability   Cr
    d   Unrealised loss in previous periods
            Asset   Dr
                Retained profits (start of period)   Cr
                Accumulated depreciation   Cr
                Deferred tax liability   Cr

8   Elimination of intercompany dividends (post-acquisition profits):
    a   Interim dividends
            Dividends income   Dr
                Interim dividend (in retained profits)   Cr
    b   Final dividends declaration
            Dividends payable   Dr
                Final dividend (in retained profits)   Cr
    c   Recognition of final dividends
            Dividends income   Dr
                Dividends receivable   Cr
    d   Final dividend recognised in next period
            Dividends income   Dr
                Retained profits (start)   Cr

COMPREHENSIVE ILLUSTRATION

From the information that follows, a consolidated worksheet will be prepared for the year ending 30 June 2007.
- Sea Ltd acquired 100% of the issued capital of Gull's Ltd on 1 July 2006 for $120 000.
- Share capital and reserves of Gull's at that date were:

	$
Paid-up capital	60 000
Retained profits	5 000

- Intercompany sales included cash sales from:

	$
Gull's to Sea	12 000
Sea to Gull's	8 000

- Gull's Ltd's opening stock at 1 July 2006 includes $2 000 of unrealised profit.
- Stock on hand of Sea Ltd at 30 June 2007 included stock to the value of $4 000. This had been purchased from Gull's who made a profit of $1 000.
- Gull's paid commission amounting to $2 000 to Sea Ltd.
- Gull's paid an interim dividend during the year.
- Gull's has proposed to pay a final dividend of $10 000 at 30 June 2007. This has not been brought to account by Sea Ltd.
- The tax rate is 30%.
- Goodwill has been impaired by $5 500.

Consolidated worksheet as at 30 June 2007

	Sea Ltd	Gull's Ltd	Eliminations Debit	Eliminations Credit	Economic entity
	$	$	$	$	$
Sales	450 000	140 000	20 000 (2)		570 000
less Cost of goods sold					
Stock 1 July 2006	20 000	8 000		2 000 (3)	26 000
Purchases	260 000	60 000		20 000 (2)	300 000
	280 000	68 000			326 000
less Stock 30 June 2007	40 000	15 000	1 000 (5)		54 000
	240 000	53 000			272 000
Gross profit	210 000	87 000			298 000
add Other revenue					
Commission	2 000		2 000 (4)		
Dividends	13 000		13 000 (6)		
	225 000	87 000			298 000
less Expenses	115 000	70 000	600 (3)	300 (5)	
			5 500 (8)	2 000 (4)	188 800
Net profit/loss	110 000	17 000			109 200
Retained profit 1 July 2006			1 400 (3)		
	25 000	33 000	5 000 (1)		51 600
Funds available for appropriation	135 000	50 000			160 800
less Interim dividends		13 000		13 000 (6)	
Final dividends	50 000	10 000		10 000 (7)	50 000
Retained profits 30 June 2007	85 000	27 000			110 800
Paid-up capital	200 000	60 000	60 000 (1)		200 000
Reserves	25 000	10 000			35 000
Creditors	30 000	5 000			35 000
Provision for taxation	50 000	–			50 000
Dividends payable	50 000	10 000	10 000 (7)		50 000
	440 000	112 000			480 800
Bank	80 000	7 000			87 000
Debtors	160 000	40 000			200 000
Stock	40 000	15 000		1 000 (5)	54 000
Deferred tax asset	10 000		300 (5)		10 300
Shares in Gull's Ltd	120 000			120 000 (1)	
Motor vehicles	30 000	50 000			80 000
Goodwill on acquisition			55 000 (1)	5 500 (8)	49 500
	440 000	112 000	173 800	173 800	480 800

* Expenses include income tax and commission.

Eliminations

1. Eliminates the investment in Gull's Ltd. The company was purchased one year prior to consolidation and the amounts eliminated are those from acquisition date.
2. Eliminates intercompany sales.
3. Eliminates the unrealised profit in opening stock, including the adjustment for income tax expense. Profit before tax $2 000, income tax $600, retained profits (after tax) $1 400.
4. Eliminates intercompany commission to prevent overstating revenues of Sea Ltd and overstating expenses of Gull's Ltd.
5. Eliminates the unrealised profit on closing stock, to prevent overstating group profits and assets in the balance sheet. Also, the income tax effect of the closing stock is reduction in income tax payable of $1 000 × .30 = $300 and a deferred tax asset.
6. Eliminates the interim dividend paid out of post-acquisition profits by Gull's Ltd to Sea Ltd.
7. Eliminates the final dividend proposed from Gull's Ltd to Sea Ltd out of post-acquisition profits.
8. Impairment loss of goodwill on acquisition in the first year.

Question 9.17

From the following information you are required to:
a complete the consolidated worksheet as at 30 June 2007;
b prepare the financial statements for the parent and the economic entity for the period ended 30 June 2007.

On 1 January 1996, East Ltd purchased all of the issued capital of West Ltd and obtained control. At this date West Ltd held the following shareholders' equity:

	$
Ordinary shares	300 000
Retained profits	100 000
General reserve	50 000

Additional information

- Goodwill has been impaired by $7 000 of which $2 000 was impaired in the current year.
- East Ltd sold land costing $120 000 to West Ltd for $170 000.
- Intercompany sales totalled $800 000.
- Unrealised profit of $20 000 was identified in the opening stock of East Ltd.
- East Ltd's closing stock included an unrealised profit of $30 000.
- East Ltd recognises all dividends.
- The tax rate is 30%.

Consolidated worksheet as at 30 June 2007

	East Ltd	West Ltd	Eliminations Debit	Eliminations Credit	Economic entity
	$	$	$	$	$
Sales	1 500 000	800 000			
less Cost of goods sold					
Stock at start	240 000	100 000			
Purchases	700 000	340 000			
	940 000	440 000			
Stock at end	114 000	80 000			
	826 000	360 000			
Gross profit	674 000	440 000			
Dividends received	50 000				
Profit on land sale	50 000				
	774 000	440 000			
Other expenses	424 000	130 000			
Profit before tax	350 000	310 000			
Income tax expense	140 000	124 000			
Profit after tax	210 000	186 000			
Retained profits 1 July 2006	20 000	45 000			
	230 000	231 000			
Interim dividends	50 000	20 000			
Final dividends	50 000	30 000			
Transfer to general reserve	20 000	15 000			
Retained profits 30 June 2007	110 000	166 000			
Ordinary shares	500 000	300 000			
General reserve	50 000	140 000			
Dividends payable		30 000			
Other liabilities	150 000	120 000			
	810 000	756 000			
Stock on hand	114 000	80 000			
Deferred tax asset	6 000	2 000			
Dividends receivable	30 000				
Other assets	110 000	674 000			
Investment in West Ltd	550 000				
	810 000	756 000			

Question 9.18

On 1 July 2006 Gold Ltd purchased all of the issued shares of Rush Ltd for $900 000. For this price the company acquired Rush Ltd's balances of accounts as follows:

Assets		Equities	
	$		$
Bank	500 000	Mortgage	200 000
Stock	100 000	Ordinary shares	600 000
Vehicles	400 000	Retained profits	200 000

Using this information and that presented below, you are required to:
a prepare a consolidated worksheet as at 30 June 2007;
b prepare a consolidated income statement for the year ended 30 June 2007; and
c prepare a consolidated balance sheet as at 30 June 2007.

Consolidated worksheet as at 30 June 2007

	Gold Ltd	Rush Ltd	Eliminations Debit	Eliminations Credit	Economic entity
	$	$	$	$	$
Sales	700 000	500 000			
less Cost of sales					
Stock	40 000	30 000			
Purchases	300 000	250 000			
	340 000	280 000			
Stock	50 000	20 000			
	290 000	260 000			
Gross profit	410 000	240 000			
Dividends revenue	12 000				
Interest revenue	8 000	10 000			
	430 000	250 000			
Expenses	130 000	100 000			
Profit (before tax)	300 000	150 000			
Taxation expense	120 000	60 000			
Net profit	180 000	90 000			
Retained profits 1 July 2006	300 000	250 000			
	–	–			
	480 000	340 000			
Interim dividend		12 000			
Final dividend	50 000	18 000			
General reserve	10 000	50 000			
Retained profits 30 June 2007	420 000	260 000			
Ordinary shares	1 000 000	600 000			
Reserves	200 000	300 000			
	1 620 000	1 160 000			
Assets					
Bank	730 000	930 000			
Debtors	150 000	100 000			
Investment – Rush Ltd	900 000				
Loan – Rush Ltd	100 000				
Vehicles	200 000	500 000			
Stock	50 000	20 000			
Deferred tax asset					
	2 130 000	1 550 000			

| | Gold Ltd | Rush Ltd | Eliminations || Economic entity |
			Debit	Credit	
Liabilities					
Creditors	50 000	80 000			
Mortgage	270 000	150 000			
Loan – Gold Ltd		100 000			
Dividends payable	50 000	18 000			
Taxation payable	140 000	42 000			
	2 130 000	390 000			

Additional information

- Goodwill has been impaired in the current year by $20 000.
- Gold Ltd's opening stock includes $5 000 in unrealised profit.
- Intercompany sales: Rush Ltd sold Gold Ltd stock valued at $20 000. This had cost Rush Ltd $15 000. Gold Ltd sold this stock for $30 000.
- Gold Ltd's closing stock includes stock from Rush Ltd of $8 000 at a mark-up of 25%.
- During the year Rush Ltd paid interim dividends and has proposed a final dividend at 30 June.
- Gold Ltd received $1 000 of interest from Rush Ltd on its loan. Gold Ltd owes Rush Ltd $30 000 for unpaid stock purchases.
- In the previous year Rush Ltd brought to account an unrealised loss on the sale of a vehicle of $50 000. The loss had no taxation implications.
- The tax rate is 30%.

CHAPTER 10
CONSOLIDATION WITH MINORITY INTERESTS

Objectives

Upon satisfactory completion of this chapter you should be able to:

- prepare a consolidated worksheet for a parent company with up to two minority subsidiaries; and
- prepare a consolidated worksheet for a parent company with one minority subsidiary and one indirect minority subsidiary.

Introduction

Companies investing in subsidiary companies may not purchase all the shares of the subsidiary to gain control. The percentage of the subsidiary not controlled by the parent is termed **minority interest**. Where a parent company has less than 100% control of a subsidiary, it must record the amount owing to the minority interest when the accounts of the parent and the subsidiary are consolidated.

This chapter considers the requirements of consolidation when the parent has investments in subsidiary companies where minority interests exist. In addition, the chapter examines situations where the subsidiary company has a controlling interest in another company.

Minority interest

AASB 127: Consolidated and Separate Financial Statements defines minority interest as the portion of the profit or loss and net assets of a subsidiary that are attributable to the interests that are not owned either directly or indirectly by the parent company.

For example, if a parent entity has purchased 100% of the issued capital of another company, there would be no minority interest as there is no equity held in the subsidiary by another. However, if a parent holds 80% of the share capital of a subsidiary, then the remaining 20% is attributed to others and is deemed minority interest. Thus, where a parent company has purchased a controlling interest in another company but has not purchased the entire share capital of the subsidiary, the percentage not owned by the parent company is called minority interest.

The minority interest is also referred to as a direct interest, as shareholders who are in the minority have a direct investment. The term 'minority interest' may also be referred to as 'direct outside equity' interest.

The following illustration shows a parent company, Parent Ltd, owning 80% of Son Ltd and 70% of Daughter Ltd. This results in a direct minority interest in Son Ltd of 20% and in Daughter Ltd of 30%.

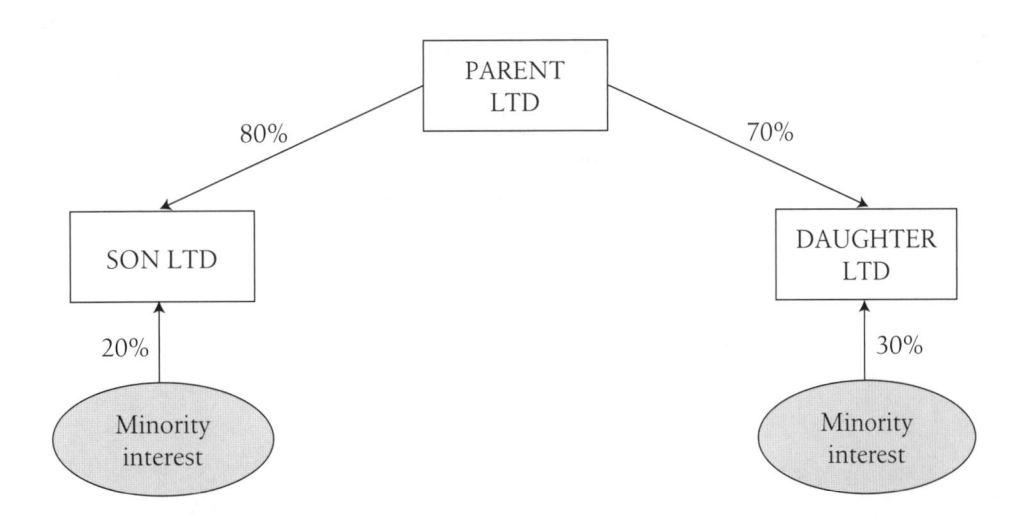

When preparing consolidated accounts where minority interests exist, AASB 127 requires the following to be reported:
- Minority interest is to be disclosed in the balance sheet as part of shareholders' equity and be shown separately from the parent company's equity.
- The profit or loss attributable to the minority interests must be disclosed separately.

Consolidation with minority interest

When consolidating the accounts where minority interest exists, it is necessary to observe the following four procedures:
1. elimination of the parent entity investment at the date of acquisition;
2. elimination of the minority interest at the date of reporting;
3. elimination of intercompany transactions and allocation of profits to the minority interest; and
4. adjustments for appropriation of profits.

Consequently, the eliminations and adjustments are normally performed on a consolidated worksheet.

Elimination of investment by the parent entity (at the date of acquisition)

On consolidation, the parent entity is required to make an adjustment to eliminate its investment in each subsidiary. The elimination values are *applicable as at the date of acquisition* of each subsidiary. The values of the elimination of the investment are made on the consolidated worksheet each time the consolidation of accounts takes place.

ILLUSTRATION

Power Ltd is in the process of consolidating its accounts on 30 June 2007. The company has the following investments in subsidiaries over which Power Ltd has control:
- an 80% ownership of the shares in Walsh Ltd acquired on 1 July 2004 at a cost of $700 000; and
- a 70% ownership of the shares in Mask Ltd acquired on 1 December 2006 at a cost of $300 000.

The balance sheets of Walsh Ltd and Mask Ltd at the respective dates of acquisition were as follows:

	Walsh Ltd 1 July 2004	Mask Ltd 1 December 2006
	$	$
Assets		
Bank	100 000	40 000
Debtors	150 000	20 000
Stock	250 000	100 000
Property and equipment	400 000	300 000
	900 000	460 000
Equities		
Creditors	100 000	10 000
Ordinary shares	550 000	250 000
Retained profits	150 000	50 000
Reserves	100 000	150 000
	900 000	460 000

The elimination entries at values applicable at the date of acquisition would be calculated as follows:

Walsh Ltd

	$	$
Purchase price of investment		700 000
Value of shareholders' equity purchased		
Ordinary shares (80% of $550 000)	440 000	
Retained profits (80% of $150 000)	120 000	
Reserves (80% of $100 000)	80 000	
Total value of shareholders' equity		640 000
Goodwill at date of acquisition		60 000

Since the date of acquisition it has been determined that the cash-generating assets acquired have been impaired as follows:

	$	$
Impairment loss – Goodwill		
From date of acquisition to start of current period	24 000	
For current period	12 000	
Total impairment loss of goodwill		36 000

Mask Ltd

	$	$
Purchase price of investment		300 000
Value of shareholders' equity purchased		
Ordinary shares (70% of $250 000)	175 000	
Retained profits (70% of $50 000)	35 000	
Reserves (70% of $150 000)	105 000	
Total value of shareholders' equity		315 000
Discount on acquisition		15 000

Note: Discount on acquisition to be credited to profits in accordance with the accounting standards.

The consolidation entries to eliminate the date of acquisition values of the subsidiaries would be as follows:

Consolidation entries

Date	Details	Debit	Credit
2007		$	$
30 June	Ordinary shares	440 000	
	Retained profits (at start)	120 000	
①	Reserves	80 000	
	Goodwill on acquisition	60 000	
	Investment in Walsh Ltd		700 000
	Elimination of investment in Walsh Ltd at 80% of values at date of acquisition		

Consolidation entries

Date	Details	Debit	Credit
		$	$
(2)	Retained profits (at start)	24 000	
	Operating expenses	12 000	
	Goodwill on acquisition		36 000
	Impairment of goodwill since date of acquisition		
(3)	Ordinary shares	175 000	
	Retained profits (at start)	35 000	
	Reserves	105 000	
	Profit and loss (Discount on consolidation)		15 000
	Investment in Mask Ltd		300 000
	Elimination of investment in Mask Ltd at 70% of values at date of acquisition		

The consolidated worksheet showing the values of the parent company and its two subsidiaries and the above elimination entries is presented opposite:

Consolidated worksheet as at 30 June 2007

	Power Ltd	Walsh Ltd	Mask Ltd	Eliminations		Minority interest		Economic entity
				Debit	Credit	Debit	Credit	
	$000s	$000s	$000s	$000s	$000s	$000s	$000s	$000s
Sales	3 100	1 500	1 000					5 600
less Cost of sales	1 400	600	400					2 400
Profit	1 700	900	600					3 200
Profit on equipment sale			125					125
Dividends income	62							62
Discount on consolidation					15 (3)			15
	1 762	900	725					3 402
Operating expenses	330	225	181	12 (2)				748
Profit (before tax)	1 432	675	544					2 654
Taxation expense	573	270	218					1 061
Profit (after tax)	859	405	326					1 593
Retained profits (start)	500	300	200	120 (1)				
				24 (2)				
				35 (3)				821
Funds to appropriate	1 359	705	526					2 414
Interim dividends	30	10	10					50
Final dividends	30	50	10					90
Transfer to reserves	100	20	50					150
Retained profits (end)	1 199	645	456					2 124
Ordinary shares	900	550	250	440 (1)				
				175 (3)				1 085
Reserves	400	200	100	80 (1)				
				105 (3)				515
Minority interest							375	375
Creditors	200	150	50					400
Dividends payable	30	50	10					90
	2 729	1 595	866					4 214
Assets								
Bank	100	200	70					370
Debtors	180	100	50					330
Stock	200	300	150					650
Dividends receivable	47							47
Property and equipment	1 202	995	596					2 793
Investment in Walsh Ltd	700				700 (1)			–
Investment in Mask Ltd	300				300 (3)			–
Goodwill on acquisition				60 (1)	36 (2)			24
	2 729	1 595	866	1 051	1 051			4 214

Eliminations

1 Elimination of investment in Walsh Ltd at 80% of date of acquisition values.
2 Impairment of goodwill since date of acquisition.
3 Elimination of investment in Mask Ltd at 70% of date of acquisition values.

Question 10.1

From the information that follows, you are required to prepare the consolidated worksheet for Casey Ltd and its subsidiaries as at 30 June 2007.

Casey Ltd purchased 90% of the shares of Barton Ltd on 1 January 2005 and gained control. The balance sheet of Barton Ltd on this date included the following:
- Ordinary shares $600 000
- Retained profits $300 000
- Reserves $200 000

On 1 August 2006 Casey Ltd gained control of Parks Ltd by acquiring 60% of the issued capital of the company. On this date, the shareholders' funds of Parks Ltd included the following:
- Ordinary shares $800 000
- Retained profits $200 000
- Reserves $400 000

Note: Goodwill has been impaired by $12 000 since the date of acquisition.

The financial statements of Casey and its subsidiaries as at 30 June 2007 are presented in the following consolidated worksheet.

Consolidated worksheet as at 30 June 2007

	Casey Ltd	Barton Ltd	Parks Ltd	Eliminations		Minority interest		Economic entity
				Debit	Credit	Debit	Credit	
	$000s	$000s	$000s	$000s	$000s	$000s	$000s	$000s
Operating profit	500	200	20					
Discount on acquisition								
Retained profit (start)	500	450	180					
Retained profits (end)	1 000	650	200					
Ordinary shares	1 500	600	800					
Reserves	250	200	450					
Creditors	50	45	10					
	2 800	1 495	1 460					
Assets								
Bank	50	150	25					
Debtors	100	20	80					
Stock	80	85	75					
Property and equipment	720	1 240	1 280					
Investment in Barton Ltd	950							
Investment in Parks Ltd	900							
Goodwill on acquisition								
	2 800	1 495	1 460					

Elimination of the minority interest (at the date of reporting)

To determine the extent of minority interest in the balance sheet on consolidation, it is necessary to calculate the proportion of the subsidiary balance sheet that is not under the control of the parent company. This is achieved by calculating the percentage of the shareholders' equity that is attributable to the minority interest at the date of reporting.

As the parent company has purchased a controlling interest in the subsidiary, the parent has a legal right to the net assets of the subsidiary. The net assets are effectively controlled by the parent company and are not under the control of the minority shareholders. Consequently, it is not appropriate for the consolidated worksheet to allocate a percentage of the net assets to the minority interest.

Consistent with this logic and in accordance with AASB 127, the consolidated worksheet must disclose the percentage of owners' equity that is attributable to the minority interest for:
- share capital;
- retained profits (losses); and
- reserves.

When calculating the minority interest's share of these items, the values of each subsidiary's balance sheet *at the date of consolidation* must be taken (not the date of acquisition values, as is the case for the elimination of the parent company's investment in the subsidiary).

ILLUSTRATION

In the previous illustration Power Ltd, the parent company, is in the process of consolidating its accounts on 30 June 2007 and has the following controlling investments in subsidiaries:
- an 80% ownership of the shares in Walsh Ltd purchased on 1 July 2004; and
- a 70% ownership of the shares in Mask Ltd purchased on 1 December 2006.

Consequently, the following minority interests must be accounted for at the date of consolidation:
- a 20% interest in Walsh Ltd; and
- a 30% interest in Mask Ltd.

At the date of consolidation, 30 June 2007, the balance sheets of the subsidiaries disclosed the following values:

Consolidated worksheet as at 30 June 2007

Account	Walsh Ltd	Mask Ltd
	$	$
Net profit	405 000	326 000
Retained profits (start)	300 000	200 000
Funds for appropriation	705 000	526 000
Interim dividends	(10 000)	(10 000)
Final dividends	(50 000)	(10 000)
Transfers to reserve		(50 000)
Retained profits (end)	645 000	456 000
Ordinary shares	550 000	250 000
Reserves	200 000	100 000
Creditors	150 000	50 000
Dividends payable	50 000	10 000
	1 595 000	856 000
Assets		
Bank	200 000	70 000
Debtors	100 000	50 000
Stock	300 000	150 000
Property and equipment	995 000	596 000
	1 595 000	866 000

The minority interest value in each of the subsidiaries at the date of consolidation is calculated as follows:

Walsh Ltd

	$
Ordinary shares (20% of $550 000)	110 000
Retained profits at start (20% of $300 000)	60 000
Reserves at end (20% of $200 000)	40 000
Minority interest in Walsh Ltd	**210 000**

Mask Ltd

	$
Ordinary shares (30% of $250 000)	75 000
Retained profits at start (30% of $200 000)	60 000
Reserves at end (30% of $100 000)	30 000
Minority interest in Walsh Ltd	**165 000**

The minority interests in Walsh Ltd and Mask Ltd would be aggregated for inclusion in the consolidated accounts as follows:

Aggregated minority interest

	Walsh Ltd	Mask Ltd	Total
	$	$	$
Ordinary shares	110 000	75 000	185 000
Retained profits (at start)	60 000	60 000	120 000
Reserves (at end)	40 000	30 000	70 000
Aggregated minority interest	**210 000**	**165 000**	**375 000**

The aggregated minority interest would be included in the minority interest column in the consolidated worksheet on 30 June 2007 by recording each component as a reduction (debit) against the respective components of shareholders' equity, and crediting the aggregated amount against the minority interest account.

An elimination journal entry recording this entry could be prepared as follows:

Consolidation entries

Date	Details	Debit	Credit
2007		$	$
30 June	Ordinary shares	185 000	
	Retained profits (at start)	120 000	
	Reserves	70 000	
	Minority interest		375 000
	Elimination of minority interests in Walsh Ltd (20%) and Marks Ltd (30%)		

The consolidated worksheet including this entry is shown as follows:

Consolidated worksheet as at 30 June 2007

	Power Ltd	Walsh Ltd	Mask Ltd	Eliminations Debit	Eliminations Credit	Minority interest Debit	Minority interest Credit	Economic entity
	$000s	$000s	$000s	$000s	$000s	$000s	$000s	$000s
Sales	3 100	1 500	1 000					5 600
less Cost of sales	1 400	600	400					2 400
Profit	1 700	900	600					3 200
Profit on equipment sale			125					125
Dividends income	62							62
Discount on consolidation					15 (3)			15
	1 762	900	725					3 402
Operating expenses	330	225	181	12 (2)				748
Profit (before tax)	1 432	675	544					2 654
Taxation expense	573	270	218					1 061
Profit (after tax)	859	405	326					1 593
Retained profits (start)	500	300	200	120 (1)				
				24 (2)				
				35 (3)		120		701
Funds to appropriate	1 359	705	526					2 294
Interim dividends	30	10	10					50
Final dividends	30	50	10					90
Transfer to reserves	100	20	50					150
Retained profits (end)	1 199	645	456					2 004
Ordinary shares	900	550	250	440 (1)				
				175 (3)		185		900
Reserves	400	200	100	80 (1)				
				105 (3)		70		445
Minority interest							375	375
Creditors	200	150	50					400
Dividends payable	30	50	10					90
	2 729	1 595	866					4 214
Assets								
Bank	100	200	70					370
Debtors	180	100	50					330
Stock	200	300	150					650
Dividends receivable	47							47
Property and equipment	1 202	995	596					2 793
Investment in Walsh Ltd	700				700 (1)			–
Investment in Mask Ltd	300				300 (3)			–
Goodwill on acquisition				60 (1)	36 (2)			24
	2 729	1 595	866	1 051	1 051			4 214

Reporting of minority interest

In accordance with the reporting requirements of AASB 127, the balance sheet and disclosure notes of the consolidated group would show the following information in relation to the group and the minority interest:

Balance sheet as at 30 June 2007 (Extract)

Shareholders' equity	$	Notes
Share capital	900 000	1
Reserves	445 000	2
Retained profits	2 004 000	
Minority interest	375 000	3
Total shareholders' equity	3 724 000	

Notes of disclosure

Note 3 Minority interest consists of:

	$
Share capital	185 000
Reserves	70 000
Retained profits	120 000

Question 10.2

You are required to:
a calculate the respective minority interests in the subsidiary companies in question 10.1;
b prepare a consolidated journal recording the aggregated minority interest;
c adjust the consolidated worksheet below to account for the minority interest; and
d show the shareholders' equity section of the balance sheet after consolidation (with appropriate disclosure notes).

Consolidated worksheet as at 30 June 2007

	Casey Ltd	Barton Ltd	Parks Ltd	Eliminations		Minority interest		Economic entity
				Debit	Credit	Debit	Credit	
	$000s	$000s	$000s	$000s	$000s	$000s	$000s	$000s
Operating profit	500	200	20	12 (3)				
Discount on acquisition					40 (1)			
Retained profits (start)	500	450	180	270 (1)				
				120 (2)				
Retained profits (end)	1 000	650	200					
Ordinary shares	1 500	600	800	540 (1)				
				480 (2)				
Reserves	250	200	450	180 (1)				
				240 (2)				
Minority interest								
Creditors	50	45	10					
	2 800	1 495	1 460					
Assets								
Bank	50	150	25					
Debtors	100	20	80					
Stock	80	85	75					
Property and equipment	720	1 240	1 280					
Investment in Barton Ltd	950				950 (1)			
Investment in Parks Ltd	900				900 (2)			
Goodwill on acquisition				60 (2)	12 (3)			
	2 800	1 495	1 460	1 902	1 902			

Question 10.3

The following information relates to the Angst company group. From this information you are required to:
a complete the consolidated worksheet of the company as at 30 June 2007; and
b prepare the shareholders' equity section of the balance sheet (with disclosure notes).
Angst Ltd made the following investments, giving the company control over the subsidiaries:
- On 1 July 2006: 75% of Martyr Ltd.
- On 1 January 2007: 90% of Farm Ltd.

The respective company balance sheets at the dates of acquisition revealed the following balances:

	Martyr Ltd	Farm Ltd
	$	$
Shareholders' equity		
Ordinary shares	100 000	80 000
Reserves	100 000	70 000
Retained profits	40 000	10 000

Note: Goodwill has been impaired by $6 000 in the current period and by $3 000 for previous periods.

The consolidated worksheet as at 30 June 2007 is shown as follows:

Consolidated worksheet as at 30 June 2007

	Angst Ltd	Martyr Ltd	Farm Ltd	Eliminations		Minority interest		Economic entity
				Debit	Credit	Debit	Credit	
	$000s	$000s	$000s	$000s	$000s	$000s	$000s	$000s
Operating profit	420	336	75					
Discount on acquisition								
Retained profits (start)	140	60	40					
Retained profits (end)	560	396	115					—
Ordinary shares	84	100	80					
Reserves	80	160	70					
Creditors	105	42	28					
	829	698	293					
Assets								
Bank	35	15	50					
Debtors	42	45	36					
Stock	36	28	36					
Property and equipment	382	610	171					
Investment in Martyr Ltd	160							
Investment in Farm Ltd	174							
Goodwill on acquisition								
	829	698	293					

Elimination of intercompany transactions and allocating profits to the minority interest

Once the parent's investments in the respective subsidiaries have been eliminated and the value of the minority interest has been accounted for, it is then necessary to make the normal eliminations for transactions that have taken place between the parent and the subsidiaries.

Eliminations for transactions such as intercompany sales, intercompany expenses, intercompany asset disposals, and intercompany debt and debt servicing will not have an effect on the value of minority interest, as these transactions are made within the economic entity and merely affect the true and fair view required of group accounts.

The minority interest is, however, entitled to a share of the after-tax profits of the companies in which it has a direct investment. Hence, the value of the minority interest in the consolidated worksheet will need to be adjusted to account for the share of after-tax profits or losses of the companies in which it has an investment.

As the minority interest does not have an investment in the parent company or a controlling interest in any other subsidiary company in the group, it is only entitled to a share of the profits of the subsidiary in which it has an investment.

The share of profits (losses) must first be adjusted for unrealised profits or losses. The adjustments for unrealised profits and losses that must be made are only in respect of unrealised profits that have been identified in the accounts of the company in which the minority interest has an interest. For example, if a minority interest had an interest in a subsidiary and that subsidiary had recorded an unrealised profit in its calculation of after-tax profit, then the minority interest's share of after-tax profit of the subsidiary would first have to be adjusted to eliminate the unrealised profit.

If the unrealised profit has been recorded by a company in the group in which the minority interest does not have an investment, then the unrealised profit will not affect the minority interest's share of after-tax profit (loss) of the subsidiary in which it has an investment. For example, A Ltd, which owns a majority share of B Ltd, sold goods to B Ltd at a profit, but B Ltd has not sold the goods to a party outside the group. As A Ltd has recorded the unrealised profit, and not B Ltd, then the minority shareholders of B Ltd will not be affected by the adjustment, which removes the unrealised profit from the consolidated accounts.

When calculating the minority interest's share of after-tax profit that has been affected by unrealised profits, it is necessary to adjust the profit as set out below.

Unrealised profits in opening stocks

If the unrealised profit is associated with the previous year's accounts, it is necessary to add the unrealised profit back to the after-tax profit in the current period before taking the minority interest's share in that profit. The reason for this is that the adjustment, which removes the unrealised profit from the previous year's accounts, is initially made against the opening retained profits value of the subsidiary. The subsidiary, having recorded the profit in the previous year, will not record the profit in the current period.

Hence, the consolidated worksheet will not show the profit being realised. On the assumption that the profit will be realised in the current period, it is necessary to add the unrealised profit to the subsidiary's after-tax profit to ensure that the true profit is accurately reported. From this true after-tax profit, a calculation can be made in respect of the minority interest's share in that profit.

Unrealised profits in closing stocks

Unrealised profits recorded in the current period by the subsidiary must be deducted from the subsidiary's after-tax profit before the minority interest's share in the annual profit is calculated. The reason for this is that the subsidiary will have recorded the unrealised profits in the after-tax profit for the current period, and as the profit has been inflated by the unrealised profit it must be reduced.

ILLUSTRATION

Bragge Ltd is controlled by Hall Ltd as a result of Hall's 80% ownership of share capital. For the year ended 30 June 2007 Bragge reported the following:

Retained profits (at start)	$200 000
Profit (after tax)	$600 000

Stock-related transactions included (sales from Bragge Ltd to Hall Ltd):

Unrealised profit (before tax) in opening stock of Hall Ltd	$50 000
Unrealised profit (before tax) in closing stock of Hall Ltd	$300 000

The tax rate is 30%.
The profit effect of taxation on these unrealised profits is as follows:

Unrealised profit (after tax) in opening stock

	$
Profit before tax	50 000
less Income tax (30%)	15 000
Unrealised profit (after tax)	35 000

Unrealised profit (after tax) in closing stock

	$
Profit before tax	300 000
less Income tax (30%)	90 000
Unrealised profit (after tax)	210 000

The resulting adjustments to profits and associated minority interests are:

	$
Retained profits (at start)	200 000
less Unrealised profit in opening stock (after tax)	35 000
Adjusted retained profits (at start)	165 000
Minority interest share of retained profits (at start) at 20%	33 000
Profit (after tax)	600 000
add back Unrealised profit (after tax) in opening stocks	35 000
less Unrealised profit (after tax) in closing stock	(210 000)
Adjusted profit (after tax)	425 000
Minority interest share of profits at 20%	85 000

Unrealised profits (losses) on asset disposals and associated depreciation charges

Where a subsidiary company records a profit on disposal of an asset to another company in the economic entity, which is not then sold to a party outside the group, the profit is unrealised. When preparing the consolidated accounts, the unrealised profit must be eliminated, depreciation calculations adjusted and taxation calculations amended.

The effect of removing an unrealised profit with associated depreciation and taxation adjustments is to reduce the reported profit of the subsidiary. Consequently, the share of the subsidiary company's after-tax profit that accrues to the minority interest is reduced.

ILLUSTRATION

Parker Ltd has a 70% controlling interest in Norton Ltd. For the year ended 30 June 2007 Norton Ltd reported a profit (after tax) of $400 000. Included in this profit was a profit (before tax) on an asset sold to Parker Ltd of $125 000 which had not been sold to a party outside the group. Parker depreciates assets at 20% p.a.

The associated effects of this unrealised profit on the group accounts are as follows:

	$
Unrealised profit (before tax)	125 000
less Depreciation on excess asset value at 20%	25 000
Unrealised profit (before tax)	100 000
less Income tax at 30%	30 000
Unrealised profit (after tax)	70 000

When this entire transaction is reversed, the reported profit (after tax) will be reduced by $70 000 and the outside interest in profit (after tax) reduced accordingly — that is:

	$
Profit (after tax)	400 000
less Net effect of unrealised profit on asset sale	70 000
Adjusted profit (after tax)	330 000
Minority interest share of profits at 30%	99 000

Question 10.4

From the following information on Nardoo Ltd, calculate the minority interest's share of:
a retained profits (at start); and
b profit (after tax).

Nardoo Ltd is controlled by Pace Ltd, which owns 60% of its issued capital. For the year ended 30 June 2007 the following has been reported for the group:

Retained profits (at start) of Nardoo Ltd	$250 000
Profit (after tax) of Nardoo Ltd	$600 000

Stock-related transactions (resulting from sales from Nardoo Ltd to Pace Ltd)

Unrealised profit (before tax) in closing stock of Pace Ltd	$200 000
Unrealised profit (before tax) in opening stock of Pace Ltd	$100 000

Asset-related transactions (from Nardoo Ltd to Pace Ltd)

Profit on sale of asset (before tax)	$50 000
Nardoo Ltd depreciates assets at 10% p.a.	$600 000

The tax rate is 30%.

Question 10.5

Trask Ltd holds an 80% controlling interest in Dash Ltd and a 70% controlling interest in Star Ltd. Both subsidiaries deal directly with the parent company and for the year ended 30 June report the following:

	Dash Ltd	**Star Ltd**
	$	$
Retained profits (at start)	300 000	200 000
Profit (after tax)	400 000	270 000

- Unrealised profits in stocks of Trask Ltd (arising from sales from subsidiaries).
    - Opening stocks:
      Dash Ltd reported a profit (before tax) of $50 000 on sales to Trask Ltd in the previous year. This stock remained with Trask Ltd at the end of the previous year.
    - Closing stocks:
      The closing stock of Trask Ltd contained unrealised profits (before tax) as follows:
      $30 000 as a result of sales from Dash Ltd
      $150 000 as a result of sales from Star Ltd
      Unrealised profits from asset sales.

Star Ltd sold equipment to Trask Ltd at a profit of $125 000. Assets are depreciated at 20% p.a. The tax rate is 30%.

From the information presented, you are required to calculate the outside entity interest in retained profits (at start) and profit (after tax).

Adjustments for appropriation of profits

Dividends

The appropriation of profits by a subsidiary in the form of dividends is eliminated in the normal manner by the parent company when consolidation of the group accounts takes place. That is, the share of dividends income and dividend accruals made by the parent and the subsidiary are removed from the accounts. However, the share of dividends that the minority interest is entitled to must be calculated and adjustments made to the consolidated accounts.

Dividends paid (interim) or declared (final) are returns of profits to the owners of share capital. As the value of the minority interest includes a share of the subsidiary's profit (after tax) for the current period, it is necessary to offset against this value any dividend amounts paid out or declared by the subsidiary.

Reserve transfers

Where a subsidiary has transferred profits to reserve accounts, the transfers need to be reversed. The value of the minority interest will have been increased by the share of retained profits (at start) and profit (after tax). In addition, the value of the minority interest will have been increased by the share of balance sheet reserves at the date of consolidation. (See 'Elimination of the minority interest (at the date of reporting)', pp. 312–18.)

Thus, the minority interest will have double-counted the reserve account increase. Consequently, it is necessary to decrease the value of the minority interest to eliminate the effect of double-counting.

On the other hand, if a reserve account is decreased, the value of minority interest will also decrease when the share of reserves is calculated at the date of reporting. The transfer from the reserve accounts does not have an effect on either retained profits (at start) or profit (before tax). Consequently, the transfer from the reserve will undervalue the value of minority interest. An adjustment is required to return the value of the reserve transfer back to the value of the minority interest.

ILLUSTRATION

Marvel Ltd has 80% of its share capital owned by a parent company. Minority interests account for the remaining 20%. The amount owing to minority interests at the start of the year was $200 000.

For the year ended 30 June 2007 Marvel Ltd reported the following in its income statement.

	$	$
Profit (after tax)		750 000
Retained profits (at start)		250 000
Funds to appropriate		1 000 000
less Funds appropriated		
Dividends:		
Interim	50 000	
Final	70 000	
Transfer to reserves	30 000	150 000
Retained profits (at end)		850 000

The value of the minority interest would be calculated as follows:

		$	$
Minority interest balance (at start of period)			200 000
add Share of profit (after tax) (20% × $750 000)			150 000
			350 000
less Appropriated funds:			
Dividends:			
Interim dividends (20% × $50 000)		10 000	
Final dividends (20% × $70 000)		14 000	
Transfer to reserves (20% × $30 000)		6 000	30 000
Value of minority interest after appropriations			20 000

Question 10.6

From the following information you are required to calculate the value of minority interest after the appropriation of profits.

The economic entity consists of a parent company, Loyd Ltd, and two subsidiaries, Batty Ltd and Trad Ltd. The details of the extent of minority interest and profits for the year ended 30 June 2007 are as follows:

	Batty Ltd	Trad Ltd
Share of minority interest	20%	30%
	$	$
Value of minority interest before profits	210 000	165 000
Profit (after tax)	500 000	180 000
Interim dividends	100 000	60 000
Final dividends	100 000	40 000
Transfer to reserves	50 000	Nil
Transfer from reserves	Nil	10 000

COMPREHENSIVE ILLUSTRATION

This illustration is a continuation of the previous illustrations relating to Power Ltd and its subsidiaries, Walsh Ltd and Mask Ltd. The previous illustrations covered the elimination entries to remove the parent's investment in the subsidiaries at the date of acquisition and the adjustment to recognise the values of the minority interests at the date of reporting. Hence, elimination entries 1 to 3 have already been made.

In the previous illustrations, Power Ltd, the parent company, has the following controlling investments in subsidiaries:
- an 80% ownership of the shares in Walsh Ltd; and
- a 70% ownership of the shares in Mask Ltd.

For the year ended 30 June 2007 the following intercompany transactions require elimination. The tax rate is 30%.

Unrealised profits in opening stocks of Power Ltd: Walsh Ltd sold goods to Power Ltd during the previous year at a profit (before tax) of $50 000. Power Ltd failed to sell the goods to another party.

The elimination entry (No. 4) is as follows:

Consolidation entries

Date	Particulars	Debit	Credit
2007		$	$
30 June	Retained profits (start) (Walsh Ltd)	35 000	
	Income tax expense	15 000	
④	Cost of sales (stock at start)		50 000
	Elimination of unrealised profit in the opening stock of Power Ltd		

- Intercompany sales:
  - Walsh Ltd to Power Ltd $200 000
  - Mask Ltd to Power Ltd $300 000

The elimination entry (No. 5) is as follows:

Consolidation entries

Date	Particulars	Debit	Credit
2007		$	$
30 June	Sales	500 000	
⑤	Cost of sales (purchases)		500 000
	To eliminate intercompany sales made by Walsh Ltd and Marks Ltd to Power Ltd		

- Unrealised profits (before tax) in closing stocks of Power Ltd:
  - $30 000 as a result of sales from Walsh Ltd; and
  - $150 000 as a result of sales from Mask Ltd.

The elimination entries (Nos 6–9) are:

Consolidation entries

Date	Particulars	Debit	Credit
2007 June		$	$
	Cost of sales (stock at end)	30 000	
	Stock		30 000
(6)	To eliminate unrealised profit in closing stock of Power Ltd as a result of sales from Walsh Ltd		
	Deferred tax asset	9 000	
	Income tax expense		9 000
(7)	To adjust income tax as a result of unrealised profit in closing stock		
	Cost of sales (stock at end)	150 000	
	Stock		150 000
(8)	To eliminate unrealised profit in closing stock of Power Ltd as a result of sales from Mask Ltd		
	Deferred tax asset	45 000	
	Income tax expense		45 000
(9)	To adjust income tax as a result of unrealised profit in closing stock		

- Mask Ltd sold equipment to Power Ltd at a profit of $125 000. Assets are depreciated at 20% p.a. The elimination entries (Nos 10–12) are as follows:

Consolidation entries

Date	Particulars	Debit	Credit
2007 30 June		$	$
	Profit on equipment sale	125 000	
	Property and equipment		125 000
(10)	To eliminate unrealised profit on sale of equipment made by Mask Ltd		
	Accumulated depreciation	25 000	
	Operating expenses		25 000
(11)	To record reversal of depreciation on unrealised profit on disposal of asset		
	Deferred tax asset	30 000	
	Income tax expense		30 000
(12)	Adjustment of income tax as a result of eliminating $125 000 unrealised profit on asset sale and reduction of associated depreciation expense		

- Both subsidiaries have paid dividends during the period. The parent company recognises dividends when declared.
  - Walsh Ltd has paid interim dividends of $10 000 and declared final dividends of $50 000.
  - Mask Ltd has paid interim dividends of $10 000 and declared $10 000 in final dividends.

The elimination entries (Nos 13–14) are as follows:

Consolidation entries

Date	Particulars	Debit	Credit
		$	$
(13)	Dividends income	48 000	
	Interim dividends (retained profits)		8 000
	Final dividends (retained profits)		40 000
	Elimination of interim dividends paid and declared by Walsh Ltd ($60 000 × .80)		
(13)	Dividends payable	40 000	
	Dividends receivable		40 000
	Elimination of final dividend declared by Walsh Ltd and accrued by Power Ltd ($50 000 × 0.70)		
(14)	Dividends income	14 000	
	Interim dividends (retained profits)		7 000
	Final dividends (retained profits)		7 000
	Elimination of interim dividends paid and declared by Mask Ltd ($10 000 × .70)		
(14)	Dividends payable	7 000	
	Dividends receivable		7 000
	Elimination of final dividend declared by Mask Ltd and accrued by Power Ltd ($10 000 × .70)		

Additional information

	Walsh Ltd	Mask Ltd
	$	$
Profit (after tax)	405 000	326 000
Retained profits (at start)	300 000	200 000

The calculation of the values of the minority interests in the respective subsidiaries retained profits (at start) and profits (after tax) would be as follows:

Calculation 1

Minority interest share of retained profits (at start)

	Walsh Ltd	Mask Ltd
	$	$
Retained profits (at start)	300 000	200 000
less Unrealised profit (after tax) on stock from previous period	(35 000)	
Profit after tax (after unrealised profits)	265 000	
Percentage of minority interest	20%	30%
Minority interest in retained profits (at start)	53 000	60 000

The aggregated values of minority interests in the retained profits (at start) of the economic entity are:

	$
Walsh Ltd	53 000
Mask Ltd	60 000
Minority interest share of profits (after tax)	113 000

Calculation 2

Minority interest share of profits (after tax)

	Walsh Ltd	Mask Ltd
	$	$
Profit (after tax)	405 000	326 000
add Unrealised profit (after tax) on stock from previous period	35 000	–
less Unrealised profit (after tax) on stock from current period	(21 000)	(105 000)
less Unrealised profit (after tax) on asset sale in current period	–	(70 000)
Profit after tax (after unrealised profits)	419 000	151 000
Percentage of minority interest	20%	30%
Minority interest in profit (after tax)	83 800	45 300

The aggregated values of minority interests in the profits (after tax) of the economic entity are:

	$
Walsh Ltd	83 800
Mask Ltd	45 300
Minority interest share of profits (after tax)	129 100
	129 000 rounded

Calculation 3

Minority interest share of dividends

As both subsidiaries have appropriated profits, adjustments to the value of the respective minority interests are necessary. The appropriate adjustments are shown in the following tables.

Minority interest share of Walsh Ltd:

	$
Interim dividends (20% × $10 000)	2 000
Final dividends (20% × $50 000)	10 000
Reduction in value of minority interest	12 000

Minority interest share of Mask Ltd:

	$
Interim dividends (30% × $10 000)	3 000
Final dividends (30% × $10 000)	3 000
Transfer to reserves (30% × $50 000)	15 000
Reduction in value of minority interest	21 000

The aggregated reduction of the minority interest for dividends would be:

	$
Reduction of minority interest share of Walsh Ltd	12 000
Reduction of minority interest share of Mask Ltd	21 000
Reduction in value of minority interest	33 000

The combined effects on the aggregated value of the minority interest resulting from these calculations and the adjustment of shareholders' equity accounts at the date of reporting would be as follows:

	$
Minority interest share of balance sheet items at date of reporting	
Ordinary shares (refer calculations on p. XXX)	185 000
Reserves	70 000
Retained profits (at start) – Calculation 1	114 000
Minority interest share of profits after tax – Calculation 2	129 000
	498 000
less Adjustments to minority interest for appropriated profits – Calculation 3	33 000
Net value of minority interest	465 000

The preceding consolidation journal entries and adjustments to the value of the minority interest would be recorded in the consolidated worksheet as follows:

Consolidated worksheet as at 30 June 2007

	Power Ltd	Walsh Ltd	Mask Ltd	Eliminations		Minority interest		Economic entity
				Debit	Credit	Debit	Credit	
	$000s	$000s	$000s	$000s	$000s	$000s	$000s	$000s
Sales	3 100	1 500	1 000	500 (5)				5 100
less Cost of sales	1 400	600	400	30 (6)	50 (4)			
				150 (8)	500 (5)			2 030
Profit	1 700	900	600					3 070
Profit on equipment sale			125	125 (10)				–
Discount on acquisition					15 (3)			15
Dividends income	62			48 (13)				
				14 (14)				–
	1 762	900	725					3 085
Operating expenses	330	225	181	12 (2)	25 (11)			723
Profit (before tax)	1 432	675	544					2 362
Taxation expense	573	270	218	15 (4)	9 (7)			
					45 (9)			
					30 (12)			992
Profit (after tax)	859	405	326					1 370
less Minority interest share						129		129
								1 241
Retained profits (start)	500	300	200	120 (1)				
				24 (2)				
				35 (3)				
				35 (4)			114	672

	$000s	$000s	$000s	$000s	$000s	$000s	$000s	$000s
Funds to appropriate	1 359	705	526					1 913
Interim dividends	30	10	10		8 (13)			
					7 (14)		5	30
Final dividends	30	50	10		40 (13)			
					7 (14)		13	30
Transfer to reserves	100	–	50				15	135
Retained profits (end)	1 199	645	456					1 718
Ordinary shares	900	550	250	440 (1)				
				175 (3)		185		900
Reserves	400	200	100	80 (1)				
				105 (3)		70		445
Minority interest							465	465
Creditors	200	150	50					400
Dividends payable	30	50	10	40 (13)				
				7 (14)				43
	2 729	1 595	866					3 971
Assets								
Bank	100	200	70					370
Debtors	180	100	50					330
Stock	200	300	150		30 (6)			
					150 (8)			470
Dividends receivable	47				40 (14)			
					7 (14)			–
Deferred tax asset				9 (7)				
				45 (9)				
				30 (12)				84
Property and equipment	1 202	995	596	25 (11)	125 (10)			2 693
Investment in Walsh Ltd	700				700 (1)			–
Investment in Mask Ltd	300				300 (3)			–
Goodwill on acquisition				60 (1)	36 (2)			24
	2 729	1 595	866	2124	2 124	498	498	3 971

Eliminations

1. Elimination of investment in Walsh Ltd at 80% of date of acquisition values.
2. Amortisation of goodwill on acquisition since date of acquisition.
3. Elimination of investment in Mask Ltd at 70% of date of acquisition values.
4. Elimination of unrealised profit (after tax) in opening stock.
5. Elimination of intercompany sales.
6. Elimination of unrealised profit in closing stock (Walsh Ltd's sales).
7. Tax effect adjustment on elimination 6.
8. Elimination of unrealised profit in closing stock (Mask Ltd's sales).
9. Tax effect adjustment on elimination 8.
10. Elimination of unrealised profit on asset sale.
11. Adjustment to account for overstated depreciation on asset sale.

12 Tax effect adjustment of eliminations 10 and 11.
13 Elimination of dividends paid and declared by Walsh Ltd.
14 Elimination of dividends paid and declared by Mask Ltd.

Reporting requirements of minority interest

AASB 127 requires the following information in relation to the reporting and disclosure of minority interests:

- in the income statement:
  - the portion of the net profit;
- in the balance sheet:
  - the share capital;
  - retained profits or accumulated losses; and
  - reserves.

ILLUSTRATION

Using the consolidated worksheet from the previous illustration, to comply with the reporting requirements of minority interests in the consolidated accounts the following would need to be reported.

Income statement for the year ended 30 June 2007 (Extract)

	Economic entity $
Profit before income tax	2 362 000
less Income tax attributable to profit	992 000
Net profit	1 370 000

Notes of disclosure (for the income statement)

	Parent entity interest $	Minority interest $
Profit after income tax	1 241 000	129 000
Retained profit 1 July 2006	672 000	114 000
Total available for appropriation	1 913 000	243 000
Transfers to reserves	(135 000)	(15 000)
Dividends provided for or paid to:		
Parent entity shareholders	(60 000)	
Minority interest		(18 000)
Retained profits at 30 June 2007	1 718 000	210 000

Balance sheet as at 30 June 2007 (Extract)

Shareholders' equity	$	Notes
Share capital	900 000	1
Reserves	445 000	2
Retained profits	1 718 000	
Minority interest	465 000	3
Total shareholders' equity	3 528 000	

Notes of disclosure

Note 3 Minority interest consists of:

	$
Share capital	185 000
Reserves	70 000
Retained profits	210 000
	465 000

Note: Minority interest value of retained profits (at end) is calculated as follows:

	$
Share of profit (after tax)	129 000
add Share of retained profits (at start)	114 000
	243 000
less Appropriated funds	
Interim dividends paid	(5 000)
Final dividends declared	(13 000)
Transfer to reserves	(15 000)
Value of minority interest share of retained profits (at end)	210 000

Question 10.7

The following information relates to Go Ltd and its subsidiaries. You are required to prepare:
a the consolidated worksheet for the year ended 30 June 2007;
b an extract of the income statement for the year ended 30 June 2007 showing profits before and after tax; and
c an extract of the balance sheet as at 30 June 2007 showing the shareholders' equity section.
   Go Ltd made the following investments giving the company control over the subsidiaries:
- On 1 July 2006: 60% of North Ltd.
- On 1 October 2006: 80% of East Ltd.

   The respective company balance sheets at the dates of acquisition revealed the following balances:

	North Ltd	East Ltd
	$	$
Ordinary shares	200 000	50 000
Retained profits	50 000	50 000
Reserves	160 000	60 000

Notes:
- Goodwill has been impaired by $1 000 in the current year.
- During the first year of operation ending 30 June 2007 there were no intercompany transactions. The subsidiaries did, however, appropriate profits.

The respective companies' financial statements for the year ended 30 June 2007 appeared in the consolidated worksheet as follows:

Consolidated worksheet as at 30 June 2007

	Go Ltd	North Ltd	East Ltd	Eliminations Debit	Eliminations Credit	Minority interest Debit	Minority interest Credit	Economic entity
	$000s	$000s	$000s	$000s	$000s	$000s	$000s	$000s
Sales	800	400	200					
less Expenses	300	120	80					
	500	280	120					
add Dividends income	26	—	—					
Discount on acquisition								
Profit (before tax)	526	280	120					
Income tax expense	210	120	50					
Profit (after tax)	316	160	70					
Retained profits (start)	140	60	40					
Transfer from reserves		20	—					
	456	240	110					
Interim dividends	50	20	10					
Final dividends	40	10						
Transfer to reserves			10					
Retained profits (end)	366	210	90					
Ordinary shares	400	200	50					
Reserves	80	140	70					
Minority interest								
Dividends payable	40	10						
Creditors	100	40	20					
	986	600	230					
Assets								
Bank	35	15	50					
Debtors	42	45	55					
Stock	62	28	23					
Dividends receivable	6							
Property and equipment	461	512	102					
Investment in North Ltd	240							
Investment in East Ltd	140							
Goodwill on acquisition								
	986	600	230	—	—	—	—	—

Question 10.8

The following information relates to Holly Ltd and its subsidiaries in the second year of its operation, ending 30 June 2007. You are required to prepare:
a the consolidated worksheet for the year ended 30 June 2007;
b an extract of the income statement for the year ended 30 June 2007 showing profits before and after tax; and
c an extract of the balance sheet as at 30 June 2007 showing the shareholders' equity section.
  Go Ltd's investments were as follows:
- On 1 July 2005: 60% of Space Ltd.
- On 1 October 2005: 80% of Wars Ltd.
  The balance sheets of the subsidiaries at the dates of acquisition revealed the following balances:

	Space Ltd	Wars Ltd
	$	$
Ordinary shares	200 000	50 000
Retained profits	50 000	50 000
Reserves	160 000	60 000

Notes:
- Goodwill has been amortised by $1 000 in the current year and $1 000 in the previous year.
- Discount on acquisition is to be eliminated against property and equipment.
  During the year ended 30 June 2007 the following intercompany transactions occurred:
1 Intercompany sales from subsidiary companies to the parent company:
  - Sales from Space Ltd to Holly Ltd: $80 000.
  - Sales from Wars Ltd to Holly Ltd: $20 000.
2 Unrealised profit in closing stocks: The closing stocks of Holly Ltd include an unrealised profit of $50 000 as a result of sales from Space Ltd.
3 Intercompany loan: During the year, Holly Ltd loaned Space Ltd $100 000.
  The tax rate is 30%.

The respective companies' financial statements for the year ended 30 June 2007 appeared in the consolidated worksheet as follows:

Consolidated worksheet as at 30 June 2007

	Holly Ltd	Space Ltd	Wars Ltd	Eliminations		Minority interest		Economic entity
				Debit	Credit	Debit	Credit	
	$000s	$000s	$000s	$000s	$000s	$000s	$000s	$000s
Sales	1 200	500	400					
less Expenses	650	250	120					
	550	250	280					
add Dividends income	42							
Discount on acquisition								
Profit (before tax)	592	250	280					
Income tax expense	235	100	120					
Profit (after tax)	357	150	160					
less Minority interest share								
Retained profits (start)	366	210	90					
	723	360	250					
Interim dividends	60	20	15					
Final dividends	50	30						
Transfer to reserves	10		20					
Retained profits (end)	603	310	215					
Ordinary shares	400	200	50					
Reserves	90	140	90					
Minority interest								
Dividends payable	50	30						
Creditors	120	50	30					
Loan from Holly Ltd		100						
	1 263	830	385					
Assets								
Bank	50	10	40					
Debtors	80	40	60					
Stock	100	30	20					
Dividends receivable	18							
Loan to Space Ltd	100							
Property and equipment	537	750	265					
Investment in Space Ltd	240							
Investment in Wars Ltd	138							
Goodwill on acquisition								
	1 263	830	385					

Question 10.9

JB Ltd and its subsidiaries are now at the end of their third year of operations, ending 30 June 2007. From the information provided, you are required to prepare:
a   the consolidated worksheet for the year ended 30 June 2007;
b   an extract of the income statement for the year ended 30 June 2007 showing profits before and after tax; and
c   an extract of the balance sheet as at 30 June 2007 showing the shareholders' equity section.
    JB Ltd's investments were as follows:
- On 1 July 2004:   60% of Black Ltd.
- On 1 October 2004:   80% of White Ltd.

The balance sheets of the subsidiaries at the dates of acquisition revealed the following balances:

	Black Ltd	White Ltd
	$	$
Ordinary shares	200 000	50 000
Retained profits	50 000	50 000
Reserves	160 000	60 000

Note:
- Goodwill was impaired by $2 000 in the previous year and $1 000 in the current year.
    During the year ended 30 June 2007 the following intercompany transactions occurred:
1   Intercompany sales from subsidiary companies to the parent company:
    - Sales from Black Ltd to JB Ltd: $100 000.
    - Sales from White Ltd to JB Ltd: $40 000.
2   Unrealised profit in opening stocks: The opening stocks of JB Ltd include an unrealised profit of $50 000 as a result of sales from Black Ltd in the previous year.
3   The closing inventories of JB Ltd include an unrealised profit of $30 000 arising from sales from White Ltd.
4   White Ltd recorded a profit on the sale of equipment to JB Ltd. The sale occurred on 1 July 2006. Assets are depreciated at 20% p.a.
    The tax rate is 30%.

The respective companies' financial statements for the year ended 30 June 2007 appeared in the consolidated worksheet as follows:

Consolidated worksheet as at 30 June 2007

	JB Ltd	Black Ltd	White Ltd	Eliminations		Minority interest		Economic entity
				Debit	Credit	Debit	Credit	
	$000s	$000s	$000s	$000s	$000s	$000s	$000s	$000s
Sales	1 400	600	500					
less Expenses	720	300	210					
	680	300	290					
add Dividends income	42							
add Profit on asset sale			100					
Discount on acquisition								
Profit (before tax)	722	300	390					
Income tax expense	290	120	160					
Profit (after tax)	432	180	230					
less Minority interest share								
Retained profits (start)	603	310	215					
	1 035	490	445					
Interim dividends	60	30	15					
Final dividends	40	20						
Retained profits (end)	935	440	430					
Ordinary shares	400	200	50					
Reserves	90	140	90					
Minority interest								
Dividends payable	40	20						
Creditors	100	60	40					
	1 565	860	610					
Assets								
Bank	200	40	50					
Debtors	70	50	20					
Stock	120	40	50					
Dividends receivable	12							
Deferred tax asset								
Property and equipment	815	730	490					
Investment in Black Ltd	200							
Investment in White Ltd	148							
Goodwill on acquisition								
	1 565	860	610					

Indirect minority interests

Minority interests as described and illustrated in the previous pages related to direct minority interests (DMI) – that is, the minority interests of a subsidiary directly held shares in the subsidiary. For example, Apple Ltd owns a 90% controlling interest in Orange Ltd. Thus, 10% of Orange Ltd is owned by minority interests as they have direct ownership of 10% of the company's share capital.

Minority interests may also be classified as indirect minority interests (IMI). This will occur where a parent company purchases a controlling interest in another company, and that company in turn purchases a controlling interest in a third company. This is referred to as the parent–son–grandson relationship.

For example, Apple Ltd (the parent) purchases an 80% controlling interest in Orange Ltd (the son), which in turn purchases a 75% controlling interest in Pear Ltd (the grandson). Presented diagrammatically, this would appear as follows:

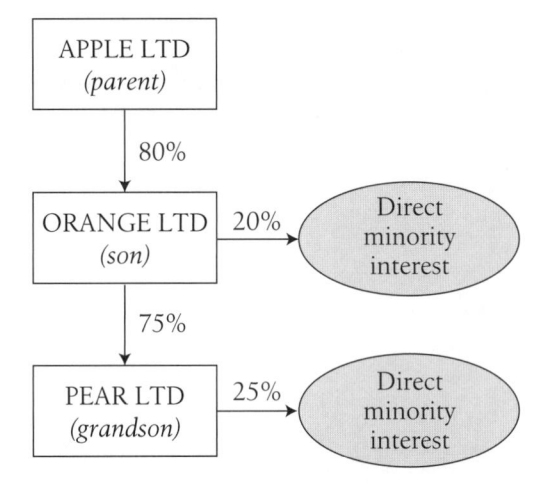

```
          APPLE LTD
           (parent)
              |
             80%
              ↓
         ORANGE LTD ──20%──▶ Direct minority interest
            (son)
              |
             75%
              ↓
          PEAR LTD  ──25%──▶ Direct minority interest
         (grandson)
```

In this illustration, there are two *direct* minority interests. These are:
- 20% of Orange Ltd; and
- 25% of Pear Ltd.

There is also an *indirect* minority interest in Pear Ltd. This is held by the direct minority interest shareholders of Orange Ltd as a result of Orange Ltd's 75% direct investment in Pear Ltd.

The amount of the minority interest is equal to the direct minority interest's interest in Orange Ltd (20%) multiplied by the interest that Orange Ltd holds in Pear Ltd (75%) – that is, 20% × 75% = 15%.

The aggregated minority interest in the economic entity is shown in the following table. The table shows the percentages of Orange Ltd and Pear Ltd which are held directly and indirectly by the minority interests.

Minority interest	Orange Ltd	Pear Ltd
Direct	20%	25%
Indirect	Nil	15%

From the parent company's (Apple Ltd) point of view, they have a direct investment in Orange Ltd of 80%. In addition, as Orange Ltd has a 75% interest in Pear Ltd, Apple Ltd has an indirect investment in Pear Ltd. The extent of this indirect investment is 80% × 75% = 60%.

Another way of viewing the ownership of Pear Ltd is to analyse who really owns the 75% of shares in Pear Ltd that Orange Ltd purchased. As Apple Ltd owns 80% of the shares of Orange Ltd (which in turn owns 75% of the shares in Pear Ltd), Apple Ltd effectively owns 60% of the shares of Pear Ltd.

Similarly, as minority interests own 20% of Orange Ltd (which in turn owns 75% of Pear Ltd), then the minority interest shareholders of Orange Ltd have the right to claim 15% of Pear Ltd. Thus, the 75% interest in Pear Ltd is held indirectly. Apple Ltd indirectly owns 60% of Pear Ltd and the direct minority interest shareholders of Orange Ltd indirectly own 15% of Pear Ltd. Minority interests who have invested directly in Pear Ltd own the remaining 25% of Pear Ltd.

So, who owns Pear Ltd? There are two categories of owners – those with a direct investment, and those with an indirect investment. The following table summarises the extent of the direct and indirect investments in Pear Ltd.

Direct investment	25%	(Held by minority interest shareholders of Pear Ltd.)
Indirect investment	15%	(Held by minority interest shareholders of Orange Ltd.)
Indirect investment	60%	(Held by Apple Ltd.)
Total investment	100%	

When consolidating the accounts so that they reflect the economic entity as a whole, it is necessary to adjust the accounts to reflect the full amount accruing to the aggregate minority interests. In the case of Apple Ltd, Orange Ltd and Pear Ltd, these are both direct and indirect – that is:

Minority interest direct investments:

20% of Orange Ltd (Held by minority interest shareholders of Orange Ltd.)

25% of Pear Ltd (Held by minority interest shareholders of Pear Ltd.)

Minority interest indirect investments:

15% of Pear Ltd (Held by minority interest shareholders of Orange Ltd.)

Question 10.10

Calculate the full extent of minority interests in each of the following company structures:

a Gamble Ltd purchased a 100% controlling interest in Lost Ltd, which in turn holds a 90% controlling interest in Casino Ltd.

b Able Ltd holds a 60% controlling interest in Wave Ltd, which in turn controls 80% of Crest Ltd.

c Davo Ltd has a 75% interest in Robbo Ltd, which gives Davo Ltd control. Robbo Ltd in turn has a controlling interest of 90% in Macka Ltd.

Accounting for indirect minority interests on consolidation

When consolidating the accounts where indirect minority interests exist, it is necessary to allocate to the minority interests a share of:

- the retained profits (at the start of each year) of the grandson company; and
- the profits (after tax) earned by the grandson company in every year.

(*Note:* The indirect minority interests *are not* entitled to a share of the dividends paid by the grandson company. Dividends can only be paid to investors who have a *direct* investment in a company.)

Allocating retained profits to an indirect minority interest

As the minority interests do not have a direct interest in the subsidiary, they are not entitled to retained profits that were in existence at the date of acquisition. They are, however, entitled to a share of **post-acquisition** profits – that is, profits earned by the subsidiary after the date of acquisition. In addition, if the subsidiary company has transferred profits to reserve accounts, the indirect minority interest is entitled to a share of the increase in the reserves since the date of acquisition.

Similar adjustments are required if reserves have been transferred back to retained profits.

The indirect minority interest share of post-acquisition retained profits of the subsidiary must first be adjusted to eliminate any unrealised profits.

ILLUSTRATION

Apple Ltd (the parent) purchases an 80% controlling interest in Orange Ltd (the son), which in turn purchases a 75% controlling interest in Pear Ltd (the grandson). The indirect minority interest in Pear Ltd is therefore 20% × 75% = 15%.

The retained profits and reserves of Pear Ltd are as follows:

	$
Retained profits:	
at date of acquisition	100 000
at 1 July 2007	900 000
Reserves:	
at date of acquisition	50 000
at 1 July 2007	250 000

The retained profits at 1 July 2007 include the following unrealised profits (before tax):
1. Unrealised profit (before tax) in opening inventory $200 000 arising from sales to Orange Ltd.
2. Unrealised profit (before depreciation and tax) on sale of equipment $125 000 to Apple Ltd sold on 1 July 2006.

The tax rate is 30%, and assets are depreciated at 20% p.a.

The first step is to adjust the retained profits at 1 July 2007 to eliminate the full effect of the unrealised profits.

Unrealised profit calculations

Unrealised profit (after tax) in opening stock:

	$
Profit before tax	200 000
less Income tax (30%)	60 000
Unrealised profit (after tax)	140 000

Unrealised profit (after tax) on equipment sale:

	$
Unrealised profit (before tax)	125 000
less Depreciation on excess asset value at 20%	25 000
Unrealised profit (before tax)	100 000
less Income tax at 30%	30 000
Unrealised profit (after tax)	70 000

The value of retained profits (at 1 July 2007) after the elimination of unrealised profits is therefore:

	$	$
Retained profits at 1 July 2007		900 000
less Unrealised profits (after tax)		
On opening stock	140 000	
On equipment sale	70 000	210 000
Adjusted retained profits		690 000

The second step is to calculate the indirect minority interest in the post-acquisition profits and reserves. The indirect minority interest is calculated as follows:

	$	$
Retained profits		
Adjusted retained profits at 1 July 2007	690 000	
less Retained profits at date of acquisition	100 000	
Post-acquisition retained profits		590 000
Reserves		
Reserves balances at 1 July 2007	250 000	
less Reserve balance at date of acquisition	50 000	200 000
Increase in retained profits and reserves		790 000
Indirect minority interest		15%
Indirect minority interest in retained profits and reserves at 1 July		118 500

Allocating annual profits (after tax) to an indirect minority interest

Indirect minority interests are entitled to a share of annual profits (after tax) after adjustments have been made for unrealised profits in the annual accounts.

In relation to the appropriation of after-tax profits, the indirect minority interests are not entitled to a share of dividends or transfers to reserves. Dividends are paid to the owners of shares of a company. These shareholders have a direct investment in the subsidiary, not an indirect investment. The dividends received by a company from its subsidiary form part of its profit (after tax) – that is, dividends income. The direct minority interest of the company will then receive a share of the company's profit. Thus, the direct minority interests will effectively obtain a share of the subsidiary's dividends. They do not receive the dividends indirectly from the subsidiary.

ILLUSTRATION

This illustration continues on from the previous illustration, where Apple Ltd owns 80% of Orange Ltd, which in turn owns 75% of Pear Ltd. The indirect minority interest in Pear Ltd is therefore 20% × 75% = 15%.

Pear Ltd made a profit (after tax) of $400 000, which included the following intercompany transactions:
1 Unrealised profit (before tax) in opening inventory $200 000 arising from sales to Orange Ltd.
2 Unrealised profit (before tax) in closing inventory $100 000 arising from sales to Orange Ltd.

The adjustments arising from these transactions are as follows.

Unrealised profit (after tax) in opening stock

As the opening balance of retained profits will have already been reduced due to the unrealised profit in opening stocks, it is necessary to increase the reported profit to bring the profit to account in the current year.

	$
Profit before tax	200 000
less Income tax (30%)	60 000
Unrealised profit (after tax)	140 000

Unrealised profit (after tax) in closing stock

	$
Profit before tax	100 000
less Income tax (30%)	30 000
Unrealised profit (after tax)	70 000

The effects of these adjustments on the reported after-tax profit of Pear Ltd and the resulting indirect minority interest share of the adjusted profit are shown in the following table.

	$
Profit (after tax)	400 000
add Unrealised profit (after tax) in opening stock	100 000
	500 000
less Unrealised profit (after tax) in closing stock	(70 000)
Adjusted profit (after tax)	430 000
Indirect minority interest	15%
Indirect minority interest's share of profits (after tax)	64 500

Question 10.11

Bears Ltd purchased an 80% controlling interest in Cats Ltd on 1 July 2004. On the same date, Cats Ltd purchased a 50% interest in Roos Ltd, which gave Cats Ltd control.

From the following information provided by Roos Ltd for the year ended 30 June 2007 you are required to determine the value of the indirect minority interest in the economic entity.

	$
Values at date of acquisition:	
Retained profits	100 000
Reserves	50 000
Values at 1 July 2006:	
Retained profits	500 000
Reserves	200 000
Profit (after tax)	704 000

Unrealised profits relate to:
1. The opening stock of Bears Ltd includes an unrealised profit (before tax) of $80 000 on sales made from Roos Ltd.
2. The closing stock of Cats Ltd includes an unrealised profit (before tax) of $150 000 as a result of sales made by Roos Ltd.
3. Roos Ltd recorded a profit on the sale of plant of $300 000. The asset was sold on 1 January 2007. The tax rate is 30%, and assets are depreciated at 20% p.a.

Question 10.12

From the following information, you are required to calculate the value of the minority interest in the economic entity at 30 June 2007.

(*Note:* You will need to calculate the respective values of the direct and indirect minority interests.)

Big Ltd purchased a 75% controlling interest in Medium Ltd on 1 January 2003. On the same day, Medium Ltd purchased 80% of the shares of Small Ltd and obtained control.

On this date the respective balance sheets included the following balances:

	Medium Ltd 1 January 2003 $	Small Ltd 1 January 2003 $
Equities		
Ordinary shares	500 000	200 000
Retained profits	100 000	50 000
Reserves	100 000	150 000
	700 000	400 000

At 30 June 2007 the respective companies' balance sheets included the following amounts:

	Medium Ltd $	Small Ltd $
Profit (after tax)	900 000	500 000
Retained profits (at start)	400 000	300 000
Funds to appropriate	1 300 000	800 000
Dividends paid	200 000	100 000
Retained profits (at end)	1 100 000	700 000
Ordinary shares	500 000	200 000
Reserves	200 000	300 000
	1 800 000	1 200 000

Additional information

The accounts of Small Ltd include the following unrealised profits:
- The opening stock of Big Ltd includes an unrealised profit (before tax) of $100 000 resulting from sales made by Small Ltd.
- The closing stock of Medium Ltd includes an unrealised profit (before tax) of $150 000 arising from sales from Small Ltd.
  The tax rate is 30%.

Consolidation with direct and indirect minority interests

When consolidating the accounts where direct and indirect minority interests exist, it is recommended that a consistent and logical pattern of elimination and adjustments occurs. The following procedures are recommended:

1. Determine the percentages of direct and indirect minority interests.
2. Eliminate the *parent entity* interest in the balance sheet values of the *son entity* at the date of acquisition (share capital, reserves and retained profits at start), recognising and adjusting the accounts for goodwill or discount on acquisition.
3. Eliminate the interest of the *son entity* in the balance sheet values of the *grandson entity* at the date of acquisition (share capital, reserves and retained profits at start), recognising and adjusting the accounts for goodwill or discount on acquisition.
4. Eliminate any intercompany transactions in the consolidated accounts, including all unrealised profits (excluding appropriations of annual profits).
5. Eliminate the effects of intercompany dividends paid by the subsidiaries and recorded by the *parent and son entities*.
6. Calculate and record the *minority interests* in the *son entity* and the *grandson entity* at the date of reporting. This will involve the following calculations:
   a. The direct minority interest of the *son entity* and *grandson entity*:
      - in the balance sheet, values at the date of acquisition (retained profits, share capital, reserves); and
      - the adjusted profits (after tax).
   b. The indirect minority interest of the *grandson entity*:
      - in the balance sheet, values at the date of acquisition (retained profits, share capital, reserves); and
      - the adjusted profits (after tax).
   c. The direct minority interest of the *son entity* and *grandson entity* in the appropriation of profits.

ILLUSTRATION

On 1 July 2003, Long Ltd acquired an 80% controlling interest in Short Ltd. On the same day, Short Ltd purchased a controlling interest in Crest Ltd of 75%.

On this date the respective subsidiary balance sheets included the following values:

	Short Ltd	Crest Ltd
	$	$
Ordinary shares	300 000	100 000
Reserves	40 000	40 000
Retained profits	200 000	100 000

The following intercompany transactions occurred during the year ended 30 June 2007:
1. Intercompany sales from subsidiary companies to the parent company:
   - Sales from Crest Ltd to Short Ltd: $120 000.
   - Sales from Crest Ltd to Long Ltd: $80 000.
2. Unrealised profit in opening stocks: The opening stock of Long Ltd includes an unrealised profit of $100 000 as a result of sales from Crest Ltd in the year 2007.
3. The closing inventories of Long Ltd include an unrealised profit of $50 000 arising from sales from Crest Ltd.

The tax rate is 40%.

The completed worksheet, including the required eliminations, follows. (*Note:* Following the worksheet are the calculations for the eliminations.)

Consolidated worksheet as at 30 June 2007

Account	Long Ltd	Short Ltd	Crest Ltd	Eliminations		Minority interest		Economic entity
				Debit	Credit	Debit	Credit	
	$000s	$000s	$000s	$000s	$000s	$000s	$000s	$000s
Sales	2 000	1 500	1 000	200 (3)				4 300
less Expenses	900	675	450	50 (5)	200 (30)			
					100 (4)			1 775
	1 100	825	550					2 525
add Dividends income	20	15		20 (6)				–
				15 (7)				
Profit (before tax)	1 120	840	550					2 525
Income tax expense	448	336	220	30 (4)	15 (5)			1 019
Profit (after tax)	672	504	330					1 506
less Minority interest share						247		247
								1 259
Retained profits (start)	400	320	150	160 (1)				
				75 (2)				
				70 (4)		81		484
	1 072	824	480					1 743
Interim dividends	45	10	20		8 (6)			
					15 (7)		7	45
Final dividends	35	15			12 (6)		3	35
Retained profits (end)	992	799	460					1 663
Ordinary shares	500	300	100	240 (1)				
				75 (2)		80		505
Reserves	80	100	60	32 (1)				
				30 (2)		35		143
Minority interest							433	433
Dividends payable	35	15		12 (6)				38
Creditors	20	40	50					110
	1 627	1 254	670					2 892
Assets								
Bank	80	150	60					290
Debtors	120	40	10					170
Stock	60	30	40		50 (5)			80
Deferred tax asset	10			15 (5)				25
Dividends receivable	12				12 (6)			–
Property and equipment	733	1 034	560					2 327
Investment in Short Ltd	432				432 (1)			–
Investment in Crest Ltd	180				180 (2)			–
	1 627	1 254	670	1 024	1 024	443	443	2 892

The calculations associated with the eliminations and adjustments are as follows:

Calculation of percentages of direct and indirect minority interests

	Direct minority interest	Indirect minority interest
Short Ltd	20%	Nil
Crest Ltd	25%	(20% × 75%) = 15%

Eliminations (and calculations)

1 Elimination of investment in Short Ltd by Long Ltd at date of acquisition.

	$	$
Retained profits (at start)	200 000 × 80%	160 000
Ordinary shares	300 000 × 80%	240 000
Reserves	40 000 × 80%	32 000

2 Elimination of investment in Crest Ltd by Short Ltd at date of acquisition.

	$	$
Retained profits (at start)	100 000 × 75%	75 000
Ordinary shares	100 000 × 75%	75 000
Reserves	40 000 × 75%	30 000

3 Elimination of intercompany sales.

4 Elimination of unrealised profit in opening stock of Long Ltd and tax effect.

Before tax	Tax at 30%	After tax
$	$	$
100 000	30 000	70 000

5 Elimination of unrealised profit in closing stock of Long Ltd and tax effect.

Before tax	Tax at 30%	After tax
$	$	$
50 000	15 000	35 000

6 Elimination of dividends paid and declared by Short Ltd.

	$	$
Interim dividends	10 000 × 80%	8 000
Final dividends	15 000 × 80%	12 000
		20 000

7 Elimination of dividends paid and declared by Crest Ltd.

	$	$
Interim dividends	20 000 × 75%	15 000

Calculations of minority interest:

Minority interests in balance sheets at date of reporting
- Share of retained profits:

			$	$	$
Direct minority interest in:	Short Ltd		320 000 × 20%	64 000	
	Crest Ltd		150 000		
	less Unrealised profit at start		70 000		
			80 000 × 25%	20 000	
Indirect minority interest in:	Crest Ltd				
	Adjusted at date of reporting		80 000		
	less Date of acquisition		100 000		
	Increase since date of acquisition		(20 000) × 15%	(3 000)	81 000

- Share of ordinary shares:

		$	$	$
Direct minority interest in:	Short Ltd	300 000 × 20%	60 000	
	Crest Ltd	100 000 × 25%	20 000	80 000

- Share of reserves:

			$	$	$
Direct minority interest	Short Ltd		100 000 × 20%	20 000	
	Crest Ltd		60 000 × 25%	12 000	
Indirect minority interest in	Crest Ltd				
	At date of reporting		60 000		
	less Date of acquisition		40 000		
			20 000 × 15%	3 000	35 000

- Share profits (after tax):

		$	$	$
Direct minority interest in:	Short Ltd	504 000 × 20%	101 000	
	Crest Ltd	330 000		
	add Unrealised profit (at start)	70 000		
	less Unrealised profit at end	(35 000)		
		365 000 × 25%	91 250	
Indirect minority interest in Crest Ltd profits (after tax)		365 000 × 15%	54 750	247 000
				443 000

- Less appropriations to direct minority interest
- Dividends paid

	$	$	$
Short Ltd	10 000 × 20%	2 000	
Crest Ltd	20 000 × 25%	5 000	
		7 000	

- Final dividends

	$		$	$
Short Ltd	15 000	20%	3 000	10 000
				433 000

Question 10.13

From the following information, you are required to prepare the consolidated worksheet as at 30 June 2007.

On 1 July 2000, Able Ltd acquired a 75% controlling interest in Cane Ltd. On the same day, Cane Ltd purchased a controlling interest in Post Ltd of 80%.

On this date the respective subsidiary balance sheets included the following values:

	Cane Ltd	Post Ltd
	$	$
Ordinary shares	400 000	80 000
Reserves	60 000	50 000
Retained profits	100 000	90 000

The following intercompany transactions occurred during the year:
1. Intercompany sales from subsidiary companies to the parent company:
   - Sales from Post Ltd to Able Ltd: $300 000.
   - Sales from Post Ltd to Cane Ltd: $200 000.
2. Unrealised profit in opening stocks: The opening stock of Able Ltd includes an unrealised profit of $50 000 as a result of sales from Post Ltd in the year 2007.
3. The closing inventories of Able Ltd include an unrealised profit of $100 000 arising from sales from Post Ltd.
   The tax rate is 30%.

Consolidated worksheet as at 30 June 2007

	Able Ltd	Cane Ltd	Post Ltd	Eliminations		Minority interest		Economic entity
				Debit	Credit	Debit	Credit	
	$000s	$000s	$000s	$000s	$000s	$000s	$000s	$000s
Sales	1 800	1 000	1 200					
less Expenses	810	440	480					
	990	560	720					
add Dividends income	90	160						
Profit (before tax)	1 080	720	720					
Income tax expense	432	220	140					
Profit (after tax)	648	500	580					
less Minority interest share								
Retained profits (start)	400	320	150					
	1 048	820	730					
Interim dividends	100	80	200					
Final dividends	200	40						
Retained profits (end)	748	700	530					
Ordinary shares	800	400	80					
Reserves	200	160	100					
Minority interest								
Dividends payable	200	40						
Creditors	30	10	50					
	1 978	1 310	760					

	Able Ltd	Cane Ltd	Post Ltd	Eliminations		Minority interest		Economic entity
				Debit	Credit	Debit	Credit	
	$000s	$000s	$000s	$000s	$000s	$000s	$000s	$000s
Assets								
Bank	120	140	100					
Debtors	200	140	90					
Stock	80	50	60					
Deferred tax asset	20							
Dividends receivable	30							
Property and equipment	1 108	804	510					
Investment in Cane Ltd	420							
Investment in Post Ltd		176						
	1 978	1 310	760					

Question 10.14

From the following information, you are required to prepare:
a the consolidated worksheet as at 30 June 2007; and
b an extract of the balance sheet as at 30 June 2007 for shareholders' equity (and associated disclosure notes).

On 1 July 2000, Hart Ltd acquired a 75% controlling interest in Pace Ltd. On the same day, Pace Ltd purchased a controlling interest in Jade Ltd of 60%.

On this date the respective subsidiary balance sheets included the following values:

	Pace Ltd	Jade Ltd
	$	$
Ordinary shares	200 000	80 000
Reserves	20 000	75 000
Retained profits	80 000	60 000

The following intercompany transactions occurred during the year:
1 Intercompany sales from subsidiary companies to the parent company:
   - Sales from Jade Ltd to Hart Ltd: $200 000.
   - Sales from Jade Ltd to Pace Ltd: $200 000.
2 On the last day of the financial year, Jade Ltd sold plant to Pace Ltd at a profit of $200 000. The profit is taxable. (The plant is not to be depreciated until the next year.)
3 The closing inventories of Hart Ltd include an unrealised profit of $100 000 arising from sales from Jade Ltd.
   The tax rate is 30%.

Consolidated worksheet as at 30 June 2007

Account	Hart Ltd	Pace Ltd	Jade Ltd	Eliminations		Minority interest		Economic entity
				Debit	Credit	Debit	Credit	
	$000s	$000s	$000s	$000s	$000s	$000s	$000s	$000s
Sales	950	860	550					
less Expenses	380	440	220					
	570	420	330					____
add Dividends income	120	30						
Profit on plant sale			200					____
Profit (before tax)	690	450	530					
Income tax expense	285	180	80					____
Profit (after tax)	405	270	450					
less Minority interest share								
Retained profits (start)	200	180	100					____
	605	450	550					
Interim dividends	50	100	50					
Final dividends	50	60						
Transfer to reserves			20					
Retained profits (end)	505	290	480					
Ordinary shares	200	200	80					
Reserves	60	100	115					
Minority interest								
Dividends payable	50	60						
Creditors	20	40	45					____
	835	690	720					
Assets								
Bank	20	10	50					
Debtors	50	20	10					
Stock	200	40	120					
Deferred tax asset	5							
Dividends receivable	45							
Property and equipment	290	491	540					
Investment in Pace Ltd	225							
Investment in Jade Ltd		129						
	835	690	720					

Question 10.15

From the following information, you are required to prepare:
a the consolidated worksheet as at 30 June 2007;
b an extract of the balance sheet as at 30 June 2007 for shareholders' equity (and associated disclosure notes).

On 1 July 2001, Hye Ltd acquired a 60% controlling interest in Flow Ltd, which in turn purchased a 75% controlling interest in Gill Ltd on the same day.

On this date the respective subsidiary balance sheets included the following values:

	Flow Ltd	Gill Ltd
	$	$
Ordinary shares	300 000	200 000
Reserves	30 000	20 000
Retained profits	100 000	40 000

Note: Goodwill is amortised over four years.

The following intercompany transactions occurred during the year:
1 Intercompany sales from subsidiary companies to the parent company:
   - Sales from Gill Ltd to Flow Ltd: $300 000.
   - Sales from Gill Ltd to Hye Ltd: $200 000.
2 The opening stock of Hye Ltd includes an unrealised profit of $50 000 as a result of sales made by Gill Ltd.
3 On the first day of the financial year, Gill Ltd sold plant to Hye Ltd at a loss of $100 000. The loss is tax-deductible. (The plant is being depreciated over five years.)
4 The closing inventories of Hye Ltd include an unrealised profit of $90 000 arising from sales from Gill Ltd.

The tax rate is 30%.

Consolidated worksheet as at 30 June 2007

Account	Hye Ltd	Flow Ltd	Gill Ltd	Eliminations Debit	Eliminations Credit	Minority interest Debit	Minority interest Credit	Economic entity
	$000s	$000s	$000s	$000s	$000s	$000s	$000s	$000s
Sales	1 400	900	800					
less Expenses	560	360	320					
	840	540	480					____
add Dividends income	120	45						____
Profit (before tax)	960	585	480					
Income tax expense	384	235	184					____
Profit (after tax)	576	350	296					
less Minority interest share								
Retained profits (start)	200	180	130					____
	776	530	426					
Interim dividends	200	120	60					
Final dividends	250	80						
Transfer to reserves			40					____
Retained profits (end)	326	330	326					
Ordinary shares	200	300	200					
Reserves	100	120	100					
Minority interest								
Dividends payable	250	80						
Creditors	20	40	45					____
	896	870	671					═══
Assets								
Bank	35	15	65					
Debtors	45	25	20					
Stock	100	20	60					
Deferred tax asset	20							
Dividends receivable	48							
Property and equipment	390	595	526					
Investment in Flow Ltd	258							
Investment in Gill Ltd		215						
Goodwill on acquisition								____
	896	870	671					═══

CHAPTER 11
SHARE CAPITAL ALTERATIONS

Objectives

Upon satisfactory completion of this chapter you should be able to:

+ differentiate between shareholders' obligations and rights of creditors;
+ identify decisions that have no effect on share capital;
+ identify decisions that lead to an alteration in share capital and make the appropriate journal adjustments;
+ prepare journal entries for the redemption of redeemable preference shares; and
+ prepare journal entries for the issue of bonus shares.

Introduction

Companies from time to time may desire to rearrange their share capital by altering share capital, reducing share capital or returning paid-up capital. When share capital is altered in a way that has the potential to affect the rights of creditors, the company must ensure that it abides by the requirements of the Corporations Law and records the adjustments in the appropriate manner.

This chapter examines the decisions made by companies which alter their share capital and the legal and bookkeeping requirements in respect of the share capital alteration.

Alteration to share capital

Subdivision of share capital (into larger or smaller amounts)

The Corporations Law allows a company to consolidate and divide its share capital into larger or smaller amounts than the existing issued share capital subject to approval by the shareholders at a general meeting.

Where a company alters the number of issued shares (either fully paid or partly paid) without altering the total value of paid-up capital, a journal entry is not required; however, amendments to members' share registers are required.

For example, a company may have issued and paid-up capital valued at $800 000 in respect of 400 000 ordinary shares. An agreed subdivision may increase the number of issued shares to 800 000 ordinary shares without changing the value of the issued shares. This action would ultimately reduce the market value of shares, as the quantity of shares has increased.

Such action may be taken at a time when the company is up for sale. Shareholders may find it easier to sell shares on the marketplace that have a lower market value.

Reduction of share capital

Authority for a company to reduce its share capital is contained in the Law, which states the rules that a company must follow when reducing its share capital. The rules have been put in place to protect the interests of shareholders and creditors by ensuring that during the share capital reduction the company considers the risk of insolvency, seeks fairness among shareholders and discloses material information.

Companies are permitted to reduce share capital regardless of the authority included in the Law as long as the company is fair and reasonable to its shareholders in the reduction, does not compromise its ability to pay creditors and it is approved by the shareholders.

Return of share capital

A company may return share capital to its owners when it is of the opinion that it has an excess of investment in the company by the owners. To return share capital to the owners, the company will need to make cash available to the shareholders and reduce their investment in the company. The conversion of share capital to cash will be made via the capital reduction account.

> **ILLUSTRATION**
>
> Enormous Ltd's balance sheet, shown below, indicated that 100 000 ordinary shares had been issued in respect of $100 000 in net assets.

Enormous Ltd
Balance sheet as at 30 June

	$
Assets	180 000
less Liabilities	80 000
Net assets	100 000
Shareholders' equity	
100 000 fully paid ordinary shares	100 000

A resolution passed at the annual general meeting on 1 August has agreed that the company has $20 000 in excess capital and that it should be returned to the shareholders. Accordingly, a return on capital is to be made at $0.20 per share (100 000 × $0.20). Two journal entries are required.

1 To record the reduction in share capital – that is:

General journal

Date	Particulars	Debit	Credit
		$	$
1 Aug	Share capital – Ordinary shares	20 000	
	Capital reduction		20 000
	To record the reduction in paid-up capital at $0.20 per share on 100 000 shares		

2 To record the payment of cash to shareholders – that is:

Cash payments journal

Date	Particulars	Chq. No.	Sundries	Bank
			$	$
1 Aug	Capital reduction		20 000	20 000

The resulting general ledger would be as follows:

General ledger

Date	Particulars	Debit	Credit	Balance
Share capital – Ordinary shares				
1 Aug	Balance			100 000 Cr
	Capital reduction	20 000		80 000 Cr
Capital reduction				
1 Aug	Ordinary shares		20 000	20 000 Cr
	Bank	20 000		–
Bank				
1 Aug	Capital reduction		20 000	20 000 Cr

The balance sheet after the reduction in share capital would be presented as follows:

Enormous Ltd
Balance sheet as at 1 August

	$
Assets	160 000
less Liabilities	80 000
Net assets	80 000
Shareholders' equity	
100 000 fully paid ordinary shares	80 000

Question 11.1

The balance sheet of Barton Ltd on 1 September is shown below.

Barton Ltd
Balance sheet as at 1 September

	$
Assets	500 000
less Liabilities	50 000
Net assets	450 000
Shareholders' equity	
150 000 fully paid ordinary shares	450 000

The annual general meeting has made the following resolutions:
1. That share capital be reduced by $0.50 per share and be returned to shareholders.
2. That the number of issued shares be doubled, without affecting the value of the issued capital.

You are required to prepare:
a the journal entries to record the resolutions; and
b the balance sheet after recording the journal entries.

Cancellation of lost share capital

Where a company has accumulated losses, it may wish to remove the losses permanently from the accounts. This can be achieved by writing the losses off against share capital, thereby reducing the amount of shareholders' equity.

ILLUSTRATION

Jarman Ltd's balance sheet as at 30 June was as follows:

Jarman Ltd
Balance sheet as at 30 June

	$
Assets	200 000
less Liabilities	20 000
Net assets	180 000
Shareholders' equity	
50 000 fully paid ordinary shares	250 000
less Retained losses	(70 000)
	180 000

A resolution passed at the annual general meeting on 1 August has agreed that the accumulated losses be written off against the shareholders' equity. Two journal entries are required.

1 To remove the accumulated losses from the accounts.

General journal

Date	Particulars	Debit	Credit
		$	$
1 Aug	Capital reduction	70 000	
	Retained losses		70 000
	To write off accumulated losses		

2 To record the reduction in share capital – that is:

General journal

Date	Particulars	Debit	Credit
		$	$
1 Aug	Share capital – Ordinary shares	70 000	
	Capital reduction		70 000
	To write off accumulated losses against paid-up capital		

The resulting general ledger would be as follows:

General ledger

Date	Particulars	Debit	Credit	Balance
Retained losses				
1 Aug	Balance	70 000		70 000 Dr
	Capital reduction		70 000	–
Capital reduction				
1 Aug	Retained losses	70 000		70 000 Dr
	Ordinary shares		70 000	–
Share capital – Ordinary shares				
1 Aug	Balance			250 000 Cr
	Capital reduction	70 000		180 000 Cr

The balance sheet after the reduction in share capital would be presented as follows:

Jarman Ltd
Balance sheet as at 1 August

	$
Assets	200 000
less Liabilities	20 000
Net assets	180 000
Shareholders' equity	
50 000 fully paid ordinary shares	180 000

Question 11.2

From the following information relating to the alterations to the share capital of Argus Ltd, you are required to:
a prepare the general ledger accounts recording the alterations to share capital; and
b prepare the shareholders' equity section of the balance sheet after the alterations.

Argus Ltd
Balance sheet as at 2 August

	$
Shareholders' equity	
400 000 fully paid ordinary shares	200 000
100 000 fully paid preference shares	300 000
	500 000
less Retained losses	(100 000)
	400 000

The annual general meeting made the following resolutions:
1 That retained losses be written off against all shares in direct proportion to the value of fully paid capital.
2 That the number of issued preference shares be halved.

Redemption of shares

When raising capital, companies may have issued preference shares under the condition that they will be bought back (redeemed) by the company at a future date.

Sections 245J and 245K permit the redemption of redeemable preference shares:
- if the shares are fully paid;
- if the redemption is financed from a new issue of shares made for the purpose of the redemption or from profits; and
- if after the redemption, the shares are cancelled.

Redemption of preference shares out of profits

Section 254K allows for the redemption of preference shares from the profits of a company which would otherwise have been paid as dividends. A capital redemption reserve account is normally used when redeeming shares from company profits.

The creation of the capital redemption reserve is used to replace the redeemed preference shares, leaving the total value of shareholders' equity intact. This practice has the effect of maintaining the responsibility of shareholders to the company's creditors, as the overall level of shareholders' equity remains constant and the balance between debt funds and equity funds remains unchanged.

Two possible scenarios could arise. The price paid per share at the time of redemption could be either:

1. at a price equal to the issue price; or
2. at a price above the issue price (at a premium).

Redemption at the issue price

ILLUSTRATION

On 1 August, Chart Ltd's shareholders' equity includes 50 000 redeemable 5% preference shares with a book value of $250 000, the original issue price being $5 per share. A decision has been made to redeem 20 000 of these shares at their issue price – that is, at a value of $100 000. This transaction requires three journal entries.

1. To reduce the value of the paid-up preference shares as a result of the redemption – that is:

General journal

Date	Particulars	Debit	Credit
		$	$
1 Aug	Share capital – Preference shares	100 000	
	Shareholders' redemption		100 000
	To redeem 20 000 preference shares at $5 per share		

2. To transfer the value of the redemption to the statutory reserve account – that is:

General journal

Date	Particulars	Debit	Credit
		$	$
1 Aug	Retained profits	100 000	
	Capital redemption reserve		100 000
	Transfer of profits		

3. To make the cash payment to the shareholders who have had their shares redeemed – that is:

Cash payments journal

Date	Particulars	Chq. No.	Sundries	Bank
			$	$
1 Aug	Shareholders' redemption		100 000	100 000

The resulting general ledger would be as follows:

General ledger

Date	Particulars	Debit	Credit	Balance
Share capital – Preference shares				
1 Aug	Balance			250 000 Cr
	Shareholders' redemption	100 000		150 000 Cr
Shareholders' redemption				
1 Aug	Preference shares		100 000	100 000 Cr
	Bank	100 000		–
Bank				
1 Aug	Shareholders' redemption		100 000	100 000 Cr
Retained profits				
1 Aug	Capital redemption reserve	100 000		100 000 Dr
Capital redemption reserve				
1 Aug	Retained profits		100 000	100 000 Cr

Redemption above the issue price (at a premium)

When a company redeems preference shares at a price per share above their issue price, the shares are said to be redeemed **at a premium**. Where a preference share is redeemed at a premium, the premium is provided for out of profits.

ILLUSTRATION

On 1 October, Holat Ltd's shareholders' equity includes 100 000 redeemable 10% preference shares with a book value of $400 000, the original issue price being $4 per share. A decision has been made to redeem 80 000 of these shares at a premium of $0.50 per share – that is, a price of $4.50 per share – deriving a total value of $360 000. The company has a retained profits balance of $500 000. The journal entries to accommodate this transaction are as follows:

1 Reduce the value of the paid-up preference shares as a result of the redemption – that is:

General journal

Date	Particulars	Debit	Credit
		$	$
1 Oct	Share capital – Preference shares	320 000	
	Shareholders' redemption		320 000
	To redeem 80 000 preference shares at their original issue price of $4 per share		

2. Transfer the value of the redemption to the statutory reserve account – that is, 80 000 shares at $4 per share ($320 000) – and record the premium payable to the shareholders at $0.50 per share ($40 000).

General journal

Date	Particulars	Debit	Credit
		$	$
1 Oct	Retained profits	360 000	
	Capital redemption reserve		320 000
	Shareholders' redemption		40 000
	To transfer funds to the capital redemption reserve at $4 per share on 80 000 shares and record a $0.50 premium on each share		

3. Make the cash payment to the shareholders who have had their shares redeemed – that is, $4.50 per share on 80 000 shares ($360 000).

Cash payments journal

Date	Particulars	Chq. no.	Sundries	Bank
			$	$
1 Oct	Shareholders' redemption		360 000	360 000

The resulting general ledger would be as follows:

General ledger

Date	Particulars	Debit	Credit	Balance
Share capital – Preference shares				
1 Oct	Balance			400 000 Cr
	Shareholders' redemption	320 000		80 000 Cr
Shareholders' redemption				
1 Oct	Preference shares		320 000	320 000 Cr
	Retained profits		40 000	360 000 Cr
	Bank	360 000		–
Bank				
1 Oct	Shareholders' redemption		360 000	360 000 Cr
Retained profits				
1 Oct	Balance		500 000	500 000 Cr
	Shareholders' redemption	40 000		460 000 Cr
	Capital redemption reserve	320 000		140 000 Cr
Capital redemption reserve				
1 Oct	Retained profits		320 000	320 000 Cr

Question 11.3

You are required to prepare the appropriate ledger accounts relating the following redemption of preference shares.

On 1 July, Trash Ltd held 200 000 preference shares which had been originally issued at $4 per share. The company has decided to redeem half of the shares at a premium of 25% of their issue price.

The balance in the retained profits account is $900 000.

Question 11.4

From the following information relating to Test Ltd, you are required to:
a record the journal entries relating to the redemption of preference shares; and
b prepare a balance sheet after the redemption.

Test Ltd
Balance sheet as at 1 November

	$
Assets	400 000
less Liabilities	120 000
Net assets	280 000
Shareholders' equity	
40 000 fully paid ordinary shares	40 000
20 000 fully paid preference shares	100 000
Retained profits	140 000
	280 000

The company has decided to redeem all preference shares at $6 per share. The shares were originally issued at $5 per share.

Redemption of preference shares from a fresh issue of shares

The redemption of preference shares from a fresh issue of shares requires the company issuing shares to the public and using the proceeds from the share issue to repay the holders of redeemed preference shares.

When shares are being redeemed and sourced from a fresh share issue, it is not necessary to make use of the capital redemption reserve as with the redemption of shares from profits. The issue of shares to source the redemption effectively maintains the balance between shareholders' equity and those of creditors. Thus, the obligation of shareholders to protect the rights of creditors is maintained.

As with the redemption from profits, shares may be redeemed at their issue price or at a premium.

Redemption at issue price

ILLUSTRATION

Trident Ltd has decided to redeem 100 000 of its 150 000 preference shares at their issue price of $1 per share. The redemption is to be sourced by a new issue of 400 000 ordinary shares which are to be issued at their issue price of $0.25 per share (that is, $100 000) which will be finalised by 1 January.

The first step is to prepare a prospectus inviting the public to purchase the shares and to allocate the shares to successful applicants. The final result of this step would see $100 000 being deposited in the company's general bank account and ordinary share capital rising accordingly.

The journal entries to record the share issue would be as follows:

General journal

Date	Particulars	Debit	Credit
		$	$
1 Jan	Trust account	100 000	
	Applications		100 000
	To record the receipt on 400 000 ordinary shares at $0.25 each		
	Applications	100 000	
	Share capital – Ordinary shares		100 000
	To record the allotment of 400 000 ordinary shares		
	Bank	100 000	
	Trust account		100 000
	To record the transfer of trust money		

The resulting general ledger would be as follows:

General ledger

Date	Particulars	Debit	Credit	Balance
Share capital – Ordinary shares				
1 Jan	Applications		100 000	100 000 Cr
Bank				
1 Jan	Trust account	100 000		100 000 Dr

The second step is to redeem the preference shares, which will require the following journal entry:

General journal

Date	Particulars	Debit	Credit
		$	$
1 Jan	Share capital – Preference shares	100 000	
	Shareholders' redemption		100 000
	To record the redemption of 100 000 preference shares		

The final step is to reimburse the shareholders who have had their shares redeemed, which requires the following journal entry:

Cash payments journal

Date	Particulars	Chq. no.	Sundries	Bank
			$	$
1 Jan	Shareholders' redemption		100 000	100 000

The resulting general ledger would be as follows:

General ledger

Date	Particulars	Debit	Credit	Balance
	Share capital – Ordinary shares			
1 Jan	Applications		100 000	100 000 Cr
	Bank			
1 Jan	Applications	100 000		100 000 Dr
	Shareholders' redemption		100 000	100 000 Cr
	Shareholders' redemption			
1 Jan	Preference shares		100 000	100 000 Cr
	Bank	100 000		–
	Share capital – Preference shares			
1 Jan	Balance			250 000 Cr
	Shareholders' redemption	100 000		150 000 Cr

Redemption at a premium

The redemption of preference shares at a premium, sourced from a new share issue, requires:
- the issue of shares to finance the nominal value of the redeemed preference shares; and
- the premium component to be sourced from profits (or a share premium reserve).

ILLUSTRATION

On 1 December, Marks Ltd is to finalise an issue of 400 000 ordinary shares at a value of $0.50 each to finance the redemption of all of its 60 000 preference shares. The preference shares have an issue price of $2 each but will be redeemed at a premium of 50% – that is, $3 per share. The company has a retained profits balance of $90 000.

Step 1 is to finalise the issue of the ordinary shares, which would result in $200 000 in cash arising from the issue of 400 000 shares at $0.50 each. The resulting journal entries would be as follows:

General journal

Date	Particulars	Debit	Credit
		$	$
1 Dec	Trust account	200 000	
	Applications		200 000
	To record the receipt on 400 000 ordinary shares at $0.50 each		
	Applications	200 000	
	Share capital – Ordinary shares		200 000
	To record the allotment of 100 000 ordinary shares		
	Bank	200 000	
	Trust account		200 000
	To record the transfer of trust money		

Step 2 is to record the issue value of the redeemed preference shares – that is, $120 000 (60 000 shares at $2 each) – and the transfer of profits for the amount of the premium – that is, $60 000 (60 000 shares at $1 each).

The journal entries required are as follows:

General journal

Date	Particulars	Debit	Credit
		$	$
1 Dec	Share capital – Preference shares	120 000	
	Shareholders' redemption		120 000
	To redeem 60 000 preference shares at $2 per share		
	Retained profits	60 000	
	Shareholders' redemption		60 000
	Transfer of profits to account for $1 premium per share on 60 000 shares		

Finally, an entry is required to pay the shareholders for the redeemed shares – that is:

General journal

Date	Particulars	Debit	Credit
		$	$
1 Dec	Shareholders' redemption	180 000	
	Bank		180 000
	Payment by shareholders for redeemed shares		

The resulting general ledger would be as follows:

General ledger

Date	Particulars	Debit	Credit	Balance
Share capital – Ordinary shares				
1 Dec	Applications		200 000	200 000 Cr
Bank				
1 Dec	Applications	200 000		200 000 Dr
	Shareholders' redemption	180 000		20 000 Cr
Shareholders' redemption				
1 Dec	Preference shares		120 000	120 000 Cr
	Retained profits		60 000	180 000 Cr
	Bank	180 000		–
Share capital – Preference shares				
1 Dec	Balance			120 000 Cr
	Shareholders' redemption	120 000		–
Retained profits				
1 Dec	Balance		90 000	90 000 Cr
	Shareholders' redemption	60 000		30 000 Cr

Question 11.5

From the following information relating to Aspray Ltd, you are required to:
a prepare the journal entries for making a fresh share issue (for the purposes of redeeming preference shares);
b prepare journal entries for redeeming the preference shares; and
c show the shareholders' equity section of the balance sheet after the redemption.

On 1 October, Marvel Ltd made the decision to redeem preference shares financed from a new issue of ordinary shares. The shareholders' equity of the company prior to the redemption was:

		$
Ordinary shares:	1 000 000 shares (@ $0.25 each)	250 000
Preference shares:	500 000 shares (@ $2 each)	1 000 000
Retained profits:		600 000
		1 850 000

The redemption is for 300 000 preference shares at their issue price plus a premium of 50% of the issue price. The redemption is to occur on 1 December.

The ordinary share issue is for 900 000 ordinary shares at their issue price of $1 each payable on application and is to be finalised by 1 November. (Assume that the ordinary share issue was fully subscribed.)

Issuing bonus shares

A bonus share is a share issued to existing shareholders at no charge to the shareholder. The bonus share may be issued in lieu of a cash dividend or where the company is attempting to resist a takeover from another company. Whatever the reason, the issue of bonus shares has the effect of increasing the issued and paid-up capital of the business.

Bonus shares are usually issued to existing shareholders on the basis of the number of shares already held. For example, bonus shares may be issued on the basis of one bonus share for every 10 shares already held.

The issue of bonus shares occurs from the capital reserves of the company, namely:
- the asset revaluation reserve; and
- the capital redemption reserve.

ILLUSTRATION

The directors of Frederick Ltd resolved on 1 June to make a bonus share issue of one $1 ordinary share for every 10 ordinary shares held in the company. At this date the company had a share capital consisting of 1 000 000 $1 fully paid ordinary shares, a share premium reserve of $50 000 and an asset revaluation reserve of $50 000. The dividend was to be paid on 30 June.

The following entries would be made in the general journal of Frederick Ltd.

1 The directors meet and declare a bonus dividend.

General journal

Date	Particulars	Debit	Credit
		$	$
1 June	Bonus dividend	100 000	
	Dividends payable		100 000
	Declaration of bonus share dividend		

2 The bonus shares are allocated from an existing capital reserve.

General journal

Date	Particulars	Debit	Credit
		$	$
30 June	Asset revaluation reserve	100 000	
	Bonus dividend		100 000
	Allocation of bonus share dividend from capital reserve and statutory reserve		

3 The bonus shares are issued to shareholders.

General journal

Date	Particulars	Debit	Credit
		$	$
30 June	Dividends payable	100 000	
	Share capital – Ordinary shares		100 000
	Issue of bonus share dividend		

Question 11.6

The company accounts of Naylor Ltd reveal the following:
- Shareholders' equity consists of 600 000 ordinary shares, each with an issue price of $2.
- Calls in arrears total $30 000 as a result of the owners of 60 000 shares failing to meet the final call of $0.50 per share.
- The reserves of the company are:
    - Retained profits: $50 000.
    - Dividend equalisation reserve: $25 000.
    - Asset revaluation reserve: $100 000.
    - Capital redemption reserve: $150 000.
- On 1 August, the company declared a bonus dividend of one fully paid bonus share at $2 each for every 20 shares already held. The bonus share is not payable to shareholders who have not paid the call on shares.
- Bonus shares are to be allocated equally from existing capital reserves on 31 August.

You are required to prepare the journal entries recording the declaration, allocation and issue of the bonus shares.

Summary of share capital alterations which reduce share capital

(*Note:* Payments to shareholders are shown in the general journal in this summary, rather than in the cash payments journal as shown throughout the chapter.)

Return of share capital

General journal

Date	Particulars	Debit	Credit
		$	$
	Share capital – Ordinary shares	XXX	
	Capital reduction		XXX
	To record the reduction in share capital		
	Capital reduction	XXX	
	Bank		XXX
	Payment to shareholders		

Cancellation of lost share capital

General journal

Date	Particulars	Debit	Credit
		$	$
	Capital reduction	XXX	
	Retained losses		XXX
	To write off accumulated losses		
	Share capital – Ordinary shares	XXX	
	Capital reduction		XXX
	To write off accumulated losses against share capital		

Redemption of preference shares out of profits at their issue price

General journal

Date	Particulars	Debit	Credit
		$	$
	Share capital – Preference shares	XXX	
	Shareholders' redemption		XXX
	To redeem preference shares at nominal value		
	Retained profits	XXX	
	Capital redemption reserve		XXX
	Transfer of profits		
	Shareholders' redemption	XXX	
	Bank		XXX
	Payment to shareholders		

Redemption of preference shares out of profits at a premium

General journal

Date	Particulars	Debit	Credit
		$	$
	Share capital – Preference shares	XXX	
	Shareholders' redemption		XXX
	To redeem preference shares at their nominal value		
	Retained profits	XXX	
	Capital redemption reserve		XXX
	Shareholders' redemption		XXX
	To transfer funds to the capital redemption reserve at the nominal value and record a premium on each share		
	Shareholders' redemption	XXX	
	Bank		XXX
	Payment to shareholders		

Redemption of preference shares at their issue price from a new issue of shares

General journal

Date	Particulars	Debit	Credit
		$	$
	Trust account	XXX	
	Applications		XXX
	To record the receipt of applicants' money on fresh share issue		
	Applications	XXX	
	Ordinary shares		XXX
	To record the allotment of ordinary shares		
	Bank	XXX	
	Trust account		XXX
	To record the transfer of trust money		
	Share capital – Preference shares	XXX	
	Shareholders' redemption		XXX
	To record the redemption preference shares		
	Shareholders' redemption	XXX	
	Bank		XXX
	Payment to shareholders		

Redemption of preference shares at a premium from a new issue of shares

General journal

Date	Particulars	Debit	Credit
		$	$
	Trust account	XXX	
	Applications		XXX
	To record the receipt of applicants' money on fresh share issue		
	Applications	XXX	
	Share capital – Ordinary shares		XXX
	To record the allotment of ordinary shares		
	Bank	XXX	
	Trust account		XXX
	To record the transfer of trust money		
	Share capital – Preference shares	XXX	
	Shareholders' redemption		XXX
	To record the redemption preference shares at nominal value		
	Retained profits	XXX	
	Shareholders' redemption		XXX
	Transfer of profits to account for premium on redeemed shares		
	Shareholders' redemption	XXX	
	Bank		XXX
	Payment to shareholders		

Issuing bonus shares

General journal

Date	Particulars	Debit	Credit
		$	$
	Bonus dividend	XXX	
	Dividends payable		XXX
	Declaration of bonus share dividend		
	Capital reserves	XXX	
	Bonus dividend		XXX
	Allocation of bonus share dividend from capital reserves		
	Dividends payable	XXX	
	Share capital – Ordinary shares		XXX
	Issue of bonus share dividend		

Question 11.7

The balance sheet of Isaac Ltd included the following information.

Isaac Ltd
Balance sheet as at 30 June

	$
Shareholders' equity	
50 000 fully paid ordinary shares	250 000
20 000 fully paid preference shares	160 000
Asset revaluation reserve	150 000
less Retained losses	(90 000)
	470 000

The company has sought and been granted the authority to implement the following alterations to share capital (which must be performed in numerical sequence):

1 Write off $70 000 of the accumulated losses against issued ordinary shares.
2 Redeem 20 000 preference shares which have an issue price of $8 each at a premium of $1 each sourced from a fresh share issue. The new shares are to be issued at $7.50 per share, with the number of shares to be issued and the resulting cash flow to be equal to the cash flow required to redeem the preference shares.
3 Reduce all fully paid ordinary shares by 50% of their book value.

You are required to:
a record the journal entries for the above share alterations; and
b prepare a balance sheet after the share alterations.

Question 11.8

The balance sheet of Harper Ltd at 30 June is presented below.

Harper Ltd
Balance sheet as at 30 June

	$
Bank	500 000
Other	1 800 000
	2 300 000
less Liabilities	600 000
Net assets	1 700 000
Shareholders' equity	
200 000 fully paid ordinary shares	200 000
100 000 fully paid preference shares	400 000
80 000 fully paid cumulative preference shares	800 000
Asset revaluation reserve	100 000
Retained profits	150 000
General reserve	50 000
	1 700 000

On 20 September, the company obtained all the legal requirements to make the following alterations to share capital:
- Issue a bonus dividend of one ordinary share for every 20 shares held. The shares are issued at $1 each.
- Redeem 30 000 preference shares at their issue price of $4 each from profits.
- Redeem 20 000 cumulative preference shares at their issue price of $10 each from a fresh issue of ordinary shares.
- Convert all issued preference shares to a value of $5 per share.

You are required to:

a prepare the appropriate journal entries to record the share capital alterations; and
b prepare a balance sheet after the share capital alterations.

CHAPTER 12
RECEIVERSHIP AND LIQUIDATION

Objectives

Upon satisfactory completion of this chapter you should be able to:
- describe the functions of a receiver and a liquidator;
- describe a statement of assets and liabilities;
- describe the priorities of creditors' claims;
- describe the priorities of shareholders in a winding-up; and
- prepare the accounting entries for a liquidation where a company has fully paid shares.

Introduction

This chapter examines two aspects of a company: its inability to repay certain debts and therefore being placed in receivership; and the situation where a company is liquidated or wound up. The differences between these terms are explored, together with the priorities of creditors and shareholders in a liquidation and the associated accounting entries.

Receivership

When a company borrows funds from lenders, it may provide security over the loan by making a charge against specific assets or a floating charge over all assets. This charge protects the lender against the inability of the company to repay the amount borrowed or the interest associated with the loan. If the company cannot repay the debt or the interest on or by the dates stipulated in the loan agreement, the lender may request the courts to place the company in the hands of a **receiver** – that is, the company is placed into receivership.

The receiver then acts on behalf of the lender by taking control of the asset or assets stipulated in the loan agreement as security for the loan. The receiver can manage the asset(s) to generate a cash flow which enables the lender to be repaid, or the receiver can sell the asset(s) and use the proceeds from the sale to repay the lender. When the lender has been repaid, the receiver's job is finished and the company's management is returned to its normal management team.

In many cases, companies that have been placed into receivership and settled their debts to their lenders are faced with poor cash flows and unprofitable trading which forces the company to be liquidated.

Liquidation

The winding up of a company due to insolvency, unprofitable trading, takeover by another company, amalgamation with another company or by ceasing its operations is referred to as **liquidation** – that is, the company is in liquidation.

Liquidation of a company can be called by the directors, in which case the liquidation is referred to as a **voluntary liquidation**, or it can be called by the courts at the request of a lender (**involuntary liquidation**).

When a company is liquidated, it is placed in the hands of a **liquidator** whose task it is to dispose of (sell) all the assets of the company and use the proceeds to repay the company's liabilities and distribute any surplus (deficit) to the company's shareholders.

Treatment of assets on liquidation

When a company is placed into liquidation, the assets of the company become the responsibility of the liquidator. In relation to the assets of the company, the liquidator must determine which assets are to be liquidated and also calculate their respective book values and realisable values.

Statement of assets and liabilities

The Corporations Law requires that a report as to the company's affairs must be prepared by the company prior to the company being placed into the hands of a receiver or being wound up (liquidated). This report, referred to as a 'Statement of Assets and Liabilities' or 'Report as to Affairs', is set out in Form 507 of the Corporations Law. The purpose of the statement is to disclose:

- the assets which are to be sold, showing both the book value and the realisable value of the asset. In addition, assets are reported in the statement as to whether they have been secured (charged) against a specific debt;
- the liabilities which are to be repaid from the proceeds from the sale of the asset(s);

- the value of liabilities that may arise in the course of receivership or liquidation – for example, liquidation costs; and
- the anticipated surplus (deficit) of funds remaining after the assets have been sold and the liabilities repaid. The surplus (deficit) is attributable to the shareholders of the company.

An extract of Form 507 showing the major components follows.

Form 507

Report as to Affairs

			Cost $	Estimated realisable value $
1	Assets not specifically charged			
	a	Interest in land		
	b	Sundry debtors		
	c	Cash on hand		
	d	Cash at bank		
	e	Stock		
	f	Work in progress		
	g	Plant and equipment		
	h	Other assets		
Subtotal				
2	Assets subject to specific charges			
	less Amounts owing under the charge			
Total assets (at book value)				
Total assets at realisable value				
3	*less* Payable in advance of secured creditors:			
	amounts owing for tax instalment deductions			
	amounts owing for employee entitlements			
4	*less* Amount owing and secured by debenture or floating charge over assets			
5	*less* Preferential claims ranking behind secured creditors			
6	Balance owing to partly secured creditors			
7	Creditors (unsecured)			
8	Contingent assets			
9	Contingent liabilities			
Estimated surplus (deficit)				

Accounting for assets on liquidation

When accounting for the liquidation of a company, there are three essential steps. These are:
1. Sell (liquidate) all of the company's assets.
2. Repay the company's creditors (liabilities).
3. Repay the company's shareholders.

To account for the sale (liquidation) of the company's assets, an account called 'Liquidation' is created. This account will be used to account for the closure of all asset accounts and the proceeds from their disposal.

In addition, the liquidator will need to establish a cash account over which the liquidator has control. This account can be called 'Cash at bank – Liquidation'. This account will be used to deposit the proceeds from the liquidated assets and then to repay creditors and shareholders.

The procedure for liquidating assets is as follows:
- Close all asset accounts (including accumulations against assets) to the liquidation account.
- Record the proceeds from the sale of the assets.

ILLUSTRATION

On 1 August, Damned Ltd was placed into liquidation. The company liquidator realised $900 000 from the sale of the company's assets. The company balance sheet at this date included the following assets at cost.

	$	$	$
Current assets			
Cash at bank		50 000	
Stock		80 000	
Debtors	110 000		
less Allowance for doubtful debts	10 000	100 000	
Total current assets			230 000
Non-current assets			
Plant and equipment	190 000		
less Accumulated depreciation	40 000	150 000	
Buildings		450 000	
Total non-current assets			600 000
Total assets			830 000

The entry to close all assets to the liquidation account would appear in the general journal as follows:

General journal

Date	Particulars	Debit	Credit
		$	$
1 Aug	Liquidation	880 000	
	Cash at bank		50 000
	Stock		80 000
	Debtors		110 000
	Plant and equipment		190 000
	Buildings		450 000
	Entry closing asset accounts at their cost value to the liquidation account		

General journal

Date	Particulars	Debit	Credit
		$	$
1 Aug	Allowance for doubtful debts	10 000	
	Accumulated depreciation	40 000	
	Liquidation		50 000
	Entry closing asset reduction accounts to the liquidation account		

The general ledger after the closure of these accounts would appear as follows:

General ledger

Date	Particulars	Debit	Credit	Balance
Cash at bank				
1 Aug	Balance	50 000		50 000 Dr
	Liquidation		50 000	–
Stock				
1 Aug	Balance	80 000		80 000 Dr
	Liquidation		80 000	–
Debtors				
1 Aug	Balance	110 000		110 000 Dr
	Liquidation		110 000	–
Allowance for doubtful debts				
1 Aug	Balance		10 000	10 000 Cr
	Liquidation	10 000		–
Plant and equipment				
1 Aug	Balance	190 000		190 000 Dr
	Liquidation		190 000	–
Accumulated depreciation				
1 Aug	Balance		40 000	40 000 Cr
	Liquidation	40 000		–
Buildings				
1 Aug	Balance	450 000		450 000 Dr
	Liquidation		450 000	–
Liquidation				
1 Aug	Cash at bank	50 000		50 000 Dr
	Stock	80 000		130 000 Dr
	Debtors	110 000		240 000 Dr
	Plant and equipment	190 000		430 000 Dr
	Buildings	450 000		880 000 Dr
	Allowance for doubtful debts		10 000	870 000 Dr
	Accumulated depreciation		40 000	830 000 Dr

The entry to record the sale of the assets would be as follows:

Cash receipts journal

Date	Particulars	Rec. no.	Sundries	Bank
			$	$
1 Aug	Liquidation		900 000	900 000

The resulting general ledger would be as follows:

Date	Particulars	Debit	Credit	Balance
	Liquidation			
1 Aug	Cash at bank	50 000		50 000 Dr
	Stock	80 000		130 000 Dr
	Debtors	110 000		240 000 Dr
	Plant and equipment	190 000		430 000 Dr
	Buildings	450 000		880 000 Dr
	Allowance for doubtful debts		10 000	870 000 Dr
	Accumulated depreciation		40 000	830 000 Dr
	Cash at bank – Liquidation		900 000	70 000 Cr
	Cash at bank – Liquidation			
1 Aug	Liquidation	900 000		900 000 Dr

As a result of the sale of $830 000 of assets at cost price for $900 000, a profit on the sale of $70 000 is recorded in the liquidation account for distribution to the shareholders. In addition, there is $900 000 in cash available to repay the company's creditors and shareholders.

Question 12.1

Lost Out Ltd was placed into liquidation by its directors on 1 November. The balance sheet of the company on this date revealed the following assets:

	$	$	$
Current assets			
Deposits at call		25 000	
Debtors	55 000		
less Allowance for doubtful debts	5 000	50 000	
Stocks on hand		75 000	
Total current assets			150 000
Non-current assets			
Machinery	250 000		
less Accumulated depreciation	50 000	200 000	
Plant		500 000	
Total non-current assets			700 000
Total assets			850 000

On 25 November, the company's liquidator realised all non-monetary assets at the following values:

Assets	$
Deposits at call	25 000
Debtors	48 000
Stocks on hand	82 000
Machinery	190 000
Plant	580 000

You are required to prepare the journal and general ledger entries recording the liquidation of the company's assets.

Treatment of liabilities on liquidation

Once a liquidator has disposed of the assets of the company in liquidation, it is necessary to determine the classes of liabilities and the order of priority in which they will be paid. Having determined the priorities of payment of the company's creditors, the funds that are at the liquidator's disposal can then be used to repay the creditors.

Priorities of creditors' claims on liquidation

When a company is placed into liquidation, certain liabilities have preference for settlement over other liabilities. The priorities for the settlement of company debts are set out in the Corporations Law and the *Income Tax Assessment Act* as follows:

Priority	Description
1	Liquidator's costs.
2	Creditors associated with a fixed charge over assets.
3	Costs and debts incurred by an administrator.
4	Amounts owing to employees for wages and superannuation. (Directors and their relatives are restricted to a maximum payment of $2 000 each.)
5	Payments owing in respect of workers' injuries.
6	Amount owing to employees for leave owing. (Annual leave and payments to directors are restricted to a maximum of $1 500.)
7	Retrenchment payments owing to employees.
8	Creditors associated with a floating charge over assets.
9	Creditors without security over company assets.

In addition to the priority of payments, the following principles of repayment of creditors apply:

1 Each category of creditors' priority must be paid out before payments take place to the next category of priority – for example, creditors with associated security over assets (priority 2) would not be paid until the liquidator's costs had been paid (priority 1), and so on.
2 All creditors in a category of priority are deemed to be equal – that is, if there are insufficient funds to repay all creditors, then the funds available to repay the next category of creditor will be distributed equally among that category. For example, if a company had used the proceeds from asset sales to repay creditors in priorities 1 to 8, and had $100 000 left to repay the creditors in priority category 9 who were owed $500 000, then the creditors in this category would receive $0.20 in each dollar ($100 000 / $500 000).

ILLUSTRATION

Damned Ltd is in the process of liquidation. The statement of assets and liabilities included the following assets showing their associated security and values and priority for settlement of creditors' payments.

Form 507

Report as to Affairs

			Cost	Estimated realisable value
			$	$
1	Assets not specifically charged			
		Debtors	100 000	90 000
		Cash at bank	50 000	50 000
		Stock	80 000	90 000
		Plant and equipment	150 000	170 000
		Total assets not specifically charged	380 000	400 000
2	Assets subject to specific charges			
		Buildings	450 000	500 000
		less Amounts owing under the charge	(150 000)	(150 000)
		Total assets subject to specific charges	100 000	350 000
	Total assets (at book value)		480 000	
	Total assets at realisable value			750 000
3	less			
		Wages owing to employees	80 000	
		Directors' fees (three directors)	10 000	
		Leave owing to one director	30 000	
7	less Trade creditors		110 000	230 000
	Estimated surplus (deficit)			520 000
	Estimated costs of liquidation $15 000			

The statement of assets and liabilities reveals that the market value of assets before identifying the security payable on the buildings is $900 000. After recognising the amount owing as security over the buildings of $150 000, there is $750 000 available to pay liabilities and shareholders. From this amount it will be necessary to repay liabilities totalling $380 000. The surplus of funds – $370 000 – can be used to pay the costs of liquidation of $15 000. This will leave $355 000 to be paid to the company's shareholders.

As a result, the creditors' payments and associated values would be as follows:

				Balance of funds available $
Funds available from asset disposals				900 000
less Creditors' payments by priority				
Priority	Description	Calculation	Total	
			$	
1	Liquidator's costs		15 000	885 000
2	Creditors with fixed charge		150 000	735 000
4	Wages owing to employees		80 000	655 000
4	Directors' fees (three directors)	(3 × $2 000)	6 000	649 000
6	Leave owing to one director	(1 × $1 500)	1 500	647 500
9	Unsecured creditors*		142 500	505 000

* Unsecured creditors comprises:

	$
Balance of directors' fees	4 000
Balance of directors' leave	28 500
Trade creditors	110 000
	142 500

Question 12.2

The following is a list of creditors of Defab Ltd which has been placed into liquidation. You are required to make a priority list of these creditors.
- GST payable
- Loans from employees
- Accrued expenses
- Employees' accrued wages
- Leave entitlements owing to employees
- Leave entitlements owing to directors
- Directors' fees owing
- Mortgage (secured over equipment)
- Trade creditors
- Debentures (secured over buildings)
- Employees' retrenchment payments
- Liquidator's expenses
- Trade creditors (with a floating charge secured over assets)
- Bank overdraft

Question 12.3

Due to insufficient cash flows, Brand Ltd has been placed into liquidation. The liquidator has realised $750 000 from the disposal of the company's assets and determined the following list of company creditors:

	$
Accounts payable	40 000
Directors' fees (five directors)	20 000
PAYG payable	12 000
Leave owing to employees	145 000
Loans from employees	15 000
Mortgage (secured over equipment)	350 000
GST payable	6 000
Wages payable	50 000

Note: Liquidation expenses are $12 000.

You are required to:

a prepare a list of creditors showing their priority of payment and the amounts that they can expect to receive from the liquidation; and

b calculate the anticipated surplus (deficit) of funds that is attributable to the shareholders of the company after liabilities have been repaid.

Question 12.4

Gonunder Ltd has been placed into receivership. The liquidator has identified the following assets at their book value and realisable value:

	Book value $	Realisable value $
Cash on hand	15 000	15 000
Trade debtors	60 000	50 000
Stock on hand	25 000	24 000
Buildings (secured by mortgage)	250 000	300 000
Other assets	150 000	120 000

The balance sheet of Gonunder Ltd includes the following liabilities:

	$	$
Current liabilities		
Accounts payable	39 125	
Taxes payable	40 000	
Bank overdraft	30 000	
Wages owing	15 000	
Leave provisions	30 000	
Accrued expenses	5 000	159 125
Non-current liabilities		
Mortgage on buildings	100 000	
Debentures (floating charge on assets)	250 000	350 000
		509 125

Additional information

- Wages owing includes $5 000 owing to one director.
- Leave provisions includes $10 000 owing to one director.
- The liquidator's costs are estimated at $25 000.

You are required to prepare a list of creditors showing their priority of payment and the amounts that they can expect to receive from the liquidation.

Accounting for liabilities on liquidation

The liquidator, having realised the company's assets and determined the priority for payment of the company's creditors, can then issue cheques from the bank account under the liquidator's control to repay the creditors.

Liquidation costs are accounted for by making a payment from the liquidator's cash at bank account (credit) and reducing (debiting) the amount in the liquidation account.

ILLUSTRATION

Damned Ltd in the previous illustrations had received $900 000 on the sale of assets which had been carried on the balance sheet at $830 000. This had resulted in a balance of $70 000 being carried in the liquidation account and $900 000 in the liquidator's bank account.

On 9 August, the liquidator paid the costs of liquidation and the company's creditors, which were as follows:

	$
Liquidation expenses	15 000
Mortgage on buildings	150 000
Wages owing to employees	80 000
Directors' fees owing	10 000
Leave owing to director	30 000
Trade creditors	110 000
Total liabilities	395 000

The journal entry to pay the costs of liquidation and repay the liabilities would be as follows:

Cash payments journal

Date	Particulars	Chq. no.	Sundries	Bank
			$	$
1 Aug	Liquidation expenses		15 000	15 000
	Mortgage on buildings		150 000	150 000
	Wages owing to employees		80 000	80 000
	Directors' fees owing		10 000	10 000
	Leave owing to director		30 000	30 000
	Trade creditors		110 000	110 000
				395 000

The general ledger after the recording of the cash payments would appear as follows:

General ledger

Date	Particulars	Debit	Credit	Balance
Mortgage on buildings				
1 Aug	Balance		150 000	150 000 Cr
9 Aug	Cash at bank – Liquidation	150 000		–
Wages owing to employees				
1 Aug	Balance		80 000	80 000 Cr
9 Aug	Cash at bank – Liquidation	80 000		–
Directors' fees owing				
1 Aug	Balance		10 000	10 000 Cr
9 Aug	Cash at bank – Liquidation	10 000		–
Leave owing to director				
1 Aug	Balance		30 000	30 000 Cr
9 Aug	Cash at bank – Liquidation	30 000		–
Trade creditors				
1 Aug	Balance		110 000	110 000 Cr
9 Aug	Cash at bank – Liquidation	110 000		–

General ledger

Date	Particulars	Debit	Credit	Balance
Liquidation				
1 Aug	Cash at bank	50 000		50 000 Dr
	Stock	80 000		130 000 Dr
	Debtors	110 000		240 000 Dr
	Plant and equipment	190 000		430 000 Dr
	Buildings	450 000		880 000 Dr
	Allowance for doubtful debts		10 000	870 000 Dr
	Accumulated depreciation		40 000	830 000 Dr
	Cash at bank – Liquidation		900 000	70 000 Cr
9 Aug	Cash at bank – Liquidation	15 000		55 000 Cr
Cash at bank – Liquidation				
1 Aug	Liquidation	900 000		900 000 Dr
9 Aug	Payments		395 000	505 000 Dr

The outcome of paying company debts is that there is $55 000 in surplus liquidation funds owing to the shareholders and $505 000 in the liquidator's bank account to distribute to shareholders.

Question 12.5

The liquidator of Marcus Ltd has realised the company's assets for $650 000, earning the shareholders a surplus of $80 000. The company has liabilities totalling $370 000 as follows:

	$
Liquidation expenses	10 000
Debentures	200 000
Wages payable	30 000
Provision for employees' leave	25 000
Directors' fees owing	5 000
Loans from finance company	30 000
Trade creditors	70 000

You are required to:
a prepare the journal entries to record the payments to extinguish liabilities on 3 June; and
b show the general ledger accounts after the payment of liabilities.

Question 12.6

From the following information relating to Sparks Ltd, which has been placed in liquidation on 6 May, you are required to prepare the journal entries to:
a liquidate the company's assets on 6 May;
b pay the company's creditors on 9 May; and
c show the liquidation account after the payment of liabilities.

Form 507

Report as to Affairs

	Cost $	Estimated realisable value $
Assets not specifically charged		
Debtors (WDV – written-down value)	25 000	25 000
Cash on hand	15 000	15 000
Stock	50 000	45 000
Equipment (WDV)	120 000	130 000
Total assets not specifically charged	210 000	215 000
Assets subject to specific charges		
Buildings	200 000	300 000
less Mortgage secured on buildings	(150 000)	(150 000)
Total assets subject to specific charges	50 000	150 000
Total assets (at book value)	260 000	
Total assets at realisable value		365 000
less		
Wages payable	15 000	
Directors' fees (two directors)	10 000	
Bank overdraft	30 000	
Trade creditors	200 000	255 000
Estimated surplus (deficit)		110 000
Estimated costs of liquidation $5 000		

Treatment of shareholders on liquidation

If funds remain after all creditors of the company have been repaid, the funds can be distributed to the company's shareholders. The distribution of these funds to the shareholders returns share capital to the shareholders. Any surplus after that represents excess funds received on the liquidation of the company's assets above their cost price.

Priorities of shareholders

When considering the allocation of funds to the shareholders, two principles must be applied. These are:

1. If the company's constitution specifies how the funds will be distributed to shareholders in the event of the company's winding up, then the constitution must be followed.
2. If the company's constitution makes no reference to how funds will be distributed, then all shareholders rank equally in the distribution.

However, in reference to the amounts owing *by* shareholders and the amounts owing *to* shareholders, specific attention may need to be given to the following situations:

- dividends owing to shareholders;
- calls in arrears by shareholders; and
- calls received in advance from shareholders.

Dividends owing to shareholders

Dividends payable to shareholders are classified as a return to shareholders and, while appearing in the balance sheet as a liability, can only be considered for payment after all other creditors have been repaid. The payment of dividends owing to shareholders may be specified in the company's constitution. If the company's constitution empowers the liquidator to pay dividends prior to the distribution of funds to shareholders, then they shall be repaid. If the company's constitution makes no reference to the payment of dividends in the event of liquidation, then they do not need to be paid.

Calls in arrears by shareholders

Where shareholders are in arrears for calls on their shares at the time of liquidation, the liquidator will be directed by the company's constitution. If the company's constitution does not direct the liquidator to pursue the calls for payment, the liquidator is entitled to declare the shares as 'forfeited', thus rendering the shareholder ineligible to participate in the return of capital or any surplus arising from the disposal of assets. Conversely, the shareholder will not be required to bear an apportionment of any deficit arising where there is a deficit of funds.

Calls in advance made by shareholders

Again, the liquidator will be guided by the company's constitution where shareholders have paid for calls in advance at the time of liquidation. If the company's constitution does not refer to calls in advance on liquidation, the liquidator must repay the calls to the shareholders, but only after all creditors have been repaid. If the company has classes of shares which have a priority right as to the repayment of capital, these shares must be paid out before calls in advance are refunded.

Distribution of funds to shareholders

The distribution of funds to shareholders will be determined by the company's constitution. If the company's constitution is silent as to the priority of distribution among the classes of shareholders, then all shareholders are treated as equal in the distribution.

The amount of cash available to be distributed to shareholders may be in excess of the share capital of the shareholders, in which case the shareholders will be entitled to a distribution of the surplus funds. On the other hand, if the cash available on distribution to the shareholders is less than the contributed equity, then the shareholders will be apportioned a proportionate share of the losses.

ILLUSTRATION (DISTRIBUTION OF SURPLUS FUNDS)

Continuing with the previous illustrations relating to Damned Ltd, which had a balance sheet showing assets of $830 000 and liabilities of $380 000, the shareholders' funds representing these net assets were as follows:

Shareholders' equity	$
Contributed equity	
Ordinary shares (100 000 shares @ $1 each)	100 000
Preference shares (50 000 shares @ $2 each)	100 000
Cumulative shares (50 000 shares @ $4 each)	200 000
	400 000
Reserves	
Retained losses	(25 000)
Asset revaluation reserve	75 000
Total shareholders' equity	450 000

During the process of liquidation:
- the assets costing $830 000 had been sold for $900 000 (a profit of $70 000);
- the sale proceeds were used to pay the company's liquidator ($15 000) and creditors ($380 000), a total of $395 000;
- the liquidator was holding cash totalling $505 000 ($900 000 less $395 000); and
- the liquidation account showed a surplus of $55 000, representing the profit made on asset disposals less the liquidator's expenses ($70 000 − $15 000).

On 15 August, the liquidator decided to distribute funds to the company's shareholders. As the liquidator has cash of $505 000, there are sufficient funds to return the value of shareholders' funds to the shareholders of $450 000 plus the profit on the disposal of assets of $55 000 – that is, $450 000 + $55 000 = $505 000.

Thus, each shareholder is entitled to the following distribution of funds based on the nominal value of contributed equity:

Class of share	Total nominal value	% of total nominal value	Share of funds available for distribution	
Ordinary shares	$100 000	100 000 / 400 000 = 25%	25% × $505 000	$126 250
Preference shares	$100 000	100 000 / 400 000 = 25%	25% × $505 000	$126 250
Cumulative shares	$200 000	200 000 / 400 000 = 50%	50% × $505 000	$252 500
	$400 000			$505 000

As a consequence of these calculations, it can be seen that all classes of shares are receiving a return of their nominal capital plus a share of the surplus funds from liquidation. This is expressed in the following table.

Class of share	Number of shares	Distributed funds	Distributed funds per share	Nominal value per share	Loss per share
Ordinary shares	100 000	$126 250	$1.2625	$1	$0.2625
Preference shares	50 000	$126 250	$2.5250	$2	$0.5250
Cumulative shares	50 000	$252 500	$5.0500	$4	$1.0500
		$505 000			

ILLUSTRATION (APPORTIONMENT OF LOSSES)

The liquidator of ABC Ltd has $500 000 cash available to repay the company's shareholders. The balance sheet at the date of liquidation showed the following:

Shareholders' equity	$
Contributed equity	
Ordinary shares (400 000 shares @ $1 each)	400 000
Preference shares (50 000 shares @ $4 each)	200 000
	600 000
Reserves	
Retained profits	15 000
Reserves	85 000
Total shareholders' equity	700 000

The distribution of the funds available to the respective classes of shareholders, based on the nominal value of contributed equity, would be as follows:

Class of share	Total nominal value	% of total nominal value	Share of funds available for distribution		
Ordinary shares	$400 000	400 000 / 600 000 = 66.7%	66.7%	$500 000	$333 500
Preference shares	$200 000	200 000 / 600 000 = 33.3%	33.3%	$500 000	$166 500
	$600 000				$500 000

The calculation shows that all classes of shares are receiving a return which is less than the nominal capital. Hence the shareholders have taken a loss on distribution. The following table shows the amount returned on each share and the loss on each share.

Class of share	Number of shares	Distributed funds	Distributed funds per share	Nominal value per share	Loss per share
Ordinary shares	400 000	$333 500	$0.83	$1	$0.17
Preference shares	50 000	$166 500	$3.33	$4	$0.67
		$500 000			

Accounting for the distribution of funds to shareholders

When accounting for the distribution of funds to shareholders, it is necessary to create an account called 'Shareholders' distribution'. This account is used as a clearing house to determine the total amount of funds that are payable to the shareholders and to apply the cash under the liquidator's control to the shareholders.

The procedure that should be adopted when using the account is as follows:

1 Transfer all shareholders' funds accounts to the shareholders' distribution account.
2 Transfer the balance of the liquidation account to the shareholders' distribution account.
3 Make payments from the cash at bank – liquidation account to the shareholders' distribution account.

ILLUSTRATION

In the continuing illustration relating to Damned Ltd, the company's balance sheet revealed the following classes and amounts of shareholders' equity:

Shareholders' equity	$
Contributed equity	
Ordinary shares (200 000 shares)	200 000
Preference shares (50 000 shares)	100 000
Cumulative preference shares (50 000 shares)	200 000
	500 000
Reserves	
Retained losses	(25 000)
Asset revaluation reserve	75 000
Total shareholders' equity	450 000

The process of liquidation and payment of liabilities has resulted in:
- a $55 000 surplus in the liquidation account;
- a $505 000 balance in the cash at bank – liquidation account; and
- each class of share is entitled to the following return:

Class of share	$
Ordinary shares	126 250
Preference shares	126 250
Cumulative preference shares	252 500

The journal entries to transfer accounts to the shareholders' distribution account would be prepared as follows:

General journal

Date	Particulars	Debit	Credit
		$	$
1 Aug	Ordinary shares	100 000	
	Preference shares	100 000	
	Cumulative preference shares	200 000	
	Shareholders' distribution		400 000
	Transferred equity accounts to shareholders' distribution account		
	Shareholders' distribution	25 000	
	Retained losses		25 000
	Transferred retained losses to shareholders' distribution account		
	Asset revaluation reserve	75 000	
	Shareholders' distribution		75 000
	Transferred reserve account to shareholders' distribution account		
	Liquidation	55 000	
	Shareholders' distribution		55 000
	Transferred liquidation account to shareholders' distribution account		

The general ledger accounts recording these transfers would appear as follows:

General ledger

Date	Particulars	Debit	Credit	Balance
	Ordinary shares			
1 Aug	Balance		100 000	100 000 Cr
15 Aug	Shareholders' distribution	100 000		–
	Preference shares			
1 Aug	Balance		100 000	100 000 Cr
15 Aug	Shareholders' distribution	100 000		–
	Cumulative preference shares			
1 Aug	Balance		200 000	200 000 Cr
15 Aug	Shareholders' distribution	200 000		–
	Retained losses			
1 Aug	Balance	25 000		25 000 Dr
15 Aug	Shareholders' distribution		25 000	–
	Asset revaluation reserve			
1 Aug	Balance		75 000	75 000 Cr
15 Aug	Shareholders' distribution	75 000		–
	Liquidation			
1 Aug	Cash at bank	50 000		50 000 Dr
	Stock	80 000		130 000 Dr
	Debtors	110 000		240 000 Dr
	Plant and equipment	190 000		430 000 Dr
	Buildings	450 000		880 000 Dr
	Allowance for doubtful debts		10 000	870 000 Dr
	Accumulated depreciation		40 000	830 000 Dr
	Cash at bank – Liquidation		900 000	70 000 Cr
9 Aug	Cash at bank – Liquidation	15 000		55 000 Cr
15 Aug	Shareholders' liquidation	55 000		–
	Shareholders' distribution			
15 Aug	Ordinary shares		100 000	100 000 Cr
	Preference shares		100 000	200 000 Cr
	Cumulative preference shares		200 000	400 000 Cr
	Retained profits	25 000		375 000 Cr
	Asset revaluation reserve		75 000	450 000 Cr
	Liquidation		55 000	505 000 Cr

Cash at bank – Liquidation

1 Aug	Liquidation	900 000		900 000 Dr
9 Aug	Payments		395 000	505 000 Dr

Payments to shareholders would appear in the cash payments journal as follows:

Cash payments journal

Date	Particulars	Chq. no.	Sundries	Bank
			$	$
15 Aug	Ordinary shareholders		126 250	126 250
	Preference shareholders		126 250	126 250
	Cumulative preference shareholders		252 500	252 500
				505 000

The finalised general ledger would be as follows:

General ledger

Date	Particulars	Debit	Credit	Balance
Shareholders' distribution				
15 Aug	Ordinary shares		100 000	100 000 Cr
	Preference shares		100 000	200 000 Cr
	Cumulative preference shares		200 000	400 000 Cr
	Retained profits	25 000		375 000 Cr
	Asset revaluation reserve		75 000	450 000 Cr
	Liquidation		55 000	505 000 Cr
	Cash at bank – Liquidation	505 000		–
Cash at bank – Liquidation				
1 Aug	Liquidation	900 000		900 000 Dr
9 Aug	Payments		395 000	505 000 Dr
15 Aug	Shareholders' liquidation		505 000	–

Question 12.7

Flop Ltd has been placed into voluntary liquidation. The liquidator has realised the company's assets at a surplus of $100 000. After paying off the company's debts, the liquidator has $600 000 in cash to distribute to the shareholders.

The company balance sheet on 1 December carried the following detail in respect of shareholders' equity:

Shareholders' equity		$
Contributed equity		
Ordinary shares (400 000 shares)		100 000
Preference shares (50 000 shares)		300 000
		400 000
Reserves		
Retained profits		10 000
General reserve		90 000
Total shareholders' equity		500 000

You are required to:
a calculate the amounts that will be distributed to the respective classes of shares on 10 December;
b prepare the appropriate journal entries to distribute funds to the shareholders; and
c show the shareholders' distribution account after the distribution of funds.

Question 12.8

From the following information relating to Casino Ltd, which is in liquidation, you are required to prepare:
a the journal entries to dispose of assets, repay creditors and distribute funds to the shareholders; and
b the general ledger accounts for liquidation, cash at bank – liquidation and shareholders' distribution.

On 1 March, Casino Ltd was placed into liquidation. The balance sheet at this date was as follows:

Casino Ltd
Balance sheet as at 1 March

Assets	$	$	$
Cash on hand		5 000	
Stocks		25 000	
Debtors	100 000		
less Allowance for doubtful debts	10 000	90 000	
Buildings (secured by debentures)		450 000	
Other assets		150 000	
Total assets			720 000
Liabilities			
Creditors		150 000	
Wages and directors' fees payable		60 000	
Debentures (secured over buildings)		250 000	
Total liabilities			460 000
Net assets			260 000
Shareholders' equity			
Contributed equity			
Ordinary shares (200 000)		200 000	
Preference shares (4 000)		40 000	
		240 000	
Retained losses		(20 000)	
Reserves		40 000	
Total shareholders' equity			260 000

Additional information

- All assets were sold on 10 March and realised their book values except for buildings. These sold for $620 000.
- The liquidator paid all liabilities on 20 March. Liquidation costs were $20 000.
- Distributions were made to shareholders on 25 March.

Question 12.9

The following information relates to Marvel Ltd, which has been placed into liquidation. From this information you are required to prepare:

a the journal entries to dispose of assets, repay creditors and distribute funds to the shareholders; and

b the general ledger accounts for liquidation, cash at bank – liquidation and shareholders' distribution.

On 5 February, Marvel Ltd was placed into liquidation. The balance sheet at this date was as follows:

Marvel Ltd
Balance sheet as at 5 February

Assets	$	$	$
Deposits at call		90 000	
Inventories		15 000	
Debtors	60 000		
less Allowance for doubtful debts	5 000	55 000	
Equipment (secured by debentures)	150 000		
less Accumulated depreciation	50 000	100 000	
Total assets			260 000
Liabilities			
Bank overdraft		40 000	
Creditors		60 000	
Provision for leave payments		10 000	
Dividends payable		20 000	
Total liabilities			130 000
Net assets			130 000
Shareholders' equity			
Contributed equity			
Ordinary shares (100 000)		100 000	
Preference shares (1 000)		100 000	
		200 000	
Retained losses		(70 000)	
Total shareholders' equity			130 000

Additional information

- All assets were sold on 12 February and realised their book values except for:
    - debtors, which realised $50 000; and
    - equipment, which realised $90 000.
- The liquidator paid all liabilities on 20 February. Liquidation costs were $10 000.
- The constitution states that dividends must be paid before distributions to shareholders.
- Distributions were made to shareholders on 28 February.

CHAPTER 13
AMALGAMATIONS AND TAKEOVERS

Objectives

Upon satisfactory completion of this chapter you should be able to:

- calculate consideration in respect to fully paid shares at an agreed value, including a share premium;
- calculate and record goodwill or write off discount on acquisition as required by the accounting standards;
- prepare the accounting entries in the purchaser's books and the vendor's books for an amalgamation; and
- prepare a balance sheet where appropriate, following the amalgamation for both the purchasing company and the selling company.

Introduction

Companies from time to time undertake expansionary activities by acquiring another business. The acquisition of another business may be through an amalgamation with the other business or via a takeover of the shares of the other business. When a company amalgamates or combines with another business, it is necessary to ensure compliance with AASB 3: Business Combinations.

This chapter examines the accounting procedures that should be applied on an amalgamation and a takeover in the books of the vendor and the buyer.

The difference between an amalgamation and a takeover

The term **amalgamation** is used when a company acquires the net assets of another company to obtain control. Other terms include **absorption**, **merger** and **reorganisation**. Under an amalgamation, the net assets of the company being acquired are absorbed into the operations of the purchasing company. The business is then identified as one single entity, with one separate legal entity status, preparing one set of financial statements.

The term **takeover** is used when a company acquires shares in another company with the aim of obtaining control. After a takeover the acquired company becomes a subsidiary of the purchasing company with its own separate legal entity status. The subsidiary owns its own assets, prepares financial statements and conducts business in its own right. The parent company is also a separate legal entity which reports separately but also consolidates the accounts of the parent and the subsidiary to report as one economic entity.

Purchase consideration

When a company purchases the assets of another company in an amalgamation or purchases another company's shares in a takeover, the purchaser makes an offer to the vendor comprising cash or shares or debentures in the purchasing company or a combination of cash, shares and debentures. This is called **purchase consideration** or **cost of acquisition**.

Cost of acquisition is defined in the accounting standards as 'the purchase consideration plus any costs incidental to the acquisition'.

The standard defines purchase consideration as 'the fair value of assets given or share capital issued, liabilities undertaken, and other securities given by the purchaser, in exchange for assets or shares of another entity'.

ILLUSTRATION

Carmen Ltd has made an offer to Miranda Ltd to purchase their net assets which have a fair value of $600 000. The offer made by Carmen Ltd comprises $100 000 cash and 400 000 ordinary shares with a nominal value of $1.25 each. The legal costs associated with the purchase amount to $15 000.

The total purchase consideration is calculated as follows:

	$
Cash	100 000
Ordinary shares (400 000 × $1.25 each)	500 000
Total purchase consideration	600 000

The cost of acquisition is:

	$
Total purchase consideration	600 000
Legal costs	15 000
Cost of acquisition	615 000

Accounting for amalgamations

When a company is amalgamated with another company, the company being amalgamated (the vendor) sells its net assets to the purchasing company. Consequently, both companies must make entries in their respective books.

The vendor must make entries to dispose of its net assets and record the consideration it receives in return for those assets. The purchaser must record the fair values of the net assets it is acquiring, the amount of goodwill it has purchased (if any) or discount on acquisition (if any), and the payment it has made to obtain the net assets.

Accounting for amalgamation by the vendor

To account for the disposal of the vendor's net assets, it is necessary for the vendor to create an account called 'Realisation'. This account will be used to:

- transfer the values of all assets and liabilities which are being realised (sold); and
- record the purchase consideration.

Any balance remaining in the realisation account after the sale will represent either:

- a profit on the amalgamation, if the purchase consideration exceeds the value of the net assets sold; or
- a loss on the amalgamation, if the purchase price is less than the value of the net assets sold.

When accounting for an amalgamation in the books of the vendor, the following procedure is recommended:

1. Transfer all assets (except cash at bank accounts) to the realisation account.
2. Transfer all liability accounts to the realisation account.
3. Record the purchase consideration owing by the purchaser.
4. Record the settlement of the purchase consideration by the vendor.
5. Transfer the balance in the realisation account to the profit (loss) on realisation account.

ILLUSTRATION

On 5 May, Mango Ltd negotiated to purchase the net assets of Tropics Ltd for a purchase consideration of $305 000 comprising:
- $130 000 cash; plus
- 100 000 ordinary shares with a nominal value of $1.25 each; plus
- $50 000 in debentures.

The balance sheet of Tropics Ltd on this date was as follows:

Tropics Ltd
Balance sheet as at 5 May (before amalgamation)

Assets	$	$
Cash at bank		5 000
Debtors	15 000	
less Allowance for doubtful debts	5 000	10 000
Equipment	360 000	
less Accumulated depreciation	35 000	325 000
Total assets		340 000
Liabilities		
Creditors		40 000
Net assets		300 000
Shareholders' equity		
Contributed equity		
Ordinary shares (300 000)		300 000

The valuation of all assets was accepted as their fair values, except equipment which was valued at $350 000.

Applying the procedures suggested, the respective journal entries in the vendor's books would be as follows:

1 Transfer all assets (except cash at bank account) to the realisation account.

General journal

Date	Particulars	Debit	Credit
		$	$
5 May	Realisation	375 000	
	Debtors		15 000
	Equipment		360 000
	Transferred assets to realisation account		
	Allowance for doubtful debts	5 000	
	Accumulated depreciation – Equipment		
	Realisation	35 000	
	Transferred assets to realisation account		40 000

2 Transfer all liability accounts to the realisation account.

General journal

Date	Particulars	Debit	Credit
		$	$
5 May	Creditors	40 000	
	Realisation		40 000
	Transferred liability to realisation account		

The realisation account in the general ledger of Tropics Ltd after these transfer entries would be as follows:

General ledger

Date	Particulars	Debit	Credit	Balance
Realisation				
5 May	Debtors	15 000		15 000 Dr
	Equipment	360 000		375 000 Dr
	Allowance for doubtful debts		5 000	370 000 Dr
	Accumulated depreciation		35 000	335 000 Dr
	Creditors		40 000	295 000 Dr

3 Record the purchase consideration owing by the purchaser.

General journal

Date	Particulars	Debit	Credit
		$	$
5 May	Purchaser's consideration	305 000	
	Realisation		305 000
	To record purchase consideration on amalgamation		

4 Record the settlement of the purchase consideration by the vendor.

General journal

Date	Particulars	Debit	Credit
		$	$
5 May	Cash at bank	130 000	
	Investment in Mango Ltd	125 000	
	Debentures in Mango Ltd	50 000	
	Purchaser's consideration		305 000
	To record purchase consideration on amalgamation		

The resulting realisation account would be as follows:

General ledger

Date	Particulars	Debit	Credit	Balance
Realisation				
5 May	Debtors	15 000		15 000 Dr
	Equipment	360 000		375 000 Dr
	Allowance for doubtful debts		5 000	370 000 Dr
	Accumulated depreciation		35 000	335 000 Dr
	Creditors		40 000	295 000 Dr
	Purchaser's consideration		305 000	10 000 Cr

5 Transfer the balance in the realisation account to the profit (loss) on realisation account.

General journal

Date	Particulars	Debit	Credit
		$	$
5 May	Realisation	10 000	
	Profit on realisation		10 000
	To transfer profit on realisation		

The finalised general ledger of Tropics Ltd would be as follows:

General ledger

Date	Particulars	Debit	Credit	Balance
Ordinary shares				
5 May	Balance		300 000	300 000 Cr
Profit on realisation				
5 May	Realisation		10 000	10 000 Cr
Bank				
5 May	Balance	5 000		5 000 Dr
	Purchaser's consideration	130 000		135 000 Dr
Investmest in Mango Ltd				
5 May	Purchaser's consideration	125 000		125 000 Dr
Debentures in Mango Ltd				
5 May	Purchaser's consideration	50 000		50 000 Dr

The balance sheet of Tropics Ltd after the amalgamation would be as follows:

Tropics Ltd
Balance sheet as at 5 May (after amalgamation)

	$	$
Assets		
Cash at bank		135 000
Investment in Mango Ltd		125 000
Debentures in Mango Ltd		50 000
Net assets		310 000
Shareholders' equity		
Contributed equity		
Ordinary shares (300 000)	300 000	
Profit on realisation	10 000	
Total shareholders' equity		310 000

Question 13.1

On 2 October, Abbott Ltd agreed to purchase the net assets of Costello Ltd for a purchase consideration of $470 000 comprising:
- $200 000 cash; plus
- 200 000 ordinary shares with a nominal value of $0.60 each; plus
- $150 000 in debentures.

The balance sheet of Costello Ltd on this date was as follows:

Costello Ltd
Balance sheet as at 2 October (before amalgamation)

Assets	$	$
Debtors	50 000	
less Allowance for doubtful debts	2 000	48 000
Machinery	600 000	
less Accumulated depreciation	148 000	452 000
Total assets		500 000
Liabilities		
Creditors		100 000
Net assets		400 000
Shareholders' equity		
Contributed equity		
Ordinary shares (800 000)		400 000

The valuation of all assets was accepted as their fair values, except machinery which was valued at $475 000.

You are required to:
a prepare the journal entries in the books of Costello Ltd to account for the amalgamation; and
b prepare Costello Ltd's balance sheet after the amalgamation.

Question 13.2

From the following information relating to the amalgamation of Sharks Ltd with Finn Ltd, you are required to prepare:
a the realisation account following the amalgamation;
b the balance sheet of Sharks Ltd after the amalgamation.

On 4 July, Finn Ltd agreed to purchase the net assets of Sharks Ltd. The purchase consideration comprised:
- $20 000 cash; plus
- 100 000 ordinary shares with a nominal value of $1.20 each; plus
- $60 000 in debentures.

The balance sheet of Sharks Ltd at the date of amalgamation was as follows:

Sharks Ltd
Balance sheet as at 4 July (before amalgamation)

Assets	$	$
Cash at bank		10 000
Inventory		20 000
Debtors	45 000	
less Allowance for doubtful debts	5 000	40 000
Government bonds		100 000
Machinery	400 000	
less Accumulated depreciation	250 000	150 000
Total assets		320 000
Liabilities		
Creditors	20 000	
Mortgage	80 000	100 000
Net assets		220 000
Shareholders' equity		
Contributed equity		
Ordinary shares (150 000)	150 000	
Preference shares (10 000)	50 000	200 000
Reserves		20 000
Total shareholders' equity		220 000

It was agreed that all assets were disclosed at their fair values, except inventory which had a fair value of $18 000.

Goodwill and discount on acquisition arising on amalgamation

The purchaser in an amalgamation will offer the vendor consideration in return for the net assets acquired. The purchase consideration and associated legal costs may be greater or less than the value of the net assets purchased.

Where the cost of acquisition is greater than the net assets acquired, the purchaser will recognise goodwill on the purchased assets. On the other hand, where the cost of acquisition is less than the net assets acquired, the purchaser will recognise a discount on acquisition.

Goodwill arising on acquisition

AASB 3: Business Combinations permits a business to bring goodwill to account when the goodwill is purchased. This will occur when the purchase consideration exceeds the net assets of the business being acquired.

ILLUSTRATION

On 30 June 2000, Global Ltd purchased the net assets of Universe Ltd which had a fair value of $500 000. The purchase consideration totalled $600 000, comprising:
- $50 000 cash; plus
- 500 000 ordinary shares with a nominal value of $1.10 each.

Global Ltd incurred $12 000 in legal costs associated with the amalgamation. The purchased goodwill is calculated as follows:

	$
Purchase consideration:	
Cash	50 000
Ordinary shares (500 000 × $1.10 each)	550 000
Total purchase consideration	600 000
add Legal costs	12 000
Cost of acquisition	612 000
less Fair value of net assets	500 000
Goodwill on acquisition	112 000

Question 13.3

From the following information, you are required to calculate:

a the purchase consideration;
b the goodwill or discount arising on acquisition.

Strang Ltd agreed to purchase the net assets of Lofty Ltd which were valued at $900 000. The fair value of the assets was $850 000. The purchase consideration comprised:
- cash of $250 000; plus
- 300 000 ordinary shares in Strang Ltd issued at $1.75 each; plus
- debentures in Strang Ltd of $225 000.

The legal expenses associated with the amalgamation, $15 000, were borne by Strang Ltd.

Discount arising on acquisition

When a company purchases another business and the purchase consideration is less than the net assets acquired, AASB 3: Business Combinations requires the difference to be brought to account as 'Discount on acquisition'.

In addition, AASB 3 requires a discount on acquisition to be included in the calculation of profit in the year in which it is incurred.

ILLUSTRATION

On 30 June 2000, Dynamic Ltd purchased the net assets of Lifter Ltd which had a fair value of $200 000. The purchase consideration totalled $180 000, comprising:
- $20 000 cash; plus
- 128 000 ordinary shares with a nominal value of $1.25 each.

The discount on acquisition is calculated as follows:

	$
Purchase consideration:	
Cash	20 000
Ordinary shares (128 000 × $1.25 each)	160 000
Total purchase consideration	180 000
less Fair value of net assets	200 000
Discount on acquisition	(20 000)

Hence the net profit of Dynamic Ltd would include the discount on acquisition in its calculation of annual profit as follows::

Profit and loss account	$
Discount on acquisition	20 000

Question 13.4

From the following information you are required to calculate:
a   the purchase consideration;
b   the goodwill or discount arising on acquisition.

Charles Ltd purchased the net assets of Brewer Ltd which were valued at $700 000. The fair value of the assets was $650 000. The purchase consideration comprised:
- cash of $150 000; plus
- 212 500 ordinary shares in Charles Ltd issued at $1.60 each; plus
- preference shares in Charles Ltd (20 000 at a nominal value of $3 each); plus
- debentures in Charles Ltd of $75 000.

The legal expenses associated with the amalgamation, $25 000, were borne by Charles Ltd.

Accounting for amalgamation by the purchaser

To account for the acquisition of the net assets on amalgamation in the books of the purchaser, it is necessary to:
1   Calculate the goodwill or discount arising from the amalgamation.
2   Record the fair values of the assets purchased from the vendor and the amount owing to the vendor as consideration. (Debtors to be recorded at cost price and the allowance for doubtful debts to be recognised. Depreciable assets to be recorded at their fair value – that is, accumulated depreciation is not recognised.)
3   Record the cost of acquisition (purchase consideration paid to the vendor).

ILLUSTRATION

This illustration uses the information given in the illustration relating to accounting for amalgamation by the vendor on pp. 396–9. That information is reproduced as follows:

On 5 May, Mango Ltd negotiated to purchase the net assets of Tropics Ltd for a purchase consideration of $305 000 comprising:
- $130 000 cash; plus
- 100 000 ordinary shares with a nominal value of $1.25 each; plus
- $50 000 in debentures.

The balance sheet of Tropics Ltd on this date was as follows:

Tropics Ltd
Balance sheet as at 5 May (before amalgamation)

Assets	$	$
Cash at bank		5 000
Debtors	15 000	
less Allowance for doubtful debts	5 000	10 000
Equipment	360 000	
less Accumulated depreciation	35 000	325 000
Total assets		340 000
Liabilities		
Creditors		40 000
Net assets		300 000
Shareholders' equity		
Contributed equity		
Ordinary shares (300 000)		300 000

The valuation of all assets was accepted as their fair values, except equipment which was valued at $350 000.

In addition, the balance sheet of Mango Ltd at the date of amalgamation was:

Mango Ltd
Balance sheet as at 5 May (before amalgamation)

Assets	$	$
Cash at bank		200 000
Shareholders' equity		
Contributed equity		
Ordinary shares (200 000)		200 000

1. Calculate goodwill or discount arising on amalgamation.

	$
Purchase consideration:	
Cash	130 000
Ordinary shares (100 000 × $1.25 each)	125 000
Debentures	50 000
Total purchase consideration and cost of acquisition	305 000
less Fair value of net assets	320 000
Discount on acquisition	(15 000)

2. Record the net assets acquired at their fair values, discount on acquisition and amount owing to the vendors. In addition, eliminate the discount on acquisition.

General journal

Date	Particulars	Debit	Credit
		$	$
5 May	Debtors	15 000	
	Equipment	350 000	
	Allowance for doubtful debts		5 000
	Creditors		40 000
	Profit and loss (Discount on acquisition)		15 000
	Vendors – Tropics Ltd		305 000
	Record the purchase of net assets on amalgamation with Tropics Ltd		

3 Record the payment of the purchase consideration to the vendor.

General journal

Date	Particulars	Debit	Credit
		$	$
5 May	Vendors – Tropics Ltd	305 000	
	Cash at bank		130 000
	Ordinary shares		125 000
	Debentures owing to Tropics Ltd		50 000
	Record the purchase of net assets on amalgamation with Tropics Ltd		

The balance sheet of Mango Ltd after the amalgamation would be as follows:

Mango Ltd
Balance sheet as at 5 May (after amalgamation)

Assets	$	$
Cash at bank*		70 000
Debtors	15 000	
less Allowance for doubtful debts	5 000	10 000
Equipment		350 000
Total assets		430 000
Liabilities		
Creditors	40 000	
Debentures owing to Tropics Ltd	50 000	
Total liabilities		90 000
Net assets		340 000
Shareholders' equity		
Share capital		
Ordinary shares (300 000)**	325 000	
Profit and loss (Discount on acquisition)	15 000	
Total shareholders' equity		340 000

* Cash at bank equals $200 000 opening balance less $130 000 cash consideration.
** Ordinary shares equals $200 000 opening balance plus $125 000 purchase consideration.

Question 13.5

In question 13.1, Abbott Ltd, the purchasing company, absorbed the net assets of the vendor, Costello Ltd. In that question you accounted for the amalgamation from the vendor's viewpoint. The details of the amalgamation were as follows:

On 2 October, Abbott Ltd agreed to purchase the net assets of Costello Ltd for a purchase consideration comprising: $200 000 cash, plus 200 000 ordinary shares with a nominal value of $0.60 each, plus $150 000 in debentures.

The balance sheet of Costello Ltd on this date was as follows:

Costello Ltd
Balance sheet as at 2 October (before amalgamation)

Assets	$	$
Debtors	50 000	
less Allowance for doubtful debts	2 000	48 000
Machinery	600 000	
less Accumulated depreciation	148 000	452 000
Total assets		500 000
Liabilities		
Creditors		100 000
Net assets		400 000
Shareholders' equity		
Contributed equity		
Ordinary shares (800 000)		400 000

The valuation of all assets was accepted as their fair values, except equipment which was valued at $475 000.

On the same date, the balance sheet of Abbott Ltd was as follows:

Abbott Ltd
Balance sheet as at 2 October (before amalgamation)

	$
Assets	
Cash at bank	250 000
Liabilities	
Creditors	50 000
Net assets	200 000
Shareholders' equity	
Contributed equity	
Ordinary shares (400 000)	200 000

You are required to account for the amalgamation in the accounts of Abbott Ltd by preparing:
a the journal entries to record the amalgamation; and
b the balance sheet of Abbott Ltd after the amalgamation.

Question 13.6

Finn Ltd purchased the net assets of Sharks Ltd in question 13.2, in which you prepared the amalgamation entries for the vendor, Sharks Ltd. From the information relating to that question and additional information which follows, you are required to account for the amalgamation for Finn Ltd, the purchaser, by:

a recording the journal entries for the amalgamation; and
b preparing Finn Ltd's post-amalgamation balance sheet.

On 4 July, Finn Ltd agreed to purchase the net assets of Sharks Ltd. The purchase consideration comprised:
- $20 000 cash; plus
- 100 000 ordinary shares with a nominal value of $1.20 each; plus
- $60 000 in debentures.

The balance sheet of Sharks Ltd at the date of amalgamation was as follows:

Sharks Ltd
Balance sheet as at 4 July (before amalgamation)

	$	$
Assets		
Cash at bank		10 000
Inventory		20 000
Debtors	45 000	
less Allowance for doubtful debts	5 000	40 000
Government bonds		100 000
Machinery	400 000	
less Accumulated depreciation	250 000	150 000
Total assets		320 000
Liabilities		
Creditors	20 000	
Mortgage	80 000	100 000
Net assets		220 000
Shareholders' equity		
Contributed equity		
Ordinary shares (150 000)	150 000	
Preference shares (10 000)	50 000	200 000
Reserves		20 000
Total shareholders' equity		220 000

It was agreed that all assets were disclosed at their fair values, except inventory which had a fair value of $18 000.

The balance sheet of Finn Ltd was as follows:

Finn Ltd
Balance sheet as at 4 July (before amalgamation)

Assets	$
Cash at bank	30 000
Liabilities	
Creditors	20 000
Net assets	10 000
Shareholders' equity	
Contributed equity	
Ordinary shares (10 000)	10 000

Question 13.7

Old Pty Ltd had been operating for 10 years and its owners decided to cease operating. The children of the owners decided to continue the company's operations, but they wanted the business to trade under the name of New Pty Ltd.

To accommodate the operations of New Pty Ltd, the following took place:
- On 1 July, New Pty Ltd was incorporated with the allocation of five ordinary shares with a nominal value of $1 each being issued to each of its three owners. The shares were paid for on the same day.
- On 5 July, New Pty Ltd absorbed the net assets of Old Pty Ltd for a cash consideration of $250 000.
- On 10 July, Old Pty Ltd was liquidated, incurring legal costs of $5 000.

The owners of New Pty Ltd absorbed all of the assets and liabilities of Old Pty Ltd except the bank account. All assets were accepted at their book values, except debtors which had a fair value of $58 000 and property and equipment which had a fair value of $120 000. The consideration paid for the net assets was $200 000 cash.

The balance sheet of Old Pty Ltd at 1 July was as follows:

Old Pty Ltd
Balance sheet as at 1 July (before amalgamation)

Assets	$	$
Cash at bank		50 000
Inventory		40 000
Debtors		60 000
Plant and equipment	400 000	
less Accumulated depreciation	300 000	100 000
Total assets		250 000
Liabilities		
Mortgage		50 000
Net assets		200 000
Shareholders' equity		
Contributed equity		
Ordinary shares (two)	2	
Reserves	199 998	
Total shareholders' equity		200 000

You are required to prepare:
a the journal entry to incorporate New Pty Ltd on 1 July;
b the journal entries to account for the amalgamation in the books of Old Pty Ltd on 5 July;
c the post-amalgamation balance sheet of Old Pty Ltd on 5 July;
d the journal entries to account for the amalgamation in the books of New Pty Ltd on 5 July;
e the post-amalgamation balance sheet of New Pty Ltd on 5 July; and
f the journal entries to liquidate Old Pty Ltd on 10 July.

Accounting for takeovers

A takeover, unlike an amalgamation, does not acquire the net assets of another company. Instead, the company indulging in the takeover purchases shares in another company to gain control of that company. As a consequence of the purchasing company gaining control, the purchasing company has effective ownership of the net assets of the other company.

The company that has had its share capital purchased by another company continues to use its net assets in the pursuit of profit for its shareholders – that is, the other company.

The company that has purchased the other company's shares also continues to pursue its separate business objectives with the net assets at its disposal (which do not include the assets of the company over which it has control).

Where a company has acquired an investment in another company which gives it control over the other company, the controlling company is required to present consolidated reports in accordance with AASB 1024: Consolidated Accounts.

Accounting for a takeover by the purchasing company

When a company takes over another company, it purchases the shares in the other company directly from the existing shareholders of that company. Thus, the ownership of the shares changes hands and gives the purchaser an investment in the company. To purchase the shares from the existing shareholders in order to obtain the investment, the purchaser must make a cash payment to the existing shareholders. Hence the cash reserves of the purchaser are reduced and an investment is acquired.

ILLUSTRATION

On 6 April, Dargo Ltd purchased all the issued and paid-up capital of 100 000 ordinary shares in River Ltd. The shares were trading on the stock exchange at $1.50 each, with Dargo Ltd paying $1.60 per share. In addition, Dargo Ltd paid $1 000 in brokerage and related costs.

The cost of acquisition is calculated as follows:

	$
Ordinary shares (100 000 × $1.60 each)	160 000
Brokerage costs	1 000
Cost of acquisition	161 000

The entry in the books of Dargo Ltd to account for the purchase of the investment in River Ltd would be as follows:

Cash payments journal

Date	Particulars	Chq. no.	Sundries	Bank
			$	$
6 Apr	Investment in River Ltd		161 000	161 000

The resulting balance sheet of Dargo Ltd would include the following:

Non-current assets	$
Investments	
Investment in River Ltd	161 000

In a takeover, the ownership of the shares of the company being purchased changes hands, with the cash being paid directly to the individual shareholders of the company. Consequently, there is no effect on the accounting records of the purchasing company. The only change that the purchasing company must record is in the Members' Register, where the registered owners of the shares must be changed from the shareholders who sold their shares to the purchasing company.

Question 13.8

On 3 August, Craven Ltd acquired all of the issued shares of Wally Ltd in a takeover. Wally Ltd has issued 200 000 shares, which Craven Ltd purchased at $1.75 each. Brokerage and related costs amounted to $15 000.

You are required to:

a   prepare the journal entry in the books of Craven Ltd to account for the takeover; and
b   show the investments section of Craven Ltd's balance sheet after the takeover.

CHAPTER 14
ACCOUNTING FOR FOREIGN CURRENCY TRANSLATIONS

Objectives

Upon satisfactory completion of this chapter you should be able to:

- translate foreign currency transactions to Australian currency;
- prepare journal entries to record foreign currency transactions;
- prepare adjustments at balance date to account for movements in foreign currency;
- record payments for foreign debt;
- prepare journal entries to capitalise foreign exchange rate variations; and
- prepare the consolidations for foreign investments.

Introduction

Australian companies are required to report their financial transactions in Australian currency. This does not pose a problem for those Australian companies that conduct their business solely within Australia. However, Australian companies that transact with other countries may conduct business in the currency of other countries.

Where an Australian company transacts in the currency of another country it may need to convert or translate the value of the transaction into Australian currency. This translation process requires the overseas currency to be converted to Australian dollars at the exchange rate between the two countries at the time of the transaction.

In addition to translating the value of the currency at the transaction date, an Australian company that owes money to the foreign company at the date of preparing its financial statements is required to convert the value of the debt to the foreign currency at the date of reporting.

The exchange rates between Australia and other countries are seldom constant, and significant variations in exchange rates can occur between the dates of incurring the debt and reporting on that debt. These variations in exchange rates will give rise to the Australian company making gains or losses on the translation in the value of the foreign debt.

This chapter examines the procedures and techniques used by Australian companies that transact in foreign currencies to ensure that the transactions are recorded in the Australian currency and that the gains or losses arising on these transactions at the date of reporting are brought to account.

Translating foreign currency transactions

Accounting Standard AASB 121: The Effects of Changes in Foreign Exchange Rates requires Australian companies to determine and apply a functional currency to overseas transactions. This is defined in AASB 121 as 'the currency of the primary economic environment in which the entity operates'.

For an Australian company this would mean recording foreign currency transactions in Australian currency using the exchange rate in effect at the date of the transaction.

When an Australian company enters into a contract with a foreign company and the resulting payment is made or received in Australian currency there is no need for the transaction to be translated in Australian currency. However, if payment is made in the currency of the foreign country the Australian company will need to translate the transaction to Australian currency.

Translation to Australian currency

Australian companies trading with foreign countries may be required by the contract to make payment in the currency of the foreign country, rather than Australian currency. Thus, the value of the transaction expressed in terms of foreign currency will not be the same value as in Australian currency, given the variation in the two countries' exchange rates.

For example, if an Australian company purchased machinery from the United States with a value of USD 100 000, it would be necessary for the Australian company to express the value of the machinery in Australian currency, referred to as AUD. If the exchange rate between the two countries at the date of the transaction was AUD1 is equal to USD0.50, then the value of the Australian machine in AUD can be determined by the following formula.

$$AUD = \frac{\text{Foreign value of transaction}}{\$0.50}$$

$$AUD = \frac{USD 100\ 000}{\$0.50}$$

$$AUD = 200\ 000$$

Question 14.1

The following table shows the transactions made between an Australian importer and various countries and the exchange rate between the countries at the date of the transaction. You are required to translate each transaction into Australian currency.

Country of transaction	Value of transaction	Exchange rate AUD
United States	USD500 000	USD0.625
United Kingdom	GBP360 000	GBP0.38
New Zealand	NZD250 000	NZD1.20
Japan	JPY800 000	JPY62
Italy	EUR93 750	EUR0.60

Question 14.2

An Australian company is considering the purchase of stock from an overseas supplier. There are three suppliers who have tendered for the supply contract. Their respective quotes and exchange rates are as follows:

Supplier's origin	Price quoted	Exchange rate AUD
Hong Kong	HKD400 000	HKD3.97
Singapore	SGD100 000	SGD0.894
Indonesia	IDR500 000 000	IDR5 200

You are required to determine the suppliers in order of lowest price.

Translation to foreign currency

Just as foreign currency transactions can be converted to Australian currency, Australian currency transactions can be converted to foreign currency.

In the previous section, foreign currency transactions expressed the value of the Australian currency in terms of a foreign currency. For example, AUD1 = USD0.50, or one Australian dollar will buy 50 US cents. Hence, if an American company had made sales in the United States of USD100 000, this would be equal to AUD200 000 (USD100 000 / USD0.50).

The Australian dollar can also be expressed from the foreign country's point of view. For example, USD1 = AUD2, or one US dollar will buy two Australian dollars.

If an Australian company had made sales in Australia of $200 000 and the amount had to be converted to US currency at USD1 = AUD2, this would be equal to USD100 000 (AUD200 000/AUD2).

To calculate the reciprocal value of the Australian exchange rate, the following formula can be applied.

$$\text{Reciprocal exchange rate} = \frac{1}{\text{Exchange rate}}$$

For example, if AUD1 = USD0.50,

$$\text{then the USD} = \frac{1}{\text{USD0.50}}$$
$$= \text{AUD2.00}$$

The reciprocal exchange rate would be applied when converting the Australian currency into equivalent foreign currency. For example, an Australian company owes an American company AUD200 000 when AUD1 = USD0.50. This is to be paid in US currency. The Australian company would need to obtain USD100 000 [AUD200 000/(1/USD0.50)].

The following table shows the value of foreign currencies converted to Australian dollars and their reciprocal rates when translated in Australian dollars.

Currency	To Australian dollars	In Australian dollars
United States dollar	USD0.49130	AUD2.03542
Japanese yen	JPY60.84529	AUD0.01644
New Zealand dollar	NZD1.18758	AUD0.84205
British pound	GBP0.34543	AUD2.89497
Indonesian rupiah	IDR5 250	AUD0.0001904
Euro	EUR0.60	AUD1.66667

Question 14.3

Calculate the value of each of the following transactions in the value of the overseas currency.

Value of transaction	Exchange rate AUD
AUD500 000	USD0.45
AUD750 000	GBP0.38
AUD250 000	NZD1.20
AUD100 000	JPY62
AUD20 000	EUR0.60

Accounting for foreign currency transactions

To account for foreign currency transactions there are three distinct steps. These are as follows:
1 Record the transaction in Australian currency at the transaction date, referred to as the spot exchange rate.
2 Adjust the financial statements at balance date to record the current Australian values of amounts owing on overseas transactions.
3 Record the settlement of the overseas liability in Australian currency at the date of settlement.

Recording a foreign currency transaction

When translating a foreign currency transaction in Australian currency it is necessary to translate not only the value of the merchandise but also the methods of settling the transaction. This may be in the form of a cash settlement, making future payments, or a combination of both.

When the entire transaction has been translated into Australian currency a journal entry can then be made to record the transaction.

ILLUSTRATION

Able Ltd, an Australian company, has purchased equipment from an American company. The contract specified a price (including transportation and insurance) of USD500 000 with a deposit of USD100 000 and the balance payable in six months.

At the date of signing the sale contract between the two companies the exchange rate was USD0.625. That is, one Australian dollar can be exchanged for $0.625 US cents.

Hence the transaction will translate to AUD800 000 (USD500 000 / 0.625).

The Australian value of the deposit of USD100 000 translates to AUD160 000 (USD100 000 / 0.625).

The balance owing on the contract of USD400 000 will be paid in six months. This amount is equal to AUD640 000 (USD400 000 / 0.625).

Able Ltd would therefore record the purchase of the equipment on the date of signing the contract as follows:

General journal

Date	Particulars	Debit	Credit
		$	$
	Equipment	800 000	
	Bank		160 000
	Bills payable		640 000
	To record purchase of equipment, deposit paid and balance owing		

Question 14.4

On 1 May, Port Ltd, an Australian company, entered into a contract with a Japanese manufacturing supplier to purchase machinery valued at JPY10 000 000. An additional cost of JPY900 000 was included to cover insurance and transport costs.

The contract required Port Ltd to pay the costs of insurance and transport in cash and to make a deposit equal to 25% of the contracted amount. The balance is payable when the shipment arrives in Australia in three months.

The exchange rate between the two countries is JPY65 to the AUD.

You are required to prepare the journal entry in Port Ltd's books to record the purchase of the asset.

Question 14.5

You are required to prepare the general journal entry to record the asset purchase in the following contract between Hoddle Pty Ltd, an Australian company, and a German supplier of Mercedes-Benz cars.

Hoddle Ltd has contracted directly with the German supplier to provide a specially built Mercedes at a cost of EUR96 050. An additional EUR2 500 is to be included to cover shipping costs.

The contract was signed on 15 March and required a deposit of 50% of the total contract price. The balance is to be paid in two instalments on 1 July and 1 September. The exchange rate on 15 March was EUR0.60 to the AUD.

Reporting foreign currency transactions at balance date

When an Australian company enters into a foreign currency transaction it may not settle the account in full at the date of the transaction, necessitating the recording of a liability in respect of the unpaid amount. This amount will be paid at a future date. Where the payment date occurs after the end-of-period reporting date, the balance sheet will show the liability in respect of the overseas transaction.

AASB 121 requires monetary items such as liabilities in respect of overseas transactions to be reported in the balance sheet at the reporting date at the closing exchange rate applicable at the date of preparing the statement (the spot rate)

The recording of an overseas liability at the spot rate will result in the company bringing to account either an exchange rate gain or loss on the overseas transaction. This will result from the difference in the exchange rates used to bring the liability to account at the transaction date and the spot rate used at the balance date to adjust the value of the overseas liability.

When a gain or loss on a foreign currency transaction is brought to account, AASB 121 requires the difference to be included in the calculation of annual profit and loss.

ILLUSTRATION

On 1 May, Able Ltd, an Australian company, had purchased equipment from an American company for USD500 000 with a deposit of USD100 000 and the balance payable in six months. The exchange rate at the transaction date was AUD1 = USD0.625.

Able Ltd recorded the following journal entry in respect of the transaction.

General journal

Date	Particulars	Debit	Credit
		$	$
1 May	Equipment	800 000	
	Bank		160 000
	Bills payable		640 000
	To record purchase of equipment, deposit paid and balance owing		

At the end of the financial year, the date of reporting, the exchange rate was AUD1 = USD0.60. This is USD0.025 less than the transaction date. Consequently, the liability in respect of the overseas transaction will be different, necessitating an adjustment to the bill payable.

The adjustment amount is calculated by recalculating the bill payable at the different exchange rates and determining the difference – that is:

	Transaction date	Balance date
Overseas liability	USD400 000	USD400 000
Exchange rate	USD0.625	USD0.60
Australian currency	AUD640 000	AUD666 667

Bill payable	as at 1 May	$640 000
	as at 30 June	$666 667
Increase in bill payable		$26 667

The adjustment reveals that as a result of the decrease in the exchange rate the company's debt on the bill payable has increased by $26 667. Therefore, the company must increase the value of the bill payable on its accounts and bring to account a loss arising from the foreign exchange transaction. This would be recorded as follows:

General journal

Date	Particulars	Debit	Credit
		$	$
30 June	Foreign exchange loss	26 667	
	Bills payable		26 667
	To record increase in bill payable arising at balance date as a result of a fall in the exchange rate from USD0.625 to USD0.60		

The foreign exchange loss represents an expense on the overseas transaction in the current year and must be closed to the profit and loss account as follows:

General journal

Date	Particulars	Debit	Credit
		$	$
30 June	Profit and loss	26 667	
	Foreign exchange loss		26 667
	To transfer the expense to profit and loss		

At the reporting date the balance sheet would show the following:

Able Ltd
Balance sheet as at 30 June (Extract)

Current liabilities	$
Bills payable	666 667

Question 14.6

The following information has been taken from question 14.4. You are required to:

a prepare the appropriate journal entries at 30 June to record any foreign exchange profits or losses; and
b prepare the current liabilities section of the balance sheet as at 30 June.

On 1 May, Port Ltd, an Australian company, entered into a contract with a Japanese manufacturing supplier to purchase machinery valued at JPY10 000 000. An additional cost of JPY900 000 was included to cover insurance and transport costs.

The contract required the Port Ltd to pay the costs of insurance and transport in cash and to make a deposit equal to 25% of the contracted amount. The balance is payable when the shipment arrives in Australia in three months.

The exchange rate between the two countries at the transaction date was JPY65 to the AUD. At the date of reporting, the exchange rate was JPY62.5 to the AUD.

Question 14.7

In question 14.5, Hoddle Pty Ltd, an Australian company, on 15 March contracted a German Mercedes-Benz supplier to provide a specially built Mercedes at a cost of EUR96 050. An additional EUR2 500 was to be paid to cover shipping costs.

The contract was signed and required a deposit of 50% of the total contract price. The balance is to be paid in two instalments on 1 July and 1 September. The exchange rate on 15 March was EUR0.60 to the AUD. At balance date, 30 June, the exchange rate was EUR0.6152 to the AUD.

You are required to:

a prepare the appropriate journal entries at 30 June to record any foreign exchange profit or loss; and
b prepare the current liabilities section of the balance sheet as at 30 June.

Payment of overseas debts

When an overseas transaction is paid, it is necessary to translate the amount owing to Australian currency at the exchange rate applicable at that date. As a result of fluctuating exchange rates, a gain or loss on the transaction may result. The gain or loss arising at this date should be reported as an item of profit or loss in the year incurred.

ILLUSTRATION

Able Ltd had contracted with an American company on 1 May to purchase equipment costing USD500 000 with a deposit of USD100 000 on this date, the balance payable in six months. The exchange rate at the transaction date was AUD1 = USD0.625.

On the transaction date, Able Ltd brought to account a liability of AUD640 000 in respect of its debt of USD400 000 (USD400 000 / USD0.625).

Bill payable

Date	Details	Debit	Credit	Balance
1 May	Equipment		640 000	640 000 Cr

On 30 June, the reporting date, the exchange rate had fallen to USD0.60. On this date Able Ltd increased the amount owing by $26 667, to $666 667 in respect of the USD400 000 debt (USD400 000 / USD0.60). As a result, a foreign exchange loss of $26 667 was brought to account.

Bill payable

Date	Details	Debit	Credit	Balance
1 May	Equipment		640 000	640 000 Cr
30 June	Foreign currency loss		26 667	666 667 Cr

On 1 November, the date of payment, the exchange rate had risen from USD0.60 to USD0.606. The USD400 000 debt was now worth AUD660 066 (USD400 000 / USD0.606), a decrease of AUD6 601.

On this date Able Ltd made a payment of $660 066 and brought to account a foreign exchange gain of $6 601. Able Ltd recorded the following journal entry in respect of this transaction.

General journal

Date	Particulars	Debit	Credit
		$	$
1 Nov	Bill payable	666 667	
	Foreign exchange gain		6 601
	Bank		660 066
	To record the payment of the bill payable and recognition of foreign exchange loss		
	Foreign exchange gain	6 601	
	Profit and loss		6 601
	Transfer of gain on foreign exchange		

The bill payable account in the general ledger would appear as follows:

Bill payable

Date	Details	Debit	Credit	Balance
1 May	Equipment		640 000	640 000 Cr
30 June	Foreign currency loss		26 667	666 667 Cr
1 Nov	Foreign currency gain	6 601		660 066 Cr
	Bank	660 066		Nil

Question 14.8

Mondo Ltd imported goods from the United States during the year. On the balance date, Mondo Ltd owed USD600 000. On this date the AUD was worth USD0.60.

Mondo Ltd made full payment for the debt on 30 October when the AUD was worth USD0.50. You are required to prepare the journal entries at 31 October.

Question 14.9

You are required to:
a   prepare the appropriate journal entries in the books of Port Ltd to settle the foreign exchange transaction; and
b   show the bill payable account.

	Transaction date	Balance date	Payment date
Date	1 May	30 June	1 August
Amount owing	JPY7 500 000	JPY7 500 000	JPY7 500 000
Exchange rate	JPY65	JPY62.5	JPY64

Question 14.10

In questions 14.5 and 14.7, Hoddle Pty Ltd, an Australian company, had contracted a German Mercedes-Benz supplier to provide a specially built Mercedes at a cost of EUR96 050. An additional EUR2 500 was to be paid to cover shipping costs.

The contract was signed on 15 March and required a deposit of 50% of the total contract price. The balance is to be paid in two instalments on 1 July and 1 September.

The exchange rates at the respective dates were as follows:

15 March:	EUR0.60 to the AUD
30 June:	EUR0.6152 to the AUD
1 July:	EUR0.6151 to the AUD
1 September:	EUR0.6159 to the AUD

You are required to:
a   prepare the appropriate journal entries to settle the overseas account on the respective payment dates; and
b   show the bill payable account.

Question 14.11

From the following information you are required to prepare all journal entries relating to the foreign currency transaction.

Karter Ltd of Melbourne entered into a contract with an Indian carpet supplier on 1 March when the exchange rate was AUD1 = INR23.8 (Indian rupees). The contract price, including shipping costs, was 4 000 000 rupees. A deposit of 500 000 rupees was paid. On 1 June another payment was made of 2 000 000 rupees. The exchange rate on this date was AUD1 = INR25.

On 30 June the exchange rate was AUD1 = INR24.4.

Karter Ltd made the final payment on 30 September when the exchange rate was AUD1 = INR23.9.

Capitalisation of exchange rate variations

In the previous illustrations Australian companies acquired supplies, stock or assets ready for immediate use from overseas. Situations may arise where the Australian company enters into a financing arrangement with an overseas supplier to provide an asset over a longer term.

Where this occurs the accounting standard allows the exchange rate losses or gains to be charged against the value of the asset – that is, the variation arising from the exchange rate fluctuation is capitalised, instead of being charged to the profit and loss account. This is similar to the capitalisation of interest on a loan against the value of an asset.

The accounting standard specifies that exchange rate variations can be included in the cost of the asset, so long as the asset meets the definition of a 'qualifying asset'.

A qualifying asset is defined as an asset under construction and being made ready for future productive use or which is being constructed under a construction contract.

ILLUSTRATION

On 1 July 2006 Jarvis Ltd contracted an American company, Amtrak Ltd, to build a special-purpose cutting machine on its Australian premises using components designed in the United States. Jarvis Ltd has determined that the asset meets the criteria of a qualifying asset under AASB 121: Foreign Currency Translation and has decided to capitalise all costs associated with the project.

The contract price was USD840 000. An immediate payment of USD 126 000 is required followed by a payment of USD400 000 on 30 June 2007 and the balance of USD314 000 on 30 June 2008.

Interest is to be paid on the balance owing on 30 June each year charged at 8% p.a.

The exchange rates on the effective dates were:

1 July 2006:	USD0.560
30 June 2007:	USD0.500
30 June 2008:	USD0.640

On signing the contract and making a payment, the following entries would be prepared.

Machinery cost:	USD840 000 / 0.56 =	$1 500 000
Bank (deposit):	USD126 000 / 0.56 =	$225 000
Amtrak (loan):	USD714 000 / 0.56 =	$1 275 000

General journal

Date	Particulars	Debit	Credit
		$	$
2006	Machinery	1 500 000	
1 July	Bank		225 000
	Amtrak Ltd (loan)		1 275 000
	To record loan and deposit on machine		

At the end of the second year, 30 June 2007:
- Interest must be paid: (USD714 000 × 0.08) / USD.50 = $114 240. The amount owing at balance date must be adjusted – that is:
  - (USD714 000 / USD0.56) = $1 275 000
  - –(USD714 000 / USD0.50) = $1 428 000 = Loss $153 000.
- A payment must be made: (USD400 000 / USD0.50) = $800 000.

The journal entries to capitalise these costs and make the payment are as follows:

General journal

Date	Particulars	Debit	Credit
2007	Machinery	114 240	
30 June	Bank		114 240
	Capitalisation of interest on loan		
	Machinery	153 000	
	Amtrak Ltd		153 000
	Capitalisation of exchange rate loss		
	Amtrak Ltd	800 000	
	Bank		800 000
	Scheduled payment of overseas loan		

The respective ledger accounts at 30 June 2007 would appear as follows:

General ledger

Date	Particulars	Debit	Credit	Balance
Machinery				
1 July 2006	Amtrak Ltd	1 500 000		1 500 000 Dr
30 June 2007	Bank (interest capitalisation)	114 240		1 614 240 Dr
	Amtrak Ltd (foreign exchange loss)	153 000		1 767 240 Dr
Amtrak Ltd				
1 July 2006	Machinery		1 500 000	1 500 000 Cr
	Bank	225 000		1 275 000 Cr
30 June 2007	Machinery (foreign exchange loss)		153 000	1 428 000 Cr
	Bank	800 000		628 000 Cr

At the end of the first year, 30 June 2008:
- Interest must be paid: (USD314 000 × 0.08) / USD0.64 = $39 250.
- The amount owing at balance date must be adjusted – that is:
  - (USD314 000 / USD0.50) = $628 000
  - –(USD314 000 / USD0.64) = $490 625 = Gain $137 375.
- A payment must be made: (USD314 000 / USD0.64) = $490 625.

The journal entries to capitalise these costs and record the payment are as follows:

General journal

Date	Particulars	Debit	Credit
		$	$
2008 30 June	Machinery	39 250	
	Bank		39 250
	Capitalisation of interest on loan		
	Amtrak Ltd	137 375	
	Machinery		137 375
	Capitalisation of exchange rate gain		
	Amtrak Ltd	490 625	
	Bank		490 625
	Scheduled payment of overseas loan		

The machinery account and the liability to Amtrak Ltd account reflecting these entries would appear as follows:

General ledger

Date	Particulars	Debit	Credit	Balance
	Machinery			
1 July 2006	Amtrak Ltd	1 500 000		1 500 000 Dr
30 June 2007	Bank (interest capitalisation)	114 240		1 614 240 Dr
	Amtrak Ltd (foreign exchange loss)	153 000		1 767 240 Dr
30 June 2008	Bank (interest capitalisation)	39 250		1 806 490 Dr
	Amtrak Ltd (foreign exchange gain)		137 375	1 669 115 Cr
	Amtrak Ltd			
1 July 2006	Machinery		1 500 000	1 500 000 Cr
	Bank	225 000		1 275 000 Cr
30 June 2007	Machinery (foreign exchange loss)		153 000	1 428 000 Cr
	Bank	800 000		628 000 Cr
30 June 2008	Machinery (foreign exchange gain)	137 375		496 025 Cr
	Bank	496 025		Nil

Question 14.12

From the following information you are required to prepare the journal entries recording the foreign currency transactions over the contract term.

Sable Ltd, an Australian company, entered into a construction contract with an American consortium named Juggernaut Ltd to build a tunnel under a river in Melbourne. The directors of Sable Ltd determined that the construction contract complied with the qualifying asset definition in the accounting standards and all costs were capitalised.

The details of the contract were as follows:
- Contract signed on 1 April 2006 for USD5 million. A down-payment of USD2 million was made on this date when the exchange rate was USD0.52 to the AUD.
- The contract was to be completed in 18 months. A payment of USD1.5 million was made on 30 June 2006 when the AUD was worth USD0.50. In addition, interest was charged on the outstanding balance at 5% p.a.
- On 30 June 2007 interest was again charged at 5% p.a. The exchange rate was USD0.48 to the AUD on this date.
- The final payment was made on 30 September 2007. Interest was charged at 5% p.a. The exchange rate was USD0.51 to the AUD.

Question 14.13

Jasper Ltd contracted a New Zealand company, White Cloud Ltd, to build a warehouse at its Sydney headquarters.

Jasper Ltd's directors determined that the contract met the requirements of a qualifying asset under the accounting standards and insisted on all appropriate costs being capitalised.

From the information that follows you are required to show the ledger accounts for the warehouse and White Cloud Ltd in the books of Jasper Ltd.
- The contract was signed on 1 January 2006 for NZD1 000 000.
- Interest is paid every January at 10% p.a. (Interest is not accrued at balance date.)
- Payments were made as follows:
    - 1 January 2006 NZD250 000
    - 1 January 2007 NZD500 000
    - 1 January 2008 NZD250 000
- Exchange rates were as follows:
    - 1 January 2006 NZD1.10
    - 30 June 2006 NZD1.15
    - 1 January 2007 NZD1.12
    - 30 June 2007 NZD1.05
    - 1 January 2008 NZD1.00

Accounting for foreign investments

Australian companies may expand their operations by establishing subsidiary companies in foreign countries or by investing in foreign companies.

Where an Australian company holds a controlling investment in a foreign country it will need to present group accounts which include the investment in the foreign operation. Before the accounts of the foreign operation are consolidated with the accounts of the Australian company it is necessary to translate the accounts of the foreign entity into Australian currency in accordance with AASB 121: The Effects of Changes in Foreign Exchange Rates.

The standard requires an Australian company that has an investment in a foreign company to report its investment in that foreign company using the **presentation currency** at the time of preparing the financial statements. According to AASB 121: 'Presentation currency is the currency in which the financial report is presented.'

An investment in a foreign country by an Australian company could take many forms. These may include:

- a self-sustaining foreign investment which operates independently, both financially and operationally, from the parent company and whose operations do not normally expose the company or group to foreign exchange gains or losses. An Australian company may, for example, have a controlling interest in a New Zealand company; however, the Australian company may allow the New Zealand company to operate completely independently from the Australian company; and
- an integrated foreign investment whose existence is financially and operationally integrated with the investing company and, as a result, exposes the investing company to foreign exchange gains or losses. An Australian company may, for example, have a controlling interest in a New Zealand company where the Australian company finances the operations of the New Zealand company, trades with that company and makes decisions on behalf of that company.

Regardless of the type of foreign investment, AASB 121 requires the financial statements of the foreign investment to be translated from that country's functional currency to the presentation currency of the Australian company – that is, the Australian currency.

The accounting standard requires the following to be applied when converting the financial currency of one country to the presentation currency of another:

a Assets and liabilities are to be translated at the exchange rate current at the date of preparing the balance sheet.

b Revenue and expense items are to be translated at the exchange rates current at the transaction date. *(In order to account for variations in the exchange rate occurring throughout the year, an average exchange rate could be applied.)*

AASB 121 does not provide any direction on the exchange rates to be applied when converting equity at the date of preparing the financial reports. The former accounting standard, ASRB 1012: Foreign Currency Translation, required the following methods of translation to be applied:

c Owner's equity at the date of investment, including share capital at acquisition and pre-acquisition reserves, is translated at the exchange rate current at the date of acquisition.

d Post-acquisition movements in owner's equity, other than retained profits (losses), shall be translated at the exchange rates current at the dates of those movements, except that where a movement represents a transfer between items within owner's equity, the movement shall be translated at the exchange rate current at the date that the amount transferred was first included in owner's equity.

e Distributions from retained profits (that is, dividends paid or proposed, or their equivalent) are translated at the exchange rates current at the dates when the distributions were proposed (or, where the approval of equity holders is not sought, at the dates when the distributions were declared).

f Post-acquisition movements in retained profits or accumulated losses, because of transfers from the profit and loss account, are brought to account by applying the exchange rates current at the transaction date *(or an average exchange rate for the reporting year).*

AASB 121 also requires gains and losses arising from exchange rate differences on consolidation to be brought to account as part of equity. An account called the foreign currency translation reserve shall be used in this text for this purpose.

Once the accounts of the foreign investment have been translated to Australian currency they can be combined with the parent company's accounts in a consolidated worksheet.

ILLUSTRATION

Aussie Ltd purchased a New Zealand company called Kiwi Ltd on 1 July 2005. Kiwi Ltd was permitted to trade in its own right and met the criteria of a self-sustaining foreign operation. On the date of acquisition, Kiwi Ltd's balance sheet was as follows:

Assets		Equities	
Bank	$30 000	Ordinary shares	$110 000
Stock	$25 000	Retained profits	$40 000
Equipment	$175 000	Loan	$80 000

The relevant exchange rates to enable a translation of the accounts of Kiwi Ltd in Australian currency are as follows:

Date	Rate	Relevance of date
1 July 2005	NZD2.00	Date of acquisition
15 March 2006	NZD1.60	Interim dividend declared
30 June 2006	NZD1.80	End of reporting period
25 June 2006	NZD1.65	Closing stock valued
Average 2005–6	NZD1.70	Average rate for year

The following worksheet shows the financial statements of Kiwi Ltd and the conversion to Australian currency in accordance with the requirements of the accounting standard.

Account	Kiwi Ltd NZD	Exchange rate NZD	Kiwi Ltd NZD	Reference to accounting standard
Sales	600 000	1.70	352 941	f
less Cost of sales				
Stock 1 July 2005	25 000	2.00	12 500	f
Purchases	360 000	1.70	211 765	f
	385 000		224 265	
Stock end	20 000	1.65	12 122	f
Cost of sales	365 000		212 143	
Gross profit	235 000		140 798	
Other expenses	94 000	1.70	55 294	f
Profit (b/tax)	141 000		85 504	
Income tax expense	42 300	1.70	24 882	f
Profit (a/tax)	98 700		60 622	
Retained profits 1 July 2005	40 000	2.00	20 000	c
Total funds available for distribution	138 700		80 622	
Interim dividend	25 000	1.60	15 625	e

Final dividend	50 000	1.80	27 778	e
Retained profits 30 June 2006	63 700		37 219	
Ordinary shares	110 000	2.00	55 000	c
Foreign currency translation reserve		Note 1	4 282	
Creditors	40 000	1.80	22 222	a
Dividends payable	50 000	1.80	27 778	a
Loan	60 000	1.80	33 333	a
Total equities	**323 700**		**179 834**	
Bank	63 700	1.80	35 389	a
Stock on hand	20 000	1.80	11 111	a
Debtors	50 000	1.80	27 778	a
Equipment	190 000	1.80	105 556	a
Total assets	**323 700**		**179 834**	

Note 1 Foreign currency translation reserve

The foreign currency translation reserve account reflects the gains and losses arising on the translation of the New Zealand currency to the Australian currency at the different exchange rates. The reserve account can be determined by analysing the changes in the accounts from the date of acquisition to the date of reporting. This includes three significant translations. These are:

1. the translation of shareholders' equity since the date of acquisition;
2. the translation of the amounts deriving profits from the date of acquisition; and
3. the translation of amounts distributed to the parent company as dividends.

The calculations to prove the foreign currency translation reserve amount in the illustration are as follows:

1. *Shareholders' funds at the date of acquisition comprised:*

   Ordinary shares $110 000
   Retained shares $40 000
   $150 000   valued at 30 June 2006   ÷ $1.80 $83 334
              valued at date of acquisition ÷ $2.00 $75 000 $8 334 gain

   (A gain is recognised, as the value of the net assets has risen.)

2. *Translation of profits from date of acquisition:*

   Profit for the reporting period 1 July 2005 to 30 June 2006

   $98 700   valued after translation on the statement $60 621
             valued at 30 June 2006   ÷ $1.80 $54 833   ($5 788) loss

   (A loss is recognised, as the value of translated profits has fallen.)

3   *Distribution of profits:*

Interim dividends

$25 000	valued at 30 June 2006	÷ $1.80	$13 889	
	valued at 15 March 2006	÷ $1.60	$15 625	$1 736 gain

(A gain is recognised, as the value of dividends has fallen.)

Net foreign currency gain   **$4 282**

Note: Final dividends are not included in the calculation, as the final dividend (Dr) and the corresponding dividends payable (Cr) are both converted at the same exchange rate, which does not cause a currency variation.

The purpose of translating the accounts of the self-sustaining foreign investment into Australian currency is to allow for the consolidation of the accounts of the parent company with the foreign investment in accordance with the Australian accounting standards.

The following consolidation worksheet illustrates the consolidation of the accounts of Aussie Ltd and Kiwi Ltd after the accounts of Kiwi Ltd were translated to Australian currency.

Consolidated worksheet as at 30 June 2006

Account	Aussie Ltd AUD	Kiwi Ltd NZD	Eliminations Debit	Eliminations Credit	Economic entity AUD
	$	$	$	$	$
Sales	200 000	352 941			552 941
less Cost of sales					
Stock 1 July 2005	30 000	12 500			42 500
Purchases	120 000	211 765			331 765
	150 000	224 265			374 265
Stock end	40 000	12 122			52 122
Cost of sales	110 000	212 143			322 143
Gross profit	90 000	140 798			230 798
Dividends revenue	43 403		43 403 (2)		0
	133 403	140 798			230 798
Other expenses	70 000	55 294			125 294
Profit (b/tax)	63 403	85 504			105 504
Income tax expense	19 021	24 882			43 903
Profit (a/tax)	44 382	60 622			61 601
Retained profits 1 July 2005	100 000	20 000	20 000 (1)		100 000
Total funds available for distribution	144 382	80 622			161 601
Interim dividend	30 000	15 625		15 625 (2)	30 000
Final dividend	100 000	27 778		27 778 (2)	100 000

Retained profits 30 June 2006	14 382	37 219			31 601
Ordinary shares	300 000	55 000	55 000 (1)		300 000
Foreign currency translation reserve		4 282			4 282
Creditors	50 000	22 222			72 222
Dividends payable	100 000	27 778	27 778 (2)		100 000
Loan	250 000	33 333			283 333
Total equities	**714 382**	**179 834**			**791 438**
Bank	60 000	35 389			95 389
Dividends receivable	27 778			27 778 (2)	0
Stock on hand	40 000	11 111			51 111
Debtors	100 000	27 778			127 778
Equipment	411 604	105 556			517 160
Investment in Kiwi Ltd	75 000			75 000 (1)	0
Total assets	**714 382**	**179 834**	**146 181**	**146 181**	**791 438**

Eliminations

1. Elimination of investment at date of acquisition.
2. Elimination of annual dividends.

Question 14.14

Using the following information you are required to prepare the consolidation worksheet for the Australian-owned company Global Ltd and its self-governing foreign investment located in Singapore, Sling Ltd, for the year ended 30 June 2006.

On 1 September 2005, Global Ltd acquired Sling Ltd's SGD100 000 ordinary shares and retained profits of SGD60 000.

The respective company account balances as at 30 June 2006 are as follows:

Account	Global Ltd AUD $	Sling Ltd SGD $
Sales	250 000	1 200 000
less Cost of sales		
Stock 1 September 2005	25 000	50 000
Purchases	150 000	480 000
	175 000	530 000
Stock end	30 000	70 000
Cost of sales	145 000	460 000
Gross profit	105 000	740 000
Dividends revenue	212 706	
	317 706	740 000
Other expenses	50 000	80 000
Profit (b/tax)	267 706	660 000
Income tax expense	80 312	99 000
Profit (a/tax)	187 394	561 000
Retained profits 1 September 2005	25 000	60 000
	212 394	621 000
Interim dividend	20 000	60 000
Final dividend	100 000	120 000
Retained profits 30 June 2006	92 394	441 000
Ordinary shares	250 000	100 000
Dividends payable	100 000	120 000
Liabilities	200 000	339 000
Total equities	642 394	1 000 000
Bank	20 000	56 500
Dividends receivable	139 535	
Stock on hand	30 000	70 000
Equipment	341 748	873 500
Investment in Sling Ltd	111 111	
Total assets	642 394	1 000 000

Additional information

Exchange rates	SGD
Date of acquisition	0.90
30 June 2006	0.86
Average 2005–6	0.84
At stock valuation 20 June 2006	0.85
Interim dividend 31 January 2006	0.82

Question 14.15

Seine Ltd is a self-governing European foreign investment of Murray Ltd, an Australian company. Murray Ltd acquired Seine Ltd on 1 July 2005 when Seine Ltd had the following share capital:

Ordinary shares	EUR450 000
Retained profits	EUR150 000

From the information that follows you are required to prepare the consolidated worksheet for Murray Ltd and Seine Ltd in Australian currency.

The appropriate exchange rates for the AUD and EUR were as follows:

Exchange rates	EUR
1 July 2005	0.60
3 June 2006	0.58
Average 2005–6	0.59
At stock valuation June 2006	0.60

Account balances for the year ended 30 June 2006 were as follows:

Account	Murray Ltd AUD $	Seine Ltd EUR $
Sales	350 000	1 180 000
less Cost of sales		
Stock 1 July 2005	15 000	118 000
Purchases	210 000	472 000
	225 000	590 000
Stock end	20 000	148 000
Cost of sales	205 000	442 000
Gross profit	145 000	738 000
Dividends revenue	431 034	
	576 034	738 000
Other expenses	30 000	78 667
Profit (b/tax)	546 034	659 333
Income tax expense	146 914	65 933
Profit (a/tax)	399 120	593 400
Retained profits 1 July 2005	15 000	150 000
Total funds available for distribution	414 120	743 400
Interim dividend	50 000	0
Final dividend	200 000	250 000
Retained profits 30 June 2006	164 120	493 400
Ordinary shares	900 000	450 000
Dividends payable	200 000	250 000
Liabilities	500 000	320 000
Total equities	1 764 120	1 513 400
Bank	150 000	112 000
Dividends receivable	431 034	
Stock on hand	20 000	148 000
Machinery	163 086	1 253 400
Investment in Seine Ltd	1 000 000	
Total assets	1 764 120	1 513 400

Question 14.16

Harvey Ltd is a self-governing Australian company owned by an American company, USA Ltd. The American company purchased all the shares in the Australian company on 1 January 2004. On this date Harvey Ltd's shareholders' equity included AUD250 000 in ordinary shares and AUD50 000 in retained profits.

You are required to translate the accounts of Harvey Ltd for the year ended 30 June 2006 to American currency in accordance with the Australian accounting standards, to assist USA Ltd in consolidating the respective accounts for the year.

The appropriate exchange rates for the AUD were as follows:

Exchange rates	AUD
Date of acquisition	0.50
1 July 2005	0.60
30 June 2006	0.65
Average 2005–6	0.63
At stock valuation June 2006	0.66
Interim dividend 31 January 2005	0.62

Account balances of Harvey Ltd as at 30 June 2006

Account	Harvey Ltd AUD $
Sales	800 000
less Cost of sales	
Stock start	50 000
Purchases	480 000
	530 000
Stock end	60 000
Cost of sales	470 000
Gross profit	330 000
Other expenses	100 000
Profit (b/tax)	230 000
Income tax expense	55 000
Profit (a/tax)	175 000
Retained profits at start	75 000
	250 000
Interim dividend	40 000
Final dividend	100 000
Retained profits at end	110 000
Ordinary shares	250 000
Dividends payable	100 000
Liabilities	800 000
Total equities	1 260 000
Cash on hand	160 000
Stock on hand	60 000
Machinery	1 040 000
Total assets	1 260 000

Disclosure of foreign exchange rate variations

Variations in exchange rates that give rise to either foreign exchange gains (losses) or a foreign exchange translation reserve must be disclosed in accordance with the requirements of both:

- AASB 121: The Effects of Changes in Foreign Exchange Rates; and
- AASB 101: Presentation of Financial Statements.

These accounting standards require the disclosure of a foreign currency translation reserve to be reported in the statement of changes in equity.

The following illustration of a statement of changes in equity incorporating the movements in foreign currencies under reserves would meet the requirements of AASB 101. The illustration includes the change to the foreign currency revaluation from the previous illustration.

Statement of changes in equity
for the year ended

	$	$
Share capital		
Balance at start of period		
Share capital issued		
Total share capital		
Reserves		
Translation reserve		
Balance at start of period		
Exchange differences on translating foreign operations	4 282	
Balance at end of period		
Asset revaluation reserve		
Balance at start of period		
Asset revaluation changes		
Balance at end of period		
Revenue reserves		
Balance at start of period		
Transfers to/from retained profits		
Balance at end of period		
Total reserves		
Retained profits		
Balance at start of period		
Profit for the period		
Transfers from reserves		
Total for appropriation		
Transfers to reserves		
Dividends (interim and final)		
Share issue costs		
Balance at end of period		
Total shareholders' equity		

Index

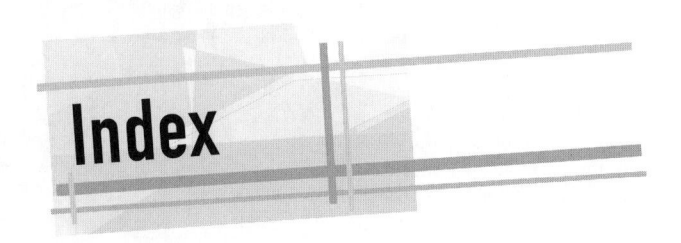

accounting records 13–14
    on liquidation 375–6, 383
accounting standards 174–81, 251–2
accruals 125, 140, 146–7, 150
    in cash flow statements 222–6
accumulated losses, amortisation 355–7
acquired goodwill 81–82
acquisition of assets 81
    above fair values 81–82
    below fair values 89–91
    cost of 395
    see also amalgamations; goodwill
adjustments for accruals 222–6
allotment money from share issue 21, 22
alteration to share capital 353
amalgamations
    accounting by purchaser 403–5
    accounting by vendor 396–9
    difference from takeovers 395
    discount on acquisition 401, 402–3
    goodwill on acquisition 401–2
    purchase consideration 395–6
    realisation account 396–9
    see also consolidated accounts
amortisation
    of accumulated losses 355–7
    of establishment costs 94–95
annual general meeting 14, 174, 251
annual leave 140, 141–2
annual profits, allocation to minority interests 340–2
annual report 174
appropriation of profits 160–5
    adjustment for 322–9
    and cash flow statements 235–7
    elimination adjustments 322–31
Articles of Association 9
asset revaluation reserves 167, 168, 242, 365–6
assets
    acquisition of 81
        above fair values 81–82
        below fair values 89–90
        cost of 395
    in amalgamations 395–406
    carrying cost 81, 118, 120
    cash 194, 195
    current assets 194–6
    disposals 320
    establishment costs as 95
    fair value of 81–82, 89–90
    intangible 95, 194–6
    inventories as 195, 196
    investments 194, 195, 196
    non-current 195, 196
        depreciation of 145–6

    disclosure of 195–9
    disposal of 275–9
    intercompany disposal of 275–8
    revaluation of 166–8
    qualifying 420
    receivables as 196
    reporting and disclosure 196–9
    revaluation of 97–9, 239
        reserves 167, 168, 242, 365–6
    statements of assets and liabilities 374–6
    in takeover 409–10
    tax base of 118–19
    treatment on liquidation 374–9
Australian Accounting Standards Board 11, 12, 174–81
Australian Business Number 8
Australian currency
    translation of foreign currency to 412–13
    translation to foreign currency 413–14
Australian Securities and Investments Commission 5, 8, 9, 11
Australian Stock Exchange 6, 11–12

balance sheet 194–212, 251
    and adjustments for accruals 222–3
    consolidated accounts with minority interests 307–8, 330–2
    examples 197–209
    format 194–5
    non-cash transactions 229–31
    overseas transactions 414–17
    reporting and asset disclosure 196–9
    reporting and equity disclosure 202–3
    reporting and liabilities disclosure 200–2
    shareholders' equity 163, 169
bonus shares
    dividend 168, 241–2
    issue 241, 365–6, 369
bookbuilding 58–9
buildings
    depreciation on 113, 149
    revaluation of 167–8
business names 2, 8
businesses
    conversion to companies 4–5, 80–92
    non-incorporated 2
    purchase price 80

calls 17, 33–40
    in advance 386
    in arrears 18
cancellation of lost share capital 355–7, 367
capacity to control subsidiaries 252
capital redemption reserves 365
capital reduction account 353
capitalisation of variations of exchange rate 419–23
carrying cost of asset 81, 118, 120

Index

carrying cost of liabilities 118–19, 121–2
cash
    as asset 194–6
    defined 215
cash at bank of liquidator 375, 383
cash distribution to shareholders 353
    on liquidation 386–7
    in takeover 409–10
cash equivalents 215
cash flow activities
    financing activities 214, 216
    investing activities 214, 215
    operating activities 214, 215, 235
cash flow statements 214–49
    adjustments for accruals 222–6
    analysis of 220
    appropriation of profits 235–7
    asset revaluations 239
    external financing 242–3
    financing activities 214, 216, 242
    format 216–17
    investing activities 215
    non-cash transactions 220
    operating activities 214, 215, 222, 235
    presentation 217–20
    share issue 241–2
cash payment to shareholders following takeover 409
Certificate of Registration 9
changes in equity statements 186–93
charges, register of 13
companies
    authorities governing 11
    constitutions 8–9
    conversion from partnership 4–5, 80–92
    conversion from proprietary to public 5–6
    conversion from sole traders 4–5, 80–87
    conversion of business to 4–5, 80–92
    establishment costs 5, 10–11, 94–5, 113
    formation of 5–6
    founding members 9, 17
    guarantee 5
    income tax rate 4
    incorporated 3
    incorporation procedures 8–9
    limited by shares 4–5
    liquidation 374–95
    no liability 5
    powers of 3
    proprietary 3–4, 5–6, 174
    public 3–6, 21–2
    registration of 3, 8, 9, 17
    Replaceable Rules 8, 9
    statutory records and registers 13–14
    unlimited liability 2, 5, 80
    see also reporting requirements
company secretary 9
consideration, purchase 395–6
consolidated accounts 251–305
    accounting standard 251–2
    capacity to control 252
    Corporations Law 260
    definition of 251–2
    with direct minority interests 307–32, 341–51

elimination adjustments 253–300, 308–26, 343–7
    with indirect minority interests 337–46
    reporting requirements 307–8, 316, 330, 343
    after takeovers 409–10
constitutions of companies 8–9
controlled entities *see* subsidiaries
conversion of business to company 4–5, 80–92
conversion of partnership to company 4–5, 80–92
conversion of proprietary company to public company 5–6
convertible notes 61
corporate reporting, *see* reporting requirements
Corporations Law 2, 5, 11–12
    on alteration to share capital 353
    on consolidated accounts 260
    incorporation of companies 8–9
    on liquidation 374–5
    reporting requirements 174
    share issue 21–2
cost of acquisition 395
creditors' claims on liquidation 379–81
currency transactions, *see* foreign currency transactions
current assets 194–6
current liabilities 194–5, 200

debentures 3, 64–65
    advantages of 62
    fixed charge 61
    floating charge 61
    interest payments on 63, 67–70
    issue of 60–1, 63, 64–7
    mortgage 61, 72
    prospectus 61, 64–5, 75–6
    redemption of 64, 70–3
    register of 13
debt 61–2
    overseas 418–19
debt capital, *see* debentures
deferred shares 19, 20
deferred tax assets 125, 154, 156
    combined with liabilities 136–8, 149–52
    reversal of 141–4
    and temporary differences 119–22, 127–30
deferred tax liabilities 131–5, 141
    combined with deferred tax assets 136–8, 149–52
    reversal of 145–9
    and temporary differences 123–5, 131–6
depreciation
    on buildings 113, 149
    on non-current assets 145–6, 178
direct minority interests 307–32, 341–51
directors 9, 13
    dividend recommendations 160, 168
    payments to 178
    reporting requirements 174
disclosure at share issue 210–11
disclosure notes 176, 177, 179
disclosure of liabilities 199–202
disclosure of non-current assets 195–9
discount on acquisition
    elimination of 260–1
    following amalgamations 401, 402–3
    and goodwill 401–3
dividends 159

bonus shares 168, 241–2
equalisation reserves 163
    final 160, 161–2, 285–8, 289–97, 299
    intercompany 280–96, 300
    interim 160–2, 283–5, 288–9, 300
    non-assessable 113, 149
    owing to shareholders on liquidation 386
    shareholder ratification of 160, 165

economic entity 251
elimination adjustments 312–16, 343–6
    for appropriation of profits 322–31
    consolidated accounts 253–300, 308–26, 343–7
    intercompany transactions 262–300, 318–21
    investment in subsidiary 253–62, 298, 308–11
    unrealised profits
        on asset disposals 320
        in closing stocks 269, 272, 298–9, 318–19
        in opening stocks 271–2, 298, 319
employee entitlements 177
entertainment expenses 113
equalisation reserves for dividends 163
equipment, as asset 195, 196
equity capital, *see* share capital
establishment costs 5, 10–11, 94–5, 113
    amortisation of 94–5
    as asset 95
    as expense 94
    as tax deduction 113
exchange rate
    capitalisation of variations 419–23
    disclosure of variations 432
    variations 412, 432
external financing 242–3
    disclosure 242–3
extraordinary revenues and expenses 177

fair value of assets 81–82
final dividends 160, 161–2, 285–8, 289–97, 299
finalisation of profit and loss account 94–109
Financial Reporting Council 12
financial reports, *see* balance sheet; income statements
financing activities 214, 216, 242
fixed charge 61
floating charge 61
foreign currency transactions
    payment of overseas debts 418–19
    presentation currency 424
    recording 414–15
    reporting requirements 415–17
    translation to Australian currency 412–13
    translation to foreign currency 413–14
    see also exchange rate; foreign investments
foreign investments 424–31
formation costs, *see* establishment costs
founding members, shares for 9, 17, 18–19, 21
fully paid shares on application 23–5

goodwill
    acquired 81–2
    in amalgamations 401–2
    discount on acquisition 401–3
    impairment of 96–7, 113, 150, 263–5, 267, 298
GST
    registration by companies 3

registration by sole traders 2
guarantee companies 5

impairment of goodwill 96, 113, 150, 263–5, 267, 298
income statements 175–9, 251
    consolidated accounts with minority interests 307–32, 337–51
    disclosure notes 176, 177, 179
    example 182–6
    extraordinary revenues and expenses 177
    formats 174–8
    and operating cash flow 222
    reconciliation of income tax 180–1
income tax
    adjustments in current period 104–6
    adjustments in next period 106–9
    calculation 103–11, 117
    company rate 4
    deferred 119–38, 149–52
    disclosure of 180–1
    non-cash transactions 229–31
    PAYG instalment system 100–11, 113
    permanent differences 113–16, 149–50
    reconciliation 180–1
    taxation loss 154–6
Income Tax Assessment Act 100, 103, 113, 117, 118
income tax expense 103, 114, 115, 127, 150, 155
income tax payable 103, 127, 150, 156
incorporation 2, 3, 8–9
indirect minority interests 337–46
intangible assets 95, 194–6
    see also goodwill
intercompany transactions 308–10
    disposal of non-current assets 275–9
    dividends 280–96, 300
    elimination adjustments 262–300, 318–21
    indebtedness and servicing 265–6, 298
    stock transactions 267–73, 298
interest payments on debentures 63, 67–70
interim dividends 160–2, 283–5, 288–9, 300
International Accounting Standards 12
International Financial Reporting Standards 12
inventories, as assets 195, 196
investing activities 214, 215
investment allowances 113–14
investments
    as assets 194, 195, 196
    foreign 424–31
    revaluation of 97–8, 113, 115, 159, 239
    in subsidiary, elimination adjustment for 253–62, 298, 308–11
issue of debentures 60–1, 63, 64–7
issue of shares, *see* share issue

Law of Corporations 2, 5, 11–12
    on alteration to share capital 353
    on consolidated accounts 260
    incorporation of companies 8–9
    on liquidation 374–5
    reporting requirements 174
    share issue 21–22
lease expenses 177
leave, long service 140, 141
liabilities
    carrying cost of 118–19, 121–2
    current 194–5, 200
    non-current 200–1

payable 200
provisions for 200
reporting and disclosure 199–202
statements of assets and liabilities 374–5
tax base of 118, 119
treatment on liquidation 379–85
limited companies 4–5
liquidation 374–95
  Corporations Law 374–5
  costs of 404
  creditors' claims 379–81
  definition of 374
  distribution of share capital 386–91
  dividends owing to shareholders 386
  priority of creditors' claims 379–80
  priority of shareholders' claims 386–92
  treatment of assets 374–8
  treatment of liabilities 379–85
  treatment of shareholders 386–92
liquidation account 375–6, 383
loans, intercompany 265–6, 298
long service leave 140, 141

Members' Register 13, 17, 19, 410
Memorandum of Association 9
minimum subscription at share issue 22, 26
minority interests, allocation of profits to 338–42
  direct 307–32, 341–51
  income statements 251
  indirect 337–46
  reporting requirements 330–2
minutes of proceedings 13
mortgage debentures 61, 72
mutual agency 2

no liability companies 5
non-assessable dividend income 113, 149
non-cash transactions 220, 229–31
non-current assets 195, 196
  depreciation of 145–6
  disclosure of 195–9
  disposal of 275–9
  intercompany disposal of 275–8
  revaluation of 166–8
  see also goodwill; property, plant and equipment
non-current liabilities, disclosure of 200–1
non-incorporated businesses 2
notes
  convertible 61
  of disclosure 176, 177, 179
  unsecured 61, 72

operating activities 214, 215, 222, 235
operating revenue 177
option holders, register of 13
ordinary shares 6, 18, 22–3
outside equity interests, see minority interests
overseas debt payment 418–19
oversubscribed share issue 22, 23, 26–8
ownership and capacity to control 252

paid-up capital, see share capital
parent companies 395
  control of subsidiaries 252–3
  definition of 251

elimination adjustment for investment 253–62, 298, 308–11
  after takeover 395
  see also amalgamations; consolidated accounts
partly paid share issue 29–32
partnership 2
  conversion to company 4–5, 80–92
payable liabilities 200
PAYG instalment system 100–11, 113
permanent differences 113–16, 149–50
plant, as asset 195, 196
preference shares 18
  redemption from fresh issue 361–5
  redemption from profits 357–61
prepaid expenses 124, 140, 146, 150
presentation currency 424
priority of creditors' claims on liquidation 379–80
priority of shareholders' claims on liquidation 386–92
profit and loss account
  finalisation of 94–109
  and operating activities 215
  see also balance sheet
profits
  allocation to minority interests 338–42
  appropriation of 160–5
    and cash flow statements 235–7
    elimination adjustments for 322–31
property, plant and equipment
  depreciation 178
  disposal of 275–9
  revaluation of 166–8
  see also equipment; non-current assets; plant
proprietary companies 3–4
  conversion to public company 5–6
  limited liability 4
  non-transferability of shares 4, 6
  reporting requirements 174
  shareholder control 6
prospectus
  for debentures 61, 64–5, 75–6
  for share issue 6, 17, 19, 21–2, 23–4, 26
provisions for liabilities 200
public companies 3
  conversion of proprietary company to 5–6
  limited liability 4
  shares
    issue 19, 21–2
    transferability 4, 6
  shareholder control of 6
  stock exchange listing 6
purchase consideration 395–6
purchase price of business 80
purchaser, accounting for amalgamations 403–5

qualifying asset 420

raising of share capital 21–22
realisation account for amalgamations 396–9
receivables, as assets 196
receivership 374
reconciliation of income tax 180–1
recording the call of share issue 50–1
redemption
  of debentures 64, 70–3
  of preference shares 357–65
reduction of share capital 353–5

refunds on share issue 22, 26, 27
register of charges 13
register of debentures 13
Register of Members 13, 17, 19, 410
register of option holders 13
registration of companies 3, 8, 9, 17
Replaceable Rules of companies 8, 9
reporting requirements
    assets 194–9
    consolidated accounts 307–8, 316, 330, 343
    Corporations Law 174
    directors' responsibilities 174
    foreign currency transactions 415–17
    liabilities 199–202
    minority interests 330–2
  at share issue 210–11
    see also balance sheet; cash flow statements; income statements
research and development costs 178
reserves 202
    accounts 159, 163–4
    for asset revaluation 167, 168, 242, 365–6
    from revenue 165–6
    transfers 330
retained earnings 163–4
retained profits 160, 161, 163, 202, 247, 271
    allocation to minority interests 338–42
retention of excess application money on share issue 40–2
return of share capital to shareholders 353–5, 366–7
revaluation
    of buildings 166–8
    of investments 97–99, 113, 115, 159, 239
    of non-current assets 166–8
    reserves 167, 168, 242, 365–6
revenue
    operating 177
    reserves 165–6

self-sustaining foreign investments 424
share capital 17–18, 202
    advantages of 62
    alterations to 353
    cancellation of lost share capital 355–7, 367
    distribution on liquidation 386–91
    raising of 21–2
    reduction of 353–5
    return to shareholders 353–5, 366–7
    subdivision of 353
    on takeover 409–10
share issue 241–2
    allotment money 21, 22
    bonus shares 241, 365–6, 369
    calls 17–18, 33–40, 386
    Corporations Law 21–2
    costs 55–58
    fully paid on application 23–5
    issue price 17
    minimum subscription 22, 26
    oversubscribed 22, 23, 26–8
    partly paid 29–32
    payable on application 33–4
    price 17
    procedure 19–20
    by prospectus 6, 17, 19, 21–2, 23–4, 26
    recording the call 50–1

    for redemption of preference shares 357–65
    refunds 22, 26, 27
    reporting and disclosure 210–11
    retention of excess application money 40–2
    transaction costs 164
    undersubscribed 26–9
    underwriters 56
shareholders 17
    cash payment following takeover 409
    control of public companies 6
    distribution account 388–9
    dividends owing on liquidation 386
    final dividends 160, 161–2, 285–8, 289–97, 299
    limited liability 4
    priority on liquidation 386–92
    in proprietary companies 6
    ratification of dividend 160, 165
    return of share capital 353–5, 366–7
    subscriber 9, 17, 19
    treatment on liquidation 386–92
shares
    bonus 241, 365–6, 369
        dividend 168, 241–2
    classes of 18
    deferred 19, 20
    for founding members 9, 17, 18–19, 21
    issue price 17
    ordinary 6, 18, 22–3
    preference 18
    redemption of 357–65, 368–9
    transferability of 4, 6
    unissued 3
    see also dividends; preference shares; share issue
sole traders 2
    conversion to companies 4–5, 80–7
stapled securities 62
statements of assets and liabilities 374–5
statements of cash flows, *see* cash flow statements
statements of changes in equity 186–93
statements of financial performance, *see* income statements
statements of financial position, *see* balance sheet
statutory records and registers 13–14
stock exchange listing of public companies 6
stock transactions, intercompany 267–73, 298
subdivision of share capital 353
subscriber shareholders 9, 17, 19
subsidiaries
    capacity to control 252
    control by parent companies 252–3
    definition of 251
    elimination adjustment for investment 253–62, 298, 308–11
    in foreign countries 424
    through takeover 395

takeovers
    cash payment to shareholders 409
    consolidated accounts 409–10
    difference from amalgamations 395
    purchase consideration 395–6
    share capital on 409–10
    subsidiaries through 395
taxation 156
    losses 154–6
    see also income tax
temporary differences 113, 117–19

combining assets and liabilities 136–8, 149–52
and deferred tax assets 119–22, 127–30
and deferred tax liabilities 123–5, 131–6
reversal of 140–50
terminology 58–9
transaction costs of share issue 164
transferability of shares 4, 6
translation
of Australian currency to foreign currency 413–14
of foreign currency to Australian currency 412–13

uncalled capital 17–18
undersubscribed share issue 26–9
unlimited liability companies 2, 5, 80
unrealised profits, elimination adjustments
on asset disposals 320
in closing stocks 269, 272, 298–9, 318–19
in opening stocks 271–2, 298, 319
unsecured notes 61, 72

vendor of business 80, 82
accounting for amalgamations 396–9

writing off, *see* amortisation